ISBN 978-1-330-83791-7
PIBN 10112027

1 MONTH OF
FREE
READING

at

www.ForgottenBooks.com

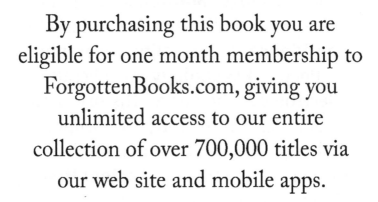

By purchasing this book you are eligible for one month membership to ForgottenBooks.com, giving you unlimited access to our entire collection of over 700,000 titles via our web site and mobile apps.

To claim your free month visit:

www.forgottenbooks.com/free112027

LABOUR CONTRACTS

A POPULAR HANDBOOK
ON THE LAW OF CONTRACTS FOR
WORKS AND SERVICES

BY

DAVID GIBBONS

Fourth Edition, revised and enlarged

WITH APPENDIX, GIVING FULL TEXT OF MANY STATUTES

By T. F. UTTLEY, Solicitor

AUTHOR OF "HINTS ON STEPHEN'S COMMENTARIES," "HINTS ON CRIMINAL LAW"
ETC: ETC.

LONDON
CROSBY LOCKWOOD AND SON
7, STATIONERS' HALL COURT, LUDGATE HILL
1892

LONDON :
PRINTED BY J. S. VIRTUE AND CO., LIMITED,
CITY ROAD.

PREFACE.

It is hoped that this portable volume on the " Labour Laws," in the present revised and enlarged edition, will be found increasingly useful by Employers and Workmen generally, as well as by members and officers of Trade Unions, and all persons who are interested in efforts for the improvement of the position of the labouring classes, many of whom have little time to study larger works upon the subject.

The usefulness of the work for purposes of reference has been materially enhanced by the Lists of Cases and of Statutes Cited which have been added to this edition ; and these lists are supplemented by a further List of Cases for Reference, which should be consulted by the student of this branch of the law. An Appendix of Statutes has also been added.

The number of Forms of Contracts between employers and workmen has been increased in the present edition, and they now include, besides a set of Working Rules to be embodied in an agreement between master and workman, a form of Engagement of Canvasser and Collector of a Trade Union, a form for Engagement of Shop Assistants, etc.

Amongst the new matters introduced in the body of the work, references have been made to such statutes as the Stamp Act, amended so recently as 1891; the Bankruptcy Act, 1883, with the amending acts; and other statutes affecting contracts for works and services which have been placed on the statute-book within the last few years, in which are included two Acts of the year 1892—namely, the Shop Hours Act, 1892, and the Betting and Loans (Infants) Act, 1892.

The reader who desires to further pursue the subject of Labour Contracts may be referred to (amongst others) the following text books and authorities thereon:—Hudson's "Building and Engineering Contracts;" Evans's "Law relating to the Remuneration of Commission Agents;" Redgrave's "Factory Acts;" Smith's "Law of Master and Servant;" Ruegg's "Employers' Liability Act," as well as the treatise of Messrs. Roberts and Wallace on the same topic, and the very recent work thereon by Mr. Minton-Senhouse.

CONTENTS.

TABLE OF CASES CITED.*

* See also Cases for Reference, *post*, p. xix.

TABLE OF STATUTES CITED.

LIST OF ADDITIONAL CASES FOR RE FERENCE ON LABOUR CONTRACTS.

1875—1880.

Contracts Generally.

Batson v. Newman, App. L.R. 1 C.P. 573.
Beeston v. Beeston, 45 L.J.R. Exch. 230 L.R. 1 Ex.D. 8.
Collins v Locke, 48 L.J.R. P.C. 68 L.R. 4 App. Cas. 674.
Diggle v. Higgs, App. 46 L.J.R. Exch. 721 L.R. 2 Ex.D. 422.
Hampden v. Walsh, 45 L.J.R. Q.B. 238 L.R. 1 Q.B.D. 189.
Harrington v. The Victoria Graving Dock Company, 47 L.J.R. Q.B.
Higginson v. Simpson, 46 L.R. C.P. 129 L.R. 2 C.P. 76.
Middleton v. Brown, App. 47 L.J.R. Chanc. 411.
Rousillon v. Rousillon, 49 L.J.R. Chanc. 338 L.R. 14 Ch.D. 331.
Thacker v. Hardy. Same v. Wheatley, App. 48 L.J.R. Q.B. 28؟
    L.R. 4 Q.B.D. 685.
Trimble v. *H*ill, 49 L.J.R. P.C. 49 L.R. 5 App. Cas. 342.

Forfeiture of Deposit by Servant.

London Tramways Co. (Lim.) v. Bailey, 47 L.R. M.C. 3 L.R. ؛
    Q.B.D. 217

Building Contracts.

The Tharsis Sulphur and Copper Co. v. McElray (H.L.Sc.), L.R. 3
    App. Cas. 1040.
Tulley v. Howling, App. 46 L.J.R. Q.B. 388 L.R. 2 Q.B.D. 182.
Walker v. London and North-Western Railway Co., 45 L.J.R. 1 C.P
    787 L.R. 1 C.P. 518.

Employers and Workmen.

Allen v. New Gas Co., 45 L.J.R. Exch. 668 L.R. 1 Ex.D. 251.
Berringer v. Great Eastern Railway Co., 48 L J.R. C.P. 400 L.R.
    C.P.*D*. 163.
Bower v. Peate, 45 L.J.R. Q.D. 446 L.R. 1 Q.B.D. 321.
Charles v. Taylor, App. L.R. 3 C.P.*D*. 492.
Clemson v. Hubbard, 45 L.J.R. M.C. 69 L.R. 1 Ex.D. 179.
Green v. Wright, L.R. 1 C.P.*D*. 591.
Goslin v. Agricultural Hall Co., 45 L.J.R. C.P. 348 L.R. C.P.*D*. 482
Lavell v Howell, 47 L.J.R. C.P. 387 L.R. 1 C.P.*D*. 161.
Newman re Ex parte Capper, App. 46 L.J.R. Bankr. 57 L.R.
    Ch. D. 724.

1880—1885.

Contracts Generally.

Corporation.

Master and Servant.

Truck.

Wages.

1886—1890.

Building Contracts.

Company.

Contracts Generally.

Bellamy v. Debenham, 45 Ch.D. 481, 63 L.T. 220.
Bristol, Cardiff, and Swansea Aërated Bread Company v. Maggs, 44 Ch.D. 616, 59 L.J. Ch.D. 472, 62 L.T. 416.
Bush v. Whitehaven Town and Harbour Trustees, 52 J.P. 292.
Hooper & Co. v. Balfour Williamson & Co., 62 L.T. 240.

Corporation.

Stevens v. Hounslow Burial Board, 61 L.T. 839, 38 R.W. 236.

Employers' Liability Act.

Brown v. Butterley Coal Company, 53 L.T. 964.
Johnson v. Lindsay, 23 Q.B. 508, 58 L.J. Q.B. 581, 37 W.R. 119.
Sweeney v. McGilvray, 14 C. of S. Cas. 105 (S.C.).
Weblin v. Ballard, 17 Q.B.D. 122, 55 L.J. Q.B. 395, 54 L.T. 532.

Employers and Workmen Act, 1875.

Patten v. Wood, 51 J.P. 549.

Infants.

Fellows v. Wood, 59 L.T. 513.
De Francesco v. Barnum (No. 1), 43 Ch.D. 165, 59 L.J. Ch. 151, 62 L.T. 40.
Ib. (No. 2), 45 Ch. D. 430, 63 L.T. 438, 39 W.R. 5.
Ib. (No. 3), 63 L.T. 514.
Holmes v. Brierley, 36 W.R. 795.
Valentini v. Canali, 24 Q.B.D. 156, 59 L.J.B. 74, 61 L.T. 731.
Johnstone v. Marks, 19 Q.B.D. 509, 57 L.J. Q.B. 6, 35 W.R. 806.
Whittingham v. Murdy, 60 L.T. 956.

Master and Servant.

Boston Deep-Sea Fishing and Ice Company v. Ansell, 39 Ch.D. 339, 59 L.T. 345 C.A.
Moore v. Palmer, 51 J.P. 196.
Pearce v. Foster, 17 Q.B.D. 536, 55 L.J. Q.B. 306, 54 L.T. 664.

Restraint of Trade.

Baines v. Geary, 35 Ch.D. 154, 56 L.J. Ch. 935, 36 W.R. 98.
Buxton, &c., Printing Co. v. Mitchell, 1 C. & E. 527.
Hill & Co. v. Hill, 55 L.T. 769, 35 W.R. 137.
Mayor of Salford v. Lever, 25 Q.B.D. 363, 39 W.R. 85.
Nicoll v. Beere, 53 L.T. 659.
Palmer v. Mallet, 36 Ch. D. 411 C.A.
Parsons v. Cotterill, 56 L.T. 839.
Stuart v. Diplock, 43 Ch.D. 343, 59 L.J. Ch. 142, 62 L.T. 333.
Watts v. Smith, 62 L.T. 453.

Ships.

The Arina, 56 L.J.P. 57, 57 L.T. 121, 35 W.R. 654.
The Justitia, 56 L.J.P. 111.

Trade Union.

Mineral Water Bottle Exchange and Trade Protection Society v. Booth, 36 Ch.D. 465, 57 L.T. 573 (C. A.).

Strick v. Swansea Tin Plate Co., 36 Ch.D. 558, 57 L.T. 392, 35 W.R. 831.

Wages.

Redgrave v. Delly, 37 W.R. 54 S.

1891—1892.

Contracts Generally.

Peninsular and Oriental SS. Co. v. McGregor & Co. and Ocean SS. Co., 7 T.L.R. 11.

Hamlyn & Co. v. Wood & Co., 65 L.T. N.S. 286.

North v. Bassett, 61 L.J.R. 177, 66 L.T. N.S. 189.

Company.

Re Anglo-Colonial Syndicate, Limited, 65 L.T. N.S. 847.

Conspiracy.

Mogul Steamship Co. v. McGregor, Gow & Co., and others, 66 L.T. N.S. 1.

Connor v. Kent, Gibson v. Lawson, Curran v. Treleaven, 61 L.J.R. (Mag.) 9.

Infants.

De Francesco v. Barnum (No. 2), 45 Ch.D. 430, 60 L.J. Ch. 63, 83 L.T. 438.

In re Soltykoff ex parte Margrett, 60 L.J. Q.B. 339, 39 W.R. 337.

Walter v. Everard, 60 L.J. Q.B. 738, 65 L.T. 443, 39 W.R. 676.

Married Woman.

Pelton Brothers v. Harrison, 65 L.T. N.S. 514.

Master and Servant.

Bound v. Lawrence, 65 L.T. N.S. 844.

De Francisco v. Barnum (No. 3), 63 L.T. 514.

Johnson v. Lindsay, 61 L.J.R. 90, 65 L.T. 97.

Lamb v. Great Northern Railway Company, 60 L.J. O.B. 489, 39 W.R. 475.

Whitworth Chemical Company v. Herdmen, 60 L.J. Ch. 428, 64 L.T. 716, 39 W.R. 433.

Restraint of Trade.

Urmston v. Whitelegg Brothers, 63 L.T. 455.

Truck.

Lamb v. Great Northern Railway Company, 65 L.T. N.S. 225.

INTRODUCTION.

MANY very important Acts of Parliament relating to the subjects treated of in this work have been passed since the last edition was issued. The Factories Acts have been much extended; measures treating more definitely of the ages at which children may be employed have been passed; trades unions. have been more thoroughly recognised; and the law generally has been made far more favourable for the workman. The full text of some of the Acts of Parliament referred to will be found in the Appendix (pp. 255—362).

Perhaps the most notable of these statutes are the Employers and Workmen Act, 1875 (38 & 39 Vic. c. 90), and the Employers' Liability Act, 1880 (43 & 44 Vic. c. 42). The Shop Hours Regulation Act, 1886 (49 & 50 Vic. c. 55), which was passed as a temporary measure, has now been superseded by the Shop Hours Act, 1892 (55 & 56 Vict. c. 62), which will be found amongst the statutes in the Appendix, and is likely to form the nucleus of future and more important legislation which will more widely extend the present provisions of the law.

The Trade Union Act of 1876 (39 & 40 Vic. c. 22) has enlarged the scope of the previous Act of 1871, and the Truck Act, 1887 (50 & 51 Vic. c. 46), has done the same service for the statute of 1831.

The Factory and Workshop Act of 1891 (54 & 55 Vic. c. 75) is one of the most important of the statutes given in the Appendix. It materially extends the Act of 1878, which so well codified the previous law on the subject. The Merchant Shipping Act of 1889 (52 & 53 Vic. c. 46) is one of interest to mariners.

The Arbitration Act, 1891 (54 & 55 Vic. c. 75), is another statute to be observed; and so also is the Partnership Law Amendment Act, 1890 (53 & 54 Vic. c. 30).

According to the Stamp Act of 1891, agreements between employers and workmen do not require stamps. This exemption applies to any agreement or memorandum for the hire of any labourer, artificer, manufacturer, or menial servant, and to any agreement or memorandum made between the master and mariners of any ship or vessel for wages on any voyage coastwise from port to port in the United Kingdom.

With regard to contracts with local authorities for work and labour, it should be borne in mind (as pointed out in Hudson's "Law of Building and Engineering Contracts") that all such contracts must be under seal in the following cases :—Contracts with municipal corporations for local improvements in cases which do not fall within the Public Health Act, 1875.*

By the Public Health Act, 1875 (38 & 39 Vic. c. 55), s. 7, all urban authorities (for definition of which,

---

* See Rawlinson on "Municipal Corporations" (eighth ed.), p. 226, note (a).

see s. 6) not then incorporated were thereby incorporated, and those already corporations remained such (Young v. Leamington (1883), 8 App. Cas., 517, *per* Lord Blackburn). The urban authorities consist of town councils in municipal boroughs, local boards in urban districts, and towns improvement commissioners which have not received municipal charters.

By s. 174 (1) of the same Act, every contract made by an urban authority, whereof the value or amount exceeds £50, shall be in writing and sealed with the common seal of such authority. The provisions of section 174 apply only to contracts which do not exceed the sum of £50 at the time they are made. Further, s. 174 (2) provides that—Every such contract shall specify the work, materials, matters, and things to be furnished, had, or done, the price to be paid, and the time or times within which the contract is to be performed, and shall specify the pecuniary penalty to be paid in case the terms of the contract are not duly performed. Sub. s. (3) provides that the urban authority shall obtain from their surveyor a previous estimate in writing of the cost and most advantageous mode of contracting.

By s. 174 (4), before any contract of the value or amount of £100 or upwards is entered into by an urban authority, at least ten days' public notice must be given, stating the nature and purpose of the proposed contract and inviting tenders for the execution of the works, and the urban authority must also take sufficient security for the due performance of the contract.

The Metropolis (states Mr. Hudson) is not included in the Public Health Act, 1875 (38 & 39 Vic. c. 55), see section 2 ; and as to the Corporation of the City of London there would appear to be no statutory provision as to their contracts, which would, therefore, be governed by the common law as to corporations. Outside the "City," the Metropolis Local Management Act, 1855 (18 & 19 Vic. c. 120), s. 149, provides that all contracts of the Metropolitan Board of Works, and every district board and vestry, for works and materials " whereof the value or amount exceeds £10, shall be in writing or print, or partly in writing and partly in print, sealed with the seal of the board or vestry " (see 52 & 53 Vict. c. 63. s. 20).*

The London County Council is now, by the Local Government Act, 1888 (51 & 52 Vic. c. 41), s. 40 (8), invested with the powers of the Metropolitan Board, and created a corporation (s. 79). The district boards of works and the vestries in the metropolis are corporations by the Act of 1855 (18 & 19 Vic. c. 120), and are not affected by the Local Government Act, 1888, except in so far as they are (s. 41 (4) (b)) constituted district councils and " urban authorities." And by s. 64 of the Metropolis Management Act, 1855 (18 & 19 Vic. c. 120), no officer or servant is to be interested in any contract (see 52 & 53 Vic. c. 69).

Further, corporations which are not municipal and not trading comprise, *e.g.*, colleges, deans, and chapters ; also various bodies constituted corporations by statute, such as boards of guardians, which are incorporated by 5 & 6 Will. IV. c. 69, s. 7, and are also rural sanitary

---

* The Public Health (London) Act, 1891 (54 & 55 Vic. c. 76) has many important sanitary clauses.

authorities under the Public Health Act, 1889 ; county councils, which by the Local Government Act, 1888 (51 & 52 Vic. c. 41, ss. 3 & 79 (3)), are the successors of the justices, and (by s. 79 of that Act) are made corporations. The county councils, except the London council, are subject to no special statutory provisions as to contracts, except as to reformatory and industrial schools, as to which the plans and costs of the build-ings must be submitted to the Home Secretary, and his consent obtained, and then the meeting of the council to consider the scheme must be advertised in accordance with 29 & 30 Vic. c. 117, and c. 118, and 35 & 36 Vict. c. 21. As to lunatic asylums, the county councils are invested with the power and duty to pro-vide and erect them under the Lunacy Act, 1890 (53 & 54 Vic. c. 5), ss. 238 and 240.

The principal statutes relating to buildings under which a contract may be unlawful, are the Factory and Workshop Act, 1878, 41 Vic. c. 16; Metallife- . rous Mines Regulation Act, 1872, 35 & 36 Vic. c. 77 ; Coal Mines Regulation Act, 1887, 50 & 51 Vic. c. 58; Metropolitan Building Act, 18 & 19 Vic. c. 122 ; Metropolitan Management Act, 18 & 19 Vic. c. 120 ; Public Health Act, 1875, 38 & 39 Vic. c. 55; Public Health Act, 1875 (Support of Sewers) Amendment Act, 1883, 46 & 47 Vic. c. 36 ; Towns Improvement Clauses Act, 1854, 17 & 18 Vic. c. 103; Public Health (Water) Act, 1878, 41 & 42 Vic. c. 25 ; Dis-used Burial Grounds Act, 1884, 47 & 48 Vic. c. 72 ; Public Health Amendment Act, 1890, 53 & 54 Vic.

c. 59 ; Public Health Buildings and Streets Act, 1888, 51 & 52 Vic. c. 52.

The by-laws made in pursuance of these Acts, if duly made and reasonable, have the force of law, according to the views of Mr. Hudson in his volume on contracts (*supra*).

In the present state of agitation between employer and employed, it is no easy matter to find a means of mediation equally acceptable to both parties. Mention is made now and again of Boards of Conciliation and the like, and labour statutes often contain arbitration clauses.

By section 24 of the Arbitration Act, 1889 (52 & 53 Vic. c. 49), it is enacted that the Act is to apply to every arbitration under any Act passed before or after the commencement of the Act as if the arbitration were pursuant to a submission, except in so far as the Act is inconsistent with the Act regulating the arbitration, or with any rules or procedure authorised or recognised by that Act.

Amongst the statutes comprising provisions relating to arbitration are the following :—5 Geo. IV. c. 96 ; 7 Wm. IV. and 1 Vic. c. 67 ; 30 & 31 Vic. c. 105 ; 35 & 36 Vic. c. 46 ; 41 Vic. c. 16 ; and more particularly 54 & 55 Vic. c. 75.

LABOUR CONTRACTS:

A POPULAR HANDBOOK ON

THE LAW OF CONTRACTS.

1. ALMOST everything that we see around us, which has been formed by the art of man, has been formed *by means of contracts.* The bread we eat, the clothes we wear, the house that shelters us, the iron road on which we travel, the puffing engine which draws us rapidly along, have become what they are by contracts. The mutual consent of men to assist each other is a contract. By contracts they combine to labour, and by contracts are produced all the necessaries and luxuries which distinguish civilised from savage life.

The idea of a contract naturally leads to the idea of law. Having ascertained what a contract is, we consider what is to be done with the man who does not faithfully perform it. Law brings the whole force of society to bear on him who fails in his engagement, to compel him to perform it, or to punish him for its breach. Law determines what contracts shall be enforced, how they shall be performed, and the consequences of their breach.

The branch of the law of contracts to which the present volume is devoted is that relating to hire of labour, and principally so far as it concerns the erection of

B

buildings and performance of other like works. Next
to the marriage contract, this is perhaps of the earliest
origin, since it has for its object the creation of property : all other contracts relating to property concern
its transfer or preservation, and may therefore be said
to be derived from and grow out of this. Contracts for
the hire of labour are of two sorts :—the contract to
perform works, whereby one man agrees to do a certain
work for another, as to build a house, and by which the
contractor is bound to find all the labour and materials,
and do everything that may be necessary for the building of the house ; and the contract to serve, whereby
one man lets his personal services to another, either for
a particular purpose or generally, and by which the
servant is bound merely to do as much as he himself
can towards the performance of the work for which he
is engaged. By the first, the relation of contractor and
employer is created ; by the second, the relation of
master and servant. The plan proposed is first to consider these two contracts together with reference to
their legal validity, and then to treat of the duties
and rights of each party to each contract separately.

With reference to their legal validity contracts for
the hire of labour, as well as all other contracts, are
divisible into contracts which the law prohibits, and
which it considers ought not to be performed, and which
may be termed bad or illegal contracts ; contracts which
it will not enforce, and which therefore need not be performed, although it is not contrary to law to perform
them, and which may be termed imperfect contracts ;
and contracts which it will enforce, and which therefore
must be performed, and which are perfect contracts.

2. Contracts which the law prohibits, or illegal contracts, are those by which something is agreed to be
done contrary to the general interests of society. They

are illegal by common law, or by statute. Contracts illegal at common law are those that so plainly violate some great principle of morality or policy, that the Courts have of their own authority held them to be contrary to law. Contracts illegal by statute are those which infringe some provision which parliament in its wisdom has considered expedient for the preservation of order, the raising of the public revenue, or the protection of particular classes from the fraud, oppression, or competition of others.

3. Of illegal contracts at common law relating to the hire of labour may be instanced a contract to print a libellous and indecent work (the 'Memoirs of Harriette Wilson'), in which case the printer, who knew its nature, failed to recover the price of the printing.[1] Best, C. J., says—"He who lends himself to that which is contrary to the laws of his country, cannot complain of not being paid for lending himself to that criminal purpose. Every servant, to the lowest, engaged in such a transaction, is prevented from recovering compensation." Any person who contributes to the performance of an illegal act by supplying a thing with a knowledge that it is going to be used for that purpose, cannot recover the price of the thing so supplied.[2] There must be an intention by the plaintiff to assist in the illegal purpose. Thus a laundress recovered the bill for washing done for a woman whom she knew to be a prostitute. Some of the articles washed were expensive dresses, and others gentlemen's nightcaps. Buller, J.—"This unfortunate woman must have clean linen, and it is impossible for the Court to take into consideration which of the articles were used for an improper purpose and

[1] Poplett v. Stockdale, 2 Car. and Payne, 200. Ry. and Moo. 337. Gale and Leckie, 2 Stark. 107.
[2] Pearce v. Brooks, L. R. 1, Ex. 217.

which were not. The plaintiff was employed generally to wash the defendant's linen, and the use which the defendant made of it cannot affect the contract."[1]

4. Contracts in total restraint of trade are also illegal and void by the common law, as oppressive on the party restrained, and injurious to society by depriving it of the industry of one of its members. A contract between a brass-founder and a firm of commission agents, that the firm should employ the brass-founder in executing orders received by them for brass-work, and that the brass-founder should not at any time work for any other person without the consent of the firm, but the firm were at liberty to employ any other person, and the brass-founder was at liberty to execute the order of any person within the city of London or within six miles, was held an unreasonable restraint of trade, and void, because the firm were not bound to. find the brass-founder with full employment.[2] A bond given to a coal-merchant by his clerk, whereby the clerk bound himself not to follow or be employed in the business of a coal-merchant for nine months after he should have left the service of his employer, was held void, as a total restraint of trade for the nine months.[3]

5. Contracts in partial restraint of trade are sometimes beneficial to trade and industry, instead of being prejudicial, since a tradesman may be enabled to dispose of his business for a valuable consideration, or may be encouraged to take a servant into his confidential employment, if he can secure the purchaser or himself against competition by a contract of this description. To render a contract in partial restraint of trade binding, it should be made upon a good consideration, and

---

[1] Lloyd v. Johnson, 1 B. and P. 340. Bowry v. Bennett, 1 Camp. 348.
[2] Young v. Timmings, 1 C. and J. 340. Sykes v. Dixon, 9 A. and E. 693.
[3] Ward v. Byrne, 5 M. and W. 548.

the restraint should not be more extensive than necessary for the protection of the party to be secured. Thus a master may lawfully bargain that his servant shall not work for any other person so long as he continnes in his employment,[1] or that he shall not work for his customers,[2] or set up business within a limited distance,[3] after he shall have quitted his service. A traveller may be restrained from travelling for any other house in the same trade over any part of the same ground.[4] On the sale of a manufacture carried on partly under patents, and partly by secret processes, the vendor may restrain himself from carrying on the same business in any part of Europe.[5]

6. A contract which is directly prohibited by statute is void, and cannot be enforced. A contract to do an act which a statute prohibits, or to do an act for the doing of which a statute has imposed a penalty, is by implication prohibited by the statute, and therefore void. A penalty implies a prohibition.[6]

If an act has been done which is expressly or by implication prohibited by statute, no compensation can be claimed for the performance; for either the parties agreed that it should be so done, in which case their contract was void, as contemplating a breach of the law, or the agreement was to do something lawful, and was not performed by the workman. Thus a printer who was employed to print a pamphlet, and did not print his name and place of residence on the first and last

---

[1] Pilkington v. Cooke, 15 M. and W. 657. Hartley v. Cummings, 5 Com. Bench. 247.

[2] Rannie v. Irvine, 7 M. and G. 969. Nicholls v. Stretton, 7 Beav. 42. 10 Q. B. 346.

[3] Mallan v. May, 11 M. and W. 668. Benwell v. Inns, 24 Beav. 307.

[4] Mumford v. Gething, 7 C. B. N. S. 305.

[5] Leather Cloth Company v. Lorsont, L. R. 9 Eq. 345.

[6] Bartlett v. Viner, Carth. 252. Cope v. Rowlands, 2 M. and W. 149.

sheets as required by statute 32 & 33 Vic. c. 34, was held not entitled to recover anything for the printing.[1] The object of the statute being to prevent the publication of libels, was understood as prohibiting the printing of books unless the name and address of the printer was printed thereon previous to publication.

Some Acts of Parliament require qualifications for certain callings. An apothecary must pass an examination by the Apothecaries' Company, and obtain a certificate of his having done so.[2] Persons in practice prior to the 1st of August, 1815,[3] and those who were army or navy surgeons before or on 1st August, 1826, are exempt from this law.[4] These and all other medical practitioners must be registered.[5] An attorney or solicitor must be admitted duly and obtain his annual certificate.[6] No one can draw deeds or legal proceedings for reward, but Counsel, Certificated Attorneys, or Solicitors, or Certificated Members of an Inn of Court.[7] An appraiser must obtain a licence from the Stamp Office.[8] A broker in the City of London must be admitted by the Court of Mayor and Aldermen.[9] In these instances it is illegal for an unqualified person to act in any of the above capacities, and if he does so, he can recover nothing for his services.

The State exercises a paternal care over our amusements, and an agreement to act or sing in an unlicensed

[1] Bensley v. Bignole, 5 B. and Ald. 335. Reference should also be made to 44 & 45 Vict. c. 60. and 51 & 52 Vic. c. 64.

[2] 55 Geo. III. c. 194, s. 21. Leman v. Fletcher, L. R. 8, Q. B. 319.

[3] S. 14.

[4] 6 Geo. IV. c. 133, s. 4. Steavenson v. Oliver, 8 M. and W. 234.

[5] 21 & 22 Vict. c. 90, s. 32.   [6] 51 & 52 Vic. c. 65.

[7] 33 & 34 Vict. c. 97, s. 60. Taylor v. Crowland Gas Company, 10 Ex. 293.

[8] 46 Geo. III. c. 43. Palk v. Force, 12 Q. B. 666.

[9] 6 Anne, c. 16, s. 4. Cope v. Rowlands, 2 M. and W. 149.

theatre, or place of entertainment, is illegal and cannot be enforced.[1]

A contract to erect a building in contravention of the Metropolitan Building Act cannot be enforced.[2] But if the parties do not contemplate infringing the Act, and it can be modified so as to make it accord with the Act, it will be so enforced.[3]

It is not every breach of a statute, or omission to comply with its requisites in the performance of a contract, which will render the contract void, or disentitle the party performing it to the price of his labour. The object of the legislature and the motives of the parties to the contract are to be regarded. If the violation of the statute is collateral to the contract, or if in the course of performing the contract a breach of a statute is committed which was not contemplated by the parties when they agreed, the contract is not rendered unlawful. The point to be ascertained is, whether the legislature intended to prohibit the contract. Thus a sale of tobacco by a party who has no licence to deal in that commodity, or who has not his name painted over his door as required by the excise laws, is not void, although the statutes relating to the excise impose penalties on those who deal in tobacco without being licensed, or without having their names painted over their doors.[4] In these cases the statutory provisions are for the regulation of the general trading of parties, and are collateral to particular contracts, though made in the course of such trading. And the price of spirits sold and delivered without a permit, or with an irre-

[1] 25 Geo. II. c. 36. 6 & 7 Vict. c. 68. De Beguis v. Armistead, 10 Bing. 107.

[2] Stevens v. Gourley, 7 C. B. N. S. 99.

[3] Cubitt v. Smith, 10 Jur. N. S. 1123.

[4] Johnson v. Hudson, 11 East, 180. Smith v. Mawhood, 14 M. and W. 452. Per Tindal, C. J., Ferguson v. Norman, 5 Bing. N. C. 84.

gular permit, may be recovered, because the violation of the statute was not contemplated by the contract.[1] The parties did not agree to infringe the statute, and were not bound to agree to observe it.

The object of the legislature is also to be considered in determining whether an agreement contrary to statute is void to all intents, or whether the parties are at liberty to make it valid by expressly dispensing with the statute. It seems that when a statute is passed for the purpose of protecting one contracting party from the fraud of the other, the benefit of the statute may be renounced by the party intended to be protected. The statute 17 Geo. III. c. 42, provided that all bricks made for sale should be of certain dimensions. Bricks were sold and delivered of smaller dimensions than specified in the statute, and the seller failed to recover the price; but the Court gave judgment against the seller on the ground that the bricks were bought as bricks of a proper size, and that the buyer did not know them to be of under size.[2]

But if the object of the legislature is to protect one party from the oppression of the other, in which case it is assumed that the party to be protected is not *sui juris*, or on equal terms with his co-contractor, or to protect the public or third persons, the contract is to all intents void, and no agreement to renounce the benefit of the law can be binding. The Truck Act and other Acts made for the protection of workmen against their employers are statutes of the one sort; the Act regulating printers is an instance of the other.

Such are some of the principles of law as to contracts rendered illegal by statutes which are applicable to contracts for works and services, and the statutes relating to such contracts.

[1] Wetherell v. Jones, 3 B. and Ad. 221.
[2] Law v. Hodson, 11 East, 300.

7. Amongst the statutes affecting general contracts for works may be mentioned those for the better observance of the Lord's day. At first it was thought sufficient to prohibit shoemakers from exposing to sale shoes, boots, buskins, startops, slippers, or pantofles.[1] The wickedness of carriers, drovers, and butchers next attracted the attention of the legislature, and they were subjected to penalties for following their callings.[2] Then came the statute 29 Car. II. c. 7, which enacts, that no tradesman, artificer, workman, labourer, or other person whatsoever, shall do or exercise any worldly labour, business, or work of their ordinary callings upon the Lord's day, or any part thereof—works of necessity and charity only excepted—it imposes a penalty of 5s.

The Act extends not to prohibit the dressing of meat in families, or dressing or selling of meats in inns, cooks' shops, or victualling-houses, for such as otherwise cannot be provided, nor to the crying and selling of milk before nine in the morning, and after four in the afternoon.

The statute does not include all persons or all works; it extends only to the persons particularly mentioned, and to others of the same class, 'ejusdem generis.' It has been decided that farmers[3] and attorneys[4] are not within the statute, that a stage-coach proprietor may lawfully agree on a Sunday to carry a passenger on a journey upon that day, and must pay for a post-chaise if he fails to perform his contract.[5] A farmer may employ himself in making his own hay without

---

[1] 1 Jac. I. c. 22. Repealed by 48 Geo. III. s. 60, which is repealed by 35 & 36 Vict. c. 97.

[2] 3 Car. I. c. 2.   [3] Rex v. Whitnash, 7 B. and C. 602.

[4] Peate v. Dicken, 1 C. M. and R. 422.

[5] Sandiman v. Breach, 7 B. and C. 96.

violating the law. He is not a labourer. A labourer means a person labouring for another: a farmer, a person who may work or not, as he likes; if he sometimes takes up a spade or a rake, he cannot on that account be called a labourer.[1]

The works made illegal by the statute are only works done by tradesmen, &c., in their ordinary callings. A contract to do on Sunday work which is not in the ordinary calling of the tradesman, or a contract which is not in his ordinary calling, that is, the usual and every-day course of his business, made on Sunday, is not illegal. Thus a contract by a farmer for the hire of a labourer, made on Sunday, is binding.[2] A contract by a farmer for letting out his stallion, though the contract be made and the purpose accomplished on Sunday, is according to law.[3] The sale of a horse on a Sunday by a person not a horse-dealer is legal;[4] but the sale of a horse on a Sunday to a horse-dealer is illegal, and no action can be brought for the price of the horse, or on a warranty given at the time of the sale.[5] The acts done on Sunday by tradesmen in their ordinary calling having simply no legal effect, except to subject them to the penalties imposed by the statute, the fact of a contract having been in part made on Sunday does not affect the validity of anything done on a subsequent week-day; and therefore, if goods are sold and delivered on the day of rest, the sale being simply void, a promise to pay for them on a subsequent week-day is, it seems, binding, as amounting to a new sale.[6] And if a contract is proposed to be made on a

---

[1] R. v. Cleworth, 4 B. and S. 933.   [2] Rex v. Whitnash, 7 B. and C. 602.

[3] Scarfe v. Morgan, 4 M. and W. 270.

[4] Drury v. Defontaine, 1 Taunt. 131.

[5] Fennell v. Ridler, 5 B. and C. 406.

[6] Williams v. Paul, 6 Bing. 653. Simpson v. Nicholls, 3 M. and W. 240.

Sunday, but completed on another day, it is binding.[1] It seems also, that in the case of a Sunday contract, if it is within the ordinary calling of the one party and not of the other, the party who has infringed the statute is bound by it, and cannot take advantage of his own wrong to excuse himself from its performance; thus, where a horse-dealer sold a horse to a gentleman and warranted it sound on a Sunday, he was held bound by the warranty. The purchaser believed him to be a stage-coachman, and did not know that he was a horse-dealer.[2] With reference to the exception of works of necessity and charity, it has been decided by the House of Lords that a barber shaving his customers on a Sunday is not a work of " necessity or mercy " within the Scotch statutes on the subject, and which have the same meaning as " necessity or charity," and that therefore he cannot compel his apprentice to do such work on Sunday.[3]

To apply these cases to contracts for works, it may be taken that if any work is done by a person to whom the statutes extend on a Sunday in his ordinary calling, no remuneration can be recovered for such work; and that if a contract is made for the performance of such work on Sunday, it is illegal, and need not be performed; and if a contract is made on a Sunday with a workman, which contract is within the ordinary calling either of the employer or the employed, it cannot be enforced by the party who has infringed the statute; but if work is on a week-day done and accepted in pursuance of such contract, the acceptance of the work will be equivalent to a new contract made on the week-day to pay the workman a reasonable remuneration for his labour, though it is doubtful whether the trans-

[1] Bloxsome v. Williams, 3 B. and C. 233.
[2] Ibid.
[3] Phillips v. Innes, 4 Cl. and Fin. 231.

action on the Sunday can be referred to at all, either to estimate the price to be paid, or to ascertain the work to be done.

The weekly division of time is singular. Days, months, and years are suggested by natural phenomena: there is nothing to suggest the week. According to the Scripture, it commenced at the creation. It is somewhat difficult to believe that the almighty Creator of the universe made it in six times twenty-four hours, and then rested twenty-four hours before He set it in motion—a motion since incessant; less so to suppose that He taught our first parents to delve and spin for six days and rest on the seventh. Certain it is that, when the Pentateuch was compiled or written, the Jews so counted and used their time, and that the origin of the custom was then unknown. The names by which we individualise its days, derived from the gods of Scandinavian mythology, denote that it prevailed with our ancestors before their conversion to Christianity. We have ten fingers, and count by ten. Acting on this idea, the French Revolutionary Government divided the month of thirty days into three weeks of ten days each.[1] This innovation did not last long— from September 20, 1793, to January 1, 1806.

The week exists, and must be accounted for. It may be accounted for by assuming the Fourth Commandment to be a divine law for the employment of time. The Jews preserved the tables of stone, on which the Commandments were engraved by eternal fingers, with the most scrupulous care. While wandering in the desert, and struggling for the dominion of Judæa, they kept them in the ark. When they thought their government established, they built the Temple to hold them; notwithstanding the tables of stone have crumbled into

---

[1] Notes and Queries, Fifth Series, vol. i. p. 281.

the smallest dust. St. Paul told the Corinthians that before his time they had been done away.[1] The Commandments have been transferred to the minds of men and carried down the stream of time by tradition (with the aid of copying, printing, and translation), are more permanently preserved than on the tables of stone in the ark, or by the Temple. The efforts of the Puseyites to expel them from our churches, and of the Brightites to exclude them from our schools, are as vain as those of the French Revolutionists to change the week from seven days to ten.

The statute which has suggested these remarks has been in force nearly two hundred years, and the decisions upon it are comparatively few, proving that it has been well observed and agrees with the disposition of the people. With respect to decisions, contrast it with the Statute of Frauds, passed about the same time, two sections of which are shortly noticed further on. It has been said that every word of these sections is worth a subsidy. If this means to the legal profession, it is far short of the truth. More than many subsidies have been spent in litigation over every letter of these celebrated sections, and the reports of the decisions of the disputed points are so numerous that they fill many volumes; and if any one has read them all, he must be an industrious man, and have had a prolonged existence. If the law is codified, we may expect an equal amount of litigation on every branch of it.

8. The statutes which regulate the employment of children and females may also be referred to as imposing restraints upon contracts relating to the hire of labour.

The first statute on the subject is the 42 Geo. III. c. 73, which relates to the employment of apprentices in mills or factories where three or more apprentices,

---

[1] 2 Cor. iii. 7—11.

or twenty or more other persons, are employed. The subsequent statutes, passed at various times, from 1833 to 1891, are embodied in the Factory and Workshop Act.[1] There are also Acts, for the regulation of coal mines[2] and metalliferous mines,[3] and for regulation of bakehouses.[4] These contain numerous minute provisions limiting the hours of labour of women and children, and for securing them leisure for their meals, holidays, and half-holidays, and for their safety, education, morals, and health. It is beyond the scope of the present work to go fully into these. But the contracts prohibited, and the places and trades to which the prohibition extends, it may be useful to mention, as showing what contracts are made illegal by the Acts.

The Factory and Workshop Act prohibits the employment of children under the age of ten years, or young persons, in any part of a factory[5] or workshop in which there is carried on the process of silvering of mirrors or making of whitelead, or melting or annealing of glass. A girl under sixteen cannot be employed for making or finishing of bricks and tiles (not being ornamented) or salt, nor a child for any dry grinding in the metal trade or the dipping of lucifer matches, nor a child under eleven in any grinding in the metal trade other than dry grinding, or in fustian-cutting.

In a factory or workshop to which the Acts of 1878 to 1891 apply no child can be employed—

    (a) During the year one thousand eight hundred and ninety-two if he is under the age of ten years; or,

    (b) After the expiration of that year if he is under the age of eleven years.

---

[1] 41 Vic. c. 16.   [2] 30 & 31 V. c. 146.

[3] 33 & 34 V. c. 62; 34 & 35 V. c. 104.   [4] 50 & 51 V. c. 58.

[5] 35 & 36 V. c. 77.

Provided that any child lawfully employed under the Factory and Workshop Act, 1878, or any Act relating to the employment of children at the time that these provisions came into force, shall be exempt from them.

A child under the age of sixteen cannot be employed in a factory without a medical certificate. In factories no child or young person under sixteen shall be employed for longer than seven days, or (in case the doctor lives over three miles from the factory) thirteen days, unless the occupier has obtained a certificate in due form under the hand of a medical man (appointed certifying surgeon to the district) of fitness for the employment, in which it must be clearly stated that the person is not incapacitated by disease or bodily infirmity for working daily during the regular hours; and the same applies to workshops. All such certificates must be produced to the inspector when called upon.

The employment in coal mines below ground, of boys under the age of twelve years, and above ground of boys under the same age is prohibited.[1] In metalliferous mines below ground, of boys under the age of twelve years; and the employment below ground, in coal mines or mines metalliferous, of girls and women, is also prohibited.[2]

The Factory Acts, 1878—1891, apply to all textile factories, that is, any premises wherein, or in the close or curtilage of which, steam, water, or other mechanical power is used to move or work any machinery employed in preparing, manufacturing, or finishing, or in any process incident to the manufacture of cotton, wool, hair, silk, flax, hemp, jute, tow, China grass, cocoa-nut fibre, or other like material, either separately or mixed together, or mixed with any other material or any fabric made thereof.

[1] 50 & 51 Vic. c. 58, s. 4.   [2] 35 & 36 V. c. 77, s. 4.

The Acts also apply to non-textile factories, that is to say, the following works, warehouses, furnaces, mills, foundries or places :—print works, bleaching and dyeing works, earthenware works, lucifer-match works, percussion-cap works, cartridge works, paper-staining works, fustian-cutting works, blast furnaces, copper mills, iron mills, foundries, metal and indiarubber works, paper mills, glass works, tobacco factories, letterpress printing works, book - binding works, flax scutch mills; so, too, to premises or places wherein or within which steam, water, or other mechanical power is used in aid of the manufacturing process carried on there; as, for instance, hat works, rope works, bakehouses, lace warehouses, ship-building yards, quarries, pit banks.

Premises coming within the Act comprise those also where manual labour is exercised by way of trade or for gain in or incidental to the making of any article, the altering, repairing, ornamenting, or finishing of any article, or the adapting for sale of any article, and wherein or within which steam, water, or other mechanical power is employed.   The Act also applies to workshops, that is, the premises enumerated above as hat works and so forth, and which are not a factory within the meaning of the Act, that is to say, do not use power.

Workshops also include premises, rooms, or places wherein manual labour is exercised by way of trade, or for gain in or incidental, like making of articles, the altering, repairing, ornamenting, or finishing of articles or adapting them for sale, and over which premises the employers have right of control.   A part of a factory or workshop may be taken to be a separate factory or workshop, but a sleeping-room is not one, nor is a place within a factory solely used for other purposes than manufacturing processes. Open-air places are a factory or workshop, but not workshops other than bakehouses conducted on the system of not employing any child, young person, or woman.[1] The winding of cotton thread, manufactured elsewhere, is a process incident to the manufacture of cotton, and the place where it is done by steam-power is a factory within the Act.[2] Weaving or plaiting cotton by steam-power round crinoline skirts is also a manufacture of cotton within the Act.[3] Every room within the building, not used as a dwelling-room, is part of the factory, though no steam-power is used in such rooms.[4]

A shipbuilding factory, in which steam is used for cutting and making iron plates, is a factory within this Act. But a ship in the course of building, in which more than fifty persons are employed, is not.[5] It is decided that the Act is confined to buildings.[6] Therefore a stone quarry, though it contains sheds, and cement works carried on principally in the open air, and in which there was no great building where workpeople were employed under cover, are not within it.[7]

It might have been thought that it was superfluous to legislate against the employment of children under the age of eight years, especially in the neighbourhood of powerful machinery which they are employed to feed, and by which they are sometimes swallowed. That it was necessary is a melancholy fact. At first the limit was nine years, but when the factory laws were revised in 1844, so valuable was the labour of children between

[1] 54 & 55 V. c. 75.   [2] Hayden v. Taylor, 4 B. and S. 519.
[3] Whymper v. Harney, 18 C. B. N. S. 243.
[4] Taylor v. Hickes, 12 C. B. N. S. 152.
[5] Palmer's Shipbuilding and Iron Company v. Chaytor, L. R. 4 Q. B. 209.
[6] Kent v. Astley, L. R. 5 Q. B. 19.
[7] Redgrave v. Lee, L. R. 9 Q. B. 363.

the age of eight and nine, or so cheap, that it was reduced to eight. The bargain in these cases is not with the child, but between a brutal operative and a still more brutal manufacturer, by which the child is sold to slavery.

There is no rule of the common law making a contract with the youngest child illegal. Before the abolition of feudal tenures, when the guardian in chivalry had the disposal in marriage of his female ward, contracts of marriage with or between children under the age of consent (twelve for the female and fourteen for the male) were not unknown nor unrecognised. Lord Coke mentions cases of a wife of the age of seven, and a husband of the age of four. If the wife attained the age of nine before the death of her husband she was entitled to dower, and the bishop was bound to find that they were joined in lawful marriage if she was above nine though under twelve, and though the husband was under fourteen. And the marriage of two little toddling children might have been made the foundation of a divorce suit.[1] Thus we see that the men from whom we inherit our lands dealt with their children in much the same manner as the landless workmen of Lancashire deal with theirs—made the most of them.

The Prevention of Cruelty to Children Act, 1889 (52 & 53 Vic. c. 54), enacts that it is an offence punishable on summary conviction with £25, with or without three months' hard labour, (a) to cause or procure a boy under fourteen or girl under sixteen to be in any street for begging or receiving alms, or inducing the giving of alms, whether under the pretence of singing, playing, performing, offering for sale, or otherwise; or (b) to cause or procure a boy or girl as aforesaid to be in any street or any premises licensed for sale of

---

[1] Co. Lit. 33. a.

intoxicants (not being licensed for entertainment) for singing, playing, or performing for profit, or offering for sale between 10 P.M. and 5 A.M., or such other extended or restricted hours (if any) as the local authority fixes; or (c) to cause or procure a child under ten to be at any time in any place, street, or premises licensed for the sale of intoxicants or licensed for public entertainments, or any circus or place of public amusement to which the public are admitted by payment, for the purpose of singing, playing, or performing for profit, or offering for sale. But the local authority may license for sale a child over seven to take part in entertainments in such premises licensed for public entertainment or circus, or place of public amusement.

The Betting and Loans (Infants) Act, 1892 (55 Vic. c. 4), enacts that if any one in order to earn commission, reward, or other profit, sends to an infant any circular, notice, advertisement, letter, telegram, or other document containing an invitation to make any bet or wager, or apply to any person or at any place for information as to any race, fight, game, sport, or other contingency upon which betting or wagering is carried on, he shall be guilty of a misdemeanour and liable, if convicted on indictment, to imprisonment with or without hard labour for a term not exceeding three months, or to a fine not exceeding £100, or to both imprisonment and fine; and if convicted on summary conviction, to imprisonment with or without hard labour for a term not exceeding one month, or to a fine not exceeding £20, or to both imprisonment and fine. Similar punishment is awarded to anyone who, for the purpose of earning interest, commission, reward, or other profit, sends to an infant any circular, &c., inviting the borrowing of money, or the application to any person or at any place with a view to obtaining information or advice as to borrowing

money. If any person send such circular, &c., to any
person at any university, college, school, or other place of
education, and such person receiving them is an infant,
the sender will be deemed to know of the infancy unless
he can prove otherwise. Similar punishments as before
are imposed on any one, except under court's authority,
soliciting an infant to make an affidavit or statutory
declaration in connection with the loan.

If any infant, who has contracted a loan which is
void in law, agrees after he comes of age to pay any
money which in whole or part represents or is agreed
to be paid in respect of any such loan, and is not a new
advance, such agreement, and any instrument, negotiable or other, given in pursuance of or for carrying
into effect such agreement, or otherwise in relation to
the payment of money representing or in respect of
such loan, is, so far as it relates to money which represents or is payable in respect of such loan, and is not a
new advance, to be void absolutely as against all persons whomsoever. For the purposes of this section any
interest, commission, or other payment in respect of
such loan is deemed to be a part of such loan.

9. Another important statute affecting the validity
of contracts made with workmen is the 1 & 2 Wm. IV.
c. 37, commonly called the Truck Act. It is entitled,
"*An Act to prohibit the payment in certain trades of
wages in goods or otherwise than in the current coin of
this realm.*" After reciting that "it is necessary to
prohibit the payment, in certain trades, of wages in
goods or otherwise than in the current coin of the
realm," it enacts, "That in all contracts for the hiring
of any artificer in any of the trades hereinafter
enumerated, or for the performance by any artificer
of any labour in any of the said trades, the wages of
such artificer shall be made payable in the current

coin of this realm only, and not otherwise ; and that if in any such contract the whole or any part of such wages shall be made payable in any manner other than in the current coin aforesaid, such contract shall be illegal, null, and void."[1]—"If in any contract hereafter to be made between any artificer in any of the trades hereinafter enumerated and his employer, any provision shall be made directly or indirectly respecting the place where, or the manner in which, or the person or persons with whom, the whole or any part of the wages due or to become due to any such artificer shall be laid out or expended, such contract shall be illegal, null, and void."[2]—"The entire amount of the wages earned by or payable to any artificer in any of the trades hereinafter enumerated, in respect of any labour by him done in any such trade, shall be actually paid to such artificer in the current coin of this realm, and not otherwise ; and every payment made to any such artificer by his employer of or in respect of any such wages, by the delivering to him of goods, or otherwise than in the current coin aforesaid, except as hereinafter mentioned, shall be illegal, null, and void."[3]—"Every artificer in any of the trades hereinafter enumerated shall be entitled to recover from his employer in any such trade, in the manner by law provided for the recovery of servants' wages, or by any other lawful ways and means, the whole or so much of the wages earned by such artificer in such trade as shall not have been actually paid to him by such employer in the current coin of this realm."[4]—"In any action, suit, or other proceeding to be hereafter brought or commenced by any such artificer as aforesaid against his employer, for the recovery of any sum of money due to any such artificer as the wages of his labour in any of the trades hereinafter enumerated, the defendant shall

[1] S. 1.   [2] S. 2.   [3] S. 3.   [4] S. 4.

not be allowed to make any set-off nor to claim any reduction of the plaintiff's demand by reason or in respect of any goods, wares, or merchandise had or received by the plaintiff as or on account of his wages, or in reward for his labour, or by reason or in respect of any goods, wares, or merchandise sold, delivered, or supplied to such artificer, at any shop or warehouse kept by or belonging to such employer, or in the profits of which such employer shall have any share or interest."[1]—"No employer of any artificer in any of the trades hereinafter enumerated shall have or be entitled to maintain any suit or action in any Court of Law or Equity against any such artificer, for or in respect of any goods, wares, or merchandise sold, delivered, or supplied to any such artificer by any such employer whilst in his employment, as or on account of his wages or reward for his labour, or for or in respect of any goods, wares, or merchandise sold, delivered, or supplied to any such artificer at any shop or warehouse kept by or belonging to such employer, or in the profits of which such employer shall have any share or interest."[2]

"If any such artificer as aforesaid, or his wife or widow, or if any child of any such artificer, not being of the full age of twenty-one years, shall become chargeable to any parish or place, and if within the space of three calendar months next before the time when any such charge shall be incurred, such artificer shall have earned or have become entitled to receive any wages for any labour by him done in any of the said trades, which wages shall not have been paid to such artificer in the current coin of this realm, it shall be lawful for the overseers or overseer of the poor in such parish or place to recover from the employer of such artificer, in whose service such labour was done,

[1] S. 5.　　　　　　　[2] S. 6.

the full amount of wages so unpaid, and to proceed for the recovery thereof by such ways and means as such artificer might have proceeded for that purpose; and the amount of the wages which may have been so recovered shall be employed in reimbursing such parish or place all such costs and charges incurred in respect of the person or persons so become chargeable, and the surplus shall be applied and paid over to such person or persons."[1]

"Provided that nothing herein contained shall be construed to prevent or to render invalid any contract for the payment or any actual payment to any such artificer as aforesaid of the whole or any part of his wages, either in the notes of the governor and company of the Bank of England, or in the notes of any person or persons carrying on the business of a banker and duly licensed to issue such notes in pursuance of the laws relating to His Majesty's revenue of stamps, or in drafts or orders for the payment of money to the bearer on demand, drawn upon any person or persons carrying on the business of a banker, being duly licensed as aforesaid, within fifteen miles of the place where such drafts or orders shall be so paid, if such artificer shall be freely consenting to receive such drafts or orders as aforesaid; but all payments so made, with such consent as aforesaid, in any such notes, drafts, or orders as aforesaid, shall, for the purposes of this Act, be as valid and effectual as if such payments had been made in the current coin of the realm."[2]

By the Truck Amendment Act of 1887 it is provided that its provisions, and those of the Act of 1831, are to extend to, and include, any workman as defined by the Employers and Workmen Act, 1875 (*see* Appendix). In the case of an advance in wages employers are for-

[1] S. 7.

[2] S. 8. Ss. 9 to 18 relate to penalties, their recovery and application. See also Truck Act Amendment Act, 1887 (50 & 51 Vict. c. 45).

bidden from making deductions save as regards covenants in husbandry. Orders for goods as a deduction from wages are considered illegal, and so are contracts with workman as to spending wages at any particular shop or particular manner. In the case of deductions from workman's wages for education, the workman is entitled to have his child's school fees paid by employer. No deduction from wages is permissible for repairing . or sharpening tools. All receipts and expenditure in respect of deductions have to be duly audited. Articles under the value of £5 made by a person at his own house or otherwise by himself or the members of his family come within the Act. These articles comprise goods knitted or otherwise manufactured of wools, worsted, yarn, stuff, jersey, linen, fustian, cloth, serge, cotton, leather, fur, hemp, flax, mohair, or silk, or of any combination thereof, or made or prepared of bone, thread, silk, or cotton lace, or of lace made of mixed materials. Penalties are imposed on employers or agents contravening the provisions. A person engaged in the same trade as an employer charged with an offence cannot act as a Justice of the Peace in hearing and determining such charge.

" Nothing herein contained shall extend to any domestic servant or servant in husbandry."[1]

" Nothing herein contained shall extend or be construed to extend to prevent any employer of any artificer, or agent of any such employer, from supplying or contracting to supply to any such artificer any medicine or medical attendance, or any fuel, or any materials, tools, or implements to be by such artificer employed in his trade or occupation, if such artificer be employed

---

[1] 1 & 2 W. IV. c. 37, s. 20. Ss. 21 and 22 relate to the magistrates qualified to act in enforcing penalties. See also Truck Act Amendment Act, 1887 (50 & 51 Vic. c. 46).

in mining, or any hay, corn, or other provender to be
consumed by any horse or other beast of burden employed by any such artificer in his trade or occupation; nor from demising to any artificer, workman,
or labourer employed in any of the trades or occupations enumerated in this Act, the whole or any
part of any tenement, at any rent to be therein reserved; nor from supplying or contracting to supply
to any such artificer any victuals dressed or prepared
under the roof of any such employer, and there consumed by such artificer; nor from making nor contracting to make any stoppage or deduction from the wages
of any such artificer for or in respect of any such rent,
or for or in respect of any such medicine or medical
attendance, or for or in respect of such fuel, materials,
tools, implements, hay, corn, or provender, or of any
such victuals dressed and prepared under the roof of
any such artificer for any such purpose as aforesaid:
Provided always, that such stoppage or deduction shall
not exceed the real and true value of such fuel, materials, tools, implements, hay, corn, and provender, and
shall not be in any case made from the wages of any
such artificer, unless the agreement or contract for
such stoppage or deduction shall be in writing, and
signed by such artificer."[1]

"Nothing herein contained shall extend, or be construed to extend, to prevent any such employer from
advancing to any such artificer any money to be by
him contributed to any friendly society or bank for
savings duly established according to law, nor from
advancing to any such artificer any money for his
relief in sickness, or for the education of any child or

---

[1] 1 & 2 W. IV. c. 37, s. 23. An agreement to deduct rent need
not be in writing: Chawner v. Cummings, *post*. See also secs. 8 and
9 of Truck Act, 1887, in Appendix.

children of any such artificer, nor from deducting or contracting to deduct any sum or sums of money from the wages of such artificer for the education of any such child or children of such artificer, and unless the agreement or contract for such deduction shall be in writing, and signed by such artificer."[1]

"In the meaning and for the purposes of this Act, all workmen, labourers, and other persons in any manner engaged in the performance of any work, employment, or operation of what nature soever, in or about the several trades and occupations aforesaid, shall be and be deemed 'artificers'; and within the meaning and for the purposes aforesaid, all masters, bailiffs, foremen, managers, clerks, and other persons engaged in the hiring, employment, or superintendence of the labour of any such artificers, shall be and be deemed to be 'employers'; and within the meaning and for the purposes of this Act, any money or other thing had or contracted to be paid, delivered, or given as a recompense, reward, or remuneration for any labour done or to be done, whether within a certain time or to a certain amount, or for a time or an amount uncertain, shall be deemed and be taken as the 'wages' for such labour; and within the meaning and for the purposes aforesaid, any agreement, understanding, device, contrivance, collusion, or arrangement whatsoever, on the subject of wages, whether written or oral, whether direct or indirect, to which the employer and artificer are parties, or are assenting, or by which they are mutually bound to each other, or whereby either of them shall have endeavoured to impose an obligation on the other of them, shall be and be deemed a 'contract.'"[2]

[1] 1 & 2 W. IV. c. 37, s. 24. See also secs. 7, 8, 9 of Truck Act, 1887 (50 & 51 Vict. c. 46), in Appendix.

[2] 1 & 2 W. IV. c. 37, s. 25. See Truck Act, 1887 (50 & 51 Vic. c. 46), in Appendix.

There have been numerous decisions under these statutes, many of which will be found noted in the Table of Cases, *supra.*

With regard to the statute 1 & 2 William IV. c. 37, it has been decided, that, with the exception of the 23rd section, it prohibits the *payment* only of wages otherwise than in money, and does not apply to deductions or charges upon wages which are agreed to at the time between the master and the workman, or which are according to the usage of trade (such usage being, in effect, part of the agreement between the parties). In this case, the balance remaining after the deduction or charge is the amount payable as wages.

A frame-work knitter was employed in weaving gloves by a middle-man, to be paid an agreed gross price per dozen pairs of glove-fingers made by him, subject to certain charges and deductions, viz., 1s. 6d. per week for the use of the frames, which were furnished by the employer; 1s. 6d. per week as a remuneration for the use of the employer's premises in which the work was to be performed, for the standing-room of the frame, and for the trouble and loss of time of the employer in procuring and conveying the materials, and for his responsibility to the master manufacturer for the due return of the manufactured articles, for sorting the goods and re-delivering them at the warehouse of the master manufacturer; 7d. per week for winding the yarn, which operation was performed by a child, whose wages were 6d. per week, and the remaining penny was for the use of the winding machinery; and 1d. in each shilling on the amount of the workman's earnings above 14s. per week, as a compensation to the middle-man for a per-centage paid to the master manufacturer on the amount of goods manufactured by machinery rented by him. These deductions were held not con-

trary to the Truck Act. It was also determined that they
were not stoppages or deductions for which an agreement in writing was required by the 23rd section.[1]

In another case, it was decided, that the statute is confined to persons who enter into contracts to employ
their personal services, and to receive payment for such
service in wages; and therefore that a sub-contractor
for excavating a certain portion of railway cutting, who
employed labourers to assist him in the performance
of his contract, was not a labourer within the meaning
of the Truck Act, although he did part of the work
himself.[2]

But if by the contract the workman is bound to give
his personal labour, although it may be a contract to
do so much work, and he may be at liberty and does
employ others to assist him, it has been held that he is
within the protection of the Act.[3]

The amount of deductions allowed by section 23 need
not be specified in the written agreement. It is sufficient if the workman agrees generally that the master
may make deductions from his wages for such matters.[4]
There must be a written agreement to authorise a deduction under ss. 23 and 24, for medical expenses or education.[5] A deduction of 6d. a week for a contribution
to a medical fund is legal.[4] The supply of materials
mentioned in section 23 means materials sold to the
workman, and not merely goods let to him. If materials
are supplied under a written agreement, it lies on the
master to prove that the true value only is charged.[6]

[1] Chawner v. Cummings, 8 Q. B. 311. Archer v. James, 2 B. and
S. 61. Moorhouse v. Lee, 4 F. and F. 354.
[2] Riley v. Warden, 2 Excheq. 59. Sharman v. Sanders, 13 C. B.
106. Ingram v. Barnes, 7 E. and B. 115. Sleeman v. Barrett, 2 H.
and C. 934.
[3] Floyd v. Weaver, 16 Jur. 289. Bowers v. Lovekin, 6 E. and B.
584.   [4] Cutts v. Ward, L. R. 2 Q. B. 357.
[5] Pillar v. Lynvi Coal Company, L. R. 4 C. P. 752.
[6] Cutts v. Ward, L. R. 2 Q. B. 357.

It seems that, although the wages are paid in money, if any constraint is put on the workman by the master, or those authorised by him, to induce the workman to spend it in a shop in which the master is interested, the payment is not sufficient. The coercion must come from the master. He is not bound by the acts of persons not authorised to hire or discharge the workmen, such as a clerk or overseer.[1] If the master has given goods instead of money in payment of wages, he has incurred a penalty under the Act, and this is not purged by the subsequent payment of the wages in money or their recovery by the workman by action at law.[2]

Chawner v. Cummings, Archer v. James, and Moorhouse v. Lee were decisions on a custom in the hosiery manufacture. It has been put an end to by 37 & 38 Vic., c. 38 (passed 30th July, 1874), which enacts as follows:—

" 1. In all contracts for wages the full and entire amount of all wages and earnings of labour in the hosiery manufacture shall be actually and positively made payable in net, in the current coin of the realm, and not otherwise, without any deduction or stoppage of any description whatever, save and except for bad and disputed workmanship.

" 2. All contracts to stop wages, and all contracts for frame rents and charges, between employer and artificers, shall be and are hereby declared to be illegal, null, and void.

" 3. If any employer shall bargain to deduct, or shall deduct, directly or indirectly, from the wages of any artificer in his employ any part of such wages for frame rent and standing or other charges, or shall refuse or neglect to pay the same or any part thereof in the current coin of the realm, he shall forfeit a sum of five pounds for every offence, to be recovered by the said

---

[1] Olding v. Smith, 16 Jur. 496.
[2] Wilson v. Cookson, 13 C. B. N. S. 496.

artificer or any other person suing for the same in the
county court in the district where the offence is committed, with full costs of suit.

"4. If any frame or machine which shall have been
entrusted to any artificer or other person by his
employer for the purpose of being used in the hosiery
manufacture for such employer, or in any process
incident to such manufacture, shall, whilst the same
shall be so entrusted, be worked, used, or employed
without the consent in writing of such employer or
other person so entrusting such frame or machine, in
the manufacture of any goods ór articles whatever for
any other person than the person by whom such frame
or machine shall have been so entrusted, then and in
every such case the artificer or other person to whom
the same shall have been so entrusted shall forfeit and
pay the sum of ten shillings for every day on any part
of which any such frame or machine shall have been so
worked, used, or employed, to be recoverable by and for
the benefit of the person who shall have so entrusted
the same, in the county court for the district where the
offence shall have been committed, with full costs of suit.

"5. No action, suit, or set-off between employer and
artificer shall be allowed for any deduction or stoppage
of wages, nor for any contract hereby declared illegal.

"6. Nothing in this Act contained shall extend to
prevent the recovery in the ordinary course of law, by
suit brought or commenced for the purpose, of any
debt due from the artificer to the employer.

"7. Within the meaning and for the purposes of this
Act, all workmen, labourers, and other persons in any
manner engaged in the performance of any employment or operation, of what nature soever, in or about
the hosiery manufacture, shall be and be deemed
'artificers;' and, within the meaning and for the purposes aforesaid, all masters, foremen, managers, clerks,

contractors, sub-contractors, middlemen, and other persons engaged in the hiring, employment, or superintendence of the labour of any such artificers shall be and be deemed to be 'employers;' and, within the meaning and for the purposes of this Act, any money or other thing had or contracted to be paid, delivered, or given as a recompense, reward, or remuneration for any labour done or to be done, whether within a certain time or to a certain amount, or for a time or for an amount uncertain, shall be deemed and taken to be the wages of such labour; and within the meaning and for the purposes aforesaid, any agreement, understanding, device, contrivance, collusion, or arrangement whatsoever on the subject of wages, whether written or oral, whether direct or indirect, to which the employer and artificers are parties or are assenting, or by which they are mutually bound to each other, or whereby either of them shall have endeavoured to impose an obligation on the other of them, shall be and be deemed a 'contract.'

"8. This Act shall not commence or take effect till the expiration of three calendar months next after the day of passing the same."

10. Illegal contracts are sometimes divisible, that is, good in part, and bad in part; and sometimes indivisible, or entirely bad.

Where two acts are agreed to be done, one legal and the other illegal, the contract is divisible, and good as to the legal act, but bad as to the other. Thus, where on the sale of a business the seller agreed not to carry on business within London or 600 miles thereof, the contract was held good so far as it restrained him from carrying on business in London, such being a reasonable restraint of trade, but void as to the 600 miles.[1]

[1] Mallan v. May, 13 M. and W. 517. Green v. Price, 13 M. and W. 695. Price v. Green, 16 M. and W. 346.

But if a single act is agreed to be done, or a sum of money to be paid in consideration of something illegal and something legal, the whole is void;[1] because the act to be done or money to be paid is in part a reward for an illegal act, and it cannot be ascertained what part or how much is to be done or paid for the legal and what part or how much for the illegal act.

It may be illegal on one side and not on the other. If one party intends to violate the law and the other does not, and is ignorant of the illegal purpose, the innocent party can enforce the contract and the guilty cannot.[2]

11. Imperfect contracts are—1, contracts made without consideration; 2, contracts made with incapable persons; 3, contracts obtained by undue means; 4, contracts not sufficiently authenticated.

Contracts considered with reference to the solemnity of their execution are of two sorts,—specialties or simple contracts. A specialty must be in writing, on paper or parchment, and sealed and delivered as a deed: a simple contract may be either in writing or verbal.

What a party agrees to do by deed, he is bound to perform, although his agreement is unilateral, that is, without anything being given or done, or agreed to be given or done, by the other contracting party: thus, if a man by deed agrees to build a house, he must do so, although he is to receive nothing for his pains. A specialty is higher in class and degree than a simple contract; and if a man first agrees to do a thing by a simple contract, and subsequently agrees to do the same thing by deed, the agreement by simple contract is merged and extinguished by the contract by deed. On the other hand, if he first agrees to do a thing by deed, and afterwards a simple contract is made that he shall

[1] Scott v. Gilmore, 3 Taunt. 226.
[2] Bloxsome v. Williams, 3 B. and C. 234. Clay v. Yates, 1 H. and N. 73. Cowan v. Milbourn, L. R. 2 Ex. 230.

do something in lieu of the thing covenanted to be done, he is bound to perform his covenant notwithstanding. A subsequent specialty extinguishes a simple contract, but a subsequent simple contract cannot vary or alter the obligation of a deed. Contracts by deed are called covenants; simple contracts are called promises or agreements.

12. Simple contracts are not binding unless founded upon a consideration, which is defined to be something given or done, or agreed to be given or done, by the promisee, beneficial to the promiser, or prejudicial to the promisee. There must be something given or done, or agreed to be given or done, by each party to the contract. The performance of a gratuitous unilateral promise is as gratuitous or honorary as the promise: this is either founded on the notion that it is not the intention of the parties that such a promise shall be binding and irrevocable, or on the notion that the party with whom the promise is made, and who neither gives nor agrees to give anything in exchange for it, loses nothing by the promise not being performed.

An action was brought against a carpenter, who had been retained by the plaintiff to repair his house before a given day, and had accepted the retainer, but did not perform the work, whereby the plaintiff's house was damaged. The action was held not maintainable, because it did not appear that the defendant was to receive any consideration, or that he had entered upon the work: had he entered upon the work, the plaintiff suffering him to do it would have been a sufficient consideration for an agreement by him to do it properly.[1]

In another case, the defendant agreed to remain with the plaintiff two years for the purpose of learning the business of a dress-maker, and left the service

[1] Elsee v. Gatward, 5 D. and E. 143.

before the expiration of the term. The Court held that she was not liable to an action, because there was no agreement on the part of the plaintiff to teach or employ her.[1]

In Sykes v. Dixon,[2] Bradley agreed to work for Sykes in making powder-flasks, and for no other person, for twelve months: he left Sykes' service within twelve months, and entered into the service of Dixon. The Court held that no action could be maintained against Dixon for harbouring Bradley, because the agreement was void for want of consideration, there being no agreement on the part of Sykes to employ Bradley. And although it was urged that an agreement to pay Bradley for his work would be implied, which would form a sufficient consideration, the Court said that would be the same in any service to which Bradley might engage himself, and was no consideration for the contract to serve for a specified time. The obligation to pay wages would arise from the service performed, and not before, and there was no express agreement to pay wages for the period during which Bradley agreed to serve. In these two cases the agreements were not signed by the master. If he had signed or agreed to the agreement, an engagement by him to employ would have been implied.[3]

A promise to reward a man for doing that which he is under a previous obligation to do is without consideration. The master of a ship promised to pay a seaman five guineas above his wages for doing some extra work in navigating the ship. The promise was void, because the seaman was previously bound to obey all the master's orders in navigating the vessel.[4]

---

[1] Lees v. Whitcomb, 5 Bing. 34. [2] 9 A. and E. 693.
[3] Whittle v. Frankland, 2 B. and S. 49.
[4] Harris v. Watson, Peake, 102.

In the course of a voyage some seamen deserted, and the captain promised to divide their wages amongst the rest of the crew. Lord Ellenborough held the promise to be void for want of consideration, saying, " Before the ship sailed from London, the sailors had undertaken to do all they could, under all the emergencies of the voyage : they had sold all their services until the voyage should be completed. If the captain had capriciously discharged the two men who were wanting, the others might not have been compellable to take the whole duty upon themselves, and their agreeing to do so might have been a sufficient consideration for the promise of an advance of wages." [1] If any extra service or extra risk be incurred beyond the risk agreed, and if the ship in the course of the voyage is undermanned, there is a consideration for an extra reward.[2]

13. It is essential to every contract that there should be two parties to it, and it is essential to the legal validity of every contract that each party to it should be in law competent to contract. If either party is incompetent, the contract is imperfect. Of such contracts, some are void and incapable of being confirmed or enforced ; others are voidable and capable of being confirmed.

A married woman is incompetent to contract, and her contract is at law absolutely void. This is because she is incapable by law of possessing property during her coverture, and therefore cannot have the means of performing a contract. She is competent to contract if the marriage is dissolved by decree of the Divorce Court, or if a judicial separation is decreed during the separation, or if she obtains a protection order from the

---

[1] Stilk v. Myrich, 2 Camp. 317 ; 6 Esp. 129.

[2] England v. Davidson, 11 A. & E. 856. Clutterbuck v. Coffin, 3 M. and G. 842. Hartley v. Ponsonby, 7 E. and B. 872.

Divorce Court or a magistrate during its continuance.[1]
If the husband has been convicted of felony and trans-
ported, during his sentence, which is civil death, she
is capable of contracting. She is capable of acting as
agent for her husband, or any other person, in making
a contract: in such case the principal, and not the
married woman, is at law the party to the contract.
That was the law prior to 1882 ; now, however, she is
entitled to more extended privileges, and can contract
to the extent of her separate property. She can also
be sued in respect thereof.

14. Although a person who is incapable of understanding the nature of a contract, from insanity or
drunkenness, cannot give that consent which is usually
essential to a contract, yet if the other party is ignorant
of his incapacity, and the contract is executed, it is
binding on the lunatic. There is an apparent though
not an actual consent by both parties, and it is more
reasonable that he should be bound than that the other
party, who trusted to his apparent capacity, should
suffer. The lunatic cannot in such case repudiate the
contract and recover money he has paid under it, and
if he has received the consideration he must pay the
price.[2] The same principle may apply to executory
contracts, though it has not as yet been extended to
them. But if the other party has notice of the insanity or drunkenness, the contract is invalid,[3] and
perhaps for necessaries furnished for the lunatic not
under control he may be liable, though the party fur-
nishing them know him to be a lunatic.[4]

15. The contracts of infants, or persons under the

[1] 20 & 21 Vict. c. 85, ss. 21 & 26 ; 21 & 22 Vict. c. 108, s. 8.

[2] Molton v. Camroux, 2 Ex. 487 ; 4 Ex. 17. Beavan v. M'Donnel,
9 Ex. 209. Campbell v. Hooper, 1 Jur. N. S. 670.

[3] Gore v. Gibson, 13 M. and W. 623. Brandon v. Old, 3 C. and
P. 440.   [4] Howard v. Digby, 2 Cl. and Fin. 621.

age of twenty-one years, are in some cases valid, in some voidable, and in some void.

Contracts to pay a reasonable price for necessaries supplied to the infant or his family are binding on him. Necessaries include necessary meat, drink, apparel, physic, and good teaching and instruction, whereby he may profit himself afterwards.[1] But if an infant has houses, and it is necessary to put them in repair, and he makes a contract for the repairs, he is not bound. No contract binds him but such as concerns his person.[2] The infant who has property ought to have a guardian to take care of it.

An agreement to serve for wages is, according to the opinion of Lord Abinger, generally speaking, binding on an infant,[3] assuming, of course, that his station in life renders it necessary for him to earn his livelihood during his infancy; and if an infant labourer deserts his service, he may, it has been said by Bayley and Littledale, JJ., be punished under the Master and Servants' Act.[4] But if the terms of the agreement are inequitable, and not beneficial to the infant, the agreement is void, and he cannot be punished for its breach: as if the agreement professes to bind the infant to serve for a term, but leaves the master free to stop his work and wages whenever he chooses.[5]

According to Fitzherbert, an infant of the age of twelve is bound by his covenant to serve in husbandry.[6] The Factory Acts may perhaps be considered as recognising the validity of the contracts to serve by infants of the age of eleven years.

[1] Co. Lit. 172, a.

[2] Per Haughton, J., Tirrell's case, 2 Rol. Rep. 271. Anon. 3 Salk. 196.

[3] Per Lord Abinger, Wood v. Fenwick, 10 M. and W. 204.

[4] Per Bayley, J., and Littledale, J., Rex v. Chillerford, 4 B. and C. 101.

[5] Reg. v. Lord, 12 Q. B. 757.   [6] F. N. B. 168.

The authority of Fitzherbert ought perhaps to be understood as confined to simple contracts of infants, since it has been held that a covenant by an infant in an apprentice deed is voidable by him.[1] The reason that an infant cannot bind himself by deed may be that the validity of his contracts depends upon the nature and amount of the consideration, and in contracts by deed the consideration is immaterial. There is said to be a custom of London by which an infant may bind himself by an apprenticeship indenture to continue after he is twenty-one. This custom is so variously stated in the Reports that it may be doubted whether it has been sufficiently uniform from time immemorial to be good, or, if uniform, whether it is not bad as unreasonable.[2] By the general law, though he cannot be sued on his covenant, he is bound by the indenture of apprenticeship to serve his master,[3] but not after he is twenty-one.[4]

A deed which may be beneficial to an infant is merely voidable by him, and, until avoided, it stands good. An infant slave in the West Indies entered into a deed by which he covenanted to serve his master for a certain term: the Court held that it was not void, because it was beneficial to the infant, inasmuch as it operated to emancipate him, and therefore a party who had seduced the infant from the service of his master was liable to an action.[5]

[*See* Infants' Relief Act, 1874 (37 & 38 Vic. c. 62), in Appendix.]

[1] Gylbert v. Fletcher, Cro. Car. 179.

[2] 21 Edw. I. 6 pl. 17. Stanton's Case, Moor, 135. Walker v. Nicholson, Cro. El. 652. Burton v. Palmer, 2 Bulst. 191. Code v. Holmes, Palm. 361, 2 Rol. 305. Mould v. Wallis, 1 Keb. 376, 512. Horn v. Chandler, 1 Mod. 271 ; 2 Keb. 687. Com. Dig. London, N. 2. Eden's case, 2 M. and S. 226.

[3] Rex v. Arundel, 5 M. and S. 257. Cooper v. Simmons, 6 H. and N. 707.

[4] Exp. Davis, 6 D. and E. 715.   [5] Keane v. Boycott, 2 H. Bl. 511.

But a contract which the Court can pronounce to be prejudicial to the infant is void, as is a bond with a penalty.[1]

16. If any fraud is practised by one party on the other in inducing him to enter into a contract, the contract may be avoided by the party defrauded. Fraud consists in some false statement which the party making it knows to be false, or some studied concealment or suppression of a material circumstance by which the other party is deceived. If the statement is obviously false, or the truth can be ascertained by the exercise of ordinary caution, the contract is not void for fraud. If a man is injured by a contract made upon such a statement, it is rather the effect of his own carelessness than of the fraud of the other. Thus, where a carrier agreed with the defendant to carry a load of wool at so much a hundredweight, and inquired of him how much it weighed, and the defendant said 8 cwt. (the wool, in fact, weighed 2000 lbs., and in consequence the carrier's horses were overstrained and killed), the Judges intimated their opinion that the carrier had no remedy, because he was in default in not weighing the goods before he received them; and he abandoned his action.[2]

A person who by false and fraudulent representations of his ability to cure a cancer without cutting, by means of sovereign remedies, induced another, afflicted with that disease, to employ him, was held not entitled to recover any remuneration for his services or medicines, by reason of the contract of employment being void for fraud.[3]

The fraud of the fraudulent party entitles the party

[1] Baylis v. Dyneley, 3 M. and S. 481.
[2] Baily v. Merrell, 3 Bulst. 94. Thwaites v. Mackerson, 3 C. and P. 341.
[3] Hupe v. Phelps, 2 Stark. 480.

defrauded to avoid the contract so soon as he discovers the fraud, and he cannot be compelled. to perform it, and may maintain an action to recover any damage he has sustained by reason of the fraud. But if he does perform his part of the contract, he cannot sue the other party upon any other contract than that actually made. A man agreed to cart away some rubbish for £15, in consequence of a fraudulent representation by his employer as to the depth of the rubbish. He performed the work, and claimed £20 as the value of his labour. It was decided that he was not entitled to more than the agreed price, since although the fraud of the defendant entitled him to avoid the contract, it did not authorise him to impose on the defendant terms to which he had not agreed: there being an express agreement as to the price, the law would not imply one. Parke, B., said, "Upon discovering the fraud, the plaintiff should immediately have declared off, and sought compensation in an action for deceit."[1]

If, after discovering the fraud, the party defrauded proceeds with the contract, or does any act by which he treats it as valid, he is bound by it. The election which the law gives to avoid the contract is an election which he may waive when he knows of his situation.[2] In cases of fraud, the contract is imperfect because of the want of the free consent of one of the contracting parties: when the party defrauded, after discovering the fraud, assents to the contract, he supplies the free consent which was wanting, and the contract becomes perfect.

17. Of contracts which are imperfect by reason of not being properly authenticated, may be instanced the

[1] Selway v. Fogg, 5 Mee. and Wels. 83. De Symons v. Minchwich, 1 Esp. 430.

[2] Campbell v. Fleming, 1 Ad. and El. 40.

simple contracts of corporations. A corporation is an artificial being, or body politic, existing by prescription, or created by charter, or Act of Parliament, or by registration under the Joint Stock Companies' Act. Railway companies are corporations by Act of Parliament: so are the guardians of the poor-law union. In the case of a corporation, the community has a legal existence distinct from the individuals composing it, and may possess property and make contracts which are binding on the corporate property.

With reference to contracts there is a distinction between corporations established for the purposes of government, of which nature are municipal corporations, the Metropolitan Board, boards of works, vestries, local boards, boards of guardians, &c., which have to be satisfied out of property with which they have been endowed for public purposes, or the rates they are empowered to levy on the portion of the public who are subject to them, and corporations established for trading purposes, such as railway and other like companies, and companies registered under the Joint Stock Companies' Acts, and which have to be satisfied out of the joint stock of the company, subscribed for the purpose of carrying on businesses with a view to profit.

A municipal corporation cannot bind themselves to pay a sum of money out of the corporation funds for making improvements within the borough unless the contract is under the common seal. The exceptions to the rule that a corporation can only bind itself by deed are—1. Cases so constantly occurring, and of such small importance, or so little admitting of delay, that to require in every such case the previous affixing of the seal, would be greatly to obstruct the every-day ordinary convenience of the body corporate, without any adequate object, in which instances the head of the corporation is considered as delegated by the rest of the members to act for them. 2. The instances of trading corporations.[1] The guardians of Billericay Union made a contract by deed with Mr. Lamprell, a builder, for building their union workhouse. The works were to be done under the superintendence of Messrs. Scott and Moffat, architects, and it was provided that if the architects required alterations or additions in the progress of the works, they should give Lamprell written instructions for the same, signed by them, and that he should not be deemed to have authority to do such additional works without such written instructions. The contract price was £5,500. Many extra works were done, which were valued by Scott and Moffat at £3,133, and there were several letters, some from Scott and some from Moffat, approving of the extra works. The guardians had paid £6,300, and had accepted and acquiesced in the additional works. An action was brought by Lamprell against the guardians for the balance of the contract price and the extra works. The Court of Exchequer, with great reluctance, decided against him, saying that his claim was apparently the most just and reasonable. The ground of the decision was, that the guardians, being a corporation, could only be bound by the deed, and the orders for the extra works were not according to the deed. They held that a written order signed by one of the architects was not sufficient to render the guardians liable, the deed requiring it to be signed by both; and that a writing signed by the architects during the progress of the extra works, or after their completion, was not sufficient. They also held that Lamprell could not appropriate the payments to the extra works, although made generally on account,

[1] Mayor of Ludlow v. Charlton, 6 M. and W. 815. 1 Williams's Notes to Saunders, 616. Note to Mellor v. Spateman.

because there was no liability on the part of the guardians to pay for any of the extras.[1]

So the guardians of a union were not bound by the appointment of a clerk or assistant to the master of the workhouse, whose duties were principally the keeping of accounts of a somewhat complicated nature, requiring some amount of skill and capacity.[2]

The hiring of a butler or cook, or the appointment of a bailiff to take cattle damage feasant, by a municipal corporation, is within the exception as a matter of frequent and ordinary occurrence, and need not be under seal.[3] So the supply of goods or rendering of occasional services necessary to be from time to time supplied or rendered, and which have been supplied or rendered under a contract in fact, made by the managing body of the corporation, is binding, though the contract is not by deed.[4] But the making a plan of one of the parishes of the union was held not to be necessary for the guardians of the union, nor incidental to the purposes for which they were created, and therefore they were not liable on a verbal order to pay for such plan.[5]

18. Trading corporations are liable on all contracts entered into for the purpose for which they are incorporated, though not under seal. It can only carry on business by agents, managers, and others, and if the contracts made by these persons are contracts which relate to objects and purposes of the company, and are not inconsistent with the rules and regulations which

[1] Lamprell v. Guardians of Billericay Union, 3 Ex. 283.
[2] Austin v. Guardians of Bethnal Green, L. R. 9 C. P. 91.
[3] Bac. Abr. Corporation, E. 3.
[4] Sanders v. St. Neot's Union, 8 Q. B. 810. Clarke v. Cuckfield Union, 1 L. and M. 81, 21 L. J. Q. B. 349. Haigh v. Bierley Union, E. B. and E. 873. Nicholson v. Bradfield Union, L. R. 1 Q. B. 620.
[5] Paine v. Strand Union, 8 Q. B. 326.

govern their acts, they are valid and binding on the company, though not under seal.[1] But a preliminary agreement to execute a contract under seal for a commercial company has been held not to be binding, the intention being that there should be a contract under seal.[2]

19. By the Companies' Clauses Consolidation Act, which relates to most companies constituted by private Acts of Parliament, in and since 1845, such as railway companies, &c., contracts may be made by the directors or committee so as to bind the company, either by deed or writing, or word of mouth, in the same cases in which contracts by deed or writing or word of mouth are binding on individuals.[3]

By the Companies' Act, 1867, relating to companies incorporated by registration, contracts, which if made by private persons should be under seal, may be under the common seal of the company. Those which between private persons should be in writing or by parol, may be made for the company by any person acting under their express or implied authority.[4]

Under these Acts companies are bound by the contracts of their agents acting in the usual course of their business, and within the general or apparent scope of their authority. And their authority may be inferred from goods and work necessary for their business being accepted and used by them or their agents at their place of business.[5] In a case in which there

[1] South of Ireland Colliery Company v. Waddle, L. R. 3 C. P. 469 ; 4 C. P. 617. Henderson v. Australian Royal Steam Navigation Company, 5 E. and B. 409. Reuter v. Electric Telegraph Company, 6 E. and B. 341.

[2] London Dock Company v. Sinnot, 8 E. and B. 347.

[3] 8 & 9 Vict. c. 16, s. 97.   [4] 30 & 31 Vict. c. 131, s. 37.

[5] Smith v. Hull Glass Company, 11 C. B. 897. Pauling v. London and North-Western Railway Company, 8 Ex. 867, per Lord Cranworth. Greenwood's Case, 18 Jur. 391. 3 De G. M. and G. 459. Walker v. Great Western Railway Company, L. R. 2 Ex. 228.

was a contract under seal with a company, governed by the Companies' Clauses Act, for the erection of pumps, engines, and machinery, extra works were done under the directions and with the approval of the company's engineer, it was decided that the company was not liable; it being considered that the engineer was not the agent of the company to order the extra works.[1]

These Acts being in the affirmative do not prevent contracts made in other modes being binding and effectual, when there is power to make them, and do not exclude any equity which may have existed before these provisions were introduced.[2]

20. The Public Health Act directs that a local board of health may enter into contracts for carrying the Act into execution, and that every contract, the value or amount of which exceeds £50, shall be in writing, and sealed with the common seal; and shall specify the work, materials, matters, or things to be so furnished, had, or done, the price to be paid, and the time or times within which the contract is to be performed, and fix some pecuniary penalty to be paid in case the terms of the contract are not performed. It also provides that, before contracting for works, the board shall obtain an estimate from the surveyor, &c.[3] These preliminaries as to the estimate, &c., are directory on the Board of Health, and, if neglected, do not render the contract invalid, and the board may be sued on the contract, although it is provided that they shall not be personally liable.[4]

[1] Homersham v. Wolverhampton Waterworks Company, 6 Ex. 147.

[2] Wilson v. West Hartlepool Railway and Harbour Company, 2 De G. J. and S. 475, 11 Jur. N.S. 126.

[3] 38 & 39 Vic. c. 55.

[4] Nowell v. Mayor of Worcester. 9 Ex. 457. See also Cole v. Green, 6 Man. and Grang. 872.

The provision as to the seal is essential. The section alone confers on the local board the power of entering into contracts, and they must exercise that power in the terms in which it is by the Act conferred upon them.[1]

If a corporation have performed its part of a contract, or does not object to the contract, the other party cannot object that the contract ought to have been, and was not, by deed.[2]

21. In cases in which the corporation is not bound at law because the contract is not under seal, and the claim of the plaintiff is for a simple money demand, he can have no relief in equity to enforce the contract; the non-payment of the price of work which has been done for them, and of which they have accepted the benefit, is not a fraud against which equity will relieve.[3] But if it is a case in which equity has jurisdiction as to decree specific performance, or as a matter of complicated account, and there has been what a court of equity considers fraud on the part of the corporation, they have jurisdiction. Thus a party who has been let into possession of land by a railway on an agreement, cannot be turned out of possession, and be liable to be treated as a trespasser, on the ground that there was no agreement. It is in the eye of a court of equity a fraud to set up the absence of an agreement when possession has been given on the faith of it;[4]

[1] Frend v. Dennett, 4 C. B. N. S. 576. Rutledge v. Farnham Board of Health, 2 F. and F. 406.

[2] Mayor of Carmarthen v. Lewis, 6 C. and P. 608. Ranger v. Great Western Railway, 5 House of Lords, 101. Fishmongers' Company v. Robertson, 5 Man. and Gr. 181. Australian Navigation Company v. Marzotti, 11 Ex. 228.

[3] Kirk v. Bromley, 2 Ph. 640. Ambrose v. Dummow Union, 9 Beav. 108. Crampton v. Varna Railway Company, L. R. 7 Ch. 562.

[4] Wilson v. West Hartlepool Railway and Dock Company, 2 De G. J. and S. 475.

and in case of a complicated account for works done for a railway company, Turner, L. J., said, " In my opinion companies, no less than individuals, must be answerable to the jurisdiction of this Court in cases of fraud; and I think that in the eye of this Court, at least, it would be a fraud on the part of this company to have desired by their engineer these alterations, additions, and omissions to be made, to have stood by and seen the expenditure going on upon them, and then to refuse payment on the ground that the expenditure was incurred without proper orders having been given for the purpose." [1] And a municipal corporation were compelled to grant a term pursuant to a resolution entered in their books, when they had allowed a wall to be built and money to be expended on the land on the faith of it.[2]

22. Some contracts are required by the statute law to be in writing. Such contracts, if not in writing, as required by the statute, are imperfect, and cannot be enforced.

The statutes which require contracts for works to be in writing are the Statute of Frauds, 29 Car. II. c. 3, and Lord Tenterden's Act, 9 Geo. IV. c. 14.

By the 4th section of the Statute of Frauds, " No action shall be brought upon any agreement that is not to be performed within a year from the making thereof, unless the agreement upon which the action shall be brought, or some memorandum or note thereof, shall be in writing, and signed by the party to be charged therewith, or some person by him thereunto lawfully authorised."

An agreement to hire a servant for a year, to com-

[1] Hill v. South Staffordshire Railway Company, 11 Jur. N. S., 193.
[2] Crook v. Corporation of Seaford, L. R. 6 Ch. 551.

mence on a future day, is within this statute;[1] but an agreement for a year's hiring, commencing at the time of making the agreement, which is the contract usually implied from a general hiring of a clerk or servant, is not.[2]

If the agreement is to be performed upon an event which may or may not happen within a year, as upon the death or marriage of one of the parties, it is not within the statute, and therefore need not be in writing.[3]

A stipulation in the contract making it defeasible within the year, does not take it out of the statute. Thus an agreement for the hire of a commercial traveller, made on the 2nd October, 1854, for his services from then until the 1st September, 1855, and from thence for a year, unless the employment was determined by three months' notice, was not enforceable because not in writing.[4]

The fact of the agreement being in part performed does not take it out of the statute.[5] But if an agreement is entirely executed on one part within a year, it is not within the statute, and the party who has fully performed his part may sue the other on the agreement, although it is not in writing.[6] To actions upon executed considerations, that is, to actions for the price of works which have been performed, whether performed within a year or beyond, the statute does not

[1] Bracegirdle v. Heald, 1 B. and Ald. 722. Snelling v. Lord Huntingfield, 1 C. M. and R. 25.

[2] Beeston v. Collyer, 4 Bing. 309. Cawthorne v. Cordrey, 13 C. B. N. S. 406.

[3] Peter v. Compton, Skin. 353. Souch v. Strawbridge, 2 C. B. 808.

[4] Dobson v. Collis, 1 H. and N. 81.

[5] Boydell v. Drummond, 11 East, 154.

[6] Donellan v. Read, 3 B. and Ad. 899. Cherry v. Heming, 4 Ex. 631.

apply, because in such case the agreement on which the action is founded is an agreement to pay the price of the work implied from its performance, and not an agreement which is not to be performed within a year.[1]

The statute requires the agreement, that is, every-thing that is agreed to be done by both parties, to be in writing; and no part of the agreement can be proved by parol. If the writing contains only the agreement of one of the parties, it stands as an agree-ment without consideration, and is of no effect. On this ground, the case of Sykes v. Dixon,[2] already re-ferred to, was decided. Nor can it be shown that the agreement of the parties was different in any respect than as contained in the writing. Thus where there was an agreement between the master and his clerk, that the one should serve the other at a specified annual salary, increasing each year, the clerk was not per-mitted to show that it was agreed that the salary should be paid quarterly, nor would the Court infer such agreement from the fact that it had been paid quarterly, the written agreement importing that it was to be paid annually.[3]

The 17th (in Revised Statutes 16th) section of the Statute of Frauds provides that "no contract for the sale of any goods, wares, or merchandise, for the price of £10 sterling or upwards, shall be allowed to be good, except the buyer shall accept part of the goods so sold, and actually receive the same, or give something in earnest to bind the bargain or in part payment, or that some note or memorandum in writing of the said bargain be made and signed by the parties to be charged

---

[1] Souch v. Strawbridge, 2 C. B. 814, per Tindal, C. J.
[2] 9 A. and E. 693.
[3] Giraud v. Richmond, 2 C. B. 835.

by such contract, or their agents thereunto lawfully authorised."

And by 9 Geo. IV. c. 14, s. 7—"The said enactment shall extend to all contracts for the sale of goods of the value of £10 sterling or upwards, notwithstanding they may be intended to be delivered at some future time, or may not at the time of such contract be actually made, procured, or provided, or fit or ready for delivery, or some act may be requisite for the making or completing thereof, or rendering the same fit for delivery."

If at the same time some ready-made goods are bought and others are ordered to be made, and the ready-made goods are delivered, the statutes are complied with, and the contract may be enforced.[1]

This last statute extends to all contracts for the manufacture of goods of the value of £10 or more, which, when manufactured, are to belong to the party ordering them : such are contracts for the sale of goods to be made.

But contracts for building or repairing houses, or for doing any works upon lands, if they may be performed within a year from the making thereof need not be in writing.

A contract to print a book is considered as a contract for work and materials, and not for the manufacture of goods, and therefore it need not be in writing.[2]

But a contract to make and fix a set of artificial teeth is a contract for the sale of goods. If the contract is such that when carried out it results in the sale of a chattel, the party cannot sue for work and labour ; but if the result of the contract is that the party has done work and labour which ends in nothing that can

[1] Scott v. Eastern Counties Railway, 12 M. and W. 33.
[2] Clay v. Yates, 1 H. and N. 73.

become the subject of sale, he cannot sue for goods sold.[1]

The written memorandum need only state all that is to be done for the party sought to be charged. Nor need it state a mere stipulation as to the mode of payment, such as that it was to be paid by cheque of the defendant's brother.[2]

23. Some contracts relating to works, if in writing, must be stamped : if unstamped, they are imperfect contracts. The Stamp Act provides generally that, save as therein appointed, no writing on which a stamp duty is imposed shall, except in criminal proceedings, be pleaded or given in evidence, or admitted to be good, useful, or available in law or equity, unless it is duly stamped in accordance with the law at the time when it was first executed.[3]

This is a defect which may be rectified. Agreements or deeds may be stamped at any time upon payment of the duty and a penalty of £10, and if they bear a sufficient stamp when produced in evidence, no inquiry is made as to when the stamp was impressed. If brought to be stamped within three months after their execution, the penalty may be wholly or partially remitted.[4]

The stamp duty, and £10 penalty, and £1 in addition, may be paid to the officer of the court on the production of unstamped instrument on the trial of a cause, and after such payment the instrument may be received in evidence. He is to give a receipt for the duty and penalty, and to account for the money to the Commissioners of Inland Revenue, and they are to stamp the instrument on production of the receipt, denoting it thereon.[5]

Every agreement, or minute, or memorandum of

[1] Lee v. Griffin, 1 B. and S. 277.
[2] Sarl v. Bourdillon, 1 C. B. N. S. 188.
[3] 54 & 55 Vic. c. 39, s. 14.   [4] S. 15.   [5] S. 14.

agreement, under hand only, whether it is only evidence of a contract, or obligatory upon the parties from its being a written instrument, is subject to a stamp duty of 6d. An agreement or memorandum the matter whereof is not of the value of £5, an agreement or memorandum for the hire of any labourer, artificer, manufacturer, or menial servant, an agreement, letter, or memorandum made for or relating to the sale of any goods, wares, or merchandise, an agreement or memorandum made between master and mariners of any ship or vessel for wages on any voyage coastwise from port to port in the United Kingdom, are exempt; [1] also an agreement entered into between landlord and tenant pursuant to subsection 6 of section 8, or subsection 2 of section 20 of the Land Law (Ireland) Act, 1881. An agreement for the hire of a fireman and stoker to a steam-vessel is within this exemption.[2] So is an agreement with an overseer in a printing-office.[3] Agreements relating to the sale of goods to be manufactured, which are required by Lord Tenterden's Act to be in writing, are also exempt.[4]

When the contract for works is by deed, it must be stamped as a deed not otherwise charged, the duty on which is 10s.[5]

The Stamp Act of 1891 has consolidated the enactments granting and relating to the stamp duties upon instruments and certain other enactments relating to stamp duties. A contract-note means the note sent by a broker or agent to his principal (except where such principal is acting as broker or agent for a principal) advising him of the sale or purchase of any stock or marketable security.

---

[1] Sched. tit. Agreement.   [2] Wilson v. Zulueta, 14 Q. B. 405.
[3] Bishop v. Letts, 1 F. and F. 401.
[4] 9 Geo. IV. c. 14, s. 8; Defries v. Littlewood, 9 Jur. 988.
[5] 54 & 55 Vict. c. 39, Sched. tit. Deed.

The duty of 6*d*. on an agreement may be denoted by an adhesive stamp, which is to be cancelled by the person by whom the agreement is first executed.[1] He must cancel it by writing on or across the stamp his name or initials, or the name or initials of his firm, together with the true date of his so writing, so that the stamp may be effectually cancelled and rendered incapable of being used for any other instrument, or for any postal purpose, or unless it is otherwise proved that the stamp was affixed at the proper time. A penalty of £10 is imposed on the person required by law to cancel an adhesive stamp who wilfully neglects or refuses to do so.[2]

The Stamp Law as to agreements under hand is very commonly evaded; parties, when they enter into agreements, not contemplating the event of a disagreement, and erroneously considering that there is no occasion to stamp an agreement which it may never be necessary to enforce by a resort to legal proceedings. The consequence is, that workmen, when they go to law with their employers, are frequently placed in a difficulty in consequence of a written agreement not being stamped. The penalty to be paid upon stamping being always a burden which it is desirable to avoid, and sometimes exceeding the amount claimed, there are frequent struggles to dispense with the production of written agreements. The rule of law on the subject is, that if from the plaintiff's evidence there appears to be an agreement in writing relating to the claim, it must be produced properly stamped; no verbal evidence can be given of its contents, or of the agreement of the parties. And even if the claim is for extra works not included in the written contract, the contract must be produced, to ascertain whether the works stated to be extras are so or not. The judge will not look at an un-

[1] S. 22. [2] S. 8.

stamped contract, to see whether it does or does not apply to the work claimed.[1] But if it is proved that the work sued for was done under a verbal order, distinct from the writing, the written contract need not be produced. In the case where this was ruled, a witness proved that the plaintiffs had been employed to do the inside work of a house under a written contract (which being unstamped could not be given in evidence), and that while the work was proceeding he heard a new order given for an entablature. Lord Tenterden said that it was not imperative on the plaintiffs to produce the contract in writing, but that they might recover for the entablature without doing so.[2]

24. The consideration of illegal contracts and imperfect contracts will assist us in forming an idea of a perfect contract. A perfect contract is the agreement of two parties that something shall be done by the one for the other. This agreement must be final and intended to be mutually binding. A tender and acceptance usually constitute an agreement,[3] and if it is customary to accept the lowest tender, and nothing is said to the contrary when the tenders are opened, the party making lowest tender may consider his tender as accepted. The plaintiff was a builder, the defendants required certain buildings erected, and their surveyor forwarded plans to the plaintiff, amongst others; the plaintiff and others sent in their tenders ; the plaintiff's was the lowest. He, the other builders and the surveyor, conceived that, according to the custom, his tender being the lowest was accepted, and partook of

---

[1] Vincent v. Cole, Moo. and Malk. 257. Jones v. Howell, 4 Dowl. 176. Buxton v. Cornish, 12 M. and W. 426 ; 1 D. and L. 585. Parton v. Cole, 6 Jur. 370. Edie v. Kingsford, 14 C. B. 759.

[2] Reid v. Batte, Moo. and Malk. 413.

[3] Allen v. Yoxall, 1 C. and K. 315.

the customary refreshment at his expense. The defendants afterwards refused to employ the plaintiff, and denied that the surveyor had any authority to accept the tender. The Judge of the County Court held that there was an acceptance and perfect contract, and his decision was upheld on appeal.[1] But, if the advertisement provides that a written contract shall be signed after the acceptance of the tender, there is no perfect contract until such written contract is drawn out and signed, and either party may withdraw before then.[2] If the contract is to be made out by an offer on one side and an acceptance on the other, and the answer is equivocal, or anything is left to be done, the two do not constitute a binding contract.[3]

If a tender refers to a specification, as if an engineer agrees to make an engine in conformity with a specification, it incorporates the whole specification as part of the contract, and the specification stipulating that the engine is to be made and delivered within two months, the engineer is bound to comply with this term.[4] The claim may be on a particular fund, and not on an individual. When by the rules of a building society the surveyor was to be paid out of the funds of the society, it was held that he had no claim on a member of the society even, for work not within the object of the society, it not appearing that the defendant had so conducted himself as reasonably to create in the plaintiff's mind the belief that he was to pay him.[5]

25. There must be two parties to a contract, the party agreeing and the party agreed with; and there

[1] Pauling v. Pontifex, 20 Law Times, 126.
[2] Kingston-upon-Hull v. Petch, 10 Ex. 611.
[3] Appleby v. Johnson, L. R. 9 C. P. 163.
[4] Wimshurst v. Daley, 2 C. B. 253.
[5] Alexander v. Worman, 6 H. and N. 100.

can be but two. However numerous the persons may
be who are parties to a contract, they constitute but
two parties; one set of persons is bound to do the act
agreed to be done, and the other set of persons is the
party for whom it is to be done, and who are entitled
to exact performance. Where several persons are the
party to a contract on one side, the law does not distinguish between the proportion of liability of each of
them, but regards each as liable for the entire performance of the contract; and this is the reason why a man
cannot contract with a partnership of which he himself
is a member, and why, when an agreement is made
between two partnerships, and the same person is a
member of both firms, it is no legal contract; in these
cases one man is a party to the contract on both sides
—is agreeing with himself, and is himself bound to
perform everything that is agreed to be performed for
him. On this ground many actions for services performed by individual members of joint stock companies
not incorporated, for the companies, have failed. In
reality, these transactions are contracts between the
member of the company performing the service and the
other members of the company, that they shall remu-
nerate him in proportion to their interest in the company; but as a Court of Law cannot ascertain the
amount of the interest of each member in the company,
it cannot take cognizance of the contract, and the only
remedy of the member who has performed the service
is in a Court of Equity.

26. It is often a question as who are the parties to
the contract. If B. is employed by A. to do work, and
B. employs C. to do the whole or part of the work, and
C. does it, there is no contract between C. and A., but
A. is liable to pay B., and B. to C.[1] Thus the drawer

---

[1] Schmaling v. Tomlinson, 6 Taunt. 147.

of a mine who was employed by the collier to assist him, the collier being employed by the agent of the proprietor, had no remedy against the proprietors for his wages, although the agent exercised the power to dismiss either the collier or the drawer.[1] But if the employment is transferred from B. to C., with the consent of A., the contract between A. and B. is at end, and there is a new contract between A. and C.[2] A person who becomes partner with the employer after the contract, and during the progress of the work, does not become liable as co-contractor, although he may give directions as to the work.[3] It is the usage of architects to have their quantities taken out by surveyors, and for the successful contractor to add the amount of the surveyor's charge to his contract. If the party proposing to build refuses to employ any builder, he is liable to the surveyor employed by his architect, it being considered that the architect has authority from him to employ the surveyor in the event of there being no contract with the builder.[4]

In a subsequent action founded on this custom, the questions left to the jury were, Was there such a custom? was it known to the parties? and did they contract on the footing of it? The verdict was for the plaintiffs.[5] When a contract to build is entered into, the surveyor taking out the quantities is the agent for the builder. The building-owner is not responsible to the builder for the negligence of the surveyor in taking out the quantities.[6]

[See now Partnership Act, 1890 (53 & 54 Vic. c. 39), in Appendix.]

[1] Exp. Eckersley, 17 Jur. 198.
[2] Oldfield v. Lowe, 9 B. and C. 73. Browning v. Stallard, 5 Taunt. 450.   [3] Beall v. Mouls, 10 Q. B. 976.
[4] Moon v. Witney Union, 3 Bing. N. C. 814. (1837.)
[5] Lansdowne v. Somerville, 3 F. and F. 236. (1862.)
[6] Scrivener v. Pask, 18 C. B. N. S. 785, L. R. 1 C. P. 715.

27. A perfect contract, when made, is in the nature of a private law, and binds the parties according to their intention in the same manner as a public law binds all persons who are subject to the legislator according to the intention of the legislator. The intention which prevails in the construction of contracts is not the private intention of the individual parties, but the intention to be collected from their expressions to each other, and which each must have understood the other to entertain. In making a contract, parties may have very dissimilar views and intentions, but they mutually profess to intend the same thing, and that which they so mutually profess is the thing. It is very improbable that a person would agree to anything that is unjust, unequal, unreasonable, or oppressive to himself; and therefore the words of a contract are to have a just and reasonable construction, and are to be understood in that sense which will make their operation equal and fair to both parties.

28. In some cases just and reasonable provisions are implied from the nature of the contract, or the terms used. For instance: if the agreement is that the workman shall do work skilfully, and that the employer shall pay, and the work is done unskilfully,—the employer says, "I did not agree to pay if the work was done unskilfully, and therefore you agreed to work for nothing in that event;"—the workman says, "That in the event which has happened, the agreement was that what is just should be done; and it is just that I should receive something for my work, though not done quite so skilfully as agreed:"—the law, interpreting the contract as equal to both parties, adopts the view of the workman. A contract of this nature is usually termed an implied contract, and is distinguished from the contract inferred from the ordinary meaning of the

words used, which is termed an express contract. An express contract and an implied contract, however, differ but in degree, the one being expressed more clearly, and the other more obscurely, by the words used.

Those provisions are implied which are necessary to make the contract effectual. Thus, a contract by a servant to serve implies a contract by a master to employ. When the words of an instrument show that its efficiency is to depend on an act to be done by one party, a contract by him is implied that he will do all in his power to bring about that act, and that if it has not been done it shall be done. A contractor agreed to execute certain paving works for a local board, to be paid out of the money when collected from the owners of the property chargeable. A contract by the board to take the steps to make the owners liable was implied.[1] And where the contract was to fix machinery to buildings of the defendant, a condition was implied that he would provide and keep up the buildings, and they having been destroyed before the work was finished, the plaintiff was held entitled to recover for what he had done.[2] There is no implied warranty that works can be executed in the manner described in the plans and specifications.[3] In cases of a personal service it is an implied condition that the servant shall continue able to serve, and if he dies or becomes unable to serve without fault on his part, the contract is dissolved.[4]

29. Another rule peculiar to written contracts may here be shortly noticed. When men reduce their con-

---

[1] Worthington v. Sudlow, 2 B. and S. 508.
[2] Appleby v. Meyers, L. R. 1 C. P. 615.
[3] Thorn v. Mayor of London, L. R. 9 Ex. 163.
[4] Taylor v. Caldwell, 3 B. and S. 835. Boast v. Firth, L. R. 4 C. P. 1. Robinson v. Davison, L. R. 6 Ex. 269.

tracts to writing, they do it for the sake of certainty.
The certainty sought for is not always attained.
Words but imperfectly describe things: whether they
profess to express the meaning of one man, as in a will,
or of two men, as in a contract, or of a body of men, as
in a statute, there are more disputes about their inter-
pretation than about anything else.   All conversations
before or at the time of making the written agreement,
and not incorporated in it, are excluded.   An omission
in a written agreement cannot be supplied, nor a patent
ambiguity removed, by oral evidence.   In a building
contract penalties were imposed for delay, but the time
for completing the building was left blank.   Evidence
that each of the parties was told verbally the day
for the completion of the building was rejected, and
the penal clause being dependent on this fell to the
ground.[1]   Parol evidence is admissible to explain a
written contract, though not to add to it.   Thus a
contract for the engagement of a servant is evidence
that at the time of the contract he was a lace-buyer
was admitted to show that he was engaged in that
capacity.[2]   But where the engagement was at a weekly
salary, parol evidence that the engagement was for a year
was rejected.[3]   A custom of trade also is admissible to
annex incidents to or interpret a written contract in a
matter as to which it is silent, if not inconsistent with
its terms; as where a building contract required the
builder to send in weekly accounts of work, he was
allowed to prove that the expression had a peculiar
signification in the building trade, and did not mean
an account of all the work done, but only of the day-
work estimated in each week, on the additions and
alterations, and the materials used in such day-work.[4]

[1] Kemp v. Rose, 1 Giff. 258.   [2] Price v. Mouat, 11 C. B. N. S. 508.
[3] Evans v. Roe, L. R. 7 C. P. 138.   [4] Myers v. Sarl, 3 E. and E. 306.

A contract was to build the walls of a house for three shillings per superficial yard of work nine inches thick. The walls were partly stone-work of two feet thick, and partly brick, and the usage was to reduce brick-work for the purpose of measurement to nine inches, but not stone-work, unless exceeding two feet in thickness. Held that the price fixed only applied to the brick-work, and that the stone-work was to be paid for on a *quantum meruit*.[1]

It has been attempted without success to control an agreement between committees of master printers and compositors as to the amount of wages by the decision of arbitrators appointed in pursuance of rules agreed to by the committees in a particular dispute between one master and his workmen. The award was held to be binding between the then litigant parties, but to have no further force or effect.[2]

30. In treating of the contract to perform works, the method proposed is, to state the general duties of each party separately. In such a contract one party, termed the contractor, agrees to perform certain works, and the other, termed the employer, agrees to pay a certain reward. The duties of the contractor are, first, to finish the work; secondly, to use care and skill in the performance; thirdly, to do it within a proper time; fourthly, to comply with the particular stipulations in the contract as to the manner of performance. The duties of the employer are, first, to pay; secondly, not to prevent but to assist the contractor in his execution of the contract.

The first duty of a contractor is to complete his contract, that is, to finish all the work he has agreed to do. If he contracts to do a specific work for a specific sum,

[1] Symonds v. Lloyd, 6 C. B. N. S. 691.
[2] Hill v. Levey, 3 H. and N. 7, 702.

he must perform the whole of the work before he is entitled to receive payment of any part of the price : so long as the work is unfinished, he is entitled to nothing.[1] The plaintiff agreed to repair three chandeliers and make them complete for £10: he returned them to the defendant, having cleaned them and repaired some icicles and drops, but not in a perfect state : the jury found that the contract had not been performed, but that the defendant had derived benefit from the work to the amount of £5. The plaintiff was nonsuited, and the Court refused to set aside the nonsuit, because he had not performed his contract. It was urged that the defendant had not returned the icicles and drops which the plaintiff had added to the chandeliers; to which it was answered, that the plaintiff ought to have demanded them.[2] In an action for work done in curing a flock consisting of 497 sheep, of the scab, it was proved that the plaintiff had declared that he did not expect to be paid unless he cured them all, and that forty out of the flock were not cured. This being evidence of a contract to cure the whole for one sum, the plaintiff failed to recover.[3]

So where the contract was to build a mill for a specified sum, and if it did not answer, to build another, the Court decided that the plaintiff could recover nothing for building the mill, unless he either proved that it had answered or had been accepted by the defendant.[4]

And where the action was on a contract to build a house for a certain sum, which the plaintiff did not complete because the defendant had refused to supply him with money as he went on, Coleridge, J., ruled that he was not entitled to receive anything under the contract until he had finished the house ; and he failed

[1] Pontifex v. Wilkinson, 1 C. B. 75, 2 C. B. 349.
[2] Sinclair v. Bowles, 9 B. and C. 92.
[3] Bates v. Hudson, 6 D. and R. 3.   [4] Davis v. Nichols, 2 Chit. 320.

to recover anything for the work done under the contract, although he recovered for extra works.[1]

The same law prevailed in a case on a contract for building a house for a certain sum, in which it appeared that the builder had omitted to put in the house certain joists and other materials of the given description and measurement. Mansfield, C. J., nonsuited the plaintiff, being of opinion, that not having performed his agreement, he could not recover upon that, and that he could not recover the value of his work. He observed, "The defendant agrees to have a building of such and such dimensions: is he to have his ground covered with buildings which he would be glad to see removed, and is he to be forced to pay for them besides? It is said he has the benefit of the houses, and therefore the plaintiff is entitled to recover on a *quantum valebant*. To be sure it is hard that he should build houses and not be paid for them; but the difficulty is to know where to draw the line; for if the defendant is to be obliged to pay in a case where there is one deviation from his contract, he may equally be obliged to pay for anything how far soever distant from what the contract stipulated for."[2]

In this case the work was done in a manner different from that specified in the contract, and was not left unfinished. It is an authority for the position, that a clear and positive deviation from the contract has the same effect as an omission to finish the work contracted for.

When payment is to be made by instalments, according to the quantity of work done, the workman must perform all the work agreed to be done to entitle him to an instalment before he can claim any payment: if he stops before an instalment is earned, he is entitled

---

[1] Rees v. Lines, 8 C. and P. 126.   [2] Ellis v. Hamlen, 3 Taunt. 52.

to nothing. An attorney covenanted with his clerk to allow him 2s. for every quire of paper that he should copy out:— the clerk copied four quires and three sheets. It was held by the Court of King's Bench, on error from the Common Pleas, that there could be no apportionment, for the covenant was to allow him 2s. for copying a quire, and not *pro ratâ;* and the judgment of the Common Pleas, which was for 8s. 3d., was reversed.[1]

The death of the workman after an instalment is payable, and before the work is complete, does not affect the right to such instalment, though the employment may involve personal confidence and is put an end to by the death. Thus, when the consulting-engineer to a railway, who was to complete the construction of the line in fifteen months, and be paid £500 by five quarterly instalments, died after the third and before the fourth quarterly instalment became payable, it was decided that his administrator was entitled to recover the unpaid instalments, including the third, although it was contended that the contract was to pay him a certain sum for certain work, and being dissolved by his death, his representative could only recover the value of the work actually done; the Lord Chief Baron saying, "His death no doubt dissolved the contract; but did not divest the right of action which had already accrued."[2]

31. But if there is no contract to do a specified quantity of work for a specified sum, the workman who works on property in the possession of his employer is entitled to be paid for his work as he proceeds; at all events, if the custom of his trade authorises such payment. A shipwright undertook to put a vessel into thorough repair; in consequence of a dispute between

[1] Needler v. Guest, Aleyn, 9.
[2] Stubbs v. Holywell Railway Company, L. R. 2 Ex. 311.

him and the ship-owner, he stopped work and demanded payment for what he had done, whilst the vessel was still unfinished. He sued for and recovered the value of his work actually done to the vessel. Lord Tenterden said,—" There is nothing in the present case amounting to a contract to do the whole repairs and make no demand until they are completed;" Littledale, J., and Parke, J., observing that the contract was to employ the plaintiff in the same way as shipwrights were ordinarily employed.[1]

32. If by the contract the work is to be finished before payment, the risk of all accidents which prevent the completion of the work is upon the workman. A printer was employed to print a book: when the work was nearly complete a fire accidentally broke out on his premises, by which the whole impression was destroyed. It was proved, that by the custom of the trade, a printer was not entitled to be paid for any part of his work until the whole was completed and delivered. The Court held that the custom was the law of the trade, and so far as it extended, controlled the general law, and therefore disallowed the printer's claim.[2] In another printer's case, the plaintiffs had been employed to print 750 copies of a work: they had printed and delivered to the defendant 210 copies of the work, when a fire broke out in their premises and destroyed all the remainder. They failed to recover anything for the printing, because the jury were not satisfied that the remaining 540 copies were all printed, completed, and ready for delivery before the fire. The defendant's counsel contended that he ought to have had notice of the work having been completed, and to take it away.

---

[1] Roberts v. Havelock, 3 B. and Ad. 404. See also Withers v. Reynolds, 2 B. and Ad. 882. Zulueta v. Miller, 2 C. B. 895.
[2] Gillett v. Mawman, 1 Taunt. 137.

This does not appear to have been adverted to by the
Judge in his summing up; but according to the custom,
as stated in Gillett v. Mawman, was necessary.[1]

But if there is no contract or custom that the work
shall be completed before payment, the workman is
entitled to be paid for what he has done, in the event
of the work being destroyed by accidental fire. Thus,
in the case of a shipwright who was employed to repair
a ship, which was burnt in the dock before the repairs
were finished, and who sued for the work he had done,
Lord Mansfield said, " This is a desperate case for the
defendant. Though compassionate, I doubt it is very
difficult for him to maintain his point. Besides, it is
stated that he paid £5 for the use of the dock." Mr.
Justice Wilmot: "So it is like a horse, which a
farrier was curing, being burnt in the owner's own
stable."[2]

33. On a contract for the manufacture of goods, the
property in the thing ordered, during the progress of
the manufacture and when made, is in the manufacturer, and remains in him until he has delivered it to
his employer, and his employer has accepted it, or until
both parties have agreed to the thing being appropriated
to the employer. This is the general legal inference
from the contract to make goods; but the parties may
agree that the property in the thing shall pass to the
employer during the progress of the work.

Until the property has passed to the employer, the
manufacturer has no right to the price, although he
may maintain an action against his employer for not
accepting the thing made. The loss, in case of accidental destruction by fire or otherwise, is the loss of

[1] Adlard v. Booth, 7 C. and P. 108.   Clay v. Yates, 1 H. and N. 73.
[2] Menetone v. Athawes, 3 Bur. 1592.   See Appleby v. Myers, L.
R. 1 C. P. 623, ante, p. 59.

the manufacturer ; and in the event of his bankruptcy, the right to the thing passes to his assignees.

Royland, a barge-builder, agreed to build a barge for Pocock. Whilst the barge was in progress, Pocock advanced him money to the whole value of the barge, and he painted Pocock's name on the stern before it was completed, and afterwards, but before the completion of the work, became bankrupt. The Common Pleas held that the barge belonged to the assignees of Royland, and not to Pocock ; Mansfield, C. J., saying that the only effect of the payment was, that the bankrupt was under a contract to finish the barge. Heath, J., appeared to think that the contract might have been performed by the delivery of any other barge within the proper time, and said that the painting the name on the stern made no difference ; and Lawrence, J., said no property vests till the thing is finished and delivered.[1]

In Atkinson v. Bell,[2] the plaintiffs, as assignees of Heddon, sought to recover of the defendants the price of some patent spinning-machines which had been made by the bankrupt for them, but which they had refused to accept : they claimed the price as a debt either for goods sold or for work done. The defendants' agent had seen the machines while being made, and knew that the bankrupt intended them for the defendants. It was held that the plaintiffs could not recover the price of the machines as a debt, though they might recover damages against the defendants for their refusal to accept them. Bailey, J., said, —" When goods are ordered to be made, while they are in progress the materials belong to the maker. The property does not vest in the party who gives the order until the thing ordered is completed ;

---

[1] Mucklow v. Mangles, 1 Taunt. 318.   [2] 8 B. and C. 277.

and although while the goods are in progress, the maker may intend them for the party ordering, he may afterwards deliver them to another, and thereby vest the property in that other. They were Heddon's goods, although intended for the defendants, and he had written to tell them so. If they had expressed their assent, there would have been a complete appropriation vesting the property in them. Then, as to the count for work and labour, if you employ a man to build a house on your land, or to make a chattel with your materials, the party who does the work has no power to appropriate the produce of his labour and your materials to any other person. Having bestowed his labour at your request on your materials, he may maintain an action against you for work and labour; but if you employ another to work up his own materials in making a chattel, then he may appropriate the produce of that labour and those materials to any other person. No right to maintain any action vests in him during the progress of the work; but when the chattel has assumed the character bargained for, and the employer accepted it, the party employed may maintain an action for goods sold and delivered; or, if the employer refuses to accept, a special action for such refusal. But he cannot maintain an action for work and labour, because his labour was bestowed on his own materials, and for himself, and not for the person who employed him."[1]

In Laidler v. Burlinson,[2] Laidler had entered into a contract for building a ship, which specified the dimensions, &c., and the price; and the plaintiff agreed to take one-fourth, the Tees Coal Company one-fourth,

---

[1] Grafton v. Armitage, 2 C. B. 336. Clay v. Yates, 1 H. and N 73. Lee v. Griffin, 1 B. and S. 272.

[2] 2 M. and W. 602.

and other persons the remainder. Laidler commenced building the ship, and the defendant paid him the whole amount of his fourth : and Harris, a member of the Tees Coal Company, inspected the work, and occasionally found fault with it, and it was improved in consequence. Before the ship was finished, Laidler became bankrupt, and at the time of his bankruptcy the ship in question was the only one in Laidler's yard. The Court held that the contract was a contract to purchase the ship when finished, and not until then, and therefore that the property was in Laidler at the time of his bankruptcy.

34. But when, after the article is completed, each party has manifested his consent that it shall be the property of the employer, he is entitled to it. In Carruthers v. Payne,[1] the plaintiff had ordered Thompson to build a chariot for him, which was completed according to order and paid for. After it was completed, the plaintiff ordered a front seat to be added, but the coach-builder being slow in the execution of this latter order, the plaintiff sent for it several times, and Thompson promised to send it. The plaintiff afterwards ordered it to be sold as it then was ; and whilst it was in Thompson's possession for sale, he became bankrupt. The Court held that the chariot belonged to the plaintiff, and not to Thompson's assignee, and distinguished the case from Mucklow and Mangles, because both the builder and the purchaser had treated the chariot as finished.

In Elliott v. Pybus,[2] the defendant had ordered a ruling-machine of the plaintiff, without any agreement as to price, and paid money on account. When finished, the plaintiff requested him to fetch it away, and pay the balance of the price. The defendant saw it com-

[1] 5 Bing. 270.   [2] 10 Bing. 512.

plete, admitted it was made to order, and requested the
maker to send it home without payment: he first
objected to the price as exorbitant, but afterwards said
he would endeavour to arrange it. He was considered
as having accepted the machine, and therefore to be
liable for the price as a debt in an action for goods bargained and sold: both parties had agreed that the
machine was the thing ordered by and made for the
defendant, and that the price was proper.

In Wilkins v. Bromhead,[1] the plaintiff had ordered
a greenhouse of Smith and Bryant for £50; when
finished, Smith and Bryant gave the plaintiff notice,
and requested him to remit the price, which he did,
and desired them to keep the greenhouse till sent for.
Before the plaintiff sent for his greenhouse, Smith and
Bryant became bankrupts, and their assignees claimed
it. The Court held that the property had passed to the
plaintiff, because there had been an appropriation on
one side, and an assent to that appropriation on the
other.

On these cases it will be observed, that in order to
vest the property in a chattel made under a contract in
the employer, there should be an agreement between
the workman and employer after the chattel is made,
that it is the thing made in pursuance of the contract,
and as to the terms upon which it is to be delivered.
The payment of the price is not essential, if the parties
are agreed as to the price to be paid. In such case the
thing belongs to the employer, and the workman has a
lien upon it for the price. The delivery of the thing is
not essential, if the parties are agreed as to the thing
to be delivered.

35. The parties may agree that the property in the
chattel to be made shall be vested in the employer

[1] 6 M. and G. 963.

during the progress of the manufacture. Contracts of this nature are frequently made for building ships.

In an action of trover by the assignees of Paton, a bankrupt, it appeared that Paton, who was a shipbuilder, had entered into a contract with Russell to build and complete a ship for him, and finish and launch her in April, 1819. Russell was to pay for her by four instalments of £750 each, by bills : the first, when the keel was laid ; the second, when they were at the light plank ; the third and fourth, when she was launched. Russell duly paid the first and second instalments, and in March, 1819, appointed a master, who superintended the building. Before the ship was finished, it was registered in Russell's name, and Paton signed the certificate of her build for the purpose of registration : the third instalment was paid at that time. Before the ship was launched, Paton became bankrupt, and Russell took possession of her and had her launched, without paying the last instalment. The Court of King's Bench held that the property of the ship was vested in Russell. Abbott, C. J., in delivering the judgment of the Court, said, "The payment of these instalments appears to us to appropriate specifically to the defendant the very ship so in progress, and to vest in the defendant a property in that ship ; and that as between him and the builder, he is entitled to the completion of that very ship, and that the builder is not entitled to require him to accept any other. But this case does not depend merely upon the payment of the instalments, so that we are not called upon to decide how far that payment vests the property in the defendant, because here Paton signed the certificate to enable the defendant to have the ship registered in his (the defendant's) name, and by that act consented that the general property in the ship should be considered from that time as being in the defendant.' They also held that the defendant was entitled to a rudder and cordage which had been bought by Paton specifically for the ship, though they were not actually attached to it at the time of his bankruptcy : but they decided that the assignees had a lien on the ship for the amount of the fourth instalment, for which Russell had not given bills at the time when he took possession, and were entitled to recover the amount of that instalment.[1]

In another case the contract for building a ship provided that it should be built under the superintendence of a person appointed by the employer, and fixed the payment of the price by instalments, regulated by particular stages in the progress of the work. The Court of Queen's Bench held, that as by the contract the vessel was to be built under a superintendent appointed by the purchaser, the builder could not compel the purchaser to accept of any vessel not constructed of materials approved by the superintendent, and the purchaser could not refuse any vessel which had been so approved : and that as soon as any materials had been approved by the superintendent, and used in the work, the fabric consisting of such materials was appropriated to the purchaser. As soon as the last of the necessary materials was approved and added to the fabric, the appropriation was complete, and the general property of the vessel vested in the purchaser, because nothing remained to be done prior to the delivery. But until the last of the necessary materials was added, the vessel was not complete ; the thing contracted for was not in existence, for the contract was for a complete vessel, and not for parts of a vessel : but they seem to have thought that the mere fact of the ship being built with the approbation of a superintendent did not vest

[1] Woods v. Russell, 5 B. and Ald. 942.

any property in the purchaser until it was completed. They decided, but with hesitation, upon the authority of Woods v. Russell, that the provision for payment regulated by particular stages of the work was made in the contract with the view to give the purchaser the security of certain portions of the work for the money he was to pay, and was equivalent to an express provision, that on payment of the first instalment the general property of so much of the vessel as was then constructed should vest in the purchaser; and that upon such payment, the rights of the parties were the same as if so much of the vessel as was then constructed had originally belonged to the purchaser, and had been delivered by him to the builder to be added to and finished, and every plank and article subsequently added became the property of the purchaser as general owner.[1]

A shipbuilder contracted to build a screw steamer for £16,000, to be paid by instalments: the four first of £1000 at specified times; £3000 on a day named, provided the vessel was plated and her decks laid; £3000 on a day named, provided she was then ready for trial; £3000 on a day named, provided she was according to contract, and properly completed; and £3000 after completion. The building was carried on under the superintendence of the employer's agent, the employer's name was punched on the keel, the instalments were paid in advance, but the building was stopped before she was decked or plated. The ship was considered as belonging to the employer, principally from the circumstance of its being built under the superintendence of the employer's agent, coupled with the payment of the instalment.[2]

[1] Clarke v. Spence, 4 Ad. and El. 448.
[2] Wood v. Bell, 5 E. and B. 772; 6 E. and B. 355.

Whilst a ship was building, and after the employer had made advances, the builder executed a bill of sale reciting the advances, and witnessing that for the security and repayment of the advances he bargained, sold, assigned, and transferred the ship then in progress, to have and to hold the said ship when it should be completed and finished. This was decided to vest the property in the employer, the intention being apparent to give him a present security on the unfinished ship.[1]

Directly the parties have agreed that the thing in progress of making shall become the property of the employer, their agreement takes effect according to their intentions;[2] and this agreement may either be expressly made in the contract of employment, or may be inferred from the provisions of the contract, as from a provision for payment of the price of the work during its progress; or the parties may agree subsequently to the original contract, as they did in Woods v. Russell, where the signature to the certificate of registry was relied upon as evidence of an agreement by both parties that the ship then unfinished should become the property of the employer.

36. In the instance of contracts for building or repairing houses, the work is not complete, and the things made for such work do not become the property of the employer, until they are actually fixed on the land, or to the house, so as to become part of it.

A builder contracted to build an hotel, and the contract provided, that in the event of his bankruptcy, his employers should take possession of *work already done* by him, and put an end to the agreement, and pay the value of the work actually done and fixed. The

[1] Reid v. Fairbanks, 13 C. B. 692.
[2] Young v. Matthews, L. R. 2 C. P. 127.

builder became bankrupt during the progress of the work. Before his bankruptcy, he delivered on the premises of his employers some wooden sash-frames, which he intended for the hotel : they were approved by the clerk of the works, and returned to him to have some iron pulleys belonging to his employers fixed to them; and the frames with the pulleys were in the builder's shop at the time of his bankruptcy. The sash-frames were decided to belong to the builder's assignees, and not to the proprietors of the hotel, because the contract was not to make goods as movable chattels, but to make and fix them to the hotel.[1] It results from this case, that if a man is employed to make a window for a house, he has not finished his contract, and can claim nothing, until he has fixed the window in the house : if it is destroyed, or lost, before it is fixed, the loss is his, and he must replace it. An agreement may be so worded as to give the employer a lien on the materials before they are used in the work,[2] or entitle him to use them in the completion of the work.[3] If materials are appropriated to the work by the workmen, with the consent of the employer, they become the property of the employer. That such an appropriation has taken place may be inferred as a conclusion of fact by a jury from circumstances.[4] A building contract provided that all materials brought upon the premises for the purpose of erecting buildings should be considered as immediately attached to and belonging to the premises, and should not be removed without the employer's consent. This

[1] Tripp v. Armitage, 4 M. and W. 687.

[2] Hawthorn v. Newcastle-upon-Tyne and North Shields Railway Company, 3 Q. B. 734, n.

[3] Baker v. Gray, 17 C. B. 462.

[4] Goss v. Quinton, 3 M. and G. 841. Williams v. Fitzmaurice, 3 H. and N. 844.

was held to give the employer a right to the materials, and protect them against an execution against the builder.[1] The builder has also an interest in them, for the purpose of using them in the building, and they cannot be seized under an execution against the employer.[2]

37. If the work is done on a chattel delivered by the employer to the workman, the contract, generally speaking, is completed, so as to entitle the workman to be paid directly the work is finished, and the employer has had notice of that fact, and a reasonable opportunity of inspecting the work, and ascertaining that it is according to order. He is bound to deliver his work, when done, upon request and upon payment of the price, but does not forfeit his right to be paid by refusing to deliver it.

A surveyor was employed to make a map and survey of a parish, the field-books and paper being provided by the employers. He finished his work, but refused to deliver the map and reference-books, except upon payment of a sum which the defendants considered excessive. They had an opportunity of inspecting the map and books. He brought an action for his demand, and the jury found that the value of his work was much less than he claimed. The Court gave judgment in his favour for the amount found by the jury. Parke, B., said, "The true state of the contract appears to me to be this: the defendants employ the plaintiff to survey a parish, and then to put down the results of his survey, first on books provided for him by the defendants, and afterwards on paper to be provided by them for him, in the shape of a map or plan; and incidental to that employment, it may be a condition that

---

[1] Brown v. Bateman, L. R. 2 C. P. 272.
[2] Beeston v. Marriott, 4 Giff. 436, 9 Jur. N. S. 960.

the plaintiff should give the defendants a reasonable opportunity of comparing the maps with the books, and both of them with the lands surveyed, in order to ascertain their accuracy. It is said that it is part of the same contract, that the plaintiff should be ready and willing to deliver the books and map to the defendants; but I do not think that is any part of the contract, although there may be an independent contract that the plaintiff should return the materials supplied by them on request, as in the case of delivery of goods to a warehouseman to keep, or, which is perhaps a closer analogy, of cloth to a tailor, to be wrought into a coat; but that is altogether collateral to the right of the tailor to sue for the debt due to him: as soon as he has worked the cloth, and given his employer an opportunity of ascertaining whether it is made to fit, he has a right to send in his bill for the work."[1]

38. Although the delivery of the thing worked on is not a condition to the right of the workman to sue for the price of his labour, he is bound to deliver it whenever his employer requests him to do so, and pays or tenders the amount due to him for his work actually done, and this although he has not finished the work contracted for, and the demand by the employer of the thing may be a breach of contract on his part. The property in the chattel is still in the employer, notwithstanding its delivery to the workman to be wrought. He has no right to keep it until the work is completed against the owner's wish, but is sufficiently recompensed by an action against the employer for the profit he would have made, had he been permitted to complete his contract.[2]

The workman is responsible to his employer if by

[1] Hughes v. Lenny, 5 M. and W. 183.
[2] Lilly v. Barnsley, 1 Car. and Kir. 344.

mistake he delivers the chattel to a wrong person. A watchmaker was employed to repair a watch; when it was repaired, he tendered it to the owner, who told him to take it to his uncle in Margaret Street, who would pay him: not finding this uncle at home, he delivered the watch to another uncle of the owner, who lost it. The watchmaker was held liable to an action for a breach of contract in not delivering the watch to the plaintiff.[1]

39. The contractor is also bound to exercise ordinary care and skill in the performance of the work, to perform it in the specified manner, and with the specified materials, if the description of materials are specified: if not, he is bound to use materials which are reasonably fit and proper for the purpose of the work.

The cases in which the degree of care and skill to be exercised in the performance of works has been discussed, are those of surgeons and other professional men; but the law established by them is applicable to every person who contracts to perform work of any description. It has been decided in the case of a surgeon, that he is bound to know and to act according to the ordinary rules and usage of his profession;[2] that he is responsible for unskilful treatment, as well as for carelessness.[3] Tindal, C. J., has thus defined the degree of skill required of a professional man: "Every person who enters into a learned profession undertakes to bring to it the exercise of a reasonable degree of care and skill. He does not undertake, if he is an attorney, that at all events you shall win your cause; nor does a surgeon undertake that he will perform a cure, nor does he undertake to use the highest possible degree of skill. There may be persons who have higher educa-

[1] Wilson v. Powis, 3 Bing. 633.
[2] Slater v. Baker, 2 Wils. 359.   [3] Seare v. Prentice, 8 East, 348.

tion and greater advantages than he has, but he undertakes to bring a fair, reasonable, and competent degree
of skill."[1] A person who holds himself out and accepts
employment as a surveyor of ecclesiastical dilapidations,
though not bound to supply minute and accurate knowledge of the law, ought to know the general rules applicable to the valuation of ecclesiastical property, and
the broad distinction which exists between the case of
a landlord and tenant and that of an incoming and outgoing incumbent. On this ground the valuers were
held responsible to their employer, the incoming incumbent, for negligence, because, in ignorance of the decision of Wise v. Metcalfe, they valued the dilapidations
to the extent only of rendering the premises habitable,
and not with a view of their being put in good and
substantial repair.[2] And a parliamentary agent is
bound to know and act upon the standing orders of
the Lords and Commons, but he is not responsible
if in a doubtful case an application to Parliament fails,
because he has put a construction upon an order different from that which afterwards prevails.[3] A house-
agent must use reasonable care and diligence in ascertaining the condition of a person before he introduces
him to the landlord as a tenant.[4] A workman employed to fix and fit up a kitchen range, if it cannot be
done in a workmanlike manner, is bound to tell his
employer so before beginning the work, and to give
him the benefit of any knowledge which a competent
workman ought to have, and which the employer may not

---

[1] Lauphiere v. Phipos, 8 C. and P. 479. Rich v. Pierpont, 3 F.
and F. 35.

[2] Jenkins v. Betham, 15 C. B. 168. Turner v. Goulden, L. R. 9
C. P. 57.

[3] Bulmer v. Gilman, 4 M. and G. 108.

[4] Hays v. Tindall, 1 B. and S. 296.

have.[1] From these authorities may be learnt the degree
of care and skill which every workman is bound to
bring to the execution of his task. He must exercise
that degree of care which a man of ordinary prudence
would exert in the conduct of his own affairs; and he
must possess and use that degree of knowledge of his
art, and skill in the practice of it, which a workman
of average knowledge and skill in the same trade
possesses. Whether or not he has been deficient in
these respects is a question of fact, to be determined,
in case of dispute, by a jury. He is not, without
orders, to try experiments, or to perform his work in
other than the ordinary way; if he does, and damage
ensues to his employer, he is answerable.[2]

40. If a chattel is delivered to the workman to be
worked on, or to be used as materials for his work, he
must take the same care to preserve it from injury,
and to prevent its loss, as a man of ordinary prudence would take of his own property. Although he
makes no charge for keeping the goods, he is not a
gratuitous bailee, who is only liable for gross negligence. The pay he is to receive for his work extends
to the taking care of the goods, and renders him a
bailee for reward and liable for to take ordinary care
of them.[3] A ship was delivered to a shipwright to be
repaired, and placed by him in his dry dock. Whilst
she lay there, during a remarkably high tide, the dock-
gates were burst open by the water, and she was forced
against another vessel and injured. The accident happened in the daytime, and all the shipwright's men
were absent. In an action against him for the injury
done to the ship, Lord Ellenborough held that it was
the duty of the defendant to have had a sufficient

---

[1] Pearce v. Tucker, 3 F. and F. 136.   [2] Slater v. Baker, 2 Wils. 359.
[3] White v. Humphrey, 11 Q. B. 43.

number of men in the dock to take measures of pre-
caution when the danger was approaching, and that
he was clearly answerable for the effects of that deficiency.[1]

A chronometer was delivered to a watchmaker to be
cleaned and repaired. He had a servant, eighteen years
of age, who had been well recommended to him, and
who slept in the shop at night for the purpose of protecting the property there. This servant, one night,
stole the chronometer and other articles, some belonging to the watchmaker and some to his customers,
which at the time of the theft were locked up in a
drawer in the shop. He had an iron chest in his shop,
in which watches belonging to himself, of great value,
were locked up, and which was not and could not
easily have been broken open. Several watchmakers
proved that it was their invariable habit to lock up at
night, in an iron safe, or some other place of equal
security, all watches, whether belonging to themselves
or in their custody for the purpose of being repaired.
Dallas, C. J., was of opinion that the defendant was
bound to protect the property against depredations
from those who were within the house. He had taken
care of his own property by locking up and securing it.
The servant had been improperly trusted, and the defendant was guilty of gross negligence in leaving him
in the care of the goods.[2] But if ordinary care is taken
of the goods, the workman is not responsible in case of
their being stolen, though they are stolen by his own
servants.[3]

[1] Leck v. Mestaer, 1 Campb. 138.
[2] Clarke v. Earnshaw, Gow. 30.   Re United Service Company,
L. R., 6 Ch. 212.
[3] Finucane v. Smith, 1 Esp. 315.   Vere v. Smith, Vent. 121, 2 Lev.
5, Co. Lit. 89 a.   Coggs v. Bernard, 2 Ld. Ray. 916, 7.   Giblin v.
M'Mullen, L. R., 2 P. C. 317.

41. The duty of the workman to use care and skill has reference to the contract with, and orders of, his employer. If the employer looks after his own property, and does not trust the workman with it, the workman is not bound to take care of it. So if he exercises his own judgment, and gives orders which are ignorant and unskilful, he cannot complain if the workman executes them. In a case in which a man went into a surgeon's shop and requested to be bled, saying that he had been relieved by that means before, and the surgeon's apprentice bled him,—Tindal, C. J., ruled that he could not complain of the surgeon, on the ground that it was improper to bleed him, because he did not consult him as to the propriety of being bled; he took that upon himself, and only required the manual operation to be performed. He was therefore bound to show want of skill in that.[1] The same principle was adverted to by Bayley, J., in an action for work done in erecting a stove in a shop, and laying a tube under the floor for the purpose of carrying off the smoke, which entirely failed. He said that if the employer had chosen to supersede the workman's judgment by using his own, he was bound to pay his bill.[2]

42. There is a distinction between the case of work being left unfinished, and of its being done improperly. It is not a condition to payment that the work shall be done in a proper and workmanlike manner; if it were so, a little deficiency of any sort would put an end to the contract and deprive a workman of any claim for payment. But under such circumstances, it has always been held that, where the contract has been executed, a jury may say what the workman really deserves to have.[3]

[1] Hancke v. Hooper, 7 C. and P. 81.
[2] Duncan v. Blundell, 3 Stark. 6.
[3] Per Tindal, C. J., Lucas v. Godwin, 3 Bing. N. C. 743.

It was at one time decided, that if the work was finished, no matter how unskilfully or improperly, the workman was entitled to the contract price, and the employer's only remedy was by cross action for the negligence, on the ground that on the completion of the work the event had happened upon which payment was to be made, and that the exercise of care and skill in the performance was not a condition precedent to the agreement to pay. Thus, in an action for the price of erecting a booth on the Bath race-ground, the plaintiff proved that the measure of the booth was settled between him and the defendant, and that he was to have twenty guineas for building it, five of which had been paid, and that he did build it of the stipulated dimensions. The defendant proved that the booth fell down during the middle of the races, owing to bad materials and bad workmanship, and that the plaintiff was fully aware of both. Buller, J., held that there was no defence to the action, especially as a particular sum was specified; but that the defendant might bring a cross action against the plaintiff for building the booth improperly.[1]

This rule was found to operate so unjustly,—an unskilful workman being usually a bad paymaster,—that it was soon altered; and it is now settled that when the work is not performed in all respects according to the contract and duties of the workman, he is not entitled to recover the contract price; but that a deduction should be made from the contract price, equal to the difference between the value of the work as it would have been, had the contract been performed, and that of the work actually done.

This appears first to have been decided in the case of Basten v. Butter,[2] which was an action by a carpenter

---

[1] Broom v. Davis, 7 East, 480, n.   [2] 7 East, 479.

against a farmer, for carpenter's work done on the farm, putting a roof on a linhay, &c. The defendant offered to prove that the work had been done in a very improper and insufficient manner, that the linhay was too weak in the roof, and after being covered with thatch, sunk in the middle, so as to let the water through, and that neither the rafters nor roof were sufficiently supported. Thompson, B., before whom the cause was tried, rejected the evidence on the authority of Broom v. Davis. The Court granted a new trial on this ground. Lord Ellenborough observed, that the action was on a *quantum meruit,* and the plaintiff ought to come into Court prepared to prove how much his work was worth, and therefore there was no injustice in suffering the defence to be entered into. Lawrence and Le Blanc, JJ., held that whether the action was on a *quantum meruit* or on a contract to pay a specific price, the plaintiff was bound to show that he had executed the work properly, and that the defendant might show that it was done improperly.

In Farnsworth v. Garrard,[1] the action was for work in rebuilding the front of a house, which, when finished, was considerably out of the perpendicular, and in great danger of tumbling down, according to some witnesses, though others said it might last for years. Lord Ellenborough said, "This action is founded on a claim for meritorious service. The plaintiff is to recover what he deserves. It is therefore to be considered how much he deserves, and if he deserves anything. If the defendant has derived no benefit from his services, he deserves nothing, and there must be a verdict against him. If the wall will not stand, and must be taken down, the defendant has derived no benefit from the plaintiff's service, but has suffered an injury. In

[1] 1 Campb. 38.

that case he might have given him notice to remove the materials. Retaining them, he is not likely to be in a better situation than if the plaintiff had never placed them there; but if it will cost him less to rebuild the wall than it would have done without these materials, he has some benefit, and must pay some damages."

In Duncan v. Blundell,[1] the plaintiff had erected a stove in the defendant's shop, and laid a tube under the floor for the purpose of carrying off the smoke. He sued for the price of his labour. The plan had entirely failed, and the stove could not be used. An attempt was made to show that the failure arose from some directions given by the defendant, but was not made out. Bailey, J., said—"When a person is employed in a work of skill, the employer buys both his labour and his judgment. He ought not to undertake the work if he cannot succeed, and he should know whether he will or not." The plaintiff was nonsuited.

Chapel v. Hicks[2] was an action on a special contract to erect buildings. The declaration contained a count on the contract and counts for money due for work: the defendant suffered judgment by default, and proved in reduction of damages that the work and building were not equal to what the defendant had contracted for. The jury returned a verdict for the full contract price; which the Court set aside, Lord Lyndhurst saying, "If the plaintiff has not performed the work in the manner which by the contract he agreed to do, he cannot recover on the contract, but must recover on the other counts of his declaration, for the work which he has done. Suppose on a contract to build a house of Baltic timber, the contractor builds it of timber of a different description; upon what principle is he entitled

[1] 3 Stark. 6.   [2] 2 C. and M. 214.

to recover, except for the work, labour, and materials?" Bayley, B., said—"The rule is, if the contract be not faithfully performed, the plaintiff shall be entitled only to recover the value of the work and materials supplied." The observations of Lord Lyndhurst in this case were either mistaken or are misreported, since the plaintiff was entitled to recover, and did recover, on the special contract, by the admission of the defendant, who, by omitting to plead, had confessed the contract, and that the plaintiff had done everything which it was necessary for him to do to recover on it. The decision supports the opinions of Lawrence and Le Blanc in Basten v. Butter, that even when the contract is specific as to the work to be done and price to be paid, the improper performance of the work renders the workman liable to an abatement of the price, but does not entirely preclude him from recovering on the contract.

The same law is applicable to the cases of workmen whose commodity is superior knowledge or skill, such as surveyors, surgeons, &c. In an action by an engineer for his services in planning and making estimates for a bridge, the defence was, that he did not bore or examine the soil for the foundation, and in consequence the company, for building the bridge, were put to an extra expense of £1600. Abbott, C. J., said—"If a surveyor who makes an estimate sues his employers for the value of his services, it is a defence that he did not inform himself, by boring or otherwise, of the nature of the soil of his foundation, and it turned out to be bad, for this goes to his right of action."[1] On another trial on the same claim, Best, C. J., stated the law to be, that unless the negligence and want of skill was to an extent that rendered the

[1] Moneypenny v. Hartland, 1 C. and P. 352.

work useless to the defendants, they must pay him and seek their remedy in a cross action: "for if it were not so," he said, "a man might by a small error deprive himself of his whole remuneration." He further observed, "that a man should not estimate a work at a price he would not contract for it; for if he did, he deceived his employer."[1]

An auctioneer, who was employed to sell a leasehold estate, failed to recover anything for his services because he had omitted to insert a condition in the particulars of sale, that the purchaser should not inquire into the landlord's title, and in consequence his employer was unable to make out a title to the purchaser, who refused to complete the purchase. Lord Ellenborough observed—"When the plaintiff proceeds upon a *quantum meruit*, the just value of his services may be appreciated; and if they are found to be wholly abortive, he is entitled to recover no compensation."[2]

So, in an action on an apothecary's bill, a defence that his treatment was unskilful was admitted. Lord Kenyon said—"In a case where the demand is compounded of skill and things administered, if the skill, which is the principal thing, is wanting, the action fails, because the defendant has received no benefit."[3]

If at any stage of the work the negligence or want of skill of the workman renders his work useless, he is entitled to no remuneration, though he may have done much work carefully and skilfully; because in cases where he does not perform his work strictly according to contract he is to be paid only the value which his whole work is to his employer.[4]

[1] 2 C. and P. 378.   [2] Denew v. Daverell, 3 Campb. 451.
[3] Kannen v. M'Mullen, Peake, 83.
[4] Braccy v. Carter, 12 A. and E. 373. Lewis v. Samuel, 8 Q. B. 685.

In claims by an attorney for remuneration for his services,[1] and by a shipowner for freight,[2] no deduction is allowed from the usual charges or the agreed freight, unless the negligence has rendered the service wholly useless.[3] And in an action by a brickmaker for making bricks, Patteson, J., is reported to have ruled that no deduction could be made from the price for bricks which were badly made, only in a trifling degree, but that if any of the bricks were so badly made as to be good for nothing, and no benefit was or could be derived from them, the employer was entitled to deduct his loss from the stipulated price.[4] This ruling is perhaps hardly consistent with the other authorities. It is submitted that the diminished value of the defective bricks and the whole price of the good-for-nothing ones should have been deducted.

43. Although the employer is entitled to make a deduction from the contract price where the work is not properly performed, and actually does so, he is also entitled to sue the workman for his breach of contract in not properly performing the work, and may recover any damage he has thereby sustained : he only abates the contract price by so much as the work done was worth less than the work agreed to be done, and does not, in all cases, deduct the whole amount of the damage he has sustained by the breach of contract.[5] He is not bound to deduct from the contract price when the work is badly done, but may pay the full amount and sue for the damage he has sustained by the inferiority of the work.[6]

[1] Templer v. M'Lachlan, 2 N. R. 136.
[2] Shiels v. Davies, 4 Campb. 119, 6 Taunt. 65.
[3] Mondel v. Steel, 8 M. and W. 871.
[4] Pardow v. Webb, Car. and Marsh, 531.
[5] Mondel v. Steel, 8 M. and W. 858. Rigge v. Burbidge, 15 M. and W. 598.
[6] Davis v. Hedges, L. R. 6 Q. B. 687.

44. A manufacturer of goods is bound to manufacture them so as to answer the purpose for which they are ordered, if he is informed of the purpose for which they are wanted, and if they are capable of being so made. If, when made, the goods do not answer the purpose for which they were ordered, the employer, after giving them a reasonable trial, and finding them defective, may give [notice of their insufficiency to the maker, and require him to take them away: after such notice they remain at his risk, and he cannot recover the price. But if the employer retains them beyond a reasonable time for trial without giving notice, or otherwise adopts them as his own, he is bound to pay their worth, but not the full contract price.[1] If he sustains damage by reason of the defective construction of the articles, he may maintain an action against the manufacturer.

The same law applies to a shopkeeper or dealer who undertakes to procure an article fit for a particular purpose, though he does not manufacture it. Each party undertakes that the article to be supplied shall be of a particular quality. A rope was ordered of a shopkeeper who dealt in ropes. He was told that it was wanted for the purpose of raising pipes of wine from a cellar. He took the order and procured a rope to be made, which his servants fixed to his customer's crane. The rope was not sufficiently strong, and broke whilst being used in raising a pipe of wine, which of course was spilled. The purchaser brought an action for its value. It was contended on the part of the seller of the rope, that it was a case of a sale of goods, and that as he did not warrant the rope, the maxim of *caveat emptor* applied. Tindal, C. J., thus distin-

---

[1] Okell v. Smith, 1 Stark. 107. Per Lord Tenterden, Street v. Blay, 2 B. and Ad. 463.

guished the case from that of an ordinary sale of goods :
"If a party purchases an article on his own judgment,
he cannot afterwards hold the vendor responsible on
the ground that the article turns out unfit for the purpose for which it was required ; but if he relies on the
judgment of the seller, and informs him of the use to
which the article is to be applied, the transaction
carries with it an implied warranty that the thing
shall be fit and proper for the purpose for which it was
required." [1]

The same law has been extended to the case of a
manufacturer who makes articles for sale, though he
does not make them to order, and sells them after they
are made.   He is understood as warranting them fit for
the purpose for which they are apparently adapted,
and for which he represents to the buyer they were
manufactured.   A man buying of a manufacturer relies
on the manufacturer's judgment, honesty, care, and
skill, rather than on his own judgment.   Copper
sheathing was sold by a manufacturer of that article
for sheathing a ship : it wore away at the end of four
months instead of lasting four years, which was the
average duration of such a commodity ; and although
no fraud was imputed to the manufacturer, he was held
liable for the injury sustained by the shipowner by
reason of the defective condition of the copper. [2]   A
barge-builder, who had sold a new barge built by himself, and which was so defectively constructed that it
was not reasonably fit for use as an ordinary barge,
was, on the same principle, held liable for damages to
the purchaser. [3]   In these cases the purchasers brought
actions for the breach of the implied warranty : they

[1] Brown v. Edgington, 2 M. and G. 279.
[2] Jones v. Bright, 5 Bing. 533.
[3] Shepherd v. Pybus, 3 M. and G. 868.

might have resisted actions for the price, had the things been wholly useless, or have abated the contract price if they were of some use; but inasmuch as the things sold and delivered were the identical things which they ordered and brought, they could not have returned them, or have refused to receive them. Thus, where a steam engine was sold to some millers, whose foreman inspected it before they bought it, and which was described as an engine of 14-horse power, but when set up proved to be only a 9-horse engine, it was held that the millers had no right to reject it, although they were entitled to an abatement of the price, and to sue for the breach of warranty.[1]

The case is different if an article of a particular description is ordered to be made or bought, which the buyer believes will answer a particular purpose, but which is wholly ineffectual to produce the end proposed. In such case the buyer exercises his own judgment as to the utility of the article, and the seller is not responsible for its failure, if he supplies the article ordered without an express warranty. He agrees to make or sell, not an article fit for a particular purpose, but a particular article. This law is applicable to many cases of orders and sales of patented things. The plaintiff ordered a machine, called Chanter's Smoke-Consuming Furnace, for his brewery. It was of no use to him, and he objected to pay for it, but was obliged.[2]

45. The contractor is also bound to finish his work within the limited time, if any time is expressly limited by the contract. If the contract does not specify the time within which it is to be performed, it must be done within a reasonable time; that is, such time as

[1] Parsons v. Sexton, 2 C. B. 899.
[2] Chanter v. Hopkins, 4 M. and W. 399. Ollivant v. Bagley, 5 Q. B. 288.

in this respect is sufficiently compensated by a cross action when the contract is by deed ; or by cross action or deduction, or both, in the case of a simple contract.

But if a sum of money is agreed to be paid expressly as a reward for diligence, performance within the time goes to the whole consideration, and is a condition precedent. The defendant agreed to purchase a house for a certain sum, and also agreed to pay £80 additional, providing the adjoining houses should be completed, i.e. roofed, sashed, and paved in front, by the 21st April, 1829, and it appeared that the pavement in front of the houses was not laid down before the 28th April, the delay being occasioned by the badness of the weather, which prevented the men from working, the plaintiff failed to recover any part of the £80.[1]

If the contract provides for a penalty, or liquidated damage, to be paid for delay beyond a specified time, the completion within the time is not a condition to payment, because the parties have expressly provided for the consequences of delay. Thus in Lamprell v. the Guardians of the Billericay Union,[2] the plaintiff covenanted completely to finish the building before the 24th of June,—and the deed contained a provision, that if he should fail in the completion of all the works within the time specified, unless hindered by fire or other cause satisfactory to the architects, he should pay the defendants £10 per week so long as the works should remain incomplete,—the time was held not to be essential, because of the weekly sum to be paid for the delay.

If a day is limited for the completion of the contract, the contractor has until the last moment of the day to finish his work ; if he has done by twelve at night, he has performed his contract.[3]

---

[1] Maryon v. Carter, 4 C. and P. 295.   [2] 3 Ex. 283.
[3] Startup v. Macdonald, 6 M. and G. 593.

If the contract is to be performed within so many months, they are understood, in the absence of any usage of trade to the contrary, to mean lunar months of four weeks each.[1] If the time is limited from the time of making the contract, or from the time of any other act or event, the day of making the contract, or on which the act or event happens, is to be excluded in reckoning the time : thus if a man on the 1st of January contracts to build a house within six months from the time of making the contract, he is bound to have built the house, at the latest, on the 18th of June.[2]

46. If the contract provides, as it frequently does, for the payment of a stipulated sum by the contractor for delay, the sum so payable is a debt from the contractor to the employer. Such a sum is liquidated damage, and not a penalty.[3] It is the sum which the parties have agreed shall be paid by the contractor to the employer for the injury from the delay, and although called a penalty in the contract it is still liquidated damage. If the payment is secured by a bond with a penalty, it is an additional circumstance to show it to be liquidated damage.[4] The distinction between a penalty and liquidated damages is, that the one is a mere nominal sum to secure the performance of the act, and if the act is not performed, only the actual damage can be recovered ; the other is a sum which is absolutely payable in the event of default, and against which there is no relief at law or in equity. If the contract provides that the contractor shall forfeit and pay the sum, such sum to be deducted from the contract price, and the employer

---

[1] Lang v. Gale, 1 Maule and Sel. 111.
[2] Lester v. Garland, 15 Ves. 248.
[3] Fletcher v. Dyche, 2 D. and E. 32.
[4] Ranger v. Great Western Railway Company, 5 House of Lords' Cases, 72.

pays the contract price without deduction, he may set off the penalty for delay against the price of extra work, or against any other claim which the contractor may have against him.[1] If by the contract the penalties for delay are to be deducted from the certificates, the employer cannot claim them in any other way.[2]

If the contract provides for the work being done before a certain day, and for a penalty being paid for delay, and the contractor is delayed by his employer in the commencement of the work or during its progress, he is not responsible for not completing the work within the time, or for the penalty : the act of his employer excuses him from the performance of his contract.[3]

A breach of contract by the employer, which does not necessarily operate to prevent the completion of the work within the time limited, and which may be sufficiently compensated in damages, does not excuse the contractor from the performance within the time, or from payment of the stipulated penalty for delay. The plaintiff covenanted with the Midland Counties Railway Company, that in consideration of £15,000, in addition to £258,629 10s. 6d., he, being provided by the company with railway bars, or rails and chairs, for temporary or permanent use, would complete a certain portion of the railway and the line of permanent railway on or before the 1st of June, 1840; and that if he should not complete the said railway by the 1st of June, 1840, he would pay to the defendants £300 for the 1st of June, and the like sum for every succeeding day, until the whole of the work should have been completed. He

[1] Duckworth v. Alison, 1 M. and W. 412.

[2] Macintosh v. Great Western Railway Company, 11 Jur. N. S. 684.

[3] Holme v. Guppy, 3 M. and W. 387. Thornhill v. Neats, 8 C. B. N. S. 831. Roberts v. Bury Improvement Commissioners, L. R. 5 C. P. 310. Westwood v. Secretary of State for India, 7 L. T. N. S. 736.

sued the company for the £15,000, and they claimed to deduct £7,500 for penalties for delay. It appeared that the railway was not finished until twenty-four days after the 1st of June, but that the company did not supply the plaintiff with bars, rails, and chairs in sufficient quantity to enable him to complete the work by the 1st of June. The Court held that the covenant by the company to supply rails, and of the plaintiff to complete by the 1st of June, were independent covenants, and that the plaintiff was not excused from the penalties by the omission of the company to supply rails, because any other construction would lead to the conclusion, which they thought an unreasonable one, that the non-supply of a single rail or chair by the time specified for its delivery, although in the result wholly immaterial to the facilities for completion, would entitle the plaintiff to receive the £15,000 given for expedition money without his giving the expedition for it.[1]

If the contractor is longer than the time limited about the work, in consequence of additional work being ordered to be done by the employer, he is not excused from the payment of the penalties for delay, if the deed allows additional time for the additional work. The plaintiff agreed to build a barn, waggon-shed, and granary, according to a specified plan, and the defendant was at liberty to order additional work. The specified work was to be finished on the 23rd of October; if not, the plaintiff was to pay £1 for every day that might be used beyond; but if the defendant required additional work, the plaintiff was to be allowed such extra time beyond the 23rd of October as might be necessary for doing and completing the same. The Court held that the circumstance of the defendant

[1] Macintosh v. Midland Counties Railway Company, 14 M. and W. 13.

ordering additional work did not exempt the plaintiff altogether from the penalty, but that he was *primâ facie* liable to the £1 per day for every day consumed after the 23rd of October, but was to be allowed out of those days so many days as were necessarily employed in doing the additional work.[1] A provision that any extra works ordered shall be executed within the original time, unless an extension of time is allowed by the architect, is binding according to its terms; and it is no excuse to a claim for penalties for delay that it was impossible to execute the extra works within the original time.[2] If the time for completing the building is omitted, the penalties for delay are displaced.[3]

47. If the contract provides that the contractor shall obtain the certificate of the employer's architect before payment, he must do so. That he shall obtain such certificate is a condition precedent to his right to payment. A builder agreed to erect certain buildings under the superintendence of A. B. Clayton, or other the architect of his employer for the time being; and the contract, after providing for payment of portions of the price during the progress of the work, stipulated that the balance found due to the builder should be paid by the employer within two calendar months after receiving the said architect's certificate that the whole of the buildings and work thereby contracted for had been executed and completed to his satisfaction. Clayton had examined and approved of the builder's charges, and had written to the employer to that effect, but had not given a certificate that he was satisfied with the manner in which the work had been done. This was

---

[1] Legge v. Harloch, 12 Q. B. 1015.
[2] Jones v. St. John's College, L. R. 6 Q. B. 115. See Roberts v. Bury Commissioners, L. R. 5 C. P. 325.
[3] Kemp v. Rose, 1 Giff. 258, *ante*, p. 60.

held to be a condition precedent to the builder's right to recover for the work, and to apply to extra and additional works, as well as those specified in the contract.[1]

In Lamprell v. the Guardians of the Billericay Union,[2] the contract provided that the builder should be paid 75 per cent. on the amount of the work from time to time actually done, to be ascertained and settled by the architects of the guardians, and the remaining 25 per cent., and the amount estimated by the architects as the value of the additional work, if any, within thirty days from the full completion of the contract; and that the builder should not be entitled to receive any payment until the works, on which such payments were made to depend, should have been completed to the satisfaction of the architects, who should examine and make a valuation of the amount so completed from time to time, and certify the same to the guardians, after which the builder should be entitled to receive the amount of payment, at the rate aforesaid, which should be then due in respect of work so certified to be completed. The Court intimated their opinion that a certificate by the architects was only necessary to enable the builder to draw 75 per cent. on account, and was not required on the completion of the contract.

In the case of an agreement between landlord and tenant that the tenant should expend £200 in altering and repairing the house, and that the alterations should be inspected and approved of by the landlord, and done in a substantial manner, and that the £200 should be allowed out of the rent,—it was held that the approval by the landlord was not a condition precedent to the allowance of the £200; that the substance of the

[1] Morgan v. Birnie, 9 Bing. 672.　　[2] 3 Ex. 283.

agreement was that the works should be properly done, and that if they were properly done, the condition was substantially complied with; that it never could have been intended that the landlord should be at liberty capriciously to withhold his approval; and if such was the intention, the condition would go to the destruction of the thing granted, and be void. The Court observed, that, in Morgan v. Birnie, the architect was appointed as an arbitrator between the parties.[1]

An architect agreed with a Committee of Visitors acting under the Act relating to lunatic asylums, to prepare the requisite probationary drawings for the approval of the committee, and all other drawings required to be submitted to the Commissioners of Lunacy and Secretary of State, pursuant to the statute, and subsequently to prepare the whole of the working drawings for a lunatic asylum for a stipulated sum, the Court of Common Pleas decided that the approval of the committee was a condition precedent to his right to be paid, and that they were the sole judges of the fitness of the plans, and that as they were a public body acting on behalf of the county, having no greater interest than any other inhabitant, they could not be considered as judges in their own cause.[2] So where, by a clause in the contract, the engineer for the time being had power to make such additions to or deductions from the work as he thought proper, and the value was to be ascertained and added or deducted from the contract price, and if any dispute arose, it was to be referred to the engineer, whose decision was to be conclusive. It was held to

---

[1] Dallman v. King, 4 Bing. N. C. 105. Parsons v. Sexton, 4 C. B. 909. Stadhard v. Lee, 3 B. and S. 368, 371.

[2] Moffatt v. Dickson, 13 C. B. 543.

be a condition precedent to the contractor's right to be paid for extras, that the amount should be ascertained, and, if the parties could not agree, it was to be ascertained by the award of the engineer.[1]

If the contract provides merely that the architect shall certify that the work was done to his satisfaction, the certificate need not be in writing.[2] If it requires a direction in writing, under the hand of the architect, for additional works, mere statements of additions, prepared and furnished by the architect, but not signed by him, are not sufficient.[3] A contract for railway works authorised the engineer, when requested by the contractors, to ascertain the extent and value of the works executed and materials provided for the works by the contractors, it was ruled that they were authorised to certify for materials provided for use though not actually fixed and used.[4]

Where a contract was that a ship should be built to the approval of G., and paid for on delivery, G.'s approval was not a condition precedent to payment.[5] Where the agreement was to sell and fix a machine at a certain price, the last instalment to be paid on the buyer being satisfied with the work within two months of its completion, it was held that the employer's satisfaction only applied to the workmanship in fixing the machine, and was not a condition to the right to the price.[6] Where a machine was to be made strong and of sound workmanship, to the approval of J., it was held that the approval was confined

[1] Westwood v. Secretary of State for India, 7 L. T. N. S. 736.
[2] Roberts v. Watkins, 14 C. B. N. S. 592.
[3] Myers v. Sail, 3 E. and E. 306.
[4] Pickering v. Ilfracombe R. C., L. R., 3 C. P. 235.
[5] Tayleur v. Blythe, 27 L. T. 101.
[6] Parsons v. Sexton, 4 C. B. 899.

to the strength and workmanship, and not to the efficiency of the machine.[1]

If a man agree to do work or supply goods to the satisfaction of the agent or servant of his employer, he cannot insist on his work or goods being accepted if the agent is not satisfied on the ground of his being dependent on his employer; the contract, although unreasonable, is binding on him;[2] and if he agrees to work to the satisfaction of a company's engineer, it is no objection that the engineer is a shareholder, and that he is not aware of it. The engineer is not like a judge, supposed to be indifferent between the parties. The stipulation that certain questions shall be decided by the engineer is in fact a stipulation that they shall be decided by the company.[3] On the same principle, where the engineer, who was to certify, had become lessee of the railway at a rent depending on the costs of the works, and the contractor, with knowledge of the fact, proceeded with the settlement of accounts, Turner, L. J., held that the engineer was not disqualified from exercising the powers vested in him by the contract.[4] But where the architect, who was to certify as to the cost of erecting a church, had given the employer an assurance that it should not exceed a fixed sum, and this was unknown to the builder, it was held that, inasmuch as this was calculated to bias his judgment, the builder was not bound by the clause as to the certificate, and the Court of Chancery exercised the judgment which the architect ought to have exercised;[5] and where the

---

[1] Ripley v. Lordan, 6 Jur. N. S. 1078.
[2] Grafton v. Eastern Counties R. C., 8 Ex. 699.
[3] Ranger v. Great Western R. C., 5 H. Lds. 88.
[4] Hill v. South Staffordshire R. C., 11 Jur. N. S. 192.
[5] Kemp v. Rose, 1 Giff. 358.

architect had contracted with his employer, unknown to the builder, that the cost of the building should not exceed a given sum, it was held to annul a clause that matters should be referred to his arbitration,[1] he having a personal interest to benefit himself by giving or withholding certificates.[2]

Where a charter-party provided that no allowance for short tonnage or deficiency in loading the ship should be made, unless the same should be certified by the defendants' presidents, agents, or chiefs and councils, or supercargoes, from whence she should receive her last despatch,—it appeared that the plaintiff had taken all proper steps to obtain the necessary certificates, but that, by the acts and defaults of the defendant's agents, it became impossible for him to obtain them, the Court held that the endeavour to obtain the certificate, so frustrated, was equivalent to performance of the condition.[3]

But in cases in which payment of the price of work is made dependent on the certificate of an architect or engineer, no action can be maintained for the price if the certificate is not obtained, though withheld by collusion with the employer. In such case the workman may maintain a special action against the employer for the breach of an implied stipulation in the contract.[4] So where there is collusion between the contractor and the architect, the certificate does not bind the employers.[5] But an action will not lie against the employer for the surveyor wrongfully and improperly refusing and neglecting to give his certificate. If he

[1] Kimberley v. Dick, L. R. 13 Eq. 1.
[2] Sharpe v. San Paulo R. C., L. R. 8 Ch. 605.
[3] Hotham v. the East India Company, 1 D. and E. 638. Macintosh v. Great Western R. C. 2 Mac. and G. 74.
[4] Milner v. Field, 5 Ex. 829. Batterbury v. Vyse, 2 H. and C. 42.
[5] South-Eastern R. C. v. Watson, 2 F. and F. 464.

refuses to exercise any judgment, the proper course, in the opinion of Willes, J., is to call upon the employer to appoint another surveyor who will do his duty.[1]

When payment is to be made on the certificate of the engineer, and matters are left to his decision, the Court of Chancery will not interfere or entertain a bill for an account with respect to such matters, unless there has been gross misconduct on his part, wilful neglect or absolute incapacity to perform his duties.[2] At first, in the case of a contract to be completed to the satisfaction of a surveyor, which had been properly performed, but the surveyor refused to certify, equity declined to interfere, because the plaintiff had a remedy at law if the certificate was improperly withheld by the surveyor, the surveyor having no right to refuse his certificate arbitrarily.[3] Afterwards it was held to be ground for relief in equity if the contractor was unable to obtain a certificate by the acts of the employer or his agent. Whether the acts arose from a fraudulent motive or not, to use them for the purpose of defeating the plaintiff's remedy constituted a fraud which the Court of Chancery would not permit the defendant to avail himself of.[4] So Cranworth, C., in holding the plaintiff bound to obtain a certificate, says, "If there were anything like fraud or unfairness in the case, different considerations might arise."[5]

[1] Clarke v. Watson, '18 C. B. N. S. '278. Stadhart v. Lee, 3 B. and S. 364.

[2] Scott v. Corporation of Liverpool, 1 Giff. 216; 3 De G. and J. 334. Cooper v. Uttoxeter Burial Board, 11 L. T. N. S. 565. Bliss v. Smith, 34 Beav. 508. Sharpe v. San Paulo R. C., L. R. 8 Ch. 507.

[3] Evan v. Churchwardens of St. Magnus, Rolls T. 1795, 6 D. and E. 716.

[4] Macintosh v. Great Western R. C., 2 Mac. and G. 74.

[5] Ranger v. Great Western R. C. 5 H. Lds. 93.

And in a case where an architect acting in a judicial character was found to have been guilty of unfair conduct, or any other misconduct, as where by withholding certificates for money which he knew to be justly due, and coercing the builder, pressed for money to pay his workmen, to abandon the contract upon payment of a sum less than the fair value of his work, the Court of Chancery interfered by putting itself in the place of the architect, and ascertaining the amount for which the architect ought to have certified.[1] A similar decision was arrived at when the architect showed his partiality by refusing to certify, or to allow any other surveyor to go over the works, and having dismissed the builder, did not trouble himself to ascertain the value of the work.[2] And collusion between the employer and architect to injure the contractor is now of itself a ground for relief in equity.[3]

The want of a certificate may, it seems, be waived by acceptance of the work.[4]

If the contract is to pay a sum assessed by a third person, the valuation when made is in the nature of an award, and binding on both parties.[5] The agreement to be bound by the certificate or decision of the surveyor is not a submission to arbitration, and cannot be made a rule of Court.[6] Nor will an agreement to refer disputes to the surveyor give the Court of Chancery jurisdiction over matters which have been decided by his certificate.[7] If the surveyor has certified an amount, and the employer has paid it, and the builder

---

[1] Ormes v. Beadel, 2 Giff. 166.
[2] Pawley v. Turnbull, 3 Giff. 70.
[3] Bliss v. Smith, 34 Beav. 508.
[4] Lamprell v. Billericay Union, 3 Ex. 305.
[5] Perkins v. Potts, 2 Chit. 399.
[6] Wadsworth v. Smith, L. R. 6 Q. B. 332.
[7] Sharpe v. San Paulo R. C. L. R. 8 Ch. 597.

asks for more, and sues for it, Chancery will not restrain him by injunction.[1] The surveyor does not in all respects resemble an arbitrator. He is responsible for negligence to his employer, and may recover his charges as agent from him.[2]

48. The great duty of the employer is to pay. *Sine pecuniâ nil*, although not mentioned by Mr. Broom, is one of the most important maxims of the law, which, like the philosopher's stone, turns, or attempts to turn, everything it touches into gold. A blow on the head, a breach of the seventh commandment, or of a lover's vow, are severally transmuted in the legal crucible into so many pounds, so many shillings, and so many pence.

The General Rule is, that when a man bestows his labour for another, he has a right of action to recover a compensation for that labour.[3] If he is employed without anything being said as to payment, the presumption is, that he is to be paid the value of his services according to the usual rate of remuneration; and in estimating the amount to be paid, the peculiar character of the services may be taken into consideration. Thus a surgeon, in suing on a general employment, may prove his skill.[4]

In the case of salvage services performed in rescuing a ship from wreck, the salvor is entitled to remuneration from the necessity of the case, although he does not work upon the retainer of the ship-owners.[5] But in other cases of services voluntarily performed in taking care of a lost thing and searching for the owner, it is doubtful whether the finder has any right to remunera-

---

[1] Baron de Worms v. Mellier, L. R. 16 Eq. 554.
[2] Jenkins v. Betham, 15 C. B. 128.
[3] Per Cur., Poucher v. Norman, 3 B. and C. 745.
[4] Bird v. M'Gahey, 2 Car. and Kir. 707.
[5] Newman v. Walters, 1 B. and P. 612.

tion for his services. It is clear that he has no lien upon the thing found.[1]

49. If the service performed is an act of friendship or kindness, no remuneration can be claimed. If a person takes a journey to become bail for another, he cannot maintain an action against such person for his trouble or loss of time in such journey, because he does not undertake the journey as work or labour, or as a person employed by the defendant, but he does it as his friend, and to do him a kindness.[2]

A step-father brought an action against his step-daughter for her board, maintenance, and education. Lawrence, J., directed the jury to consider "whether the plaintiff, at the time he began to provide for her, expected to be paid at a future time; or whether he was not acting as every moral man who married a woman having children by her former husband would act; namely, taking care of those whose interests would be most dear to the woman he had chosen for his wife. A man who married a woman with children, whether he had fortune or no fortune with her, was not bound to provide for her children. As a moral man it might be expected from him, but the law would not enforce it. That which was at first intended for a gratuity could not be afterwards converted into a debt." The jury found for the defendant.[3] In a similar case, it appeared that the step-child had some property, and that the step-father maintained and educated him in a manner superior to what he would reasonably have done had he been a member of his own family; and the step-son, when he came of age, promised to pay him for his

[1] Binstead v. Buck, 2 W. Bl. 1117. Nicholson v. Chapman, 2 H. Bl. 254.

[2] Reason v. Wirdnam. 1 C. and P. 434.

[3] Pelly v. Rawlins, Peake, Ad. Cases, 226.

board and education. The step-father recovered; the Court considering that he had given the son an education proportionable to his future prospects, but beyond his own means, upon the expectation that the son would take it into his consideration after he came of age.[1]

If services are rendered in expectation of a legacy, and not upon an understanding that they are to be paid for, there is no obligation to pay. The plaintiff brought an action for his services in transacting Mr. Guy's stock affairs. It appeared that he was no broker, but a friend; and it looked strongly as if he did not expect to be paid, but to be considered in the will. Lord Chief Justice Raymond directed the jury, that if that was the case, they could not find for the plaintiff, though nothing was given him by the will; for they should consider how it was understood by the parties at the time of doing the business; and a man who expects to be made amends by a legacy cannot afterwards resort to his action.[2] This direction was approved of in the case of an apothecary who had attended a deceased lady for eleven years, without ever sending in his bill. Tindal, C. J., there told the jury, that if the plaintiff had attended the deceased on an understanding that he was to be paid only by a legacy, he was not entitled to recover. They found for the plaintiff. The Court refused to disturb the verdict, upon the ground that it was not proved that there was any understanding that the plaintiff was not to be paid for his services except by a legacy; and that in the absence of such evidence, it must be presumed that the understanding was, that he should be remunerated in the usual way.[3]

[1] Cooper v. Martin, 4 East, 76. See Eastwood v. Kenyon, 11 A. and E. 448.

[2] Osborn v. the Governors of Guy's Hospital, 2 Str. 728.

[3] Baxter v. Gray, 3 M. and G. 771.

50. The claim of a counsel on his client is a moral one only, whether the business is litigious or nonlitigious. His fees ought to be paid at the time, and if they are not, he cannot sue for them.[1] A physician may sue for his fees unless prohibited by by-law of the College of Physicians. They have passed a by-law that no fellow of the College shall be entitled to sue for professional aid rendered by him. A licentiate, therefore, may sue, but a fellow cannot.[2] On an express contract to pay a barrister for services not relating to litigation, as for acting as returning officer on an election of guardians, or as arbitrator,[3] or as auditor of the accounts of an estate, he may recover.[4] It is said that an arbitrator cannot sue for his fees on an implied promise to pay him, but this is doubtful.[5] It is decided that he may sue on an express promise,[6] that he has a lien on the award for his fees, and that if he exacts an excessive amount, it may be recovered from him.[7]

51. If it is agreed that it shall be left to the employer whether anything and how much shall be paid for the services performed, it is optional with the employer to pay,—as where a person was employed by a committee of management for the sale of lottery-tickets, under a resolution that any service to be rendered by him should, after the third lottery, be taken into consideration, and such remuneration be made as should be

[1] Kennedy v. Broun, 13 C. B. N. S. 727. Mostyn v. Mostyn, L. R. 5 Ch. 458.

[2] 21 & 22 V. c. 90, s. 31. Gibbon v. Budd, 2 H. and C. 92.

[3] Egan v. Kensington Union, 3 Q. B. 935, n. Kennedy v. Broun, 13 C. B. N. S. 729.

[4] Lowndes v. Earl of Stamford, 18 Q. B. 425.

[5] Virany v. Warne, 4 Esp. 46. Re Coombs, 4 Ex. 841. Marsack v. Webber, 6 H. and N. 5.

[6] Hoggins v. Gordon, 3 Q. B. 466.

[7] Barnes v. Braithwaite, 2 H. and N. 569.

deemed right, it was held that no action could be maintained.[1]   But if only the amount of payment is left to the employer, he is bound to award some amount; and if he fails to do so, a jury may award to the workman such a sum as the employer, acting *bonâ fide*, would and ought to have awarded.   The plaintiff entered into the defendant's service upon the terms contained in a letter written by the plaintiff, in which he said,—"The amount of payment I am to receive I leave entirely to you."   Having served him for six weeks, he was held entitled to recover the value of his services, though the defendant had awarded him nothing.[2]   The plaintiff agreed to accept the appointment of secretary to a company at a salary of £300, if the company was registered.   "If not," he said, "I shall be satisfied with any remuneration for my time and labour you may think me deserving of, and your means can afford."   It was held that there was no contract to pay for his services.   It was a liability in honour, not in contract, and the Court preferred Taylor v. Brewer to Bryant v. Flight.[3]   If the amount of remuneration is to be fixed by a third person, no action can be maintained if he has not fixed the amount.[4]

Where a surgeon delivered a bill with a blank for his attendance, Lord Kenyon considered that he left the amount of his remuneration to the generosity of his patient, and could not recover more than he was willing to give him.[5]   And an attorney, after delivering his bill, cannot increase the amount of his charges,

---

[1] Taylor v. Brewer, 1 Maule and Sel. 290.

[2] Bryant v. Flight, 5 M. and W. 114.   Bird v. M'Gahey, 1 C. and K. 707.

[3] Roberts v. Smith, 4 H. and N. 315.

[4] Owen v. Bowen, 4 C. and P. 93.

[5] Tuson v. Batting, 3 Esp. 192.

though he may recover for items which have been omitted by mistake.[1]

52. If the engagement of the employer in Bryant v. Flight had been—"I will pay the amount your services are worth, but will not be personally liable,"—the condition, leaving it optional with the employer to pay or not to pay, would have been repugnant and inconsistent with his engagement to pay; and as the engagement and its condition could not stand together, the condition would have been rejected, according to the principle by which agreements are construed against the party professing to bind himself and in favour of the other party. This is the law adverted to by Tindal, C. J., in Dallman v. King, and was the ground of the decision in Furnival v. Coombes.[2] In that case the plaintiff had agreed by deed, with the churchwardens and overseers of the parish of St. Botolph, Aldgate, to repair Aldgate church for a certain sum of money, which they covenanted to pay, but annexed to their covenant a proviso, that nothing in the deed should extend, or be construed to extend, to any personal covenant of, or obligation upon, the churchwardens and overseers, or anywise personally affect them, their executors, administrators, goods, estates, and effects, in their private capacity; but should be, and was intended to be, binding and obligatory upon the churchwardens and overseers for the time being, and their successors, as such churchwardens and overseers, but not further or otherwise. The Court held that, inasmuch as churchwardens and overseers could not bind their successors, the proviso that they should not be personally bound to pay was repugnant to the covenant, and void.

[1] Loveridge v. Botham, 1 B. and P. 49. Eyre v. Shelley, 8 M. and W. 154.

[2] 5 M. and G. 736.

A cross engagement by a contractor to exonerate one of several employers from personal responsibility is not open to this objection. A person employed in- the formation of a railway company sued one of the provisional committeemen for his services. He pleaded that he became a committeeman on the other's engagement to indemnify him, and the plea was adjudged good.[1]

53. Commission is a reward bargained for by an agent, measured, not by the amount of the labour of the agent, but by the benefit derived by the employer from his services. The word has passed from the employment to its fee, probably because the agent thinks most of the latter.

Generally an agent employed to negotiate a sale is entitled to commission if the relation of buyer and seller is really brought about by the act of the agent, although the actual sale has not been effected by him, and the parties cannot, by their agreement and completing the business without his interference, deprive him of his right.[2] On the sale of a ship through a ship-broker, the broker who first introduces the buyer is, by custom, entitled to commission.[3] An agent who was to have a commission on all goods bought by customers introduced by him was entitled to commission on orders accepted by his employer, though he did not execute them.[4] If the transaction is not fairly within the terms of the employment, the agent is not entitled to

---

[1] Connop v. Levy, 11 Q. B. 769.

[2] Green v. Bartlett, 14 C. B. N. S. 685. Wilkinson v. Martin, 8 C. and P. 1. Murray v. Currie, 7 C. and P. 584. Mansell v. Clements, L. R. 9 C. P. 139.

[3] Cunard v. Von Oppen, 1 F. and F. 716.

[4] Lockwood v. Levick, 8 C. B. N. S. 603. See also Bray v. Chandler, 18 C. B. 715. Lara v. Hill, 15 C. B. N. S. 45.

commission.[1] He is not entitled to commission on a sale to a company in which he is a shareholder.[2] If the agent does not find the purchaser, he is not entitled to commission in the event of a sale.[3] Though an auctioneer, by the custom of business, is entitled to a commission on a sale of an estate after he has been employed to sell, and has advertised it for sale, though not sold through him, the publicity he gives the matter, and his connection, are considered as conducing to the sale.[4]

If the principal breaks his contract, and thereby prevents the agent from earning his commission, he is entitled to a reasonable remuneration for his services performed. Thus where an agent was to be paid a commission if he found a purchaser at a price named, and he found one, but the negotiation failed because the principal was not prepared to come forward as he ought, he was held entitled to recover upon an implied contract.[5] A broker employed to dispose of the shares for a commission to be paid when all the shares were allotted, and the company wound up voluntarily before the shares were disposed of, succeeded in recovering for his services on the ground that the company had, by their own act, prevented the allotment of shares.[6] But if the act or default of the employer, which prevents the commis-

---

[1] Warde v. Stewart, 1 C. B. N. S. 88. Fullwood v. Akerman, 11 C. B. N. S. 737. Alder v. Boyle, 5 C. B. 635. Biggs v. Gordon, 8 C. B. N. S. 638. Leakey v. Lucas, 14 C. B. N. S. 491.

[2] Salomons v. Pender, 3 H. and C. 639.

[3] Simpson v. Lamb, 17 C. B. 603. Gibson v. Crick, 2 F. and F. 766. Antrobus v. Wickens, 4 F. and F. 291. Green v. Mules, 30 L. J. C. P. 343.

[4] Driver v. Cholmondeley and Rainey v. Vernon, 9 C. and P. 559.

[5] Prickett v. Badger, 1 C. B. N. S. 296.

[6] Inchbald v. the Western Neilgherry Coffee Company, 17 C. B. N. S. 733. Queen of Spain v. Parr, 21 L. T. N. S. 555.

sion being earned, is not a breach of his contract, the case is different.[1]

When payment is to be made out of a certain fund, there is no claim if there is no fund.[2]

54. It has been mentioned, in considering the duty of the workman to perform his work with skill and care, that although the work is not properly performed, the workman is entitled to be paid for its value. In cases also in which conditions precedent to payment have not been observed, as if it is not finished, or not finished in time, where to finish the work, or to finish it in time, is a condition precedent to payment, the employer is bound to pay the value of the work if he accept the work, or encourages the workman to proceed, or acquiesces in his proceeding, after the contract has been broken by him. A landlord agreed with his tenant to pay him for building a tap-room, provided it was built according to a plan to be agreed upon, and completed within two months. No plan was agreed upon, but the tenant built a tap-room. He did not complete it within two months. After the two months had elapsed, the landlord said that the chamber over the tap-room would be a useful room, and inquired when it would be finished. He also said, that if the tenant did not finish it soon, he, the landlord, would finish it; that the expense would be nothing to the tenant, as it would all fall upon him, the landlord. The Court gave judgment in favour of the tenant. They said,—"It is a settled rule, even in the case of a deed, that if there be a condition precedent, and it is not performed, and the parties proceed with the performance

---

[1] Bull v. Price, 7 Bing. 737. Moffatt v. Lawrie, 15 C. B. 583. Simpson v. Lamb, 17 C. B. 603.

[2] Higgins v. Hopkins, 3 Ex. 163. Laidman v. Entwistle, 7 Ex. 632.

of other parts of the contract, although the deed cannot take effect, the law will raise an implied assumpsit. Here, although the plaintiff cannot put his case upon the written agreement, he may go upon the agreement raised on so many of the facts of the case as are applicable. In Ellis v. Hamlen[1] there was no acquiescence by the defendant. Here is an acquiescence: for, first, the defendant uses all this building; secondly, he sees it go on, and never objects; thirdly, he sees a delay and says, Why does not the plaintiff go on, the expense is nothing to him; the expense will be mine? And he says, respecting the room above, that it will be very convenient."[2]

The mere taking possession of land on which a building is erected, as to which the conditions have not been fulfilled, does not raise an inference of a waiver of the conditions of the special contract, or of entering into a new one. If indeed the employer does anything coupled with taking possession which prevents the performance of the special contract, as if he forbids the surveyor to enter to inspect the works, or if, the failure in complete performance being very slight, he uses any language or does any act from which acquiescence may be reasonably inferred, the case may be very different.[3] And so it has been held in the case of a company who desired by their engineer alterations, additions, and omissions to be made, and stood by and saw the expenditure going on, and then refused payment on the ground that the estimate was increased without proper orders having been given for the purpose, they were precluded from objecting that the contractor had forfeited his right to payment by not finishing his work at the time

---

[1] 3 Taunt. 52.
[2] Burn v. Miller, 4 Taunt. 745. Davis v. Nicholls, 2 Chit. 320. Lucas v. Godwin, 3 Bing. N. C. 744.
[3] Munro v. Butt, 8 E. and B. 753.

appointed, by having taken possession of and used the works, and made payments after the times fixed for their completion, and when, according to their contention, the right to such payments had been forfeited.[1]

In such a case, a new contract to pay the value of the work is implied from the acceptance. Such a contract may also be implied if the employer absolutely refuses to perform, or renders himself incapable of performing, his part of the contract,[2] or if the special contract is by mutual consent rescinded. The money becomes due when the special contract is at an end, and not when the work was done.[3]

55. If the contract is to do several things for a single sum, the employer cannot resist payment because all the things contracted to be done have not been performed. The plaintiff covenanted to teach the defendant the art of bleaching materials for making paper, and to permit him, during the continuance of a patent, which the plaintiff then had, to bleach such materials according to the specification in the patent. The defendant, in consideration thereof, paid the plaintiff £250, and covenanted to pay him £250 more. In an action for the £250, it was held not necessary for the plaintiff to show that he had taught the defendant the art of bleaching, because it did not go to the whole consideration. The plaintiff was entitled to an action against the defendant for the non-payment of the £250, and the defendant to another against the plaintiff for not teaching him.[4] But in such case, if the contract is

---

[1] Hill v. South Staffordshire Railway Company, 11 Jur. N. S. 193.

[2] Keys v. Harwood, 2 C. B. 905. De Bernardy v. Harding, 8 Ex. 822. Prickett v. Badger, 1 C. B. N. S. 296.

[3] Crosthwaite v. Gardner, 18 Q. B. 640.

[4] Campbell v. Jones, 6 D. and E. 570. Stavers v. Curling, 3 Bing. N. C. 355. Mills v. Blackall, 11 Q. B. 358.

a simple contract, and not a covenant, the defendant may give the plaintiff's breach of contract in evidence in mitigation of damages. The plaintiff, in consideration of £220 10*s.* to be paid by the defendant, agreed to sell, and plant on the defendant's land, a quantity of trees, and to keep them in order for two years after the planting. The Court held that the defendant might show, in reduction of damages, that trees of an inferior quality to those agreed for were planted, and that they were not kept in order.[1]

56. If work has been done in a manner different from that specified in the contract, the employer is not bound to pay the contract price, nor the value of the work done. He is bound to pay the contract price, less the amount it will take to alter the work, so as to make it correspond with the specification.[2] This should be understood as applying to a case in which the employer either has, or intends to have, the work altered, and made to correspond to the original contract. If he has accepted the inferior work, and does not intend to have it altered, then it seems reasonable that the workman should recover the value of the inferior work, taking the contract price as the criterion of the value of the works specified; that is, that he should have so much less than the contract price, as the inferior is less valuable than the work contracted to be performed. For instance: if a builder has contracted to build a house with the best bricks at the price of inferior bricks, and he uses inferior bricks, and his employer accepts and uses the house, he ought not to recover the contract price, because he has not performed his contract, nor ought he to recover the value of the bricks used, because that might be as much or more than the contract

---

[1] Allen v. Cameron, 1 C. and M. 832.
[2] Thornton v. Place, 1 Moo. and Rob. 218.

price, and he must suffer for breaking his contract; nor
ought the employer to be allowed for pulling down and
rebuilding the house with the best bricks, because he
does not intend to do so, but is content to accept the
house built with inferior bricks. But the difference in
value between the bricks agreed to be used and those
actually used, should be deducted from the contract
price; and by this means the builder will lose so just
as much as he expected to gain by his roguery.

57. In cases in which there are contracts to do works
for certain sums, employers are frequently called upon to
pay more than the sums specified, in consequence of the
contracts having been departed from, or for works extra
the contracts. The rule in cases of deviations from contracts has been thus stated by Lord Kenyon: "Where
additions are made to a building which the workman
contracts to finish for a certain sum, the contract shall
exist as far as it can be traced to have been followed,
and the excess only paid for according to the usual rate
of charging. I admit, that if a man contracts to work
by a certain plan, and that plan is so entirely abandoned that it is impossible to trace the contract and say
to what part of it the work shall be applied, in such
case the workman shall be permitted to charge for the
whole of the work by measure and value, as if no contract at all had ever been made."[1]

If a workman is employed under a contract for a
certain sum, and the work is done, with the consent of
his employer, in some manner different from the manner
specified in the contract, he is not entitled to more than
the contract price, unless the deviations are of such a
nature that the employer must have known that they
would increase the expense, or unless the workman in-

---

[1] Pepper v. Burland, Peake, 139.   See also Ranger v. Great
Western R. C., 5 H. of Lds. C. 118.

formed his employer, before departing from the contract, that such would be the consequence of the departure. In an action on a carpenter's bill, in which the work was done in altering a house which was originally undertaken on a contract for a fixed sum, but alterations were subsequently made in the original plan, and the plaintiff claimed to abandon the contract, and recover a measure and value price for all the work done,—Lord Tenterden observed—"A person intending to make alterations of this nature generally consults the person whom he intends to employ, and ascertains from him the expense of the undertaking; and it will very frequently depend on this estimate whether he proceeds or not. It is therefore a great hardship upon him if he is to lose protection of this estimate, unless he fully understands that such consequences will follow, and assents to them. In many cases he will be completely ignorant whether the particular alterations suggested will produce any increase of labour and expenditure; and I do not think that the mere fact of assenting to them ought to deprive him of the protection of his contract. Sometimes, indeed, the nature of the alterations will be such, that he cannot fail to be aware that they must increase the expense, and cannot therefore suppose that they are to be done for the contract price. But where the departures from the original scheme are not of that character, I think a jury will do wisely in considering that a party does not abandon the security of his contract by consenting that such alterations shall be made, unless he is also informed, at the time of the consent, that the effect of the alteration will be to increase the expense of the work." [1]

If work is within the contract, it cannot be claimed as an extra because it is omitted from the specification.

[1] Lovelock v. King, 1 Moo. and Rob. 60.

Thus, when a contract was to complete a house, and the flooring was omitted from the specification, the builder had no right to claim it as an extra.[1]

A contract for building a ship for the Portuguese government, provided that no charges were to be demanded for extras, but any addition made by an order in writing by Sir J. Sartorius was to be paid extra at a price to be previously agreed for in writing. Orders not in writing were given by the agents of the government, and executed. They were held to form part of the contract, and not to be paid for as extras.[2] And where there was a similar contract, and the employer himself gave a verbal order for extra work, it was held that there should be something beyond an order to entitle the builder to payment.[3] But if the builder is told, or led to believe, by the employer or his authorised agent, that he is to be paid extra for the work, the case is different.[4]

When extra works have been done in addition to the contract, the workman is entitled to be paid for such works, although he has not performed his contract,[5] and although the time for the payment of the contract price has not arrived.[6]

Extras are sometimes provided for by the contract, and sometimes by subsequent agreement, and are to be paid for accordingly.[7]

58. The consideration of the duty of the employer to pay involves that of the right of the workman to receive

---

[1] Williams v. Fitzmaurice, 3 H. and N. 844.

[2] Russell v. De Bandeira, 13 C. B. N. S. 149.

[3] Franklin v. Darke, 3 F. and F. 65; 6 L. T. N. S. 291.

[4] Wallis v. Robinson, 3 F. and F. 307. Eccles v. Southern, 3 F. and F. 142. Hill v. South Staffordshire Railway Company, 11 Jur. N. S. 193.

[5] Rees v. Lines, 8 C. and P. 126.

[6] Robson v. Godfrey, 1 Stark. 275. Holt, N. P. C. 236.

[7] Ranger v. Great Western R. C., 5 H. of Lds. 99.

payment, and leads to that of his remedies to enforce it. He may not only maintain an action at law, but in the case of a chattel delivered to him to be worked upon, he has a lien upon or right to detain the chattel until the amount due for his work bestowed upon it is paid. This right of lien, generally speaking, exists wherever a movable thing has been delivered to a workman to be improved or altered, and he has improved or altered it by bestowing his labour upon it. Thus a shipwright has a lien on a ship delivered to him to be repaired ;[1] and a farmer has a lien on a mare delivered to him to be covered by a stallion.[2] But there is no lien when the thing is not altered, nor its value improved, by the labour of the workman bestowed upon it ;[3] or when no labour is bestowed upon and mixed up with the thing itself.[4] Nor is there any lien when its existence is inconsistent with the agreement of the parties ; as if credit is agreed to be given for payment of the price of the labour ; or if the understanding is that the employer is to have and use the thing occasionally whilst the work is going on, as in the case of a livery-stable keeper, or an agister of cows. In the one case the owner of the horse is entitled to have and use it whenever he wishes, in the other the owner of the cows is entitled to milk them, which rights are considered to be inconsistent with a right of lien.[5]

A right of lien is lost by the workman relinquishing the possession of the thing. If, therefore, he delivers the thing to the owner, or pledges it, his lien is gone.[6]

---

[1] Exp. Ockendon, 1 Atk. 235.
[2] Scarfe v. Morgan, 4 M. and W. 270.
[3] Stone v. Lingwood, 1 Str. 651.
[4] Steadman v. Hockley, 15 M. and W. 553.
[5] Jackson v. Cummins, 5 M. and W. 350.
[6] Scott v. Newington, 1 Moo. and Rob. 252.

It is lost if he refuses to deliver it upon tender of the amount due ;[1] or if he claims a right to detain for any cause other than his lien :[2] but he does not lose his lien merely by demanding more for his work than he is entitled to.[3] When a chattel is made for another it may be provided that the property shall not pass until the price is paid, and that the maker shall be entitled to recover possession in case of nonpayment, and this, although called a lien in the agreement, is not strictly a lien, but a continuation of the workman's property.[4]

A workman who keeps a chattel by virtue of his lien is not, in the absence of express agreement, entitled to charge for keeping it.[5]

59. It is also the duty of the employer not to do any act which will prevent the workman from performing his contract, and also to do every act agreed to be done by him, to enable the workman to perform his contract. If, by the employer doing or omitting to do any act, the workman is prevented from performing his contract, he is excused from the performance, and is, so far as he has been disabled by the employer, entitled to recover from the employer any damage he may have sustained by the act or omission of the employer.

A publication was commenced by some booksellers, called "The Juvenile Library," and they employed an author to write a volume for it, on Costume and Ancient Armour, for £100. When he had written a considerable part of the work, they abandoned the publication. He refused to allow them to publish his work separately, and commenced an action, and re-

[1] Jones v. Tarleton, 9 M. and W. 675.
[2] Boardman v. Sill, 1 Campb. 410.
[3] Scarfe v. Morgan, 4 M. and W. 270.
[4] Walker v. Clyde, 10 C. B. N. S. 381.
[5] British Empire Shipping Company v. Somes, E. B. and E. 353, 8 H. of Lds. 338.

covered £50, although he had not finished or tendered his work, they having exonerated him from so doing by abandoning the publication.[1] A tenant covenanted to expend £100 in substantial repairs and improvements to a dwelling-house, under the direction and with the approbation of some competent surveyor, to be named by the landlord. The landlord failed to recover against the tenant for not expending the money upon the premises, because he had not named a surveyor.[2] In the case already mentioned, in which the calico-printer demanded from the engraver rollers sent to be engraved, before the work was finished, Rolfe, B., expressed his opinion that the engraver, who was bound to deliver the rollers when demanded, would have a right of action for being prevented from completing the work.[3]

So in the case of Hotham v. East India Company,[4] the plaintiff, having been prevented from obtaining the certificates by the act and default of the agents of the Company, was in the same situation as if he had obtained them. And in Dallman v. King,[5] it was the duty of the landlord to approve of the repairs, if substantially done; and therefore, by improperly withholding his approbation, he could not defeat the tenant's right to the allowance. And in Bryant v. Flight,[6] it was the duty of the defendant to award to the plaintiff a reasonable remuneration for his services, and his not doing so did not prevent the plaintiff recovering. And in Holme v. Guppy,[7] the defendant not having given the plaintiff possession of the ground

[1] Planché v. Colburn, 8 Bing. 14. Inchbald v. Western, &c., Company, 17 C. B. N. S. 733.

[2] Coombe v. Green, 11 M. and W. 480.

[3] Lilley v. Barnsley, 1 C. and K. 344, ante, s. 38. Davis v. Mayor of Swansea, 8 Ex. 808. Kewley v. Stokes, 2 C. and K. 435.

[4] 1 D. and E. 638, ante, s. 47.   [5] 4 Bing. N. C. 105, ante, s. 49.
[6] 5 M. and W. 114, ante, s. 51.   [7] 3 M. and W. 387, ante, s. 46.

for three weeks after the date of the contract, and he being delayed for a week by the default of the masons employed by the defendant, excused him from finishing his work within the time specified, and from payment of the penalties provided for delay.

When the words of a contract show that its efficiency is to depend upon an act to be done by one party, there is a contract by that party that he will do all that lies in his power to bring about that act, and that if it is not already done it shall be done. Thus, on a contract with a Board of Health to do works under the Public Health Act, the contractor was to be paid when the money was collected from the owners of the property chargeable, a contract by the Board of Health to exercise the powers vested in them by the Act to enforce payment of the moneys was implied.[1]

When plans and specifications for a work are prepared by an engineer for the employer, there is no contract by the employer that the specification is sufficient, and that it is reasonably practicable to execute the work in the mode prescribed; as to those matters the contractor can and should judge for himself before he enters into the contract.[2]

A contract is also implied by the employer that the work agreed for does not infringe the rights of others, and if it does, without the knowledge of the workman, the employer is bound to indemnify him.[3]

If the workman who has not stipulated for payment before the work is finished refuses to proceed without security, the employer is justified in withdrawing from the contract.[4]

---

[1] Worthington v. Sudlow, 2 B. and S. 508.
[2] Thorn v. Mayor, &c., of London, L. R. 9 Ex. 163.
[3] Dixon v. Fawcus, 3 E. and E. 537.
[4] Pontifex v. Wilkinson, 1 C. B. 75, 2 C. B. 349.

60. Contracts sometimes contain a power for the employer to dismiss the contractor in certain events. These powers are reasonably construed. It was provided that if the contractor should from bankruptcy, &c., be prevented from or delayed in proceeding with the works, or should not proceed therein to the satisfaction of the surveyor, the contract should, at the option of the employers, become void, and *the amount already paid* be considered as the full value of the works, and provision was made for payment by instalments. It was read by the Court " the amount, *if any*, already paid," and decided that the employers were entitled to dismiss the contractor, although no payment had been made.[1]

A deed provided that the work might be taken out of the contractor's hands if he failed to comply with a notice in writing given him by his employer's engineer to rectify improper work, or proceed with due expedition. A notice requiring him to supply all proper and sufficient materials for the due prosecution of the work and to proceed with due expedition was held sufficiently particular, though if the engineer had required any work altered it should have been more particular.[2] A contract empowered the architect to extend the time for completing the works in certain specified cases, and also empowered the employers, in case the contractor should not, in the opinion and according to the determination of the architect, make such due progress as would enable the works to be completed by the time fixed, to take the works out of the contractor's hands. The completion of the works within the agreed time was prevented by the default and breach of contract of the employers, and the architect not having ex-

---

[1] Davis v. Mayor of Swansea, 8 Ex. 808.
[2] Pauling v. Mayor of Dover, 10 Ex. 750.

tended the time, they dismissed him. It was ruled in the Exchequer Chamber, reversing the judgment of the Common Pleas, that they had no power to do so, because the terms of the contract did not make the architect judge as to whether there had been a breach of contract on the part of the employers. The Court says—"When the effect of giving such a construction to the contract is to put one party completely at the mercy of the other, it ought not to be so construed unless the intention is pretty clearly expressed. The employers ought to take care to select words which the contractor could not misapprehend if such was their object," and as the contract did not expressly make the architect judge as to whether or not there had been a breach of contract by the employer, the ordinary rule prevailed that the default of the employer excused the delay of the contractor, and the power to dismiss could not be acted upon. It was also held that in cases in which the architect had power to extend the time the contractor could not claim an extension when none had been granted.[1] A contract empowered the employers to enter and employ workmen, and deduct the cost from the money payable to the contractor, if the works did not proceed as rapidly and satisfactorily as required by them. It was held to be no plea that the works proceeded as rapidly and satisfactorily as the employers could reasonably and properly require ; but that so long as the employers acted *bonâ fide* under an honest sense of dissatisfaction, although it might be unfounded and unreasonable, they were entitled to insist on the condition.[2] If the architects are to ascertain and decide as to whether there has been delay or unsatisfactory conduct without appeal, before the employers

[1] Roberts v. Bury Commissioners, L. R. 4 C. P. 755, 5 C. P. 310.
[2] Stadhart v. Lee, 3 B. and S. 365.

take possession of the works, the agreement cannot be made a rule of Court as a submission to arbitration, as this would in effect be an appeal against their decision.[1] If the power to dismiss is improperly exercised, the contractor does not become entitled to be paid for the work irrespective of the contract, but has his remedy in damages for the wrongful act of the employer.[2] Unless the case is so clear as to be almost undisputed, an injunction will not be granted to restrain the employer from taking the works out of the contractor's hands, on the ground of comparative injury: the contractor, if improperly dismissed, having an adequate remedy in damages, the injury to the employer by having the work done in an improper and insufficient manner being greater.[3] On the same principle, when the contractor becomes bankrupt, the employer will not be restrained from taking the works out of the hands of the assignees. If there are any stipulations showing that confidence was placed in the unusual skill of the contractors, or if it is provided that they shall set out the works and be responsible for any errors, and provide and employ such number of workmen as the architect deems necessary, it is doubtful whether the assignees have the right to proceed with the works.[4]

A power to take the works from the contractor, and use plant, is in the nature of a penalty to secure the performance of the works, and the employer who exercises it is bound to account to the contractor for the value of his property taken possession of, or is entitled to be allowed the sum properly expended in

[1] Wadsworth v. Smith, L. R. 6 Q. B. 332.
[2] Ranger v. Great Western Railway Company, 5 H. of Lds. 95.
[3] Garrett v. Banstead Railway Company, 4 De G. J. and S. 462. Munro v. Wivenhoe Railway Company, 11 Jur. N. S. 612.
[4] Knight v. Burgess, 10 Jur. N. S. 166.

completing the works against what would have been
payable to the contractor under the contract had he
completed it.[1] Where the power was that, on default
of the contractor, his employers (a railway company)
might take the execution of the works out of his hands,
use his plant, and that, in addition to all other rights,
the plant which might then be on the works should
become the absolute property of the company, and be
valued or sold, and the amount of the valuation or sale
credited to the contractor in reduction of the moneys,
if any, recoverable from him by the company, Lord
Romilly held that the power to use the plant implied
that it continued the property of the contractor, and
that it did not become the property of the company unless
they had sustained loss or expense; and he restrained
them from removing the plant, except so far as necessary for opening the line.[2]

61. The contract between master and servant is, that
the servant shall serve the master in a particular
capacity, for a definite or indefinite time, in consideration of wages to be paid by the master; and that the
master shall pay wages, in consideration of the service
to be rendered by the servant. The general duties of
the servant upon this contract are to serve, and serve
properly: the general duties of the master are to
employ, and pay wages.

First, it is the duty of the servant to serve for the
time prescribed by the contract. To ascertain the
extent of this duty, the duration of the period must be
determined. The general understanding of parties is,
that a general hiring of a servant, without any circumstance to show that a less time was meant, is a hiring

[1] Ranger v. Great Western Railway Company, 5 H. of Lds. 107.
[2] Garrett v. Salisbury, &c., Railway Company, L. R. 2 Eq. 358.

for a year.[1] The reason given is, that both master and servant may have the benefit of all the seasons.[2] This rule applies to the cases of all servants who are hired in a permanent capacity for an indefinite time, such as servants in husbandry, domestic servants, trade servants, reporters to newspapers, &c.[3]

62. The hiring of a domestic or menial servant, though for a year, is subject to be determined at any time by a month's warning on the part of the master or the servant, or by payment of a month's wages by the master in lieu of warning.[4] This custom applies, although the contract between the master and servant is in writing, if the written agreement does not negative or is not inconsistent with it.[5]

A head gardener, who had the management of a gentleman's hot-houses and pineries, at the wages of £100 a year, with a house within the master's grounds, and the privilege of taking two apprentices, and who had five under-gardeners employed for his assistance, was held to be a menial servant within the custom, whom his master was entitled to dismiss upon a month's notice. Lord Abinger said, "I should have been inclined to have told the jury that the plaintiff was a menial servant; for though he did not live in the defendant's house, or within the curtilage, he lived in the grounds within the domain."[6]

---

[1] Co. Litt. 42, b. Rex v. Seaton v. Beer, Cald. 440. Rex v. Macclesfield, 3 D. and E. 76. Rex v. Worfield, 5 D. and R. 506.

[2] Per Best, C. J., Beeston v. Collyer, 2 C. and P. 609.

[3] See Holcroft v. Barber, 1 C. and K. 4. Baxter v. Nurse, 1 C. and K. 10.

[4] Archard v. Hornor, 3 C. and P. 349. Robinson v. Hindman, 3 Esp. 235. Turner v. Mason, 14 M. and W. 116, per Parke, B.

[5] Johnson v. Blenkinsop, 5 Jur. 870. Mentzer v. Bolton, 9 Ex. 518.

[6] Nowlan v. Ablett, 2 C. M. and R. 54.

A huntsman has been held to be a menial servant within the custom, Erle, C. J., saying that the law applied "when the service was of such a domestic nature as to require the servant to be frequently about his master's person or grounds; and when, if any ill-feeling should arise between them, the constant presence of the servant would be a source of infinite irritation and annoyance to the master." Byles, J., said, "menial would seem to be derived from *ménage*, one of the retinue or attendance." [1]

A governess is not a domestic or menial servant within this rule. The position which she holds in a family, and the manner in which she is usually treated in society, place her in a very different situation from that which mere menial and domestic servants hold. [2]

63. A trade servant, servant in husbandry, [3] or other servant not menial, who is engaged for a year, cannot be dismissed until the end of the year. If the contract is not determined at the end of the first year, but the relation is continued, a new contract is understood to be made to serve for another year, on the same terms as those of the preceding year's service, and so from year to year, until either party puts an end to the relation at the end of some year. But neither party can lawfully determine the relation of master and servant during the currency of any year.

The plaintiff had been for many years in the service of the defendant as his clerk, in his business of army agent, at a salary of £500 a year, which was at first paid quarterly, but afterwards monthly. His service commenced on the 1st March, 1811, and he was discharged on the 23rd December, 1826. He recovered £83 damages for his discharge. On an application to

---

[1] Nicoll v. Greaves, 17 C. B. N. S. 27.
[2] Todd v. Kerrick, 8 Ex. 151.   [3] Lilley v. Elwin, 11 Q. B. 742.

set aside the verdict, on the ground that there was no evidence of a yearly hiring, Best, C. J., observed, " It would be indeed extraordinary, if a party in the plaintiff's station of life could be turned off at a moment's notice, like a cook or scullion. If a master hire a servant without mention of time, that is a general hiring for a year ; and if the parties go on four, five, or six years, a jury are warranted in presuming a contract for a year in the first instance, and so on for each succeeding year, as long as it pleases the parties. It is not necessary for us now to decide whether six months, three months, or any notice be requisite to put an end to such a contract; because, under the circumstances of the present case, after the parties had consented to remain in the relation of employer and servant, from 1811 to 1826, we must imply an engagement to serve by the year, unless reasons are given for putting an end to the contract." [1]

In an action by a reporter for the *Morning Post* newspaper, on a contract to employ him for a year, it was held to be no plea that the defendant tendered the plaintiff a reasonable sum above his wages in lieu of notice, and on his refusal to accept it, gave him notice of his intention to put an end to the service a reasonable time before his dismissal, because it did not appear that the notice expired with the year, and by the terms of the contract, the service could only be determined with the year.[2] And an agreement between master and servant for the servant to serve three years at the master's option, at a yearly salary, is a yearly hiring, and the master can only determine the service at end of a year.[3]

---

[1] Beeston v. Collyer, 4 Bing. 309. Huttman v. Boulnois, 2 Car. and Payne, 510.

[2] Williams v. Byrne, 7 A. and E. 177. [3] Down v. Pinto, 9 Ex. 327.

The cases do not establish that in the case of a contract to serve and employ from year to year, any notice is necessary to determine the relation of master and servant at the end of a year. If any such notice is necessary, it must be so either by the express agreement of the parties, or by the general understanding and practice of masters and servants in similar cases. There is no reason for any such notice, since each party knows that the contract of service will expire, if not renewed, at the end of each year.

In Fairman v. Oakford,[1] Pollock, C. B., says :— "There is no inflexible rule that a general hiring is a hiring for a year. Each case depends on its own circumstances. From much experience of juries, I have come to the conclusion that the usual indefinite hiring of a clerk is not a hiring for a year, but rather one determinable by three months' notice." The plaintiff having on a former occasion accepted a month's salary from his master on his dismissal, it was found that the hiring was determinable by a month's notice. When by custom of trade the hiring is determinable by a month's notice, it applies when there is an agreement in writing for a year, with a provision that the master will, if the business prospers, add to the salary at the end of the year.[2]

64. The circumstance of the wages being payable weekly or monthly is a circumstance to show that the hiring and service is to be for a week, and from week to week, or for a month, and from month to month, and not for a year. Thus, where a pauper had hired himself as a plumber and glazier, for board, lodging, and wages of six shillings per week, he was held to be a weekly and not a yearly servant.[3] In another case, as

[1] 5 H. and N. 635.   [2] Parker v. Ibbetson, 4 C. B. N. S. 346.
[3] Rex v. Dedham, Bur. S. C. 653.

to the settlement of a pauper who had been hired as an ostler, at four shillings per week, in which it was decided that he was a weekly servant, Buller, J., thus stated the law: "If there be anything in the contract to show that the hiring was intended to be for a year, the reservation of weekly wages will not control the hiring. But if the reservation of weekly wages be the only circumstance from which the duration of the contract is to be collected, it must be taken to be only a weekly hiring."[1] A similar decision was come to in a case where the servant was to have four shillings a week, except in the harvest time, when his wages were to be increased to ten shillings and sixpence a week, and afterwards to be reduced to four shillings. The provision for an increase of wages at harvest time did not make him an annual servant.[2] And in another, where the agreement was that the servant should have eight shillings per week, and two guineas for the harvest.[3]

But if the parties show an intention to bind themselves to serve and employ for a longer period than a week, the reservation of weekly wages does not control the time of service, and the period for service is a year. Thus, where a farm servant was hired at three shillings a week the year round, with liberty to go on a fortnight's notice, the Court held it to be an express contract to serve the year round, with power for either party to determine it by a fortnight's notice.[4] A miller hired a servant at three shillings and ninepence per week, with liberty of parting on a month's notice on either side. This was held to be an annual hiring,

---

[1] Rex v. Newton Toney, 2 D. and E. 453. Rex v. Odiham, 2 D. and E. 622. Evans v. Roe, L. R. 7 C. P. 138.

[2] Rex v. Droitwich, 3 Maule and Sel. 243.

[3] Rex v. St. Mary, Lambeth, 4 Maule and Sel. 315.

[4] Rex v. Birdbrook, 4 D. and E. 245.

determinable by a month's notice, the provision for the month's notice showing that the parties intended to bind themselves to serve and employ for more than a week.[1]

In an action by a warehouseman against his employer, the agreement was: "William Cash engages to pay Thomas Fawcett £12 10s. per month for the first year, and advance £10 per annum until the salary is £180, from the 5th March, 1832." This was held to be a contract for a year, because by agreeing to pay £12 10s. per month for *the first year*, the parties contemplated that the service was to continue for one year, at all events, and that it might continue for four, in which case there was to be a yearly advance of salary.[2]

A contract by an author to write tales for a weekly publication, extending over the period of a year, for which he was to be paid £10 a week for each number, was held to be a contract for a year. His agreement to furnish matter week by week did not make it a weekly engagement. The weekly payments were instalments.[3]

An agreement for twelve months certain, and to continue from time to time, until three months' notice given by either party to determine the same, may be determined by notice at the end of the twelve months.[4] An agreement for twelve months certain, after which either party to be at liberty to terminate it by three months' notice, may be put an end to at the end of the twelve months without notice.[5] An agreement at a yearly

[1] Rex v. Humpreston, 5 D. and E. 205. Rex v. Great Yarmouth, 5 Maule and Sel. 114. Rex v. St. Andrew in Pershore, 8 B. and C. 679.

[2] Fawcett v. Cash, 5 B. and Ad. 904. Davis v. Marshall, 4 L. T. N. S. 216.

[3] Stiff v. Cassell, 2 Jur. N. S. 348.

[4] Brown v. Symons, 8 C. B. N. S. 208.

[5] Langton v. Carleton, L. R. 9 Ex. 57.

salary, determinable by a three months' notice, may be determined by notice at any time.[1]

65. The nature of the service is also an important circumstance to be taken into consideration, in order to ascertain whether the understanding of the parties was that the employment should be for a year. In a case in which it appeared that the plaintiff had been employed to write articles for a new monthly publication,—he had written an article each month, and been paid £10 per month,—the jury found that he was not employed for the year, notwithstanding it was proved that the usual engagement of editors, sub-editors, and reporters to newspapers was annual.[2] In another case, the plaintiff had been engaged as editor of a new review, at three guineas a week, with a progressive increase of salary according to the sale of the review. The custom, that the engagement of editors, &c., to newspapers was for a year, unless otherwise expressed, was proved. The jury found that the contract was not for a year's service, but for a week, and so on from week to week. The Court refused to disturb the verdict, on the ground that it was not an inflexible rule that contracts for services, without any definite arrangement as to time, were contracts for a year, but a presumption to be raised from contracts of the same kind; and that the circumstance that the publication was new, was material to be taken into consideration.[3] In these two cases, the plaintiffs, having been employed to serve the defendants as editors of new publications, which might not answer, their services might not be required for a year.

The presumption that the hiring was general for a

---

[1] Ryan v. Jenkinson, 25 L. J. Q. B. 7.
[2] Holcroft v. Barber, 1 C. and K. 4.
[3] Baxter v. Nurse, 1 C. and K. 10 ; 6 M. and G. 935.

year cannot be made in a case in which there is no evidence of the hiring, and in which occasional payments have been made by the master, but not at any fixed and definite periods.   In such case the occasional payments warrant the inference of a hiring at will, and a servant may recover the value of his services, although he has not served a year.[1]

Nor does the presumption apply when the duration of the service is expressed to be at the will of either of the parties.   Thus, a boy who entered into the service of a farmer, for meat and clothes, as long as he had a mind to stop, was held to be a servant at will, and not for a year.[2]

66. A man may contract to serve for his life, but it is said that the contract in such case should be by deed.[3]   The authority referred to does not warrant this position.   It was an action of debt against executors, in which the plaintiff counted that he was retained by the testator for the term of his life in peace and war, at 100 shillings a year, and that his salary was in arrear for two years.   It was objected that the action was brought against executors, and no speciality was shown, and judgment was given against the plaintiff.   The action failed, not because the contract was invalid, but because an action of debt on simple contract did not lie against executors, which depended on the old law of law wager.[4]

67. Personal considerations being the foundation of the contract between master and servant, the death of

[1] Bayley v. Rimmell, 1 M. and W. 506.

[2] Rex v. Christ's Parish, York, 3 B. and C. 459.   Rex v. Great Bowden, 7 B. and C. 249.

[3] Wallis v. Day, 2 M. and W. 273.

[4] 2 Hen. 4, 14, pl. 12.   Bro. Laborers, pl. 44.   Vin. Abr. Master and Servant, N. 5.

either party puts an end to the relation.[1] And where an agent was employed in a partnership business carried on by two partners, the Court held that the relation was determined by the death of one of the partners.[2] But the parties may agree that the contract shall continue to the executors. Thus, when an apprentice was bound to a tradesman and his executors carrying on the same business, the death of the master did not determine the apprenticeship; but his executrix, who continued his business, was bound to teach him, and he bound to serve her.[3] It is also an implied condition that the servant should continue able to serve, and if he is disabled without fault on his part, he is excused from serving for a time, if the illness is temporary; or if permanent, and such as entirely disables him from performing the contract, it has the effect of death.[4] In such case the servant should forthwith give the master notice of his illness, and if he incurs any expense by reason of the failure to give notice, he has a claim on the servant for an indemnity.[5] The case of permanent illness not only excuses the servant from serving, but entitles the master to put an end to the contract, and dismiss. If he does not dismiss him, but takes his chance of recovery, he is bound to pay his wages during his illness, and until he elects to dismiss him.[6] There is also an implied warranty by the servant that he is of skill reasonably competent to the task he undertakes, and, if he is not, the master may dismiss him.[7]

68. If the hiring is at so much for the service, or so

[1] Farrow v. Wilson, L. R. 4 C. P. 744.

[2] Tasker v. Shepherd, 6 H. and N. 575.

[3] Cooper v. Simmons, 7 H. and N. 707.

[4] Boast v. Firth, L. R. 4 C. P. 1. Robinson v. Davison, L. R. 6 Ex. 269.

[5] Robinson v. Davison.   [6] Cuckson v. Stones, 1 E. and E. 248.

[7] Harmer v. Cornelius, 5 C. B. N. S. 236.

much for a year, or other period of time, the servant
must perform the whole service, or serve for the whole
period, before he is entitled to any wages; and if, from
any cause, he does not perform the whole service, or
serve the whole time, he is entitled to no part of the
wages, because the contract is to pay a certain sum for
a certain service, and not to pay that sum, or a portion
of it, for part of the service.

Throgmorton was appointed by the Earl of Plymouth,
by writing, to receive his rents, and the Earl agreed to
pay him £100 per annum for his service. Throgmorton died three-quarters of a year after his appointment,
and his executrix brought an action for £75. Judgment was given against her, because, without a full
year's service, nothing could be due, and the year's
service was in the nature of a condition precedent.
There was no difference between wages and rent, or an
annuity; and it being one consideration and one debt,
could not be divided.[1] It has been attempted, but
without success, to apply the Apportionment Act[2] to
the case of salary payable for services when the
employment was determined before the salary became
due.[3]

If the agreement is to pay wages so much a month
for a voyage, the wages are due at the end of each
month, and this is not controlled by the master agreeing to pay wages in consideration of the services to be
duly performed. They do not make the due performance of the month's service a condition precedent to
the right to recover any wages.[4]

Cutter v. Powell[5] was an action by the administrator

[1] Countess of Plymouth v. Throgmorton, 1 Salk. 65.
[2] 4 & 5 W. IV. c. 22, now 33 & 34 Vic. c. 35.
[3] Lowndes v. Earl of Stamford, 16 Jur. 903.
[4] Button v. Thompson, L. R. 4 C. P. 330.
[5] 6 D. & E. 320 ; 2 Smith, Leading Cases, 1.

of a sailor, who had died during a voyage from Jamaica to Liverpool, for his services as second mate, from the time of entering the ship until the day of his death. The terms of his engagement were contained in the following note, signed by the defendant: "Ten days after the ship 'Governor Parry,' myself master, arrives at Liverpool, I promise to pay to Mr. T. Cutter the sum of 30 guineas, provided he proceeds, continues, and does his duty as second mate in the said ship from hence to the port of Liverpool. Kingston, July 31st, 1793." The Court held that the plaintiff was not entitled to recover anything, because the defendant only engaged to pay the intestate on condition of his doing his duty on board during the whole voyage; and he was to be entitled either to thirty guineas or to nothing; for such was the contract between the parties.

If the servant is dismissed for misconduct before any wages have become payable by the terms of the contract, he is entitled to nothing. In an action for wages by a yearly servant of a farmer, who had been dismissed during the year for misconduct, Lord Ellenborough observed,—"If the contract be for a year's service, the year must be completed before the servant is entitled to be paid." The servant abandoned his action by withdrawing a juror.[1] In another action, by the foreman of silk manufacturers, who was to have wages at the rate of £80 per year for his services from January to June, when he was dismissed for misconduct, —the Court held that the plaintiff was not entitled to recover anything; Parke, J., observing, that the *primâ facie* presumption was that the plaintiff was hired for a year, and there was nothing to rebut that presumption; and having violated his duty before the year expired, so as to prevent the defendants from having his services

---

[1] Spain v. Arnott, 2 Stark. 256.

for the whole year, he could not recover wages *pro ratâ*.[1]

The same law was acted upon in Ridgway v. the Hungerford Market Company,[2] in which the plaintiff had been appointed clerk to the company at a salary of £200 a year, which was payable quarterly, and had been dismissed for misconduct during a quarter. Lord Denman said, that if a party hired for a certain time so conduct himself that he cannot give the consideration for his salary, he shall forfeit the current salary, even for the time for which he has served. The other Judges said, that in such case he shall not recover his salary. The latter expression is the more correct, as by reason of the dismissal before the salary becomes due, the event has never happened on which it was to become due, namely, service for the whole of the period agreed.

In Lilley v. Elwin,[3] the plaintiff was a farm labourer, hired generally at £10 10s. for the year, and was discharged for misconduct at the end of ten months,—the Court decided that he was entitled to no wages, saying, "If the plaintiff had been guilty of disobedience of orders, and unlawfully absenting himself from his work, so as to justify his discharge, and the defendant had discharged him, the plaintiff was entitled to nothing; the contract being £10 10s. for the year, and no part of the wages being due till the end of the year. If, on the other hand, the discharge was not justifiable, the plaintiff was at liberty to treat that discharge as a rescinding of the contract by the defendant, and sue for his wages *pro ratâ* up to the time of the unjustifiable discharge."

According to Hulle v. Heightman,[4] even where the

---

[1] Turner v. Robinson, 5 B. and Ad. 789.   [2] 5 Ad. and El. 171.
[3] 12 Jur. 623.   [4] 2 East, 145.

servant is improperly discharged by the master before any wages have become due, he is not entitled to recover wages as wages, because the whole of the stipulated service has not been performed; but his remedy is for damages, for the master's breach of contract for preventing him from serving. This decision is disapproved by Mr. Smith,[1] on the ground that the act of the master operates as a rescission of the contract by him, which act the servant may adopt, and sue the master for the value of his services on a contract inferred from the fact of the master having accepted the services actually rendered. This view appears to have been adopted by the Court in Lilley v. Elwin.

In Crocker v. Molyneux[2] a servant was hired at thirty guineas and a suit of clothes: he was dismissed before the end of the year, and commenced an action for the clothes. Lord Tenterden ruled that if he was improperly dismissed whereby he was prevented from becoming entitled to the clothes, he had his action for that; but he could not maintain an action of trover, because he had no property in the clothes until he had served a year.

But if the servant improperly leaves the service after wages have become due, he does not forfeit those wages.[3]

69. It may be provided that misconduct shall operate as a forfeiture of wages, and in such case wages payable but not paid are forfeited,[4] and a mere continuation in the service will not condone the forfeiture. There must be a new consideration to create a liability to pay the wages forfeited.[5]

[1] 2 Leading Cases, 11. [2] 3 C. and P. 470.
[3] Taylor v. Laird, 1 H. and N. 266.
[4] Taylor v. Carr, 4 L. T. N. S. 415. Walsh v. Walley, L. R. 9 Q. B. 367.
[5] Monkman v. Shepherdson, 11 A. and E. 411.

70. When the wages are *at the rate of* so much per year, and not so much per year, they are divisible; and if the servant is discharged without notice during the year, he may sue for his wages up to the time of his dismissal as a debt, and can only recover them in that shape.[1] And perhaps in such case he is entitled to wages up to the time of his dismissal, if he is dismissed for misconduct. The case of Turner v. Robinson, already cited, is to the contrary. There the Court appear to have considered that no wages were due until the end of the year, although they were made payable *at the rate of* £80 per year. In the case of a domestic servant, the wages are payable *de die in diem*, in proportion to the period of service.[2]

71. It is also the duty of the servant to serve properly. He must obey the just and reasonable commands of his master. He should be careful and faithful to his master's interests and property committed to his charge, and behave with decency, and consistent with his character as servant. If he is guilty of wilful disobedience of the master's lawful command, or habitual neglect of the duties of his service, or conducts himself with dishonesty towards his master, or with gross indecency in the master's house and in relation to his service, or acts in a manner inconsistent with his station of servant, he violates an essential condition of the contract, and may be dismissed. But a disobedience not wilful and contumacious, or of an order which he is not bound to obey, or which does not properly appertain to the character of his service,[3] or a neglect which is not seriously injurious to the

---

[1] Hartley v. Harman, 11 A. and E. 798.

[2] Per Lawrence, J., Cutter v. Powell, 6 D. and E. 326. Huttman v. Boulnois, 2 C. and P. 512.

[3] Price v. Mouat, 11 C. B. N. S. 508.

master's interests, does not justify the master in dismissing the servant.

72. The wilful disobedience of a just and reasonable command of the master, which the servant on entering into the service has contracted to obey, is a breach of duty which authorises the master to put an end to the contract of service, and to dismiss the servant.

The command must be just and reasonable, and have reference to the service which the servant has contracted to perform.[1] The servant is not bound to risk his safety in the service of the master, but may, if he think fit, decline any service in which he reasonably apprehends injury to himself.[2]

A master told his servant to go with the horses to the marsh, which was a mile off, before dinner. It was the servant's usual dinner hour, and dinner was then ready. The servant said that he had done his due, and would not go till he had had his dinner. The master told him to go about his business. He went accordingly, and brought an action for his wages. Lord Ellenborough said,—"If the plaintiff persisted in refusing to obey his master's orders, I think he was warranted in turning him away. There is no contract between the parties except that which the law makes for them; and it may be hard upon the servant, but it would be exceedingly inconvenient if the servant were permitted to set himself up to control his master in his domestic regulations. After a refusal, on the part of the servant, to perform his work, the master is not bound to keep him on as a burthensome and useless servant to the end of the year."[3]

A carpenter was employed to repair a gentleman's

[1] 2 Jacquot v. Bourra, 7 Dowl. 348.
[2] Per Lord Abinger, Priestley v. Fowler, 3 M. and W. 6.
[3] Spain v. Arnott, 2 Stark. 256.

house in the country. He sent his servants down to do the work. In consequence of a complaint from the gamekeepers, the men were directed not to go into the preserves. One of them afterwards went into the preserves, and was dismissed. Coleridge, J., left it to the jury to say, whether the workman did not go down to Staunton (the name of the seat) on the understanding and undertaking that he was to conduct himself decorously and properly,—and whether the master was not justified in dismissing him. He observed, that if the master employed men who acted so as to disoblige his customers, by going into their gardens and preserves, when they were told not, he would soon find that he was injured in his business, and would lose his custom, because gentlemen would not employ him. The jury found that the master was justified in dismissing the workman.[1]

In an action for dismissing a domestic servant, the defendant pleaded that the plaintiff asked for leave of absence, which he refused; but she nevertheless left his service, and remained absent all night, and until the following morning, wherefore he discharged her. She replied, that she requested leave of absence, because her mother had been seized with sudden sickness, and was in imminent danger of death; and because the defendant wrongfully and unjustly refused his permission she went without, and did not cause any hindrance to him in his domestic affairs, and was not guilty of any improper omission or unreasonable delay in her duties. The Court gave judgment against the plaintiff, on the ground that her replication did not allege that she gave notice to the defendant of her mother's illness. Pollock, C. B., remarked,—"It is very questionable whether any service to be rendered to any other person

---

[1] Read v. Dunsmore, 9 C. and P. 588.

than the master would suffice as an excuse; she might go, but it would be at the peril of being told that she could not return." Parke, B., said,—" *Primâ facie* the master is to regulate the time when his servant is to go out from and return to his home. Even if the replication had stated that he had had notice of the cause of her request to absent herself, I do not think it would have been sufficient to justify her in disobedience to his order." Alderson, B., said,—" There may, undoubtedly, be cases justifying a wilful disobedience of an order of the master; as, when the servant apprehends danger to her life or violence to her person from the master, or when, from an infectious disorder raging in the house, she must go out for the preservation of her life." [1]

A man was engaged by a farmer as a waggoner, but during harvest he worked in the field generally. The practice was, during harvest, to work until eight in the evening. The waggoner refused to work till that hour, because, he said, that strong beer of good quality was not allowed him, according to a pretended custom, and the beer supplied being, as he alleged, very bad small beer, and not so good as water. There was no such custom as to beer, and his master discharged him for this refusal to work. The Court of Queen's Bench held that he was justified in so doing.[2]

In an action by a courier for his wages, it appeared that his mistress had dismissed him before his year's service was up, because, in getting into her carriage at Padua, she had desired him not to stop at a particular hotel, where she had been before, but at another; but he, notwithstanding, did stop at the forbidden hotel, and, when remonstrated with, said he had not been told; and at the second hotel was sulky, and neglected to

---

[1] Turner v. Mason, 14 M. and W. 112.
[2] Lilley v. Elwin, 11 Q. B. 742.

come on two or three occasions when rung for, and was insolent in manner at Florence. Parke, J., told the jury that there was a contract for a year, with an implied agreement that if there was any moral misconduct, either pecuniary or otherwise, wilful disobedience, or habitual neglect, the defendant should be at liberty to part with the plaintiff; and that, in his opinion, no such conduct had been proved. The jury found for the plaintiff.[1]

A clerk wrote for £140, including £30 due to himself for salary. The master remitted him £100 for business purposes; he applied £30 towards his salary, and the master dismissed him. The judge left it to the jury to decide whether the clerk had been guilty of any wrongful and improper misappropriation of money or disobedience of orders. They found for the plaintiff. The Court refused to disturb the verdict, but appear to have considered that if the clerk had known that the master did not intend him to pay himself out of the £100, there would have been a wilful disobedience sufficient to justify the dismissal.[2]

73. In an action by a servant for a month's wages, on the ground of his having been discharged without warning, it was proved that he had been negligent in his conduct, frequently absent when his master wanted him, and often slept out at nights. Lord Kenyon ruled that the plaintiff was not entitled to recover, on account of his misconduct.[3]

A surgeon attempted to justify the dismissal of his pupil and assistant, with whom a premium had been paid, from his service, because he had occasionally come to his house intoxicated, and at such late hours that he could not compound the medicines, on which occasions

[1] Callo v. Brouncker, 4 C. and P. 518.
[2] Smith v. Thompson, 8 C. B. 44.
[3] Robinson v. Hindman, 3 Esp. 234.

he had ordered the shopboy to compound them. Lord Denman said,—that the assistant coming home intoxicated was not of itself a sufficient cause for dismissing him ; but that his employing the shopboy to compound the medicines, if thereby real danger was occasioned to the master's business, was. He considered the case as intermediate between that of an apprentice, who cannot be dismissed for misconduct, and that of a servant who can.[1] A teacher of French and drawing in a school did not return to the school for a long and unreasonable time after the holidays had expired ; but it did not appear that the master was obliged to hire another, or that the teacher's department was not adequately filled, or that the master was delayed or injured in the matter in which he would have employed the teacher during the time of his absence. The neglect was held not sufficient to entitle the master to dissolve the contract and dismiss the teacher, though it might be a breach of contract by the teacher, and support an action against him at the master's suit.[2]

The neglect to justify a dismissal must be such as to cause an injury to the master, and as demonstrates that it will be injurious to the master to continue the servant in his employ. And so a disobedience, not wilful and contumacious, which will justify a dismissal, must be such as to occasion an injury and loss to the master.[3] It must go to the whole consideration, a question somewhat difficult to decide.[4]

74. If the servant is absent during the period of service in consequence of temporary sickness, it is not

[1] Wise v. Wilson, 1 C. and K. 662. See also Lacy v. Osbaldiston, 8 C. and P. 80.

[2] Filleul v. Armstrong, 7 A. and E. 557.

[3] Cussons v. Skinner, 11 M. and W. 161.

[4] Gould v. Webb, 4 E. and B. 933. Lomax v. Arding, 10 Ex. 734.

a neglect or breach of duty. The master is bound to provide and take care of him during his sickness, and cannot dismiss him, or even deduct his wages for the time during which he is sick.[1]

If the servant, towards the expiration of his period of service, absents himself without the leave, or even in disobedience of the master, for the purpose of seeking another engagement at a usual time, it is not a breach of his contract. A farm servant, hired for a year, three days before his year's service was up, asked leave of his master to go to a statute fair, to be hired for the next year. The master refused leave, but the servant went. The Court held that the master was not justified in dismissing him for this cause. " Consider," said they, " how the case stands with regard to the servant. He knew his master designed to part with him at the year's end, and therefore it was high time for him to look out for another place. To this end, he applied in a very proper manner for leave to go to the statute fair, which was a place where, in all likelihood, he might have provided himself, and not be obliged to lie idle all the year, it being usual for people in the country to go thither to hire their servants. The master, like an unreasonable man, refused so reasonable a request. As therefore the request was reasonable, and upon a just ground on the side of the servant, and the refusal unreasonable on the side of the master, we think the servant's going afterwards, without leave, is no forfeiture of his former service."[2]

The servant is entitled to holidays sanctioned by the

[1] Rex v. Islip, 1 Str. 423. Rex v. Christchurch, ¡Bur. S. C. 494. Rex v. Sharrington, 2 Bott. 322. Rex v. Maddington, Bur. S. C. 675. Chandler v. Grieves, 2 H. Bl. 606, *n.* Rex v. Sudbrook, 1 Smith 59, per Le Blanc, J. Exp. Harris, 1 De Gex, 165; 9 Jur. 497.

[2] Rex v. Islip, 1 Str. 423. Rex v. Polesworth, 2 B. and Ald. 483.

custom of trade, though there is a written agreement, and no mention of holidays in it.[1]

75. Any act of dishonesty by the servant during the service, to the injury of the master's property or business, is a breach of duty which will justify his dismissal, as well as render him liable to an action. An accountant employed by a joint stock company, at an annual salary, entered in their books, under the orders of the managing director and the secretary, a sum of £1080 as paid for salt, which to his knowledge had been spent in the purchase of shares. It was held that the company were justified in dismissing him as an improper person to fill the situation of their accountant.[2] A manufacturer was held justified in dismissing his foreman, because he had advised his apprentice to abscond from his service, and assisted him to go to America. The manufacturer also recovered damages in an action against the foreman.[3] The manager of a business buying goods in which his master dealt, as agent for another, is misconduct which justifies his dismissal.[4]

But a traveller who solicits his master's customers to deal with him when his service is at an end is not guilty of a breach of his relative duty. In an action against the defendant, who had been the plaintiffs' traveller, for seducing their customers, Lord Kenyon observed,— "The conduct of the defendant in this case may perhaps be accounted not handsome, but I cannot say that it is contrary to law. The relation in which he stood to the plaintiffs, as their servant, imposed on him a duty which is called of imperfect obligation, but not such as can

[1] Rex v. Stoke-upon-Trent, 5 Q. B. 303.
[2] Baillie v. Kell, 4 Bing. N. C. 638. See also Willetts v. Green, 3 C. and K. 59.
[3] Turner v. Robinson, 6 C. and P. 15 ; 5 B. and Ad. 789.
[4] Horton v. McMurtry, 5 H. and N. 667.

enable the plaintiffs to maintain an action.   A servant,
while engaged in the service of his master, has no right
to do any act which may injure his trade or undermine
his business; but every one has a right, if he can, to
better his situation in the world; and if he does it by
means not contrary to law, though the master may be
eventually injured, it is *damnum absque injuriâ*.   There
is nothing morally bad, or very improper, for a servant
who has it in contemplation, at a future period, to set
up for himself, to endeavour to conciliate the regard of
his master's customers, and to recommend himself to
them, so as to procure some business from them as well
as others.   In the present case, the defendant did not
solicit the present orders of the customers; on the contrary, he took for the plaintiffs all those he could
obtain : his request of business for himself was prospec-
tive, and for a time when the relation of master and
servant between him and the plaintiffs would be at an
end." [1]

76. The understanding of the parties on a contract
between master and servant is, that the servant shall
conduct himself with morality and decency while in the
master's service; and if he is guilty of any breach of
duty in this respect, the master may dismiss him.   A
female servant, hired for a year, was dismissed because
she was with child.   Lord Mansfield said,—"I think
the master did not do wrong.   Shall he be bound to
keep her in his house ?   To do so would be *contra bonos
mores*, and in a family where there are young persons,
both scandalous and dangerous." [2]   So a master was
held to be entitled to discharge a man who had got his
female servant with child.[3]   A clerk and traveller, who
had been hired for a year, and lived and boarded in the

---

[1] Nichol v. Martyn, 2 Esp. 732.   [2] Rex v. Brampton, Cald. 11.
[3] Rex v. Welford, Cald. 57.

master's house, made an assault upon his female servant, with intent to ravish her, for which he was dismissed; and it was held rightly.[1]

But the fact of the servant having been the father of a bastard child before the master hired him, or being guilty of a crime of that description out of his master's house, does not justify his dismissal. It is not seducing the master's servant, or turning his home into a brothel.[2]

77. An act of a servant, inconsistent with his character of servant, is a breach of his duty which justifies the master in dismissing him. The Directors of the Hungerford Market Company resolved to dismiss their clerk, which resolution he, according to the duties of his office, entered in a book, and under it subjoined a protest by himself against the proceeding, and they at once dismissed him. Lord Denman desired the jury to say whether the entry of the protest by the clerk justified his dismissal without notice. They found that it did.[3] A wine-merchant dismissed his clerk, because he claimed to be a partner. He was held justified; because, having disclaimed being a servant, if the master had suffered him to go on in his employment, the nature of his situation might have been doubtful, and evidence that he really was a partner.[4]

78. When a master dismisses his servant for misconduct, he need not at the time of his dismissal state the cause; and if he assigns an insufficient cause for the dismissal, and a sufficient one exists, he may justify the dismissal on the ground which existed, though he can-

---

[1] Aikin v. Acton, 4 C. and P. 208.

[2] Per Lord Mansfield, in Rex v. Westmeon, Cald. 129.

[3] Ridgway v. the Hungerford Market Company, 3 Ad. and El. 171.

[4] Amor v. Fearon, 9 Ad. and El. 548.

not do so on the cause assigned;[1] and this though, at the time of the dismissal, he did not know of the cause. His right to dismiss depends on the misconduct of the servant, and not upon his knowledge of it, and if he is justified in dismissing the servant, no inquiry can be made into his motive for doing so.[2]   But in the case of a curate whom a rector had agreed to employ until, by fault by him committed, he should be lawfully removed, it was decided that the rector could not exercise the power of removal, without notifying to the curate the cause.[3]

If, after knowledge of the servant's misconduct, the master continues him in his service, and accepts his services, it may amount to a condonation of the misconduct,[4] and the master cannot, on any subsequent cause of displeasure, dismiss the servant for the previous misconduct.

79. If the wages was payable *pro ratâ*, and not lost by reason of the misconduct, or if the servant is not dismissed, the misconduct may be taken into consideration in estimating the value of the servant's services, and he is not entitled to his full wages, as he would have been had he served faithfully and properly.[5] A shopman to a silversmith sued for four quarters wages.   He had during his service embezzled silver spoons and money, received by him for his master.

---

[1] Ridgway v. the Hungerford Market Company, 3 Ad. and El. 171. Baillie v. Kell, 4 Bing. N. C. 638.   Mercer v. Whall, 5 Q. B. 466.

[2] Willetts v. Green, 3 C. and K. 59.   Spotswood v. Barrow, 5 Ex. 110.   Cussons v. Skinner, 11 M. and W. 161.   Smith v. Allen, 3 F. and F. 157 contra.

[3] Martyn v. Hind, 1 Doug. 142.   Cowp. 437.

[4] Per Ld. Denman, 3 Ad. and El. 174.   Per Blackburn, J., Phillips v. Foxall, L. R. 7 Q. B. 680.   See Monkman v. Shepperdson, 11 A. and E. 411.

[5] Baillie v. Kell, 4 Bing. N. C. 638.

Lord Tenterden ruled, that if the servant habitually embezzled his master's property, the amount embezzled is immaterial, and although the amount of wages may exceed it, he is not entitled to anything.[1] So an agent who had made profits by selling his own spirits mixed with those of his principals, and destroyed books of account, was disallowed his commission.[2]

In one case, Alderson, B., had refused to allow the defendants to go into evidence of misconduct in an action for salary; saying, that if the plaintiff was guilty of misconduct, and the defendants did not put an end to the contract when they might, and he continued to perform the work, he was entitled to be paid for it.[3] This was an action by a dissenting minister for his services, and the misconduct imputed probably did not diminish the value of the service performed.

80. It results from the duty of the servant to serve, that the master is entitled to what his servant produces in his capacity of servant. If he hires him to invent, he is entitled to his inventions. Thus a calico-printer is entitled to a book provided by himself, in which his head-colourman enters the processes for making colours, although such book contains processes of the colourman's own invention. The inventions are the property of the master.[4] If the master is the inventor of a machine or process for which he is entitled to a patent, he may include in his patent subordinate improvements suggested or invented by his servants.[5] And if he employs servants or agents to make such improvements, he is, it seems, entitled to

---

[1] Brown v. Croft, 6 C. and P. 16.
[2] Gray v. Haig, 20 Beav. 219.
[3] Cooper v. Whitehouse, 6 C. and P. 545.
[4] Makepeace v. Jackson, 4 Taunt. 770.
[5] Allen v. Rawson, 1 C. B. 551.

letters patent for those improvements, the same as if they were his own invention.[1] But if the principal invention is discovered by the servant, the master is not entitled to a patent; because he is not the inventor, and by the patent law a monopoly can only be granted to the first and true inventor within this realm of a new manufacture.[2] A person who merely suggests the subject and employs and pays an author to write a drama or literary work, is not by virtue of the employment entitled to the exclusive right of representation or copyright, because the statutes vest such right in the author, and require the transfer of such a right to be in writing.[3] The case is different of a person who plans a work and employs others to assist him in different parts of it;[4] and the Copyright Act gives a qualified copyright to the publisher or proprietor of an encyclopædia or work published periodically or in parts in the contributions to such work.[5]

81. It also results from this duty that the master is entitled to the services of the servant, and may maintain an action against one who wrongfully deprives him of them, either by an act of violence, as by so beating the servant as to disable him from serving the master;[6] or by negligence, as by negligent driving over the servant;[7] or against a surgeon who, employed to cure the servant of a wound, administers unwholesome medicines on purpose to make the wound worse.[8]

[1] Bloxam v. Elsee, 1 C. and P. 564.

[2] Rex v. Arkwright, 8 Taunt. 395. 1 Davies, P. C. 61. Winter v. Wells, 1 Webster, P. C. 132. Baker v. Shaw, 1 Webster, P. C. 126.

[3] Shepherd v. Conquest, 17 C. B. 427.

[4] Barfield v. Nicholson, 2 Sim. and St. 1. Hatton v. Kean, 7 C. B. N. S. 268.

[5] 5 & 6 Vict. c. 45, s. 18. Sweet v. Benning, 16 C. B. 459.

[6] Bac. Abr. Master and Servant, O.

[7] Martinez v. Gerber, 3 Man. and Gr. 88.

[8] Roll. Abr. 82. Rol. Rep. 124. 2 Bulst. 332.

So he may sue any one who knowing the servant to be such entices him away, or continues to employ him in his service after notice.[1] And he may sue either for damages for the wrong, or for the value of the servant's work as a debt.[2] It is upon this principle that the ordinary action for seduction is founded; the female seduced always being stated and proved to be the servant of the plaintiff at the time of the seduction. The principle has been applied to the case of employer and employed. A theatrical manager has been held entitled to sue a rival manager for damages, who knowingly prevented a songstress from performing her engagement;[3] but for an assault upon a singer by which he was disabled from singing, it has been decided that no action lies.[4] Nor has the master any claim if the injury to the servant is the breach of a contract with the servant, as for an injury to a railway passenger.[5]

82. To enforce the duty of obedience, the master is entrusted with the power of correction. He may correct and punish his servant for abusive language, neglect of duty, &c.; but the chastisement must be moderate and usual, and he cannot delegate this power to another.[6] Thus an upper servant cannot justify beating an under one.[7]

83. A contract between a master and servant, by which the servant agrees to serve for a certain time,—a year, for instance,—and the master agrees to pay wages, or salary, for the year's service, creates the relation of master and servant for the prescribed period;

[1] Blake v. Lanyon, 6 D. and E. 221.
[2] Lightly v. Clouston, 1 Taunt. 112.
[3] Lumley v. Gye, 2 E. and B. 216.   [4] Taylor v. Neri, 1 Esp. 386.
[5] Alton v. Midland Railway Company, 19 C. B. N. S. 213.
[6] Bac. Abr. Master and Servant, N.
[7] Reg. v. Huntley, 3 C. and K. 142.

and the master is bound to continue that relation for the whole time. He is not bound to provide the servant with any particular work, or to keep him continually at work; but he is bound to retain him in his service; and if he dismisses him, and puts an end to the relation of master and servant before the expiration of the year, he breaks the contract, and is answerable to the servant in an action for damages. This was decided in an action on an agreement between an attorney and a company, by which it was agreed that the plaintiff, as solicitor of the company, should receive and accept a salary of £100 a year, in lieu of rendering an annual bill of costs for general business transacted by the plaintiff for the company as such solicitor; and that he should, for such salary, advise and act for the company on all occasions, in all matters connected with the company, with certain exceptions, and attend the secretary, the directors, and meetings of proprietors, when required. He complained that the company did not retain or employ him as their attorney, but dismissed him from being their attorney before the expiration of a year from his appointment. The Common Pleas gave judgment against the plaintiff, on the ground that there was no agreement by the company to retain and employ, but merely to pay him his salary. The Exchequer Chamber held that the agreement being to give a certain salary for one year at least, to the plaintiff, who engaged for it to give his services, if required, created the relation of attorney and client, and amounted to a promise to continue that relation at least for a year, though the company were not bound to furnish him with business, as an attorney and solicitor, at all events, or to require his advice, or use his services, as an attorney, whenever they had occasion to require the service of an attorney. "Medical advisers," they said, "may be employed, at a salary, to be ready in case of illness; members of theatrical establishments, in case their labours should be needed; household servants, in performance of their duties when their masters wish: in these, and other similar cases, the requirement of actual service is distinct from the employment by the party employing. If it is held that such a contract as this was for service and pay respectively; and that although the employer determines the relation by an illegal dismissal, yet the employed may entitle himself for the whole time by being ready to serve, that doctrine, if sanctioned, will be of pernicious consequence in case of a business being discontinued or a dismissal for misconduct without legal proof. According to the plaintiff's construction, the agreement creates the relation of employer and employed; and the illegal determination of the relation entitles him to indemnity, the measure of damage being the actual loss, which may be much less than the wages, when another employment may be easily obtained. According to the defendant's construction, it is a contract for service and pay; and the whole salary, for all the time comprised in the contract, becomes due, if the plaintiff served, or was ready to serve." This judgment was affirmed by the House of Lords upon the opinion of a majority of the judges.[1]

If an agreement between master and servant provides that the master shall be at liberty to dismiss the servant on giving him a month's notice, or paying him a month's wages, it implies an obligation by the servant to serve, and the master to employ, until the agreement is put an end to by the notice or payment of wages. In an action for harbouring the servant of a glass-

[1] Elderton v. Emmens, 4 C. B. 479. 6 C. B. 160. Emmens v. Elderton, 13 C. B. 495; 4 H. of Lds. C. 624.

maker, it appeared that there was an agreement between the glass-maker and his workman, that the workman should serve the glass-maker for seven years, and should not, during the term, work for any other person; that during any depression of the trade, he should be paid a moiety of his wages; that if he should be sick or lame, the master should be at liberty to employ any other person in his stead, without paying him any wages; that the master should pay him, so long as he continued to be employed, wages by the piece, and £8 per annum in lieu of house-rent and firing, and should have the option of dismissing him from his service upon giving him a month's wages or a month's notice. It was objected that this agreement was void for want of mutuality, and as an unreasonable restraint of trade, there being no obligation on the master to employ; but the Court held that an obligation by the master to employ was necessarily to be inferred from the option to dismiss, and that the obligation to serve, and the restraint on the workman against working for any others, were co-extensive with the obligation to employ.[1]

In another action for seducing the servant of a glass and alkali manufacturer, the agreement between the master and servant was, that the servant should for seven years serve the plaintiff or his partners, or such of them as should carry on the trade or business then carried on by him as a glass and alkali manufacturer, and that the servant should not, during the term, work for any other person; that the plaintiff should, so long as the servant continued to be employed for him or his partners, pay him twenty-four shillings per week for 1,200 tables; and the plaintiff agreed to find the workman some other description of work, provided he did

[1] Pilkington v. Scott, 15 M. and W. 657.

not require 1,200 tables, so that his wages should not be less than twenty-four shillings per week, except when a furnace should be out, when the servant engaged to work for twenty-one shillings per week. In case the servant should be sick or lame, or otherwise incapacitated to perform, or should not perform the work and service aforesaid and his engagement with the plaintiff, or in case he should not in his opinion have conducted himself properly, or as he ought to do, or if the plaintiff or his partners should discontinue the business during the term of seven years, they should be at liberty to retain any other person in lieu of the servant, and should not be obliged to make any payment. Upon an objection taken to this agreement, it was held to impose on the master an obligation to employ for seven years, provided the trade was carried on so long, and on the servant to serve during the same period; and that he was only restrained from working for others so long as the master was bound to employ and he was bound to serve.[1] And an agreement by which the servant is to work exclusively for the master for twelve months, in consideration of which the master is to pay him every week such wages as the articles made by him amount to, with a proviso for determining the service upon notice, implies an engagement to provide a reasonable quantity of work whilst the relation of master and servant continues.[2]

An agreement between a collier and a coal company, the collier to serve them in consideration of wages (not specifying the amount) to be paid to him fortnightly, and the company not to dismiss him without twenty-eight days' notice, was held to imply an obligation by the

[1] Hartley v. Cummings, 5 C. and B. 247.
[2] Regina v. Welch, 2 E. and B. 357.

employers to find the servant in work, as it would be perfectly illusory to hold otherwise.[1]

But if the master merely engages to pay wages to the servant in proportion to the work to be done by him, he does not bind himself to find him work. An agreement was made between the owners of a colliery and some colliers, that the colliers should for a year do such work as might be necessary for carrying on the colliery, and as they should be required to do by the owners; that the owners should pay them wages in proportion to the work done; that during all the times the mines should be laid open, the parties hired should continue the servants of the owners, and when required, except when prevented by sickness, they should perform a full day's work on each and every working day. It was held that the owners were not bound to employ the colliers at work at reasonable times for a reasonable number of working days during the term : it was quite optional with them to set the labourers to work.[2]

In Aspdin v. Austin,[3] the plaintiff agreed to manufacture cement for the defendant; the defendant, on condition of the plaintiff performing his agreement, agreed to pay him £4 weekly during two years following the date of the agreement, and £5 weekly during the next year, and also to receive him into partnership at the expiration of three years. The Court of Queen's Bench decided that this agreement did not bind the defendant to employ the plaintiff in manufacturing cement, but merely to pay wages in case the plaintiff did manufacture the cement, or was ready and willing to do so, and was prevented by the defendant. They said, "Where parties have expressly covenanted to perform certain acts, they cannot be held to have im-

---

[1] Whittle v. Frankland, 2 B. and S. 49.

[2] Williamson v. Taylor, 5 Q. B. 175.   [3] 5 Q. B. 671.

pliedly covenanted for every act convenient or even necessary for the perfect performance of their express covenants. Where parties have entered into written engagements with express stipulations, it is not desirable to extend them by an implication: the presumption is, that having expressed some, they have expressed all the conditions by which they intend to be bound under the instrument. It is assumed that the defendant, at however great a loss to himself, was bound to continue his business for three years; but the defendant has not covenanted to do so; he has covenanted only to pay weekly sums to the defendant, on condition of his performing what on his part is a condition precedent."

And on the same principle they held, in Dunn v. Sayles,[1] that the defendant was not liable for refusing to allow the plaintiff's son to remain in his service, but dismissing him therefrom, the plaintiff having covenanted that his son should serve the defendant for five years in the art of a surgeon-dentist, and should attend nine hours each day; and the defendant having covenanted that he would, during the five years, in case the son should faithfully perform his part of the agreement, but not otherwise, pay him certain weekly sums during the five years.

In Elderton v. Emmens, the Exchequer Chamber cited these two cases, and professed not to overrule them. In Worthington v. Sudlow,[2] Crompton, J., said that Aspdin v. Austin had been attacked, if not overruled, in the House of Lords. But in Churchward v. the Queen,[3] Cockburn, C. J., said that he thought the decision right. In this last case Churchward covenanted that he would, to satisfaction of the Lords of the Admiralty, convey the mails which they or the Postmaster-General should require; and the Admiralty, in consideration of

[1] 5 Q. B. 685.   [2] 2 P. and S. 514.   [3] L. R. 1 Q. B. 191.

his so doing, covenanted to pay him £18,000 a year out of moneys to be provided by Parliament; and it was held that there was no implied covenant to employ. The Lord Chief Justice saying, "Although a contract may on the face of it appear to be obligatory only upon one party, there are occasions on which you must imply corresponding obligations on the other. When the act to be done by the party binding himself can only be done upon something of a corresponding nature being done by the opposite party, you would then imply a corresponding obligation; as if a man engages to work, and he is only to be paid by the measure of the work, the contract necessarily presupposes, on the party who engages him, an obligation to supply the work." [1] Agreeably to this, it has been held that when a workman had received all the money he was to receive for his services, he could not sue for wrongful dismissal. [2]

84. If the master who is under an obligation to employ his servant, wrongfully dismisses him from his service before the period for employment has expired, the remedy of the servant is by action for the wrongful dismissal, and not for his wages. He cannot maintain an action for his wages, unless he has actually served all the time for which he claims wages. [3] He may maintain an action for wrongful dismissal, directly he has been dismissed; he need not wait until the period for which he has agreed to serve is out. [4] And if the master refuses to employ the servant before the period agreed for the service has commenced, it is a breach of

[1] L. R. 1 Q. B. 195.

[2] Rutledge v. Farnham Board of Health, 2 F. and F. 406.

[3] Archard v. Horner, 3 C. and P. 319. Smith v. Hayward, 7 A. and E. 544. Fewings v. Tisdal, 1 Ex. 295, overruling Gandell v. Potigny, 4 Camp. 375.

[4] Paganini v. Gandolfi, 2 C. and P. 371. Dunn v. Murray, 9 B. and C. 780.

contract which entitles the servant to treat the contract at an end, and at once to sue for damages.[1]

85. It is also the duty of the master to pay wages in consideration of the service performed. If the relation of master and servant has subsisted, it will, in most cases, be presumed that there was an agreement, or understanding, that the servant should be paid the value of his services, although it does not appear that the parties have agreed to the amount.[2] But if relations live together, and perform acts of service for each other, the probability is, that such acts are performed by way of kindness or duty, and not for reward. Thus, when an illegitimate daughter had lived in her father's house, and acted as his servant for several years, though when first she came to him he had hired her as a servant for a year, at fifty shillings wages, she was considered not to have been his servant at wages during the subsequent years.[3] And where a man who had lived in his brother's house, and assisted him in carrying on his business, afterwards made a claim for his services, it was left to the jury to say, whether the parties came together on the terms that the one was to be paid by the other for his services.[4] A slave who came to England with his master, and continued with him, was held not entitled to wages from the simple circumstance of service. If an express agreement to pay wages had been made between him and his master, he would have been en-. titled to wages for his services after the making of such agreement, but not for previous service.[5] The circumstance of a female servant cohabiting with her master,

---

[1] Hochster v. De la Tour, 2 E. and B. 678.
[2] Bayley v. Rimmell, 1 M. and W. 506.
[3] Rex v. Sow, 1 B. and Ald. 178.
[4] Davies v. Davies, 9 Car. and Payne, 87.
[5] Alfred v. Fitzjames, 3 Esp. 3.

is material to show that there was no contract of hiring and service, or to pay wages.[1]

86. If a person has entered into the service of another, and served him under a special contract which has been rescinded and put an end to by the parties; it will be presumed that the master has agreed to pay the servant for the value of his services. The defendant agreed with the plaintiff's father to take him on trial, and to take him as his apprentice if he approved of him. The plaintiff served him for two years upon this understanding, and the defendant then sent him away, and refused to bind him as an apprentice. The jury finding that the contract was at an end, and that each party had treated it as rescinded, it was held that the plaintiff was entitled to a reasonable remuneration for his services.[2] On the same principle was decided the case of a clerk who engaged himself for a year, at an annual salary, whose master became bankrupt before any salary was due, and who left shortly after the bankruptcy, his services being no longer required : he was held entitled to a *pro ratâ* salary for the period during which he had served, the contract of service having been dissolved by mutual consent, and it being understood to be on the terms that he should be paid for his services actually rendered.[3] When the master gave up business without dismissing the servant, the servant being ready and willing to serve during the agreed period, recovered his salary on the ground of a constructive service.[4] A superintendent of packets, in the service of a steam packet company, whose salary was payable quarterly, on the 20th October. tendered his resignation, which was

---

[1] Bradshaw v. Haward, Car. and Marsh, 591.
[2] Phillips v. Jones, 1 A. and E. 333.
[3] Thomas v. Williams, 1 A. and E. 685.
[4] Cook v. Sherwood, 3 F. and F. 729.

accepted on the 13th December, no salary having then become due,—it was held, that although no new contract arises by implication of law upon the dissolution of special contract, in respect of services performed under such special contract previous to its dissolution, yet it ought to have been submitted to the jury, as to whether the parties did or did not, upon the dissolution of the contract, come to a new agreement to pay for the services under it, and for which no wages had become due by the contract.[1] A carman was engaged by some tea-merchants, at the wages of £160 per annum, payable quarterly. At the expiration of the first month of his service, he was guilty of misconduct, for which they dismissed him ; but, at their request, he worked for them two days after his dismissal. The jury considered that the dismissal was accompanied by a new contract to pay him a month's wages for the services actually performed, in consideration of his remaining in their service two days after his dismissal.[2] If the servant is wrongfully dismissed before his salary is due, he may rescind the contract, and recover a *pro ratâ* salary for the time he has served, or he may sue for damages. If he elects to sue for damages, he cannot recover wages.[3] But if the servant is properly dismissed for misconduct before his wages are due, he cannot recover anything.[4] If the contract is for three months' notice or three months' salary, and the servant is dismissed without notice, he is entitled to the salary as liquidated damages.[5]

87. Wages are sometimes payable upon condition. An agreement between master printers and compositors

[1] Lamburn v. Cruden, 2 M. and G. 253.
[2] Hurcum v. Stericker, 10 M. and W. 553.
[3] Goodman v. Pocock, 15 Q. B. 576.
[4] Lilly v. Elwin, 11 Q. B. 742.
[5] East Anglian Railway Company v. Lythgoe, 10 C. B. 726.

provided that printing advertisements on wrappers was
—"Standing advertisements and stereo blocks forming a
complete page, and when collected together making one or
more complete pages on a wrapper, not to be charged,
the compositor only to charge for his time in making
them up; the remainder of the matter in such wrappers,
including standing advertisements or stereo blocks not
forming a complete page, to be charged according to a
scale." It was held by the Courts of Exchequer and
Exchequer Chamber, that for every page of the adver-
tising sheet not filled with standing advertisements the
compositor was entitled to charge according to the scale;
the first branch of the agreement applying to the pages
filled with standing advertisements, the second to the
others.[1]

88. Sometimes it is agreed that the servant shall have
a percentage on the profits. Such an agreement does
not constitute him a partner, but it may entitle him to
a discovery and account of the profits.[2] He may be entitled to overhaul the books and accounts of the master's
business, and to a percentage on the profits from year
to year. The Court is bound to see that a *bond fide*
estimate has been made, and not an estimate made at
the mere arbitrary will of the employer.[3]

If a servant is allowed to occupy his master's house
during his service, and as part of his remuneration, he
acquires no interest therein, not even to the extent of a
tenancy at will; but must quit when dismissed from
the service, whether rightly or wrongly, or when
required to do so by the master.[4]

---

[1] Hill v. Levey, 3 H. and N. 7—702.
[2] Harrington v. Churchward, 6 Jur. N. S. 576.
[3] Rishton v. Grissell, L. R. 5 Eq. 326.
[4] White v. Bayley, 10 C. B. N. S. 227. Lake v. Campbell, 5 L. T.
N. S. 582.

89. The value of things lost or injured by the neg-ligence of a servant cannot be deducted from his wages, unless there is an agreement to that effect between the master and servant. If there is such an agreement, it is tantamount to an agreement that the balance of wages only shall be paid, after deducting the value of the things lost or injured.[1] Nor can the master, with-out an agreement to that effect, deduct money he has paid to a medical man whom he has called in to attend the servant whilst sick.[2] If the servant has not agreed to pay doctor, or master's reimbursement, the calling doctor in will be an act of generosity by the master.

If the servant is an infant, the master cannot deduct from the wages any payments he may have made for the servant, unless they have been made in the purchase of necessaries. Payments made for the servant do not operate to discharge or satisfy the wages, as do pay-ments made to her after the wages have become due; but they constitute a debt due from the servant to the master, and may be set off against the wages, if the servant is legally liable to repay them, but not other-wise. An infant, as has been stated, is not bound by contracts, unless for necessaries suitable to her degree; and therefore, in the case now put, is not liable to repay the advances. In an action by a servant-of-all-work for wages earned by her when under twenty-one, the master claimed to deduct £1 10s. which he had paid for a silk dress for her, £4 10s. for a reticule and lace for caps; also payment for coach fares. Bayley, J., held that he was not entitled to the deductions, saying, "Pay-ments made on account of wages due to an infant for necessaries, and which could not be avoided, are valid

---

[1] Le Noir v. Burton, 4 Campb. 134. Cleworth v. Pickford, 7 M. and W. 314.

[2] Sellen v. Norman, 4 C. and P. 80.

payments ; but an infant cannot bind herself for things which are not necessary.[1]

90. On the bankruptcy of the master, or the winding up of a company under the Companies Act, 1862, the wages or salary of a clerk or servant in the employment of the bankrupt or company at the date of the receiving order or commencement of the winding up, not exceeding four months' wages or salary, and not exceeding £50, and wages not exceeding £25 of any labourer or workman in the employment of the bankrupt or company at the same date not exceeding two months' wages, are to be paid in priority of all other debts, *pari passu* with certain rates and taxes. If the property of the bankrupt is insufficient to meet them they are to rebate in equal proportions.[2] But where any labourer in husbandry has entered into a contract for the payment of a portion of his wages in a lump sum at the end of the year of hiring, he shall have priority in respect of the whole of such sum, or a part thereof, as the Court may decide to be due under the contract, proportionate to the time of service up to the date of the receiving order, or the commencement of the winding up.

A corresponding provision in a former Act was held to extend to a clerk who had lent money to the bankrupt, and was taken into his service at a salary in consequence of the loan.[3] A music-master and a drillmaster employed by a school-master are held to be servants within this clause.[4] Servants are entitled to immediate payment out of the assets in hand, and are not to be postponed because the trustee intends to take proceedings against the debtor which may exhaust them.[5]

---

[1] Hedgeley v. Holt, 4 Car. and Payne, 104.   [2] 51 & 52 Vic. c. 62.
[3] Ex parte Harris, 1 De Gex, 165, 9 Jur. 497.
[4] Exp. Walter, L. R. 15 Eq. 412.   [5] Exp. Powis, L. R. 17 Eq. 130.

On the winding-up of a company a servant has no preferential claim for his wages. He is entitled to prove on the footing of having had notice of discharge when the order to wind up was made.[1]

91. A master is not bound to provide his servant with medical attendance or medicines. Although Lord Kenyon held, that in the case of a menial servant who fell sick and was supplied with medicines whilst under the master's roof, the master was liable, on the ground that the servant formed part of his family, and that he was bound, during the period of service, to find him with all necessaries, and, amongst others, medicines and medical advice,[2] yet this opinion has been over-ruled. The event of the servant falling sick during the service is an event not contemplated by the parties when the relation is contracted; and it has been remarked, that if masters were bound to provide their servants with necessary medicines and medical advice, many masters who are obliged to employ servants would be unable to perform their engagements. The extent of a master's liability, in the event of the servant's sickness, is to pay him his wages, and provide him with ordinary food.[3] On the trial of an indictment against a master for causing the death of his apprentice by neglecting to provide him with proper nourishment, Patteson, J., told the jury, that by the general law, a master was not bound to provide medical advice for a servant; yet that the case was different with respect to an apprentice, and that a master was bound, during the illness of his apprentice, to provide him with proper medicines.[4]

[1] Re General Rolling Stock Company, L. R. 1 Eq. 346.
[2] Scarman v. Castell, 1 Esp. 270.
[3] Wennall v. Adney, 3 B. and P. 241. Sellen v. Norman, 4 C. and P. 80. Cooper v. Phillips, 4 C. and P. 581.
[4] Regina v. William Smith, 8 C. and P. 153.

It is a misdemeanor at Common Law for a master to neglect to provide necessaries for a servant to the injury of his health, if by contract he is bound to do so, and the servant is of tender years under the master's control, and unable to take care of himself.[1] If the servant is in a helpless state and unable to take care of herself, and the master leaves her with insufficient food or lodging, so as to cause death, it is manslaughter; but if she has the exercise of free will and chooses to stay in a service of such great hardship, and bad food and lodging, that death supervenes, the master is not criminally responsible.[2] By Stat. 24 & 25 Vict. c. 100, s. 20, it is a misdemeanor punishable by penal servitude for three years, or imprisonment for not exceeding two years, with or without hard labour, for a master or mistress, who is legally bound to provide food, clothing, or lodging for an apprentice or servant, wilfully and without lawful excuse, to refuse or neglect to provide the same, or unlawfully and maliciously to do or cause to be done any bodily harm to the apprentice or servant to the danger of life or permanent injury of health. By 14 & 15 Vict. c. 11, provision is made for the safety of servants under sixteen, hired from workhouses.

92. The relation of master and servant often involves a bailment of the person of the servant to the master. The servant has to trust himself in the master's building, or mine, or ship, or carriage, or scaffold, or in the midst of his machinery, and in doing so frequently carries his life in his hand, and is in peril of losing it if the master's things, amongst which he has to work, are defective or are improperly used. The case is complicated by the circumstances that the servant is in some respects capable of taking care of himself, and

[1] Rex v. Ridley, 2 Campb. 160.　　[2] Reg. v. Smith, 11 Jur. N. S. 695.

sometimes it is part of the duty of his service to take care of the things which put him in peril. The bailment or relation is mutually beneficial, and, in the nature of a hiring, and subject to the above qualification, would seem to impose on the master the duty of taking ordinary care of the servant.

In Priestley v. Fowler, which is the first case on this subject, and is said to have introduced a new chapter into the law,[1] and has frequently been referred to as the leading case on the subject,[2] this principle is apparently recognised. A butcher ordered his servant to go in a van loaded with goods. In consequence of the van being in bad repair, and overloaded, it broke down on the journey, and the servant was injured. It was held that the master was not liable. Lord Abinger, in delivering the judgment of the Court, stated the law to be,—That the mere relation of master and servant could not imply an obligation, on the part of the master, to take more care of the servant than he might be reasonably expected to take of himself;—that he was bound to provide for the safety of the servant, in the course of his employment, to the best of his judgment, information, and belief. The servant was not bound to risk his safety in the service of his master, and might, if he thought fit, decline any service in which he reasonably apprehended injury to himself; and in most cases in which danger might be incurred, if not in all, he was just as likely to be acquainted of the probability and extent of it as his master.[3]

In a subsequent case, the Court say,—" The master is bound to take due care not to expose his servant to unreasonable risks. The servant, when he engages to run

[1] Per Byles, J., Clarke v. Holmes, 7 H. and N. 947.
[2] Vose v. Lancashire and Yorkshire Railway Company, 2 H. and N. 734. Riley v. Baxendale, 6 H. and N. 448. Clarke v. Holmes, 7 H. and N. 947.   [3] Priestley v. Fowler, 3 M. and W. 1.

the risks of his service, has a right to understand that the master has taken reasonable care to protect him from such risks by associating with him only persons of ordinary skill and care."[1]

But the same Court, when differently constituted, afterwards held that there was no contract by the master to take due and ordinary care not to expose the servant to extraordinary danger and risk in the course of his employment.[2]   In Morgan v. Vale of Neath Railway Company,[3] Blackburn, J., on this subject cites with approbation the dictum of Shaw, C. J.,—"The servant does not stand towards the master in the relation of a stranger, but is one whose rights are regulated by contract express or implied."

In two Scotch appeals to the House of Lords, the law has been administered more favourably for the servant. In each case a miner had been killed by a stone falling on him.   In the first the question was whether the rashness of the workman contributed to the accident, and disentitled his family to compensation.   He had often complained to the defendant's manager of the stone, and requested him to remove it.   The manager said there was no danger, and, after some delay, sent men to remove the stone.   They found the deceased filling his hutch with coal under the stone, and waited until he had finished.   While the deceased was filling his hutch, the stone fell and killed him.   The Judge told the jury that the plaintiff could not recover.   The House of Lords held that there was evidence for the jury of the negligence of the defendants, or their manager, for whom they were responsible, in not removing the stone before, and of the miner's death not having been caused by his own extraordinary rashness.

---

[1] Hutchinson v. York, Newcastle, and Berwick R. C., 5 Ex. 343.
[2] Riley v. Baxendale, 6 H. and N. 445.   [3] 5 B. and S. 579.

The Lord Chancellor (Lord Cranworth) said, "The law of Scotland is, and I believe it to be entirely conformable to the law of England also, that where a master is employing a servant in a work, particularly in a work of a dangerous character, he is bound to take all reasonable precautions that there shall be no extraordinary danger incurred by the workman. A case has been put by Mr. Bovill of a rope going down to a mine. I take it that in England, just as in Scotland, if a master of a man negligently puts a rope that is so defective that it will break with the weight of a man, he is responsible to the workman, just as he would be responsible for his negligence to a stranger. I believe by the law of England, just as by the law of Scotland in the actual state of the case with which we have to deal, a master employing servants upon any work, particularly a dangerous work of this sort, is bound to take care that he does not induce them to work under the notion that they are working with good and sufficient tackle, whilst he is employing improper tackle, and being guilty of negligence, his negligence occasioning loss to them."[1] In the other, the workman was killed by a stone falling from the top of the shaft in consequence of the planking being rotten, whilst he was being drawn up from the mine. He was coming up, not at the usual hour, or in course of business, but for the purpose of stating some grievance; on this ground the Court of Session held his widow and family not entitled to compensation. The House of Lords held that he was to be considered as in the employment of the master whilst being drawn out of the mine, though for his own purposes, and that his death being caused by the machinery used in drawing up being in a defective state from neglect, the master was responsible. Lord Cranworth, Chancellor, said, the law of

[1] Patterson v. Wallace, 1 Macqueen, 748.

England was the same in this respect as the law of Scotland.[1]

In a subsequent case,[2] Lord Cranworth said that these cases proceeded on a principle established in many preceding cases, that when a master employs his servant in a work of danger he is bound to exercise due care in order to have his tackle and machinery in a safe and proper condition, so as to protect the servant against unnecessary risks. The master is liable for an accident to the servant if it has been caused by personal negligence on his part, as when a labourer was injured by a fall of a scaffold from its being built of defective put logs, and one of the masters told a labourer who was breaking them to break no more.[3] And where one of two masters in partnership acted as banksman to a mine, and was guilty of negligence, the Court held them both liable, saying, "Although the chance of injury from the negligence of fellow-servants may be supposed to enter into the calculations of a servant in undertaking the service, it would be too much to say that the risk of danger, from the negligence of a master when engaged in their common work, enters in like manner into his speculation. From a master he is entitled to expect the care and attention which the superior position and presumable sense of duty of the latter ought to command. The relation of master and servant does not the less subsist because, by some arrangement between the joint masters, one of them takes on himself the functions of a workman."[4]

---

[1] Marshall v. Stewart, 2 Macqueen, 30.

[2] Barton Hill Coal Company v. Reid, 3 Macq. 267, and per Byles J., Searle v. Lindsay, 11 C. B. N. S. 439; per Lord Campbell, Ormond v. Holland, E. B. and E. 105.

[3] Roberts v. Smith, 2 H. and N. 213. Webb v. Rennie, 4 F. and F. 608.

[4] Ashworth v. Stanwix, 3 E. and E. 701. Mellors v. Shaw, 1 B. and S. 437.

And if a master induces the servant to engage in a dangerous employment, as to work on a ladder which the master knows to be defective, but the servant does not, or other dangerous employment, he is liable for any injury that ensues to the servant.[1] So it is a breach of contract, if he compels the servant to serve on a service more dangerous than contemplated, as when the crew of a ship were engaged for an ordinary mercantile voyage, and the ship was employed in aid of a belligerent.[2] If the things of the master on or with which the servant has to work have a latent defect, and by reason thereof inflict injury upon him, the master is not liable unless he knew, or ought to have known, of the defect.[3] If the defect or danger is patent, and is or may be known to the servant, the master is not liable.[4] The knowledge of the servant of the defect is only evidence that he has agreed to encounter the risk. If it appears that he has not, but that the master has agreed to repair it, the master is liable to him for an injury caused by it. When a servant entered into the employment, machinery was properly fenced; on its ceasing to be so, the manager of the works, on the remonstrance of the servant, promised, in the presence of the master, it should be made good. It was therefore certain that at the time when the contract was entered into, it was contemplated

---

[1] Williams v. Clough, 3 H. and N. 258. Ogden v. Rummens, 3 F. and F. 751. Davies v. England, 10 Jur. N. S. 1235. Watling v. Oastler, L. R. 6 Ex. 73.

[2] Burton v. Pinkerton, L. R. 2 Ex. 340.

[3] Priestley v. Fowler, 3 M. and W. 1. Mellors v. Shaw, 1 B. and S. 441, 443. Couch v. Steel, 3 E. and B. 402. Ormond v. Holland, E. B. and E. 102. Potts v. Port Carlisle Company, 2 L. T. N. S. 283. Moffatt v. Bateman, L. R. 3 P. C. 115.

[4] Seymour v. Maddox, 16 Q. B. 326. Skipp v. Eastern Counties Railway Company, 9 Ex. 223. Assop v. Yates, 2 H. and N. 768. Griffiths v. Gidlow, 3 H. and N. 648. Smith v. Dowell, 2 F. and F 238.

that the machinery should be fenced. Through the negligence of the master in not having the machinery fenced, the servant was exposed to danger to which he ought not to have been subjected, and the injury of which he complained having thus arisen, the master was justly and properly liable.[1]

93. The principle enunciated in Priestley v. Fowler being that the master is not liable to his servant for the consequences of the negligence of others, it has been held that he is not liable to his servant for an injury caused by the negligence of his fellow-servant. The servant of a railway company, while proceeding in a train, was killed by a collision of trains caused by the negligence of other servants of the company having charge of the train. The Court put the case of a master employing A. and B., two of his servants, to drive his cattle to market. If, by the unskilfulness of A., a stranger is injured, the master is responsible; not so if A., by his unskilfulness, hurts himself. Suppose, then, by the unskilfulness of A., B., the other servant, is injured while they are jointly engaged in the same service, then we think he has no claim against the master. They have both engaged in a common service, the duties of which impose a certain risk on each of them, and in case of negligence on the part of the other, the party injured knows that the negligence is that of his fellow-servant, and not of his master. He knows, when he engages in the service, that he is exposed to the risk of injury, not only from his own want of skill and care, but also from the want of it on the part of his fellow-servant; he must be supposed to have contracted as between himself and his master

[1] Clarke v. Holmes, 7 H. and N. 937; 6 H. and N. 349. Gallagher v. Piper, 16 C. B. N. S. 692. Murphy v. Smith, 19 C. B. N. S. 365. Holmes v. Worthington, 2 F. and F. 533. Watling v. Oastler, L. R. 6 Ex. 73.

that he would run this risk. But he has a right to understand that the master has taken ordinary care to protect him from such risks, by associating him only with persons with ordinary skill and care.[1]

On the same principle the following actions have failed. The widow of a bricklayer sued for his loss. He was killed by a fall of a scaffold, on which he was at work. It was constructed by men employed by the defendant, and they used an unsound leger-pole, which was the occasion of the fall. The defect in the pole had previously been pointed out to the foreman, but there was no evidence that he was an improper person to employ as foreman.[2] A painter was injured by the fall of a scaffold which was insecurely erected by a person employed by the master. The person so employed was incompetent, but it was not shown that the master knew of his incompetency, or had been guilty of any want of care in his selection.[3]

A bricklayer, in the employ of builders, was injured by a defective ladder. The workmen had complained of it among themselves, but their complaints had not been communicated to the masters. It was the duty of the gate-keeper to examine all implements used in the works. The masters were held not liable, there being no evidence of personal negligence, either by interference in the work, or by hiring servants, or in choosing implements.[4]

A workman in a mine was killed, while being raised to the surface, through the negligence of the engine-man. The workman and engineman were held by the House of Lords, on an appeal from Scotland, to be

---

[1] Hutchinson v. York, Newcastle, and Berwick Railway Company, 5 Ex. 343.

[2] Wigmore v. Jay, 5 Ex. 354.   [3] Tarrant v. Webb, 18 C. B. 797.

[4] Ormond v. Holland, E. B. and E. 102.

fellow-servants engaged in a common employment.[1] A tub of water fell upon a workman employed in sinking a pit, because his fellow-workman neglected to use a jiddy provided by the master. The plaintiff had complained, in the presence of the defendant, that the jiddy was not used. Byles, J., directed the jury that they might find for the plaintiff if they thought that the omission to use the jiddy existed by the defendant's order, or with his sanction. The Court overruled this, saying that it was enough for the defendant to find the jiddy, and he was not bound to see it used.[2] An engineer on a steam-vessel was injured by a defective winch, which the chief engineer, who was a competent man, had neglected to have repaired. Williams, J., said that, to take the case out of the common rule, there must be reasonable evidence to show that the masters were to blame either in respect of their not having provided proper machinery, or not having retained competent workmen.[3] The guard of a railway train was killed by the train running off the line through the negligence of the ganger of plate-layers, whose duty it was to keep the rails in order. They were held to be fellow-servants, because they were engaged in a common object, viz., that passengers shall be conveyed in trains that were safe on rails which were free from danger.[4] A labourer was injured by a fall from a scaffold, owing to its faulty construction, through the negligence of the general manager of the master's works. He had been their general manager for about twenty-five years. The manager and the labourer were held by the majority of the Common Pleas to be

[1] Bartonshill Coal Company v. Reid, 3 Macq. 266.
[2] Griffith v. Gidlow, 3 H. and N. 648.
[3] Searle v. Lindsay, 11 C. B. N. S. 429.
[4] Waller v. South-Eastern Railway Company, 2 H. and C. 102. Lovegrove v. London and Brighton Railway Company, 16 C. B. N. S. 669.

fellow-servants. Williams, J., entertained a doubt as to whether he was not rather a deputy-master, intended to stand in the place of the defendants, than a fellow-workman; but thought there was not sufficient evidence. Byles, J., held that he was general agent for the defendants, and that they were liable.[1] A carpenter, employed by a railway company to mend the roof of a shed, was thrown from a ladder by the negligence of the porters of the company in moving an engine. He and the porters were held to be fellow-servants engaged in a common employment, within the rule. Blackburn, J., in whose judgment Mellor, J., concurred, said, " A servant who engages for the performance of services for compensation does, as an implied part of the contract, take upon himself, as between himself and his master, the natural risks and perils incident to the performance of such services, the presumption of law being that the compensation was adjusted accordingly; or, in other words, that those risks are considered in his wages." "If the master has, by his own personal negligence or malfeasance, enhanced the risk to which the servant is exposed beyond those natural risks of the employment, which must be presumed to have been in contemplation when the employment was accepted, as, for instance, by knowingly employing incompetent servants, or supplying defective machinery, or the like, no defence founded on this principle can apply." " I quite agree that the employment must be common in this sense, that the safety of the one servant must, in the ordinary and natural course of things, depend on the care and skill of the other." [2] The judgment was affirmed in Error,[3] Erle, C. J., observing that the principle was put very clearly by Blackburn, J., in his

---

[1] Gallagher v. Piper, 16 C. B. N. S. 669.
[2] Morgan v. Vale of Neath Railway Company, 5 B. and S. 570.
[3] 5 B. and S. 736.

judgment; and Pollock, C. B., adding that, by a decision in favour of the plaintiff, they would open a flood of litigation, the end of which no one could foresee. A labourer in a mine, under twenty-one years, was injured by the fall of a stone, which the overlooker neglected and refused to prop up, although the danger was pointed out to him by the plaintiff, but threatened to dismiss him unless he went on with his work. The Exchequer Chamber held that the young labourer and the overlooker were fellow-servants, and that he was not a deputy-master for whose negligence the mine-owners were responsible.[1] A boy of sixteen was employed in a lucifer-match factory. Simlack was the general manager, and engaged him; under him was Debor, who took his place when absent. The boy was set to stir a dangerous compound by Debor, and injured by an explosion. The Court held that he and Debor were fellow-servants, Erle, C. J., saying that there was evidence that Simlack was placed by the defendant in the position of vice-principal, but not that Debor was.[2] Where the master retained the control of the establishment, and employed a manager or foreman, the manager or foreman was held to be a servant, and not the master's representative.[3]

The same principle has been applied to exempt from liability a contractor who employed a sub-contractor to do part of his work, and did the other part by his own servants—for the death of a servant of the sub-contractor, caused by one of the contractor's servants letting something fall upon his head. The sub-contractor's servant was considered as in the same position as a servant of the contractor, and engaging to run the

---

[1] Hall v. Johnson, 3 H. and C. 589.
[2] Murphy v. Smith, 19 C. B. N. S. 361.
[3] Feltham v. England, L. R., 2 Q. B. 33.

risk of accidents caused by the negligence of those associated with him in a common employment.[1]

A person who volunteers to associate himself with the servants, and assist them in their work, is in no better position than a servant, and cannot, therefore, sue the master for an injury sustained by the negligence of the servants.[2]

It makes no difference as to the liability of the master that the negligence of the servant for which he is sued was committed before the servant injured was in his employ. It is not negligence for which he is liable. All that he is bound to do, in the event of his not personally superintending and directing the work, is to select proper and competent persons to do so, and furnish them with adequate resources for the work.[3]

It was a term of the employment of a labourer employed by a railway company that he should be carried by train to and from his work. He was, while returning from his work by train, in the service of the company, and they were, therefore, not liable to him for the negligence of the guard who had the management of the train.[4] Where a master conveyed his servant to his work in his buggy, not as one of the terms of his employment, he was held to have contracted for no greater degree of care and skill than would be required from a person who was driving another gratuitously, and liable only for negligence of a gross description.[5]

On the other hand, in Ainsworth v. South-Eastern

[1] Wiggett v. Fox, 11 Ex. 832 ; 5 H. and N. 147. Normile v. Braby, 4 F. and F. 962.

[2] Degg v. Midland Railway Company, 1 H. and N. 773. Potter v. Faulkner, 1 B. and S. 800.

[3] Wilson v. Merry, L. R. 1 Sc. 326. Brown v. Accrington Cotton Company, 3 H. and C. 511.

[4] Tunney v. Midland Railway Company, L. R. 1 C. P. 291.

[5] Moffatt v. Bateman, L. R. 3 P. C. 115.

Railway Company,[1] tried before Lord Wensleydale in 1847, ten years after Priestley v. Fowler, and three years before Hutchinson v. York, Newcastle, and Berwick Railway Company, an action brought by the executrix of a labourer, employed by the company to remove chalk, while being carried to his work in their trucks, through the negligence of the engine-driver, the plaintiff recovered, the Judge leaving it to the jury to say whether negligence—that is, want of reasonable care in the company or their servants—was made out. The point that the engine-driver and the labourer were fellow-servants was not raised either by the counsel for the defendants (Channel, Serjt., Shee, Serjt., and Bodkin) or the Judge.

Where a collier was killed while being lowered into the mine through the breaking of a rope, the owner of the colliery superintended the working of it, and allowed a rule made under the statute for its regulation, which required the rope to be tested every morning, to be entirely neglected, and kept in his employment a banksman who he knew habitually disregarded the rule, the Court held that he was guilty of most culpable negligence, and would have been responsible for the death of the servant had there not been contributory negligence on his part.[2] Where a girl under sixteen entered into the employment of rope manufacturers, and was set to work at a machine consisting of revolving rollers worked by steam-power, of which she had had no experience, and while doing as she was bid by the foreman got her hand caught, and lost her arm, Cockburn, C. J., directed the jury that the foreman was put by the defendants in their place to employ the plaintiff, and they were responsible for his negligence, and that there was evidence both of

[1] 11 Jur. 758.
[2] Senior v. Ward, 1 E. and E. 385.

negative and positive negligence on his part—negative in not giving her proper instructions, and positive in directing her to do the act which caused the accident.[1] A railway company employed a person of an inferior grade, who had been a mere ganger or foreman of navvies, to pull down a bridge, a work which required care and skill. Crompton, J., held that there was some evidence, though slight, of negligence on their part in the employment of an incompetent servant; but the evidence being met by proof that the man was of competent skill, the plaintiff, who sued for the loss of her husband who was killed through the negligence of the ganger, failed.[2]

If the servant in the course of his employment is brought into contact, or has to work with, the servants of another, not the master of his master, and is injured by their negligence, he has an action against the master of the negligent servants, as in the case of two railway companies owning a station in common, and the servant of one company being run over by the engine of the other;[3] or where the plaintiff is acting for his master in receiving goods from a warehouse, and the defendant's servants are engaged in delivering and negligently let them fall on the plaintiff.[4]

The true principle which should prevail on this subject would seem to be indicated by Lord Abinger in Priestley v. Fowler, that the master is bound to take the same degree of care of his servant as he can reasonably be expected to do of himself. If a chattel

[1] Grizzle v. Frost, 3 F. and F. 622.

[2] Edwards v. London and Brighton Railway Company, 4 F. and F. 530.

[3] Vose v. Lancashire and Yorkshire Railway Company, 2 H. and N. 728. Warburton v. Great Western Railway Company, L. R., 2 Ex. 30.

[4] Abrahams v. Reynolds, 5 H. and N. 143. See also Fletcher v. Peto, 3 F. and F. 368; Murray v. Currie L. R. 6 C. P. 24.

is let to hire to a man, the hirer is bound to the utmost
care, such as the most diligent father of a family uses,[1]
explained to mean ordinary diligence.[2]   It may be
doubted whether the principle has been correctly
carried out, and whether the master ought not to be
responsible to the servant.

If a horse is hired and injured by the defective
carriage or the carelessness of the servant of the hirer,
the hirer is liable.   In countries where slavery was
an institution (the Roman Empire and the Southern
States of America), on the bailment of a slave the
law was the same as on the bailment of a horse; why
should it be different in the case of a man who owns
himself and lets himself out to hire?   It may be
doubted, therefore, whether the principle enunciated
by Lord Abinger was not departed from in his decision;
and such departure has not been increased by the subsequent decisions, whether the master ought not to be
responsible to the servant for the defects in all those
instruments, human or mechanical, with which he
carries on his business, from the use of which he
derives the profit, which are under his control, and with
which the servant is brought into contact for the master's
benefit, and for which defects the master has, or can
have if he pleases, a remedy for all ill-consequences to
himself.   The reasons given for limiting the liability of
the master to the consequences of his personal negligence, viz., that the servant knows of the perils of the
service and incurs them with his eyes open, and that he
agrees to incur them in consideration of his wages, do
not agree with fact.   The first proves too much.   The
servant's knowledge is the same of the perils he incurs
from the master's personal negligence, and from the
defects of his instruments.   An officer of Engineers,

---

[1] Coggs v. Bernard, 2 Ld. Ray, 916.

[2] Jones, 86, 7, 120; 1 Smith, L. C. 169.

holding an appointment from the Board of Trade, and travelling as a passenger by express train, is more aware of the perils of his journey than a country boy, employed to clean the lamps or shift the carriages, of the danger of his work.

As to the agreement to encounter the risk in consideration of his wages, it may be fairly argued that the wages a servant receives is a mere compensation for the wear and tear of his bones and muscles, and not more than sufficient to find him in the necessaries of life. Very few, if any, are able to lay by anything, or to pay for the education of their children; when their health fails, they are too often the recipients of charity. The employers frequently leave millions behind them.

To suppose that a workman bargains for, or that a master would give, in addition to compensation for services, sufficient to enable the servant to pay the premiums on an accident insurance, is an instance of the power of imagination. The servants who are injured by defective machinery and negligence of other servants are the youngest, the most ignorant, whose wages are the lowest. The number of actions which have been brought for these causes are so many protests against the doctrine—declarations by those who know best that the supposition on which it is grounded is not fact; men will not be torn to pieces by machinery without complaining.

[*See* Employers' Liability Act, 1880 (43 & 44 Vic. c. 42), in Appendix. This Act throws upon the employer the onus of disproving his liability for personal injury inflicted upon a servant by reason of the act or omission of a fellow-servant: otherwise the master is liable for compensation not exceeding the aggregate earnings of three previous years.]

94. By the Factory Act, several provisions are made

for the protection of persons engaged in factories; amongst others it is enacted, that every hoist or teagle, and every fly-wheel directly connected with the steam, or water, or other mechanical power, whether in the engine-house or not, and every part of a steam-engine and water-wheel shall be securely fenced, and every wheel-race not otherwise secured shall be securely fenced close to the edge of the wheel-race, and all dangerous parts of the machinery, and every part of the mill-gearing shall either be securely fenced or be in such position, or of such construction, as to be equally safe to every person employed in the factory as it would be if it were securely fenced.[1] All fencing has to be constantly maintained in an efficient state while the parts required to be fenced are in motion, or are being used for the purpose of any manufacturing process.[2]

On this, it has been held that if a person has been injured for want of the fencing required by the Act, he may sue the occupiers of the factory for damages.[3] That it only requires the machinery to be fenced whilst in motion for a manufacturing process.[4] That a vertical shaft which was not being used for any manufacturing process, and was situate in a room in which no such process was being carried on, need not be fenced, although in motion by the steam power of the factory which was working other shafts in other parts of the factory.[5] That it is the duty of the mill-owner towards all persons to fence his machinery other than mill gearing, and not merely towards young persons and children.[6] That all parts of the machinery should be fenced, and not merely those which are so near the floor as to be

---

[1] See 54 & 55 Vic. c. 75, and 41 Vic. c. 16.

[2] 41 Vic. c. 16; see also 54 & 55 Vic. c. 75.

[3] Caswell v. Worth, 5 E. and B. 849.

[4] Coe v. Platt, 6 Ex. 752; 7 Ex. 460.   [5] Coe v. Platt, 8 Ex. 923.

[6] Coe v. Platt, 6 Ex. 752. Britton v. Great Western Cotton Company, L. R. 7 Ex. 130.

dangerous,[1] and that the mill-owner is not liable to a person injured by the unfenced machinery, if his own negligence contributes to his injury.[2]

95. The master is not bound to give the servant a character.[3] If, in giving the servant a character, he states anything prejudicial to the servant, he is not liable, unless his statement is not only false, but malicious. In giving a character he is bound to state that which he really believes to be true; and the presumption is that he has done so.[4]

96. If a person falsely personates a master, and gives a false character to a person offering himself for a servant,—or if a person offers himself as a servant with a false character, he is liable to a penalty of £20, and, on default of payment, may be committed to prison for a term not exceeding three months nor less than one month.[5]

97. The ordinary remedy for a breach of contract by action at law for damages, is in most cases practically inapplicable to disputes between master and servant; the servant being too poor to pursue it against the master, and incapable of paying the expenses, if used against him. The Legislature has therefore provided cheap and summary remedies and modes of proceedings, as well for as against servants, in several cases. By these statutes the servant, without the necessity of taking any formal proceedings, or employing a lawyer, may have the master summoned before a Magistrate, if he does not pay his wages, and may recover the wages due; and may also, in some cases, be discharged from the contract to serve. Many breaches of contract, and acts of misconduct, on the part of servants, are treated

[1] Dodd v. Shephard, 5 E. and B. 857.
[2] Caswell v. Worth, 5 E. and B. 849. [3] Carrol v. Bird, 3 Esp. 201.
[4] Edmondson v. Stephenson, B. N. P. 8. Rogers v. Clifton, 3 B. and P. 587. Gardner v. Slade, 13 Q. B. 796.
[5] 32 Geo. III. c. 56.

as crimes, and punishable summarily with more or less severity,—especially the embezzlement of the master's property intrusted to the servant to be worked upon, which differs in nothing from theft.

Other statutes provide for the settlement, by arbitration, of disputes between masters and their workmen, in particular manufactures, relating either to the amount of wages to be paid, or the quality of the work done. The arbitrators are to be either a magistrate or a master and a workman of the trade concerning which the dispute arises, chosen in a manner calculated to secure their impartiality.

As it would exceed the limits of this work to set out the statutes relating to disputes between masters and servants at length, such an abstract of their contents is given as shows the particular persons and cases to which they apply, and the punishments which may be inflicted.

By 20 Geo. II. c. 19, complaints, differences, and disputes between masters or mistresses and servants in husbandry hired for one year or longer, or artificers, handicraftsmen, miners, colliers, keelmen, pitmen, glassmen, potters, and other labourers employed for any certain time, or in any other manner, may be heard and determined by one or more Justice or Justices of the Peace of the county, riding, city, liberty, town corporate, or place where the master or mistress inhabits. The Justice may order the payment of so much wages to the servant as seems just, provided the sum in question does not exceed £10 with regard to any servant in husbandry, nor £5 with regard to any artificer, handicraftsman, miner, collier, keelman, pitman, glassman, potter, or labourer. If not paid within twenty-one days, it may be levied by distress and sale of the master's goods. In case of any misdemeanor, miscarriage, or misbehaviour of the servant in his service, the Justice may commit the offender to the House of Correction, there to remain and be corrected and held to hard labour for a reasonable time, not exceeding one calendar month, or may abate part of the wages, or may discharge the servant. In case of misusage, refusal of necessary provision, cruelty, or other ill-treatment by the master of the servant, the Justice may discharge the servant. From the decision of the Justice, except in the case of a commitment, there is an appeal to the Quarter Sessions.

By 27 Geo. II. c. 6, the provisions of 20 Geo. II. c. 19 are extended to tinners and miners employed in the stannaries in the counties of Devon and Cornwall.

By 31 Geo. II. c. 11, the provisions are extended to servants in husbandry, though hired for a less time than a year.

By 6 Geo. III. c. 25, if any artificer, calico-printer, handicraftsman, miner, collier, keelman, pitman, glassman, potter, labourer, or other person, contracts with any person, for any time or times, and absents himself from his service before the term of his contract is completed, or is guilty of any other misdemeanor, a Justice of the county or place where the artificer is found, may, on the complaint of the employer, his steward, or agent, grant his warrant for the apprehension of the servant, and may, after hearing the case, commit him to the House of Correction for a term not exceeding three months nor less than one month. This provision as to punishment is in effect repealed by 4 Geo. IV. c. 34.[1]

By 4 Geo. IV. c. 34, if any servant in husbandry, artificer, calico-printer, handicraftsman, miner, collier, keelman, pitman, glassman, potter, labourer, or other person, contracts with any person or persons to serve

[1] R. v. Youle, 6 H. and N. 753.

him, her, or them, for any time or times, or in any
other manner, and does not enter into or commence the
service according to the contract (the contract being in
writing and signed by the contracting parties), or,
having entered into the service,[1] absents himself from
the service before the term of the contract, whether it
be in writing or not, is completed, or neglects to fulfil
the same, or is guilty of any other misconduct or misdemeanor in the execution of the contract or otherwise
respecting the same, a Justice of the county or place
where the servant contracted, or was employed, or is
found, may issue his warrant to apprehend the servant,
and, after examination, may commit him to the House
of Correction, there to remain and be held to hard
labour for a time not exceeding three months, and
abate a proportional part of his wages for the period of
his imprisonment, or may punish the offender by
abating the whole or part of his wages, or may discharge him from his service.

If the master resides at a considerable distance from
the parish or place where his business is carried on, or
is absent for a long period of time, either beyond the
seas or at a considerable distance from the place of his
business, and intrusts his business to the management
and superintendence of a steward, agent, bailiff, foreman or manager, a Justice of the county or place where
the servant is employed may summon the steward, &c.,
to answer the complaint of the servant touching the
non-payment of his wages, and may make an order on
the steward for the payment of the wages due, provided
the sum in question does not exceed £10. If not paid
within twenty-one days, the amount may be levied by
distress and sale of the goods of the master.

---

[1] Rex v. Lewis, 1 Dowl. and L. 822.   Lindsay v. Leigh, 11 Q. B.
455, and Askew's Case, 2 L. M. and P. 429.

The Justice may order payment of wages to any persons named in the Acts 20 Geo. II. c. 19, and 31 Geo. II. c. 11, within such period as he shall think proper; and in case of non-payment the same may be levied out of the goods of the master. The order of the Justice under 4 Geo. IV. c. 34, is final and conclusive.[1] If there is no evidence of the relation of master and servant, the decision of the magistrate may be impeached, but not if there is evidence both ways.[2]

By 10 Geo. IV. c. 52, the provisions of 4 Geo. IV. c. 34 are extended to persons hired or employed to make felt or hat, or to prepare or work up woollen, linen, fustian, cotton, iron, leather, fur, hemp, flax, mohair, or silk manufactures, or any manufacture made up of wool, fur, hemp, flax, cotton, mohair, or silk, or any of those materials mixed one with another, and to journeymen dyers, and to servants and apprentices employed in the dyeing of felt or hat, or any woollen, linen, fustian, cotton, leather, fur, flax, mohair, or silk materials. By the Master and Servant Act, 1867,[3] which applies only to contracts of service within the meaning of the above, and some other Acts mentioned in its schedule, the following provisions are substituted for such of the enactments of the former Acts as would have applied if the Act of 1867 had not passed.[4]

" Wherever the employer or employed shall neglect or refuse to fulfil any contract of service, or the employed shall neglect or refuse to enter or commence his service according to the contract, or shall absent himself from his service, or wherever any question, difference, or dispute shall arise as to the rights or liabilities of either of the parties, or touching any misusage, misdemeanor, misconduct, ill-treatment, or injury to

[1] Reg. v. Bedwell, 4 E. and B. 213. [2] Re Bailey, 3 E. and B. 607.
[3] 30 & 31 Vict. c. 141. [4] S. 3.

the person or property of either of the parties under any contract of service, the party feeling aggrieved may lay an information or complaint in writing before a Justice, or Magistrate, setting forth the grounds of complaint, and the amount of compensation, damage, or other remedy claimed for the breach or non-performance of such contract, or for any such misusage, misdemeanor, misconduct, ill-treatment, or injury to the person or property of the party so complaining ; and upon such information or complaint being laid, the Justice, or Magistrate shall issue or cause to be issued a summons or citation to the party so complained against, setting out the grounds of complaint, and the amount claimed for compensation, damage, or other remedy, as set forth in the said information or complaint, and requiring such party to appear, at the time and place therein appointed, before two Justices or before a Magistrate, to answer the matter of the information or complaint, so that the same may be then and there heard and determined." [1]

After provisions for serving the summons and securing appearance, it enacts that " upon the hearing of any information or complaint under the provisions of this Act two Justices, or the Magistrate, after due examination, and upon the proof and establishment of the matter of such information or complaint, by an order in writing under their respective hands, in their or his discretion, as the justice of the case requires, either shall make an abatement of the whole or part of any wages then already due to the employed, or else shall direct the fulfilment of the contract of service, with a direction to the party complained against to find forthwith good and sufficient security, by recognizance or bond, with or without sureties, to the satisfaction of a

[1] S. 4.

Justice or Magistrate, for the fulfilment of such contract, or else shall annul the contract, discharging the parties from the same, and apportioning the amount of wages due up to the completed period of such contract, or else where no amount of compensation or damage can be assessed, or where pecuniary compensation will not in the opinion of the Justices or Magistrate, meet the circumstances of the case, shall impose a fine upon the party complained against, not exceeding in amount the sum of twenty pounds, or else shall assess and determine the amount of compensation or damage, together with the costs, to be made to the party complaining, inclusive of the amount of any wages abated, and direct the same to be paid accordingly; and if the order shall direct the fulfilment of the contract, and direct the party complained against to find good and sufficient security as aforesaid, and the party complained against neglect or refuse to comply with such order, a Justice or Magistrate may, if he shall think fit, by warrant under his hand, commit such party to the common gaol or house of correction within his jurisdiction, there to be confined and kept until he shall so find security, but nevertheless so that the term of imprisonment, whether under one or several successive committals, shall not exceed in the whole the period of three months : provided always, that the two Justices or Magistrate may, if they or he think fit, assess and determine the amount of compensation or damage to be paid to the party complaining, and direct the same to be paid, whether the contract is ordered by them or him to be annulled or not, or, in addition to the annulling of the contract of service and discharge of the parties from the same, may, if they or he think fit, impose the fine as hereinbefore authorised, but they or he shall not under the powers of this Act be authorised

K

to annul, nor shall any provisions of this Act have the effect of annulling, any indenture or contract of apprenticeship that they or he might not have annulled or that would not have been annulled if this Act had not been passed.[1]

Where it is alleged by any party to a contract of service that the condition of a recognizance or bond entered into or given for the fulfilment of the contract under the provisions of this Act has not been performed, two Justices or a Magistrate, being satisfied thereof, after hearing the parties and the sureties (if any), or in the absence of any party or surety not appearing after summons or citation in that behalf, may order that the recognizance or bond be enforced for the whole or part of the sum thereby secured, as to the Justices or Magistrate seems fit ; and the sum for which the same is so ordered to be enforced shall be recoverable accordingly in a summary manner under the Acts described in the second schedule to this Act.[2]

Where on the hearing of an information or complaint under this Act an order is made for the payment of money, and the same is not paid as directed, the same shall be recovered by distress of the goods and chattels of the party failing to pay, and in default thereof by imprisonment of such party, according and subject to the Acts below ;[3] but no such imprisonment shall be for more than three months, or be with hard labour.[4]

From and after the expiration of the term of any such imprisonment as aforesaid, the amount of fine, compensation, or damages, together with the costs, so assessed and directed to be paid by any such order as aforesaid, shall be deemed and considered as liquidated

[1] S. 9.   [2] S. 10.   [3] 11 & 12 Vict. c. 43 ; 28 & 29 Vict. c. 127.
[4] 30 & 31 Vict. c. 141, s. 11.

and discharged, and such order shall be annulled accordingly, and the said parties exonerated from their respective obligations under the same : provided always, that no wages or any portion thereof which may be accruing due to the employed under any contract of service after the date of such order shall be assessed to the amount of compensation or damages and costs directed to be paid by him under any such order or warrant of distress, or be seizable or arrestable under the same.[1]

Where Justices or a Magistrate impose any fine or enforce any sum secured by a recognizance or bond under this Act, they or he may, if they or he think fit, direct that a part, not exceeding one-half, of such fine or sum, when recovered, be applied to compensate an employer or employed for any wrong or damage sustained by him by reason of the act or thing in respect of which the fine was imposed, or by reason of the nonfulfilment of the contract of service.[2]

Where on the hearing of an information or complaint under this Act it appears to the Justices or Magistrate that any injury inflicted on the person or property of the party complaining, or the misconduct, misdemeanor, or ill-treatment complained of, has been of an aggravated character, and that such injury, misconduct, misdemeanor, or ill-treatment has not arisen or been committed in the *bonâ fide* exercise of a legal right existing, or *bonâ fide* and reasonably supposed to exist, and further, that any pecuniary compensation or other remedy by this Act provided will not meet the circumstances of the case, then the Justices or Magistrate may, by warrant, commit the party complained against to the common gaol or house of correction within their or his jurisdiction, there to be (in the dis-

---

[1] S. 12.   [2] S. 13.

cretion of the Justices or Magistrate) imprisoned, with or without hard labour, for any term not exceeding three months.[1]

Any party convicted by two Justices or the Magistrate under the provisions of the last preceding section may appeal against the conviction upon finding good and sufficient security, by recognizance or bond, with or without sureties, to the satisfaction of a Justice or Magistrate, to prosecute the said appeal at the next general court of quarter sessions of the peace, to be holden in and for the county or place wherein such conviction shall have been made, and to abide the result of the said appeal according to the usual procedure of such Court, and to pay such costs as that Court may direct, which costs that Court is hereby empowered to award.[2]

No wages shall become payable to or recoverable by any party for or during the term of his imprisonment under any warrant of committal under this Act.[3]

Nothing in the Act is to prevent employer or employed from enforcing their respective civil rights and remedies for any breach or non-performance of the contract of service by any action or suit in the ordinary courts of law or equity in any case where proceedings are not instituted under this Act; nor shall anything in this Act affect the provisions of the Act of the fifth year of King George IV., c. 96:

Nor to interfere with the usual and accustomed mode of procedure in any Court of criminal judicature for the trial of indictable offences relating to wilful and malicious injuries to persons or property committed by masters, workmen, servants, or others, either at common law or under the several statutes made and now in force

---

[1] S. 14.   [2] S. 15.   [3] S. 17.

for the punishment of such offences, but so that no person be twice prosecuted for the same offence.[1]

Except as in this Act expressly otherwise provided, every order or determination of a Justice, Justices, or a Magistrate, shall be final and conclusive, notwithstanding anything in any of the enactments described in the first schedule to this Act.[2]

The word "employer" includes any person, firm, corporation, or company who has entered into a contract of service with any servant, workman, artificer, labourer, apprentice, or other person, and the steward, agent, bailiff, foreman, manager, or factor of such person, firm, corporation, or company:

The word "employed" any servant, workman, artificer, labourer, apprentice, or other person, whether under the age of twenty-one years or above that age, who has entered into a contract of service with any employer:

The words "contract of service" any contract, whether in writing or by parol, to serve for any period of time, or to execute any work, and any indenture or contract of apprenticeship, whether such contract or indenture has been or is made or executed before or after the passing of this Act:

The word "magistrate" means in England, except in the City of London, a stipendiary Magistrate, and in the City of London means the Lord Mayor or an Alderman, sitting at the Mansion House or at the Guildhall:

The word "Justice" means Justice of the Peace:

The words "Two Justices" mean two or more Justices assembled and acting together:

The words "Justice," "Two Justices," "Magistrate," respectively mean a Justice, two Justices, a Magistrate,

---

[1] S. 19. [2] S. 22.

having jurisdiction in the county or place where any contract of service is according to the terms thereof to be executed, or where the party against whom any information, complaint, or proceeding is to be laid' or taken under this Act happens to be.[1]

98. The statute 20 Geo. II. c. 19 extends to every description of labourer, whether employed for a certain time or to do certain work. A man was employed to dig a well, for which he was to receive two shillings a foot; he was at liberty to employ whom he pleased to assist him. It was held that he was a labourer within the statute, and that Justices had jurisdiction to order the payment of his wages. Lord Ellenborough distinguished between his case and that of a journeyman employed in an art, trade, or mystery, or other workman employed in a branch of it. The labourer appears to have been bound to devote his whole time to the work until it was finished.[2]

And a person employed by a calico-printer as a designer to make drawings of the patterns which are engraved on the printing rollers, and subsequently transferred in colours to the fabric itself, is an artificer within the statute 4 Geo. IV. c. 34, or if not an artificer, he may be included within the term "other persons." He is the person who sets the whole in motion, and contributes in a most material degree to the calico-printing manufacture, and may be punished by a Magistrate for a breach of his contract to serve.[3]

An agreement between a shipbuilder and six skilled handicraftsmen to plank a vessel at £5 a ton, and whereby they agreed to exclusively serve him and to

---

[1] S. 2.

[2] Lowther v. the Earl of Radnor, 8 East, 113. Ex parte Gordon, 1 Jur. N. S. 683.

[3] Ex parte Ormrod, 1 D. and L. 825.

employ assistants, is within the statute 4 Geo. IV. c. 34. The words of the statute embrace all contracts for services by handicraftsmen, either for time or in any other manner. The party must be in the exclusive service of the employer, either for a given time or until the completion of work; but whether hired by the day or the quantity of work done is immaterial.[1] With respect to the payment of wages earned the Magistrate has jurisdiction, though the contract is not for any certain time.[2]

Workmen agreed to serve a potter for wages by time, and he made a sub-agreement with another to pay him according to the quantity of work and he pay the workmen their wages. The workmen were held to be servants of the potter.[3] When the service has not commenced, it seems that the contract must be in writing to give the Magistrate jurisdiction. Such contract may be inferred from several writings referring one to the other.[4]

A person employed by an attorney to take care of goods which had been seized under a writ of execution was held not to be a labourer within the statute. The Court held the term "labourer" confined to those labourers the rate of whose wages Justices were empowered to fix by the statute 5 Eliz. c. 4, and that the Legislature had principally in view out-door and country labour; and that the party in that case was not within the statute, because he was employed and paid for the exercise of care and fidelity, and not for manual labour.[5]

---

[1] Lawrence v. Todd, 14 C. B. N. S. 554.
[2] Taylor v. Carr, 2 B. and S. 334.
[3] Willett v. Boote, 6 H. and N. 26.
[4] Crane v. Powell, L. R. 4 C. P. 123.
[5] Branwell v. Penneck, 7 B. and C. 536.

Under the 4th Geo. IV. c. 34, the relation of master
and servant must exist to authorise the Magistrate to
interfere. If the contract is to do certain work, by
which the workman is not bound to devote his whole
time to the performance of the work, but may take in
and do other work for other persons, it is not a contract
to serve, and does not create the relation of master and
servant, and therefore the Magistrate has no jurisdiction under the statute : thus where Hardy had contracted to weave certain pieces of silk goods at certain
prices, and neglected his work, whereupon the Magistrate committed him under the statute, he recovered
damages in an action against the Magistrate for false
imprisonment.[1] A waller contracted to build a wall for
a certain price in a certain time. He refused to complete his work, and was committed to prison by a
Magistrate. It was decided that the Magistrate had
no jurisdiction, because the contract did not create the
relation of master and servant. It did not bind him to
employ his whole time in the work, and not to work
for any other person until it was finished, as appeared
to have been the case in Lowther v. Earl Radnor.[2] On
the same principle a man was discharged from custody
who had been committed to prison by a Magistrate,
because, having entered into a contract to print certain
pieces of woollen cotton goods, he had neglected to
perform his contract.[3]

It has also been decided that the 6th Geo. III. c. 53
does not extend to domestic servants, the words " other
persons " in that statute being confined to servants of
the same class as those specially mentioned, that is,
servants in husbandry, or some trade or business.[4]

[1] Hardy v. Ryle, 9 B. and C. 603.
[2] Lancaster v. Greaves, 9 B. and C. 628.
[3] Ex parte Johnson, 7 Dowl. 702.
[4] Kitchen v. Shaw, 6 A. and E. 729. Ex parte Hughes, 18 Jur. 447.

Nor is a bailiff or superintendent of a farm a servant within the Act.[1]

99. Although the language of the statute 4 Geo. IV. c. 34 is general, and empowers the Magistrate to punish a servant who absents himself from his service, it must be understood in a qualified sense, and as prohibiting merely an absence without lawful excuse. Before the Magistrate can commit, he must be convinced that there was no lawful excuse for the absence, and must express his conviction on the face of his warrant.[2] He ought not to convict unless satisfied that the servant absented himself without lawful excuse, knowing at the time that he had not such excuse.[3] When a servant entered into a contract to serve a master while he was under a prior contract of service and refused to enter the said service, he had lawful excuse for doing so, and could not be convicted.[4] But when the servant deserted because his master would not act upon an arbitration, it was held not to be a lawful excuse.[5] A conviction of the servant for leaving the service does not put an end to the contract, and if after he has suffered imprisonment he refuses to serve he may be convicted again, and has no lawful excuse for absenting himself.[6] The statute does not empower the Magistrate to punish in a case of misconduct which is not reasonably within the execution of the contract; otherwise, the Magistrate might inflict a heavier or slighter punishment than the servant was liable to by law. If

[1] Davis v. Ld. Berwick, 3 E. and E. 549.
[2] Seth Turner's case, 9 Q. B. 80. Re Hammond, 9 Q. B. 92. Re Gerwood, 2 E. and B. 952.
[3] Rider v. Wood, 2 E. and E. 338.
[4] Ashmore v. Horton, 2 E. and E. 360.
[5] Willett v. Boote, 6 H. and N. 26.
[6] Exp. Baker, 7 E. and B. 679; 2 H. and N. 219. R. v. Youle, 7 H. and N. 753. Unwin and Clarke, L. R. 1 Q. B. 417.

in the course of his service, the servant is guilty of a felony, such as stealing or embezzling his master's property, he is entitled to have his case considered by a jury, and the Magistrates have no jurisdiction to decide it.[1]

100. By the 20th Geo. II. c. 19, the Magistrate might commit the servant to the House of Correction, there to remain, *and be corrected.* In the other statutes it is not specified that the servant is to be corrected. This correction means whipping; and if the proceeding is taken under the first statute, it is a necessary part of the sentence; if under the other, it cannot be inflicted.[2]

Under 4 Geo. IV. c. 34, the Magistrate has jurisdiction to entertain a complaint made after the contract of service has ended.[3] Under 20 Geo. II. c. 19, the Magistrate may make a deduction from the amount agreed to be paid, on the ground that there has been no meritorious performance of the contract; for instance, that the servant's work has been badly done.[4] Under 4 Geo. IV. c. 34, s. 3, he may order wages already due to be abated.[5] Under 4 Geo. IV. c. 34, if he ordered the servant to be imprisoned he was bound to order an abatement of the wages during the imprisonment.[6] A decision of the complaint by the County or other competent Court cannot be re-opened by a proceeding under the statutes.[7] If under the Act of 1867 the Magistrates order the servant to fulfil the contract, and order him to be imprisoned in case of default, the subsequent

---

[1] Ex parte Jacklin, 2 D. and L. 103.

[2] Rex v. Hoseason, 14 East, 605.   Wood v. Fenwick, 10 M. and W. 195.

[3] Rex v. Proud, L. R. 1 C. C. R. 71.

[4] Sharp v. Hainsworth, 3 B. and S. 139.

[5] Re Biggins, 5 L. T. N. S. 605.   [6] Re Baker, 2 H. and N. 219.

[7] Routledge v. Hislop, 2 E. and E. 549.

order is, it seems, inoperative. He should be summoned after he has made default.[1]

101. Another mode of settling disputes between masters and workmen is by arbitration, under the statute 5 Geo. IV. c. 96. The following subjects of dispute between masters and workmen, and between workmen and those employed by them in any trade or manufacture, may be arbitrated under the statute :—Disagreements respecting the price to be paid for work done or in the course of being done, whether such disputes respect the payment of wages agreed on, or the hours of work agreed on, or damage done to the work, or delay in finishing the work, or the not finishing the work in a good and workmanlike manner, or according to contract, or to bad materials ;—cases where the workmen are employed to work a new pattern which requires them to purchase new implements, or to make alterations upon old implements for the working thereof, and the masters and workmen cannot agree upon the compensation to be made to the workmen in respect thereof ;—disputes respecting the length, breadth, or quality of pieces of goods, or, in the case of the cotton manufacture, the yarn thereof, or the quantity and quality of the wool thereof ;—disputes respecting the wages or compensation to be paid for pieces of goods made of any great or extraordinary length ;—disputes in the cotton manufacture respecting the manufacture of cravats, shawls, policat, romal, and other handkerchiefs, and the number to be contained in one piece of such handkerchiefs ;—disputes arising out of, for, or touching the particular trade or manufacture, or contracts relative thereto, which cannot be otherwise mutually adjusted and settled ;—disputes between masters and persons engaged in sizing or ornamenting goods.

[1] Crane v. Powell, L. R. 4 C. P. 123.

But Justices are not authorised to establish a rate of wages, or price of labour or workmanship, at which the workman shall in future be paid, unless with the mutual consent of both masters and workmen. Complaints by a workman as to bad materials must be made within three weeks of his receiving the same,— complaints for any cause within fourteen days after the cause of complaint has arisen.[1]

Whenever such subjects of dispute arise, either the master or workmen may demand and have an arbitration. They may come before, or agrèe by writing under their hands to abide by, the decision of any Magistrate of the place where the complainant resides, and he may decide the dispute. If the parties do not appear before the Magistrate, or do not agree to refer the dispute to him, he may summon one party on the complaint of the other, and on the return of the summons, if the cause of complaint continues, he may nominate four or six persons resident in or near the place where the dispute has arisen, one half being master manufacturers, or agents, or foremen of masters, and the other half workmen in the particular manufacture : out of the masters so nominated, the master is to choose one, and out of the workmen, the workman is to choose one, and the two so chosen have full power to settle the dispute.[2]

If either of the arbitrators refuses or delays to accept the arbitration, or neglects to act therein for two days, the Magistrate may appoint another in his stead. If the second arbitrator does not attend, the first may act by himself.[3] The Magistrate is to appoint a time and place of meeting, and to give notice to the arbitrators and parties to the dispute, and to certify the nomination

---

[1] S. 2, 7 Wm. IV., and 1 Vict. c. 67, s. 1.
[2] S. 3, 7 Wm. IV., and 1 Vict. c. 67, s. 2. [3] S. 4.

and appointment in a form prescribed. The arbitrators are to examine the parties and their witnesses, and to determine the dispute within two days after their nomination, exclusive of Sunday. Their decision is final and conclusive.[1] If the complaint is by a workman, of bad warps or utensils, the place of meeting is to be at or as near as may be to the place where the work is carrying on; in other cases, at or as near as may be to the place where the work was given out.[2] If either fails to attend the appointment of arbitrators, the Magistrate may appoint one for him, out of the persons proposed for the absentee's selection.[3] The arbitrators are to inspect the work, if necessary, and to examine the parties and their witnesses.[4] They have power to compel the attendance of witnesses, and to punish them if they refuse to give evidence, by complaining to a Magistrate, who may commit the refractory witness for not more than two calendar months nor less than seven days.[5]

If the arbitrators cannot, within three days, agree, they are to go before the Magistrate by whom they were appointed, or, in his absence, before another of the district where the meeting was held, and state to him the points on which they differ, and he is to decide the case upon their statement within two days.[6] If one of the arbitrators refuses to go before the Magistrate, he may, after summoning him, decide the case on the statement of the other.[7]

In all cases in which masters and workmen agree that their disputes shall be decided by arbitration, whether the cases are those mentioned in the Act or not, and although the mode of arbitration is different from that prescribed by the Act, the award has the same effect

---

[1] S. 5. [2] S. 6. [3] S. 7. [4] S. 8.
[5] S. 9. [6] S. 10. [7] S. 11.

as an award under the Act, and may be enforced in the same way.[1]

If the work has been delivered by an agent or servant of the master, the proceedings may be taken against the agent or servant, and are binding on the principal; and if the business is carried on by a partnership, proceedings against one partner are binding on all.[2] If the master becomes bankrupt, or assigns his property, the award may be enforced against the assignees or trustees, who must satisfy the workmen out of the property assigned.[3] If the complainant is a married woman, or infant, proceedings may be taken in the name of the husband of the married woman, or of the father; or if he be dead, of the mother; or if both be dead, of one of the kindred, or of the surety under an apprentice deed of the infant.[4]

Either party may appoint a deputy in the matter of the arbitration.[5]

If the parties agree, a ticket may be delivered by the manufacturer to the workman, with the work; which ticket, in the event of dispute, is evidence of all things mentioned therein.[6] The master may keep a duplicate of the ticket, which is evidence if the workman does not produce the original.[7]

If a master does not, by himself, his clerk, or foreman, object to work within twenty-four hours after he has received it, he is not allowed afterwards to make any complaint in respect of the work so received.[8]

The parties may agree to extend the time limited by the act for making the award. This agreement must be written on the back of the Magistrate's certificate, and certified and signed by each party in the presence of a

---

[1] S. 13.   [2] S. 14.   [3] S. 16.   [4] S. 17.
[5] S. 15.   [6] S. 18.   [7] S. 19.   [8] S. 20.

witness.[1] The award should be written on the back of the certificate, and should be in a form prescribed by the Act.[2] When the award has been performed, the party in whose favour it is made should give an acknowledgment on the back of the certificate, in a prescribed form.[3]

The arbitrators, or Magistrate when he decides the dispute, have power to settle the expenses of the arbitration, including compensation for loss of time.[4]

The award may be enforced by distress and imprisonment.[5]

By a subsequent Act, called the Arbitration (Masters and Workmen) Act, 1872,[6] it is enacted that,

1. The following provisions shall have effect with reference to agreements under this Act:

(1.) An agreement under this Act shall either designate some board, council, persons or person as arbitrators or arbitrator, or define the time and manner of appointment of arbitrators or of an arbitrator; and shall designate, by name or by description of office or otherwise, some person to be, or some person or persons (other than the arbitrators or arbitrator) to appoint an umpire in case of disagreement between arbitrators:

(2.) A master and a workman shall become mutually bound by an agreement under this Act (hereinafter referred to as " the agreement ") upon the master or his agent giving to the workman and the workman accepting a printed copy of the agreement:

Provided that a workman may, within forty-eight hours after the delivery to him of the

---

[1] S. 21.   [2] S. 22.   [3] S. 23.   [4] S. 31.
[5] S. 24.   [6] 35 & 36 Vict. c. 46.

agreement, give notice to the master or his agent that he will not be bound by the agreement, and thereupon the agreement shall be of no effect as between such workman and the master :

(3.) When a master and workman are bound by the agreement they shall continue so bound during the continuance of any contract of employment and service which is in force between them at the time of making the agreement, or in contemplation of which the agreement is made, and thereafter so long as they mutually consent from time to time to continne to employ and serve without having rescinded the agreement. Moreover, the agreement may provide that any number of days' notice, not exceeding six, of an intention on the part of the master or workman to cease to employ or be employed shall be required, and in that case the parties to the agreement shall continue bound by it respectively until the expiration of the required number of days after such notice has been given by either of the parties :

(4.) The agreement may provide that the parties to it shall, during its continuance, be bound by any rules contained in the agreement, or to be made by the arbitrators, arbitrator, or umpire as to the rate of wages to be paid, or the hours or quantities of work to be performed, or the conditions or regulations under which work is to be done, and may specify penalties to be enforced by the arbitrators, arbitrator, or umpire for the breach of any such rule :

(5.) The agreement may also provide that in case any of the following matters arise they shall be determined by the arbitrators or arbitrator, viz. :

    a. Any such disagreement or dispute as is mentioned in the second section of the principal Act; or

    b. Any question, case, or matter to which the provisions of the Master and Servant Act, 1867, apply ;

and thereupon in case any such matter arises between the parties while they are bound by the agreement the arbitrators, arbitrator, or umpire shall have jurisdiction for the hearing and determination thereof, and upon their or his hearing and determining the same no other proceeding shall be taken before any other court or person for the same matter ; but if the disagreement or dispute is not so heard and determined within twenty-one days from the time when it arose, the jurisdiction of the arbitrators, arbitrator, or umpire shall cease, unless the parties have, since the arising of the disagreement or dispute, consented in writing that it shall be exclusively determined by the arbitrators, arbitrator or umpire :

    A disagreement or dispute shall be deemed to arise at the time of the act or omission to which it relates :

(6.) The arbitrators, arbitrator, or umpire may hear and determine any matter referred to them in such manner as they think fit, or as may be prescribed by the agreement :

(7.) The agreement, and also any rules made by the arbitrators, arbitrator, or umpire in pursuance of its provisions, shall in all proceedings as well before them as in any court be evidence of the terms of the contract of employment and service between the parties bound by the agreement:

(8.) The agreement shall be deemed to be an agreement within the meaning of the thirteenth section of the principal Act for all the purposes of that Act:

(9.) If the agreement provides for the production or examination of any books, documents, or accounts, subject or not to any conditions as to the mode of their production or examination, the arbitrators, arbitrator, or umpire may require the production or examination (subject to any such conditions) of any such books, documents, or accounts in the possession or control of any person summoned as a witness, and who is bound by the agreement, and the provisions of the principal Act, for compelling the attendance and submission of witnesses, shall apply for enforcing such production or examination.

By 8 and 9 Vict. c. 77, manufacturers of woollen, worsted, linen, cotton, or silk hosiery, are bound to deliver to the workman, with the materials, a ticket of the materials and work to be done, containing certain specified particulars, under a penalty not exceeding £5; and the ticket, or duplicate kept by the manufacturer, is evidence in case of disputes. If the dispute relates to the improper or imperfect execution of the work, the work must be produced, and if not produced, must be taken to be properly executed. Power is given to the Magistrate to summon witnesses, and a penalty of £2 is imposed on a witness who has been paid or tendered his reasonable expenses, and does not attend in obedience to the summons.

By 8 and 9 Vict. c. 128, manufacturers of silk goods, or goods made of silk mixed with other materials, are bound to deliver to the weavers, unless both parties by writing under their hands agree to dispense therewith, a ticket stating the count or richness of the warp or cane; the number of shoots or picks required in each inch; the number of threads or weft to be used in each shoot; the name of the manufacturer, or the style or firm under which he carries on his business; the weaver's name, with the date of the engagement; the price in sterling money agreed on for executing each yard imperial standard measure of thirty-six inches of such work in a workmanlike manner; and are bound to make and preserve, until the work has been completed and paid for, a duplicate of the ticket: the ticket or duplicate is evidence in cases of disputes. If the subject of dispute relates to the improper or imperfect execution of the work, it must be produced; if not, it must be taken to be sufficiently and properly executed. Witnesses may be summoned, and if, on being paid or tendered their expenses, they disobey the summons, they are liable to a penalty of £5.

Jurisdiction is given to two Justices to order payment of wages to weavers, together with costs for loss of time, and to authorise weavers, in cases where their wages are not paid, to return their work unfinished, and to fine manufacturers for neglecting to pay wages,—£5 for the first offence, £10 for the second, and £5 extra for every subsequent offence, unless they have delivered to the weavers, within twenty-four hours after their refusal to pay, a note in writing, stating their reasons, and that they intend to have the work arbitrated.

102. A subject connected with the Law of Contracts between master and servant is the law relating to the combination between workmen, for the purpose of compelling masters to raise their wages or alter the conditions of their service. Such combinations are the reverse of the contracts already treated of,—contracts being combinations to work, and combinations being contracts not to work. Combinations between workmen for the purpose of placing them on an equality with their employers produced combinations between employers to enable them to resist the workmen. They were both illegal on common law principles as agreements in restraint of trade,[1] but they have now been legalised, and the law as to violence, molestation, and threat, by which workmen sought to enforce their resolutions, has been defined, by the Trade Union Act, 1871 (34 & 35 Vict. c. 31), as follows:

Criminal Provisions.

2. The purposes of any trade union shall not, by reason merely that they are in restraint of trade, be deemed to be unlawful, so as to render any member of such trade union liable to criminal prosecution for conspiracy or otherwise.

3. The purposes of any trade union shall not, by reason merely that they are in restraint of trade, be unlawful so as to render void or voidable any agreement or trust.

4. Nothing in this Act shall enable any court to entertain any legal proceeding instituted with the object of directly enforcing or recovering damages for the breach of any of the following agreements, namely,

---

[1] Hilton v. Eckersley, 6 E. and B. 47. Hornby v. Close, L. R. 2 Q. B. 143. Farrer v. Close, L. R. 4 Q. B. 602.

(1.) Any agreement between members of a trade union as such, concerning the conditions on which any members for the time being of such trade union shall or shall not sell their goods, transact business, employ, or be employed:

(2.) Any agreement for the payment by any person of any subscription or penalty to a trade union:

(3.) Any agreement for the application of the funds of a trade union,—

    a. To provide benefits to members; or,

    b. To furnish contributions to any employer or workman not a member of such trade union, in consideration of such employer or workman acting in conformity with the rules or resolutions of such trade union; or,

    c. To discharge any fine imposed upon any person by sentence of a court of justice; or,

(4.) Any agreement made between one trade union and another; or,

(5.) Any bond to secure the performance of any of the above-mentioned agreements.

But nothing in this section shall be deemed to constitute any of the above-mentioned agreements unlawful.

    5. The following Acts, that is to say,

(1.) The Friendly Societies Acts, 1855 and 1858, and the Acts amending the same;

(2.) The Industrial and Provident Societies Act, 1867, and any Act amending the same; and

(3.) The Companies Acts, 1862 and 1867,

shall not apply to any trade union, and the registration of any trade union under any of the said Acts shall be void, and the deposit of the rules of any trade union made under the Friendly Societies Acts, 1855 and 1858, and the Acts amending the same, before the passing of this Act, shall cease to be of any effect.

Registered Trade Unions.

6. Any seven or more members of a trade union may by subscribing their names to the rules of the union, and otherwise complying with the provisions of this Act with respect to registry, register such'trade union under this Act, provided that if any one of the purposes of such trade union be unlawful such registration shall be void.

7. It shall be lawful for any trade union registered under this Act to purchase or take upon lease in the names of the trustees for the time being of such union any land not exceeding one acre, and to sell, exchange, mortgage, or let the same, and no purchaser, assignee, mortgagee, or tenant shall be bound to inquire whether the trustees have authority for any sale, exchange, mortgage or letting, and the receipt of the trustees shall be a discharge for the money arising therefrom; and for the purpose of this section every branch of a trade union shall be considered a distinct union.

8. All real and personal estate whatsoever belonging to any trade union registered under this Act shall be vested in the trustees for the time being of the trade union appointed as provided by this Act, for the use and benefit of such trade union and the members thereof, and the real or personal estate of any branch of a trade union shall be vested in the trustees of such branch, and be under the control of such trustees, their respective executors or administrators, according to their respective claims and interests, and upon the death or removal of any such trustees the same shall

vest in the succeeding trustees for the same estate and interest as the former trustees had therein, and subject to the same trusts, without any conveyance or assignment whatsoever, save and except in the case of stocks and securities in the public funds of Great Britain and Ireland, which shall be transferred into the names of such new trustees; and in all actions, or suits, or indictments, or summary proceedings before any court of summary jurisdiction, touching or concerning any such property, the same shall be stated to be the property of the person or persons for the time being holding the said office of trustee, in their proper names, as trustees of such trade union, without any further description.

9. The trustees of any trade union registered under this Act, or any other officer of such trade union who may be authorised so to do by the rules thereof, are hereby empowered to bring or defend, or cause to be brought or defended, any action, suit, prosecution, or complaint in any court of law or equity, touching or concerning the property, right, or claim to property of the trade union; and shall and may, in all cases concerning the real or personal property of such trade union, sue and be sued, plead and be impleaded, in any court of law or equity, in their proper names, without other description than the title of their office; and no such action, suit, prosecution, or complaint shall be discontinued or shall abate by the death or removal from office of such persons or any of them, but the same shall and may be proceeded in by their successor or successors as if such death, resignation, or removal had not taken place; and such successors shall pay or receive the like costs as if the action, suit, prosecution, or complaint had been commenced in their names for the benefit of or to be reimbursed from the funds of such trade union, and the summons to be issued to such

trustee or other officer may be served by leaving the same at the registered office of the trade union.

10. A trustee of any trade union registered under this Act shall not be liable to make good any deficiency which may arise or happen in the funds of such trade union, but shall be liable only for the moneys which shall be actually received by him on account of such trade union.

11. Every treasurer or other officer of a trade union registered under this Act, at such times as by the rules of such trade union he should render such account as hereinafter mentioned, or upon being required so to do, shall render to the trustees of the trade union, or to the members of such trade union, at a meeting of the trade union, a just and true account of all moneys received and paid by him since he last rendered the like account, and of the balance then remaining in his hands, and of all bonds or securities of such trade union, which account the said trustees shall cause to be audited by some fit and proper person or persons by them to be appointed; and such treasurer, if thereunto required, upon the said account being audited, shall forthwith hand over to the said trustees the balance which on such audit appears to be due from him, and shall also, if required, hand over to such trustees all securities and effects, books, papers, and property of the said trade union in his hands or custody; and if he fail to do so the trustees of the said trade union may sue such treasurer in any competent court for the balance appearing to have been due from him upon the account last rendered by him, and for all the moneys since received by him on account of the said trade union, and for the securities and effects, books, papers, and property in his hands or custody, leaving him to set off in such action the sums, if any, which he may have

since paid on account of the said trade union; and in such action the said trustees shall be entitled to recover their full costs of suit, to be taxed as between attorney and client.

12. If any officer, member, or other person being or representing himself to be a member of a trade union registered under this Act, or the nominee, executor, administrator, or assignee of a member thereof, or any person whatsoever, by false representation or imposition obtain possession of any moneys, securities, books, papers, or other effects of such trade union, or, having the same in his possession, wilfully withhold or fraudulently misapply the same, or wilfully apply any part of the same to purposes other than those expressed or directed in the rules of such trade union, or any part thereof, the court of summary jurisdiction for the place in which the registered office of the trade union is situate, upon a complaint made by any person on behalf of such trade union, or by the registrar, or in Scotland at the instance of the procurator fiscal of the court to which such complaint is competently made, or of the trade union, with his concurrence, may, by summary order, order such officer, member, or other person to deliver up all such moneys, securities, books, papers, or other effects to the trade union, or to repay the amount of money applied improperly, and to pay, if the court think fit, a further sum of money not exceeding twenty pounds, together with costs not exceeding twenty shillings; and, in default of such delivery of effects, or repayment of such amount of money, or payment of such penalty and costs aforesaid, the said court may order the said person so convicted to be imprisoned, with or without hard labour, for any time not exceeding three months: provided, that nothing herein contained shall prevent the said trade union, or

L

in Scotland Her Majesty's Advocate, from proceeding
by indictment against the said party; provided also
that no person shall be proceeded against by indictment if a conviction shall have been previously obtained for the same offence under the provisions of this
Act.

Registry of Trade Union.

13. With respect to the registry, under this Act, of
a trade union, and of the rules thereof, the following
provisions shall have effect :

(1.) An application to register the trade union
and printed copies of the rules, together with
a list of the titles and names of the officers,
shall be sent to the registrar under this Act:

(2.) The registrar, upon being satisfied that the
trade union has complied with the regulations
respecting registry in force under this Act,
shall register such trade union and such
rules:

(3.) No trade union shall be registered under a
name identical with that by which any other
existing trade union has been registered, or
so nearly resembling such name as to be likely
to deceive the members or the public:

(4.) Where a trade union applying to be registered has been in operation for more than a
year before the date of such application, there
shall be delivered to the registrar before the
registry thereof a general statement of the
receipts, funds, effects, and expenditure of
such trade union in the same form, and showing the same particulars, as if it were the
annual general statement required as herein-

after mentioned to be transmitted annually to the registrar:

(5.) The registrar upon registering such trade union shall issue a certificate of registry, which certificate, unless proved to have been withdrawn or cancelled, shall be conclusive evidence that the regulations of this Act with respect to registry have been complied with:

(6.) One of Her Majesty's Principal Secretaries of State may from time to time make regulations respecting registry under this Act, and respecting the seal (if any) to be used for the purpose of such registry, and the forms to be used for such registry, and the inspection of documents kept by the registrar under this Act, and respecting the fees, if any, to be paid on registry, not exceeding the fees specified in the second schedule to this Act, and generally for carrying this Act into effect.

14. With respect to the rules of a trade union registered under this Act, the following provisions shall have effect:

(1.) The rules of every such trade union shall contain provisions in respect of the several matters mentioned in the first schedule to this Act:

(2.) A copy of the rules shall be delivered by the trade union to every person on demand, on payment of a sum not exceeding one shilling.

15. Every trade union registered under this Act shall have a registered office to which all communications and notices may be addressed; if any trade union under this Act is in operation for seven days without having such an office, such trade union and every officer thereof shall each incur a penalty not exceeding

five pounds for every day during which it is so in operation.

Notice of the situation of such registered office, and of any change therein, shall be given to the registrar and recorded by him: until such notice is given the trade union shall not be deemed to have complied with the provisions of this Act.

16. A general statement of the receipts, funds, effects, and expenditure of every trade union registered under this Act shall be transmitted to the registrar before the first day of June in every year, and shall show fully the assets and liabilities at the date, and the receipts and expenditure during the year preceding the date to which it is made out, of the trade union; and shall show separately the expenditure in respect of the several objects of the trade union, and shall be prepared and made out up to such date, in such form, and shall comprise such particulars, as the registrar may from time to time require; and every member of, and depositor in, any such trade union shall be entitled to receive, on application to the treasurer or secretary of that trade union, a copy of such general statement, without making any payment for the same.

Together with such general statement there shall be sent to the registrar a copy of all alterations of rules and new rules and changes of officers made by the trade union during the year preceding the date up to which the general statement is made out, and a copy of the rules of the trade union as they exist at that date.

Every trade union which fails to comply with or acts in contravention of this section, and also every officer of the trade union so failing, shall each be liable to a penalty not exceeding five pounds for each offence.

Every person who wilfully makes or orders to be made any false entry in or any omission from any such general statement, or in or from the return of such copies of rules or alterations of rules, shall be liable to a penalty not exceeding fifty pounds for each offence.

17. The registrars of the friendly societies in England, Scotland, and Ireland shall be the registrars under this Act.

The registrars shall lay before Parliament annual reports with respect to the matters transacted by such registrars in pursuance of this Act.

18. If any person with intent to mislead or defraud gives to any member of a trade union registered under this Act, or to any person intending or applying to become a member of such trade union, a copy of any rules or of any alterations or amendments of the same other than those respectively which exist for the time being, on the pretence that the same are the existing rules of such trade union, or that there are no other rules of such trade union, or if any person with the intent aforesaid gives a copy of any rules to any person on the pretence that such rules are the rules of a trade union registered under this Act which is not so registered, every person so offending shall be deemed guilty of a misdemeanour.

Legal Proceedings.

19. In England and Ireland all offences and penalties under this Act may be prosecuted and recovered in manner directed by The Summary Jurisdiction Acts.

In England and Ireland summary orders under this Act may be made and enforced on complaint before a court of summary jurisdiction in manner provided by The Summary Jurisdiction Acts.

Provided as follows :

1. The "Court of Summary Jurisdiction," when

hearing and determining an information or complaint, shall be constituted in some one of the following manners ; that is to say,

    (A.) In England,

        (1.) In any place within the jurisdiction of a metropolitan police magistrate or other stipendiary magistrate, of such magistrate or his substitute :

        (2.) In the city of London, of the Lord Mayor or any alderman of the said city :

        (3.) In any other place, of two or more justices of the peace sitting in petty sessions.

    (B.) In Ireland,

        (1.) In the police district of Dublin metropolis, of a divisional justice :

        (2.) In any other place, of a resident magistrate.

In Scotland all offences and penalties under this Act shall be prosecuted and recovered by the procurator fiscal of the county in the Sheriff Court, under the provisions of The Summary Procedure Act, 1864.

In Scotland summary orders under this Act may be made and enforced on complaint in the Sheriff Court.

All the jurisdictions, powers, and authorities necessary for giving effect to these provisions relating to Scotland are hereby conferred on the sheriffs and their substitutes.

Provided that in England, Scotland, and Ireland—

2. The description of any offence under this Act in the words of such Act shall be sufficient in law.

3. Any exception, exemption, proviso, excuse, or qualification, whether it does or not accompany the description of the offence in this Act, may be proved by the defendant, but need not be specified or negatived in the information, and if so specified or negatived, no proof in relation to the matters so specified or negatived

shall be required on the part of the informant or pro-secutor.

20. In England or Ireland, if any party feels ag-grieved by any order or conviction made by a court of summary jurisdiction on determining any complaint or information under this Act, the party so aggrieved may appeal therefrom, subject to the conditions and regula-tions following :

> (1.) The appeal shall be made to some court of general or quarter sessions for the county or place in which the cause of appeal has arisen, holden not less than fifteen days and not more than four months after the decision of the court from which the appeal is made :

> (2.) The appellant shall, within seven days after the cause of appeal has arisen, give notice to the other party and to the court of summary jurisdiction of his intention to appeal, and of the ground thereof :

> (3.) The appellant shall immediately after such notice enter into a recognizance before a justice of the peace in the sum of ten pounds, with two sufficient sureties in the sum of ten pounds, conditioned personally to try such appeal, and to abide the judgment of the court thereon, and to pay such costs as may be awarded by the court :

> (4.) Where the appellant is in custody the justice may, if he think fit, on the appellant entering into such recognizance as aforesaid, release him from custody :

> (5.) The court of appeal may adjourn the appeal, and upon the hearing thereof they may con-firm, reverse, or modify the decision of the court of summary jurisdiction, or remit the

matter to the court of summary jurisdiction
with the opinion of the court of appeal
thereon, or make such other order in the
matter as the court thinks just, and if the
matter be remitted to the court of summary
jurisdiction the said last-mentioned court
shall thereupon re-hear and decide the information or complaint in accordance with
the opinion of the said court of appeal. The
court of appeal may also make such order as
to costs to be paid by either party as the
court thinks just.

21. In Scotland it shall be competent to any person
to appeal against any order or conviction under this
Act to the next Circuit Court of Justiciary, or where
there are no Circuit Courts to the High Court of
Justiciary at Edinburgh, in the manner prescribed by
and under the rules, limitations, conditions, and restrictions contained in the Act passed in the twentieth
year of the reign of His Majesty King George the
Second, chapter forty-three, in regard to appeals to
Circuit Courts in matters criminal, as the same may be
altered or amended by any Acts of Parliament for the
time being in force.

All penalties imposed under the provisions of this
Act in Scotland may be enforced in default of payment
by imprisonment for a term to be specified in the summons or complaint, but not exceeding three calendar
months.

All penalties imposed and recovered under the provisions of this Act in Scotland shall be paid to the
sheriff clerk, and shall be accounted for and paid by
him to the Queen's and Lord Treasurer's Remembrancer on behalf of the Crown.

22. A person who is a master, or father, son, or

brother of a master, in the particular manufacture, trade, or business in or in connection with which any offence under this Act is charged to have been committed shall not act as or as a member of a court of summary jurisdiction or appeal for the purposes of this Act.

Definitions.

23. In this Act—

The term Summary Jurisdiction Acts means as follows:

As to England, the Act of the session of the eleventh and twelfth years of the reign of Her present Majesty, chapter forty-three, intituled "An Act to facilitate the performance of the duties of justices of the peace out of sessions within England and Wales with respect to summary convictions and orders," and any Acts amending the same :

As to Ireland, within the police district of Dublin metropolis, the Acts regulating the powers and duties of justices of the peace for such district, or of the police of such district, and elsewhere in Ireland, "the Petty Sessions (Ireland) Act, 1851," and any Act amending the same.

In Scotland, the term "misdemeanor" means a crime and offence.

The term "trade union" means such combination, whether temporary or permanent, for regulating the relations between workmen and masters, or between workmen and workmen, or between masters and masters, or for imposing restrictive conditions on the conduct of any trade or business, as would, if this Act had not passed, have been deemed to have been an unlawful combination by reason of some one or more of its purposes being in restraint of trade : provided that this Act shall not affect—

1. Any agreement between partners as to their own business ;

2. Any agreement between an employer and those employed by him as to such employment ;

3. Any agreement in consideration of the sale of the goodwill of a business or of instruction in any profession, trade, or handicraft.

[*See* also Trade Union Act Amendment Act, 1876 (39 & 40 Vic. c. 22), in Appendix.]

FIRST SCHEDULE.

Of Matters to be provided for by the Rules of Trades Unions registered under this Act.

1. The name of the trade union and place of meeting for the business of the trade union.

2. The whole of the objects for which the trade union is to be established, the purposes for which the funds thereof shall be applicable, and the conditions under which any member may become entitled to any benefit assured thereby, and the fines and forfeitures to be imposed on any member of such trade union.

3. The manner of making, altering, amending, and rescinding rules.

4. A provision for the appointment and removal of a general committee of management, of a trustee or trustees, treasurer, and other officers.

5. A provision for the investment of the funds, and for an annual or periodical audit of accounts.

6. The inspection of the books and names of members of the trade union by every person having an interest in the funds of the trade union.

SECOND SCHEDULE.

Maximum Fees.

	£	s.	d.
For registering trade union	1	0	0
For registering alterations in rules . . .	0	10	0
For inspection of documents	0	2	6

103. By the Act to amend the Criminal Law relating to Violence, Threats, and Molestation,[1]

1. Every person who shall do any one or more of the following acts; that is to say,

    (1.) Use violence to any person or any property,

    (2.) Threaten or intimidate any person in such manner as would justify a justice of the peace, on complaint made to him, to bind over the person so threatening or intimidating to keep the peace,

    (3.) Molest or obstruct any person in manner defined by this section,

with a view to coerce such person,—

    (1.) Being a master to dismiss or to cease to employ any workman, or being a workman to quit any employment or to return work before it is finished;

    (2.) Being a master not to offer or being a workman not to accept any employment or work;

    (3.) Being a master or workman to belong or not to belong to any temporary or permanent association or combination;

    (4.) Being a master or workman to pay any fine or penalty imposed by any temporary or permanent association or combination;

    (5.) Being a master to alter the mode of carrying on his business, or the number or description of any persons employed by him,

shall be liable to imprisonment, with or without hard labour, for a term not exceeding three months.

A person shall, for the purposes of this Act, be deemed to molest or obstruct another person in any of the following cases; that is to say,

---

[1] 34 & 35 Vict. c. 32.

(1.) If he persistently follow such person about from place to place :

(2.) If he hide any tools, clothes, or other property owned or used by such person, or deprive him of or hinder him in the use thereof :

(3.) If he watch or beset the house or other place where such person resides or works, or carries on business, or happens to be, or the approach to such house or place, or if with two or more other persons he follow such person in a disorderly manner in or through any street or road.

Nothing in this section shall prevent any person from being liable under any other Act, or otherwise, to any other or higher punishment than is provided for any offence by this section, so that no person be punished twice for the same offence.

Provided that no person shall be liable to any punishment for doing or conspiring to do any act on the ground that such act restrains or tends to restrain the free course of trade, unless such act is one of the acts hereinbefore specified in this section, and is done with the object of coercing as hereinbefore mentioned.

Legal Proceedings.

2. All offences under this Act shall be prosecuted under the provisions of The Summary Jurisdiction Acts.

Provided as follows :—

(1.) The " Court of Summary Jurisdiction," when hearing and determining an information or complaint, shall be constituted in some one of the following manners ; (that is to say,)

(a.) In England,

(i.) In any place within the jurisdiction of a metropolitan police magistrate or other stipendiary magistrate, of such magistrate or his substitute:

(ii.) In the city of London, of the Lord Mayor or any alderman of the said city:

(iii.) In any other place, of two or more justices of the peace sitting in petty sessions.

(*b.*) In Scotland, of the Sheriff of the county or his substitute.

(*c.*) In Ireland,

(i.) In the police district of Dublin metropolis, of a divisional justice:

(ii.) In any other place, of a resident magistrate.

(2.) The description of any offence under this Act in the words of such Act shall be sufficient in law.

(3.) Any exception, exemption, proviso, excuse, or qualification, whether it does or not accompany the description of the offence in this Act, may be proved by the defendant, but need not be specified or negatived in the information, and if so specified or negatived, no proof in relation to the matters so specified or negatived shall be required on the part of the informant or prosecutor.

3. In England and Ireland, if any party feels aggrieved by any order or conviction made by a court of summary jurisdiction on determining any complaint or information under this Act, the party so aggrieved may appeal therefrom, subject to the conditions and regulations following:

(1.) The appeal shall be made to some court of general or quarter sessions for the county or place in which the cause of appeal has arisen, holden not less than fifteen days and not more than four months after the decision of the court from which the appeal is made :

(2.) The appellant shall, within seven days after the cause of appeal has arisen, give notice to the other party and to the court of summary jurisdiction of his intention to appeal, and of the ground thereof :

(3.) The appellant shall immediately after such notice enter into a recognizance in the sum of ten pounds before a justice of the peace, with two sufficient sureties in the sum of ten pounds, conditioned personally to try such appeal, and to abide the judgment of the court thereon, and to pay such costs as may be awarded by the court:

(4.) Where the appellant is in custody the justice may, if he think fit, on the appellant entering into such recognizance as aforesaid, release him from custody :

(5.) The court of appeal may adjourn the appeal, and upon the hearing thereof they may confirm, reverse, or modify the decision of the court of summary jurisdiction, or remit the matter to the court of summary jurisdiction with the opinion of the court of appeal thereon, or make such other order in the matter as the court thinks just, and, if the matter be remitted to the court of summary jurisdiction, the said last-mentioned court shall thereupon re-hear and decide the information or complaint in accordance with the opinion of the said court of appeal. The court of appeal may also make such order as to costs to be paid by either party· as the court thinks just.

4. In Scotland it shall be competent to any person to appeal against any order or conviction under this Act to the next Circuit Court of Justiciary, or where there are no Circuit Courts to the High Court of Justiciary at Edinburgh, in the manner prescribed by and under the rules, limitations, conditions, and restrictions contained in the Act passed in the twentieth year of the reign of His Majesty King George the Second, chapter forty-three, in regard to appeals to Circuit Courts in matters criminal, as the same may be altered or amended by any Acts of Parliament for the time being in force.

All offences under this Act shall be prosecuted by the procurator fiscal of the county.

5. A person who is a master, father, son, or brother of a master in the particular manufacture, trade, or business in or in connection with which any offence under this Act is charged to have been committed shall not act as or as a member of a court of summary jurisdiction or appeal for the purposes of this Act.

Definitions.

6. In this Act—

The term Summary Jurisdiction Acts shall mean as follows :

As to England, the Act of the session of the eleventh and twelfth years of the reign of Her present Majesty, chapter forty-three, intituled "An Act to facilitate the performance of the duties of Justices of the Peace out of Sessions within England and Wales with respect to Summary

Convictions and Orders," and any Acts amending the same ;

As to Scotland, "The Summary Procedure Act,
1864 ; "

As to Ireland, within the police district of Dublin
metropolis, the Acts regulating the powers and
duties of justices of the peace for such district
or of the police of such district, and elsewhere
in Ireland, "The Petty Sessions (Ireland) Act,
1851," and any Act amending the same.

A combination amongst workmen to raise the price of
labour is a violent and unnatural interference with the
laws of demand and supply which regulate the price
of labour, and is more injurious to the workmen themselves than to any one else. The immediate effect of a
combination is to throw the parties to it out of employment, and deprive them of their means of support. If
successful, it raises the price of the commodity, and
diminishes the demand for it, and for the labour of the
workmen employed in producing it. A combination
has sometimes the effect of compelling masters to intro-
duce new workmen into their trades : and while it
decreases the fund to be divided amongst the labourers,
increases the number of those who are to be supported
by it. It tends therefore to diminish the demand for
labour, and to increase the supply of it. It can never
be ultimately successful, because the superfluous labourers who are deprived of work by the first consequence of the combination, must go on competing
for employment until the demand for their work is
increased so as to employ them all, which it cannot be
until prices and wages are brought to their former
level, or below it.

The only mode by which workmen's wages can be

permanently and effectually raised, is by the demand
for labour increasing faster than the supply. This
may happen in the case of particular workmen, by an
improvement in their skill beyond that of their fellows.
In the case of the general body of workmen in a particular trade, their condition may be improved by an
extension of the demand for the commodities they produce, which can only be caused by producing the
things more quickly and cheaply, and thereby increasing the class of persons who use them. But the condition of the general body of workmen can only be
improved by an increased production of the necessaries
and conveniences of life, so that there may be enough
for all. If these increase in sufficient quantity, every
workman will be enabled to have them, however low
his wages; if they do not, he cannot, however high his
wages. Thus, supposing a sufficient quantity of stockings are not manufactured for every person in the
kingdom, some must go without; but if more than
sufficient are manufactured, every workman will be
able to have stockings, because the prices must fall so
as to be within the means of the workman who receives
the lowest wages, or the stockings must remain unsold
and useless to the manufacturer.

Combinations are usually entered into upon the
supposition that the workman does not receive his fair
share of the profits of the manufacture. Upon this
subject the observations in the *Edinburgh Review* are
worthy of attention. "The capitalist and the workman are joint agents,—co-operative partners, in fact,—
in the production of a certain article (say cotton cloth),
and joint sharers in the profit arising out of the sale.
The capitalist supplies funds, machinery, and superintendence; the workman supplies handicraft skill and
manual labour. At the end of the year, or of some

shorter period, the net returns are to be divided between them, in a proportion either formally agreed upon or tacitly decided by custom.

"But the labourer is a poor man; he has no store in his cupboard, and no money in his purse. He must purchase food, clothing, and shelter from day to day, and therefore cannot wait until the end of the year to receive his share of the common gain. The capitalist, therefore, should advance to him what it is thought probable that his share will amount to, minus, perhaps, the interest on the advance, and possibly some further small deduction to compensate the risk of having over-estimated the workman's share.

"But further, the results of a manufacturing enterprise are sometimes not profit, but loss,—always occasional loss,—frequently loss for years together,—sometimes even loss on the whole. But the workman, who could not bear to wait, can still less bear his share of the loss: the capitalist has therefore to encounter all the losses, for he cannot call upon the labourer to refund the wages he has received.

"The original compact (tacit or formal) by which the division of profits would have been otherwise determined has thus become modified, for the convenience of the workmen, into the form in which we at present see it. The workman receives his share of the profits before any profits are made; he receives his share in years in which no profit is made; he receives it in years in which profits are turned into losses; he receives it sometimes when the master is being gradually ruined in the partnership, which, if he be but prudent, will have enriched it. What deductions from his original share should be made in consideration of all these predicates? It is evident that, in common justice, he cannot expect to receive as much as if he waited till profits were realised, and bore his proportion of losses when losses were incurred.

"The workman's wages, then, are his share of the profits commuted into a fixed payment. This commuted share he is sure of receiving as long as the manufacturing enterprise in which he is engaged actually goes on. The capitalist alone endures all the losses, alone furnishes all the advances, alone encounters the risk of ruin, and receives only the share of profit which may remain over after the labourer's commuted share is paid. The workman's share is a first mortgage,—the capitalist's share is only a reversionary claim."[1]

It may be added, that when capitalists receive more than their just share of profits, their capital increases faster than they can find use for it, and they embark it in undertakings by which they employ labour to the profit of the labourer, but to their own loss. This is generally true; unprofitable speculation, or, in other words, the employment of labour which is solely beneficial to the labourer, being the natural result of the too rapid accumulation of capital: although there are some men who, from peculiar sagacity or good fortune, choose only profitable investments of capital, and avoid the bad; and others who, from different causes, adopt an opposite course. The result is the same to the labourer, for, however capital is employed, it is always to his advantage.

All the money or capital in the world is constantly being used in the employment of labour: the faster it circulates, the more labourers are employed, and the better is their condition. The combination of and stoppage of work by workmen does not hasten the circulation of capital, and therefore is not the remedy for the evils they suffer. On the contrary, the circula-

[1] Edinburgh Review, April, 1849, p. 427.

tion of capital is increased by the subordination of the workman to his employer. The more complete this subordination, the greater is the confidence of the capitalist in the labourer, and the more readily is he induced to employ his capital.

A combination is always an evil, because it involves a stoppage of work : the things which would have been produced in the interval are lost to the consumer : the wages that would have been earned are lost to the workman ; the profits that would have been made are lost to the employer, and the circulation of capital is impeded.

FORMS OF CONTRACTS.

I.—*Contract to build a House, &c., under the Superintendence of a Surveyor; with a Surety for the
Builder.*

AGREEMENT made the   day of   , in the year of
our Lord   , between T. G., of   , Builder,
of the first part; T. C., of   , of the second
part; and J. B., of   , of the third part.
WHEREAS the said J. B. is possessed of a piece of ground
situate   , upon which he is desirous of
erecting a dwelling-house and offices according to the
elevation, plans, and specifications prepared for that
purpose by W. M., surveyor, and under the direction
and to the satisfaction of the said W. M. or other surveyor for the time being of the said J. B., his executors,
administrators, or assigns, which said elevation, plans,
and specifications are marked with the letters A, B, C,
D, E, F, and G, and are signed by the said T. G., T. C.,
and J. B., and the said specification is contained in the
schedule hereunder written, or hereunto annexed; AND
the said T. G. has proposed to erect and complete the
said dwelling-house and offices, and to make and
execute all other works mentioned and specified in the
said elevation, plans, and specifications, within the time
hereinafter limited for that purpose, and according to
the stipulations and agreements hereinafter contained,
at or for the price or sum of £4,480, which proposal
the said J. B. hath agreed to accept of the said T. G.,
together with the said T. C. as his surety, entering into
the agreements hereinafter contained:

M

Now it is hereby witnessed, That the said T. G. and T. C. do for themselves, their heirs, executors and administrators, and each and every one of them doth for himself, his heirs, executors, and administrators, hereby agree with and to the said J. B., his executors, administrators and assigns, in manner following: (that is to say,) that he the said T. G. shall at his own costs and charges forthwith erect and complete, make and execute, with all proper and necessary materials, workmanship and labour of the best kinds in every respect, and in the most substantial and workmanlike manner, upon the said piece of ground, a dwelling-house and offices behind the same, with the appurtenances and all other works, matters and things mentioned and specified in the same elevation, plans, and specification, under the direction and to the satisfaction of the said W. M. or other the surveyor for the time being of the said J. B., his executors, administrators or assigns; And for that purpose shall find and provide all proper and necessary materials, tools, scaffolding, cartage, cordage, and other implements and machinery: and shall make good all damages which may be occasioned either to the said dwelling-house, offices, and works, or any of them, or to adjoining buildings by the execution of the same works or any of them: and shall cleanse all bog-holes, drains, and cesspools in or about the premises, and cart and clear away at such times and in such manner as shall or may be directed by the said W. M. or other surveyor as aforesaid, all surplus earth and waste or useless materials, implements and machinery which may from time to time remain during the execution of the same works, or at the completion thereof; And also shall pay and discharge all fees now due, or hereafter to become due, to the district surveyor or surveyors in respect of the premises, and shall indemnify the said J. B., his executors, administrators and assigns, of and from the same fees, and all claims and demands on account thereof: AND shall at his own costs and charges from time to time, until the said dwelling-house, offices, and works shall be erected, completed, made, and executed, and the said J. B., his executors, administrators or assigns, shall take possession of the premises, insure or cause to be insured, in the joint names of the said J. B., his executors, administrators or assigns, and of the said T. G., his executors, or administrators, and for the sum of £   , all and singular the erections and buildings for the time being standing on the said piece of ground, to the full value thereof, in some or one of the public insurance offices in London or Westminster, and shall deliver the policy of insurance to the said J. B., his executors, administrators and assigns, and shall produce and show to the said J. B., his executors, administrators or assigns, the receipts for the premium and duty attending such insurance from time to time, when requested so to do; and that in case of fire, all the moneys to be recovered by virtue of such insurance shall forthwith be applied in reinstating the premises, under the direction and to the approbation of the said W. M. or other surveyor as aforesaid: AND that the said· T. G. shall well and sufficiently cover in, or cause to be covered in, the dwelling-house and offices so to be erected as aforesaid, before the   day of   ; and shall complete, make and execute, or cause to be completed, made and executed, all and singular the said dwelling-house, offices, and other works in manner aforesaid, and according to the true intent and meaning of these presents before the   day of   ; AND that if the said T. G., his executors or administrators, shall not so well and sufficiently cover in the

M

said dwelling-houses and offices before the said
day of   , or shall not so complete, make and
execute the said dwelling-house, offices, and works,
before the said   day of   , they the said
T. G. and T. C. shall pay to the said J. B., the sum of
£5 for every week during which the said dwelling-
house and offices shall remain uncovered in after the
said   day of   , and the like sum for
every week the said dwelling-house, offices, and works
shall remain unfinished after the said   day of
            ; which sums may be recovered as liquidated
damages, or may be deducted from the sums payable
to the said T. G. under this agreement. PROVIDED
ALWAYS, that in case the said J. B., his executors,
administrators or assigns, or his or their surveyor,
shall require any extra or additional works to be done,
or shall cause the works to be delayed in their commencement or their progress, the said T. G. shall be
allowed to have such additional time for covering in
and finishing the said buildings and works, beyond the
said days above fixed, as shall have been necessarily
consumed in the performance of such extra or additional
works, or as shall have been lost by the delay caused
by the said J. B., his executors, administrators or
assigns, or his or their surveyor as aforesaid; and the
said payments for delay shall not become payable until
after the expiration of such additional time or times.

AND the said T. G. and T. C. do hereby further
agree with the said J. B., that in case the said W. M.
or other surveyor as aforesaid shall be dissatisfied with
the conduct of any workman employed by the said
T. G. in the said works, or with any materials used or
brought upon the said premises for the purpose of being
used in the said works, and shall give notice thereof in
writing under his hand to the said T. G., he the said

T. G. will forthwith discharge such workman from the said works and remove the said materials; and that in case the said T. G. shall not in the judgment of the said W. M. or other surveyor as aforesaid, employ a sufficient number of workmen in the execution of the said works, or have on the premises a sufficient quantity of materials, tools or implements of proper quality for the said works, and the said W. M. or other surveyor as aforesaid shall by writing under his hand require the said T. G. to employ an additional number of workmen, or bring upon the premises an additional quantity of material, tools or implements of proper quality, and shall specify in such notice the number and description of additional workmen to be employed, and the quantity and description of additional materials, tools or implements to be supplied, and the said T. G. shall forthwith employ in the said works such additional number of workmen, and shall forthwith bring upon the premises such additional quantity of materials, tools or implements for the said works; and that in case he shall refuse or neglect for the space of seven days to comply with any such notice or request, it shall be lawful for the said W. M. or other surveyor as aforesaid to dismiss and discharge the said T. G. from the further execution of the said works, and for the said J. B., his executors, administrators and assigns, to employ some other person to complete the same; and that in such case the sum agreed to be paid to such other person to complete the said works (such sum being approved by the said W. M. or other surveyor as aforesaid) shall be deducted from the said sum of £4,480, and the balance, after making any other deductions which the said J. B. shall be entitled to make under this agreement, shall be paid by the said J. B. to the said T. G. in full for the work done by him, at the expiration of one month after he shall have been so discharged as aforesaid: AND it is hereby further agreed by and between the parties hereto, that all the materials brought upon the said piece of ground for the purpose of being used in the said buildings, except such as shall be disapproved of by the said W. M. or other surveyor as aforesaid, shall, immediately they shall be brought upon the said premises, become the property of the said J. B., and shall be used in the said works.

AND the said J. B. doth hereby, in consideration of the work so agreed to be done by the said T. G., agree with the said T. G., that he, the said J. B., shall pay to the said T. G. for the same the said sum of £ in manner following : that is to say, the sum of £150 within one week after the said W. M. or other surveyor as aforesaid shall have certified in writing to the said J. B., his executors, administrators or assigns, under his hand, that work to the value of £200 has been done under this agreement, and the further sum of £150 within one week after the said W. M. or such other surveyor shall have certified as aforesaid, that further work to the value of £200 has been done under this agreement, and so on shall pay £150 for every £200 worth of work so certified as aforesaid, until the whole of the said work shall be finished, and shall pay the balance remaining unpaid within one month after the said work shall have been completed and finished to the satisfaction of the said W. M. or such other surveyor, and the said W. M. or such other surveyor shall have certified to the said J. B. that the said works have been completed and finished to his satisfaction. PROVIDED ALWAYS, and it is hereby further agreed by the parties hereto, and particularly by the said T. G. and T. C., that if the said J. B., his executors, administrators or assigns, shall at any time or times be desirous of making any alterations or additions in the erection or execution of the said dwelling-house, offices, and other works, then and in such case the said T. G. shall erect, complete, make and execute the said dwelling-house, offices, and other works, with such alterations and additions as the said J. B., his executors, administrators or assigns, or the said W. M. or such other surveyor, shall from time to time direct by writing under his or their hand or hands, and to the satisfaction of the said W. M. or such other surveyor; and the sum and sums of money to be paid or allowed between the said parties in respect of such alterations and additions shall be settled and ascertained by the said W. M. or such other surveyor, whose determination shall be final. PROVIDED ALSO, and it is hereby further agreed, that in the settling and ascertaining the said sum or sums of money, the said W. M. or such other surveyor shall not include any charge for day-work, unless an account thereof shall have been delivered to the said J. B., his executors, administrators or assigns, or the said W. M. or such other surveyor, at the end of the week in which the same shall have been performed. PROVIDED ALSO, and it is hereby further agreed, that no such alteration or addition shall release the said T. G. and T. C., their executors or administrators, or any or either of them, from the observance and performance of the agreements herein contained on the part of the said T. G., his executors or administrator, to be observed and performed, so far as relates to the other parts of the said dwelling-house, offices, and works; but that the same agreements shall in all respects be observed and performed in like manner as if no such alteration or addition had been directed. PROVIDED ALSO, and it is hereby agreed, that if the said W. M. shall die, or cease to act as the surveyor of the said J. B., his executors, administrators, or assigns, and the said T. G., his executors or administrators, shall be dissatisfied with the surveyor for the time being, to be appointed by the said J. B., his executors, administrators or assigns, then it shall be lawful for the said T. G., his executors or administrators, at his own expense, to employ a surveyor on his behalf in the adjustment of the accounts, to act with the surveyor for the time being of the said J. B., his executors, administrators or assigns; and in case of disagreement between such two surveyors, they shall be at liberty to nominate a third; and the said three surveyors, or any two of them, shall and may exercise all the powers and discretion which the said W. M. could or might have exercised under or by virtue of these presents, if he had lived and continued to act as the surveyor of the said J. B., his executors, administrators or assigns. And it is hereby further agreed, that if the said T. G., his executors or administrators, shall so employ a surveyor on their behalf, he shall be nominated within ten days after the said T. G. shall be informed of the surveyor for the time being appointed by the said J. B., his executors, administrators or assigns, and notice in writing shall forthwith be given of such nomination to the said J. B., his executors, administrators or assigns. IN WITNESS, &c.

SCHEDULE.—[The Specification referred to by the foregoing Articles of Agreement.]

II.—*Sub-contract between a Builder and a Carpenter.*

AGREEMENT made the   day of   , in the year of
our Lord   , between T. G., of   , Builder,
and C. D., of   , Carpenter.

WHEREAS the said T. G. hath entered into a contract
with J. B., of, &c., to erect a dwelling-house and offices
according to certain plans, elevations, and specifications
referred to in the said contract, under the superintendence of W. M. or other surveyor of the said J. B., and
which contract is dated the   day of   ; now it
is hereby agreed, that in consideration of the sum of
£   , to be paid by the said T. G. to the said
C. D. as hereinafter mentioned, the said C. D. shall do all
the carpenter's work necessary to be done for the completion of the said contract, and referred to in the said
plans and specifications, and provide all materials, tools
and implements necessary for the performance of such
work, and shall do the same in all things according to
the said contract and specifications, and shall in all
things abide by, perform, fulfil and keep the said terms
and stipulations of the said contract, so far as the same
are or shall be applicable to such carpenter's work; and
that in case the said T. G. shall become liable to pay
any penalties under the said contract in consequence
of the delay of the said C. D. in the performance of
the work agreed to be performed by him, the said C. D.
shall pay to the said T. G. the amount of such penalties;
and that in case the said W. M. or other surveyor
appointed to superintend the works under the said contract shall disapprove of the work done by the said
C. D. or the materials used by him, or the manner in
which such work is done, it shall be lawful for the said
T. G. to dismiss and discharge the said C. D. from the

further performance of such work, and employ some other person to complete the same; and that in such case the money which the said T. G. shall pay to the said other person for the completion of the said works shall be deducted from the sum which would otherwise be payable to the said C. D. under this agreement; AND that for the considerations aforesaid, the said T. G. shall pay to the said C. D. the sum of £   , in manner following : 75 per cent. on the price and value of the work done by the said C. D. during any week, to be paid to him on the Saturday in every week during the continuance of the said works, and the balance within one month after the completion of the said dwelling-house and offices.

III.—*Contract to do Repairs or perform other Works not under the Superintendence of a Surveyor.*

AGREEMENT made the   day of   , in the year of our Lord   , between A. B. of, &c., and C. D. of, &c.

A. B. agrees to do all the works hereunder specified in the best and most workmanlike manner, and to provide for such works all necessary materials and things of the best quality, and to complete and finish the said works on or before the   day of   next; and in case the said works shall not be finished on or before the said day of   , to pay or allow to the said C. D., out of the moneys payable under this agreement, the sum of £1 for each day during which the said works shall remain unfinished after the said   day of   ; and that in case the said C. D. shall require any additions or alterations to be made to the works hereunder specified, to execute such additions and alterations in the best and most workmanlike manner, with materials of the best quality : AND it is hereby agreed, that in case any additional works shall be required by the said C. D., or in case the said C. D. shall delay the execution of the said works, the said A. B. shall have such additional time for the performance of the said works, after the said   day of   , as shall have been consumed in the execution of such additional works, or as the time during which the said C. D. shall have delayed the said works, and that the payments for delay shall not be payable until after the expiration of such additional time : AND it is hereby further agreed, that materials brought upon the premises of the said C. D. for the purpose of being used in the said works, shall, if of proper description and quality, immediately become the property of the said C. D. ; AND the said C. D. agrees to pay to the said A. B. for the said works the sum of £   within one week after the same shall be finished : AND it is hereby agreed, that in case of any addition or alterations being made in or to the said works, the price of such additions or alterations shall be estimated in proportion to the said sum of £   for the whole of the said works, and such price so estimated shall be either added to or deducted from the sum of £   .

IV.—*Agreement for Engagement of Canvasser and Collector of Trade Unions.*

THIS AGREEMENT made this   day of   , 18 , between A. B. of   , C. D. of   , and E. F. of   (hereinafter called the employers), of the one part, and X. Y. of   (hereinafter called the collecting clerk), of the other part, witnesseth that :—

1. The employers agree to employ the collecting clerk to canvass for members and to collect fees and subscriptions for the   district of the   Union of   , hereinafter called the Society, whereof the employers are trustees, and the collecting clerk agrees to accept such employment from them personally on the conditions, terms and conditions hereinafter set forth.

2. The collecting clerk shall faithfully and diligently canvass for members, and shall collect subscriptions and other moneys for the society for and on behalf of the employers.

3. All moneys collected by the collecting clerk shall be, and from the time of collection shall be, deemed to be the moneys of the employers.

4. The collecting clerk shall keep a true and faithful account of all moneys so collected, and shall account for the same to the employers as and when required, and shall pay over all such moneys not less that once in every week to the employers, or to such person and at such place as the employers shall from time to time order, without any deduction.

5. At the time of each such payment of moneys collected the employers shall pay to the collecting clerk as his sole remuneration a sum equal to the amount of the entrance fees, and one-eighth part of the subscriptions collected by him, and then duly paid over.

6. The collecting clerk shall not, during the continuance of this agreement, act in a like capacity for any person or association other than the employers.

7. The district within which the collecting clerk

8. The collecting clerk shall keep the employers indemnified and guaranteed against any default on his part, whether through loss or otherwise, by giving security to be approved by the employers to the amount of £ , and shall renew or replace such security as required.

9. This agreement shall be terminable by one month's notice in writing on either side, but if the collecting clerk shall at any time violate any of the provisions hereof, or neglect his duty, the employers may terminate the agreement and discharge him without notice.

Witness our hands,—

A. B., C. D., E. F. ; Employers.

X. Y. ; Collecting Clerk.

V.—*Agreement for Engagement of a Shop Assistant.*

AN AGREEMENT made the day of , 18 between A. B. of , &c., and C. D. of , &c.

1. A. B. agrees to engage C. D. to be an assistant in A. B.'s shop and premises, No. 5, Street, , or in such other place in as A. B. shall decide, from the day of next, and C. D. agrees to become such assistant.

2. The hours during which C. D. shall attend to his duties shall be from A.M. to P.M., except on Saturday, when the hours shall be from A.M. to P.M.

3. C. D. shall be paid for his services £ every Friday, and shall reside on the premises, having a bedroom to himself, and a fire in winter, and board and lodging and washing, in addition to his salary.

4. This engagement may be ended by either party giving to the other, at any time (one) month's notice in writing.

A. B., C. D. ; Witness E. F.

VI.—*Another Form of Contract of Service.*

An Agreement made between A. B. of   and C. D. of   .   The said A. B. agrees to hire the services of the said C. D., and the said C. D. agrees to render to the said A. B. his services at all fair and reasonable times in the capacity of   for the term of   , commencing on the day of :   , and terminating on the   day of   .   And it is further agreed that the said A. B. shall pay to the said C. D. as such servant as aforesaid wages at the rate of   by the   and that such wages shall be paid on the day of each   .   A. B., C. D.

VII.—*Agreement between Master and Workman, embodying Working Rules.*

The subjoined form of agreement between a master and workman may be written or printed after trade rules (*see below*), both being signed by the parties :—

I, A. B., master   in   , agree to employ C. D., a journeyman   in   , and I, the said C. D., agree to serve the said A. B. as a journeyman   aforesaid, upon the terms of the foregoing trade rules, signed by us of even date herewith.   Dated this   day of   , 18   .

(Signed) A. B., C. D.

VIII.—*Trade Rules to be embodied in Agreement between Master and Workman.* (See above, Form VII.)

WORKING RULES FOR   DISTRICT.

Rule 1.—The working time for   in summer shall be   hours per day for the first five days of the week and   hours on Saturday.

Work to commence at   A.M., and to cease at P.M., except on Saturday, when work shall cease at noon.

There shall be allowed half an hour for breakfast each day, and on the first five days of the week one hour for dinner.

Rule 2.—From the second Monday in   and the following weeks the working time shall be hours per day for each of the first five days of the week, and   hours on Saturday.

Work to commence at   A.M. each day and to cease at   P.M., except on Saturday, when work shall cease at   noon.

There shall be allowed half an hour for breakfast for each day, and on the first five days of the week half an hour for dinner.

Rule 3.—That the minimum rate of wages be   d. per hour; this clause to apply to all   wherever employed, and at whatever class of work.

Rule 4.—That no time beyond the hours be worked except when necessary, and then to be paid at the rate of time and a half from the ordinary time of ceasing work until   P.M., and double time from   P.M. until the ordinary time of commencing work next morning.

On Saturdays double time to commence from noon, and continue for all time worked until the ordinary time of starting on Monday morning. Bank Holidays and Christmas Day to be paid for the same as Sundays.

Rule 5.—One notice to terminate the engagement on either side, and all wages due to be paid at the expiration of such notice.

Rule 6.—That all sent to country jobs be paid London rate of wages, with per day in addition as country money. Employers to pay lodgings, rail, and 'bus fares to and from, and if the workman is discharged through no fault of his own his time travelling home to be paid for.

Rule 7.—That payment of wages commence at noon on Saturdays, and to be paid on the job, but if otherwise arranged walking time at the rate of three miles per hour to be allowed to get to the pay-table at .

Rule 8.—That no part of a workman's wage be deducted for charitable, benefit club, or insurance purposes under any circumstances (or except by mutual agreement, and in writing).

That the employer shall provide a suitable place on all jobs in which workmen can have their meals.

Rule 9.—The wages earned on Saturday only to be kept in hand as back time.

Rule 10.—The London District shall comprise the area contained within a radius of 12 miles from Charing Cross, and in which these rules shall be in force.

APPENDIX OF STATUTES.

I. TRUCK ACT, 1831.

(1 & 2 WILL. IV. CAP. 37.)

WHEREAS it is necessary to prohibit the payment, in certain trades, of wages in goods, or otherwise than in the current coin of the realm; be it therefore enacted by the King's most excellent majesty, by and with the advice and consent of the Lords Spiritual and Temporal, and Commons, in this present Parliament assembled, and by the authority of the same, That in all contracts hereafter to be made for the hiring of any artificer in any of the trades hereinafter enumerated, or for the performance by any artificer of any labour in any of the said trades, the wages of such artificer shall be made payable in the current coin of this realm only, and not otherwise; and that if in any such contract the whole or any part of such wages shall be made payable in any manner other than in the current coin aforesaid, such contract shall be and is hereby declared illegal, null, and void.

2. And be it further enacted, That if in any contract hereafter to be made between any artificer in any of the trades hereinafter enumerated, and his employer, any provision shall be made directly or indirectly respecting the place where, or the manner in which, or the person or persons with whom, the whole or any part of the wages due or to become due to any such artificer shall be laid out or expended, such contract shall be and is hereby declared illegal, null, and void.

3. And be it further enacted, That the entire amount of the wages earned by or payable to any artificer in any of the trades hereinafter enumerated, in respect of any labour by him done in any such trade, shall be actually paid to such artificer in the current coin of this realm, and not otherwise; and every payment made to any such artificer by his employer, of or in respect of any such wages, by the delivering to him of goods, or otherwise than in the current coin aforesaid, except as hereinafter mentioned, shall be and is hereby declared illegal, null, and void.

4. And be it further enacted, That every artificer in any of the trades hereinafter enumerated shall be entitled to recover from his employer in any such trade, in the manner by law provided for the recovery of servants' wages, or by any other lawful ways and means, the whole or so much of the wages earned by such artificer in such trade as shall not have been actually paid to him by such his employer in the current coin of this realm.

5. And be it further enacted, That in any action, suit, or other proceeding to be hereafter brought or commenced by any such artificer as aforesaid, against his employer, for the recovery of any sum of money due to any such artificer as the wages of his labour in any of

the trades hereinafter enumerated, the defendant shall not be allowed to make any set-off, nor to claim any reduction of the plaintiff's demand, by reason or in respect of any goods, wares, or merchandize had or received by the plaintiff as or on account of his wages or in reward for his labour, or by reason or in respect of any goods, wares, or merchandize sold, delivered, or supplied to such artificer at any shop or warehouse kept by or belonging to such employer, or in the profits of which such employer shall have any share or interest.

[See now section 6 of Truck Act, 1887, *infra*.]

6. And be it further enacted, That no employer of any artificer in any of the trades hereinafter enumerated shall have or be entitled to maintain any suit or action ¦in any court of law or equity against any such artificer, for or in respect of any goods, wares, or merchandize sold, delivered, or supplied to any such artificer by any such employer, whilst in his employment, as or on account of his wages or reward for his labour, or for or in respect of any goods, wares, or merchandize sold, delivered, or supplied to such artificer at any shop or warehouse kept by or belonging to such employer, or in the profits of which such employer shall have any share or interest.

[See now section 5 of Truck Act, 1887, *infra*.]

7. And be it further enacted, That if any such artificer as aforesaid, or his wife or widow, or if any child of any such artificer, not being of the full age of twenty-one years, shall become chargeable to any parish or place, and if within the space of three calendar months next before the time when any such charge shall be incurred such artificer shall have earned or have become entitled to receive any wages for any labour by him done in any of the said trades, which wages shall not have been paid to such artificer in the current coin of this realm, it shall be lawful for the overseers or overseer of the poor in such parish or place to recover from the employer of such artificer in whose service such labour was done the full amount of wages so unpaid, and to proceed for the recovery thereof by all such ways and means as such artificer himself might have proceeded for that purpose ; and the amount of the wages which may be so recovered shall be applied in re-imbursing such parish or place all costs and charges incurred in respect of the person or persons to become chargeable, and the surplus shall be applied and paid over to such person or persons.

8. Provided always, and be it further enacted, That nothing herein contained shall be construed to prevent or to render invalid any contract for the payment, or any actual payment, to any such artificer as aforesaid, of the whole or any part of his wages either in the notes of the Governor and Company of the Bank of *England*, or in the notes of any person or persons carrying on the business of a banker, and duly licensed to issue such notes in pursuance of the laws relating to His Majesty's Revenue of Stamps, or in drafts or orders for the payment of money to the bearer on demand, drawn upon any person or persons carrying on the business of a banker, being duly licensed as aforesaid, within fifteen miles of the place where such drafts or orders shall be so paid, if such artificer shall be freely consenting to receive such drafts or orders as aforesaid, but all payments so made with such consent as aforesaid, in any such notes, drafts, or orders as aforesaid, shall for the purposes of this Act be as valid and effectual as if such payments had been made in the current coin of the realm.

9. And be it further enacted, That any employer of any artificer in

any of the trades hereinafter enumerated, who shall, by himself or by the agency of any other person or persons, directly or indirectly enter into any contract or make any payment hereby declared illegal, shall for the first offence forfeit a sum not exceeding ten pounds nor less than five pounds, and for the second offence any sum not exceeding twenty pounds nor less than ten pounds, and in case of a third offence any such employer shall be and be deemed guilty of a misdemeanor, and, being thereof convicted, shall be punished by fine only, at the discretion of the court, so that the fines shall not in any case exceed the sum of one hundred pounds.

10. [The first part of this clause has been repealed by schedule to Truck Act, 1887.] Provided always, That no person shall be punished as for a second offence under this Act unless ten days at the least shall have intervened between the conviction of such person for the first and the commission by such person of the second offence, but each separate offence committed by any such person before the expiration of the said term of ten days shall be punishable by a separate penalty, as though the same were a first offence; and that no person shall be punished as for a third offence under this Act, unless ten days at the least shall have intervened between the conviction of such person for the second and the commission by such person of the third offence; but each separate offence committed by any such person before the expiration of the said term of ten days shall be punishable by a separate penalty, as though the same were a second offence; and that the fourth or any subsequent offence which may be committed by any such person against this Act shall be enquired of, tried, and punished in the manner hereinbefore provided in respect of any third offence; and that if the person or persons preferring any such information shall not be able or shall not see fit to produce evidence of any such previous conviction or convictions as aforesaid, any such offender as aforesaid shall be punished for each separate offence by him committed against the provisions of this Act by an equal number of distinct and separate penalties, as though each of such offences were a first or a second offence, as the case may be; and that no person shall be proceeded against or punished as for a second or as for a third offence at the distance of more than two years from the commission of the next preceding offence.

11. [Repealed by schedule to Truck Act, 1887.]

12. [Repealed by schedule to Truck Act, 1877.]

13. And be it further enacted, That no person shall be liable to be convicted of any offence against this Act committed by his or her copartner in trade, and without his or her knowledge, privity, or consent; but it shall be lawful, when any penalty, or any sum for wages, or any other sum, is ordered to be paid under the authority of this Act, and the person or persons ordered to pay the same shall neglect or refuse to do so, to levy the same by distress and sale of any goods belonging to any copartnership, concern, or business in the carrying on of which such charges may have become due or such offence may have been committed; and in all proceedings under this Act to recover any sum due for wages it shall be lawful in all cases of copartnership for the justices, at the hearing of any complaint for the nonpayment thereof, to make an order upon any one or more copartners for the payment of the sum appearing to be due; and in such case the service of a copy of any summons or other process, or of any order, upon one or more of such copartners, shall be deemed to be a sufficient service upon all.

14. And it is declared and enacted, That in all cases it shall be deemed and taken to be sufficient service of any summons to be issued against any offender or offenders by any justice or justices of the peace, under the authority of this Act, if a duplicate or true copy of the same be left at or upon the place used or occupied by such offender or offenders for carrying on his, her, or their trade or business, or at the place of residence of any such offender or offenders, being at or upon any such place as aforesaid, the same being directed to such offender or offenders by his, her, or their right or assumed name or names.

15 and 16. [Both these sections repealed by schedule to Truck Act, 1887.]

17. And be it further enacted, That no conviction, order, or adjudication made by any Justices of the Peace under the provisions of this Act shall be quashed for want of form, nor be removed by certiorari or otherwise into any of his Majesty's superior Courts of Record; and no warrant of distress, or commitments in default of sufficient distress, shall be held void by reason of any defect therein, provided it be therein alleged that the party has been convicted, and there be a good and valid conviction to sustain the same.

18 and 19. [Both these sections repealed by schedule to Truck Act, 1887.]

20. And be it further enacted, That nothing herein contained shall extend to any domestic servant.

21 and 22. [Both these sections repealed by schedule to Truck Act, 1887.]

23. And be it further enacted and declared, That nothing herein contained shall extend or be construed to extend to prevent any employer of any artificer, or agent of any such employer, from supplying or contracting to supply to any such artificer any medicine or medical attendance, or any fuel, or any materials, tools, or implements to be by such artificer employed in his trade or occupation, if such artificers be employed in mining, or any hay, corn, or other provender to be consumed by any horse or other beast of burden employed by any such artificer in his trade and occupation; nor from demising to any artificer, workman, or labourer employed in any of the trades or occupations enumerated in this Act the whole or any part of any tenement at any rent to be thereon reserved; nor from supplying or contracting to supply to any such artificer any victuals dressed or prepared under the roof of any such employer, and there consumed by such artificer; nor from making or contracting to make any stoppage or deduction from the wages of any such artificer, for or in respect of any such rent; or for or in respect of any such medicine or medical attendance; or for or in respect of such fuel, materials, tools, implements, hay, corn, or provender, or of any such victuals dressed and prepared under the roof of any such employer; or for or in respect of any money advanced to such artificer for any such purpose as aforesaid: provided always, that such stoppage or deduction shall not exceed the real and true value of such fuel, materials, tools, implements, hay, corn, and provender, and shall not be in any case made from the wages of such artificer, unless the agreement or contract for such stoppage or deduction shall be in writing, and signed by such artificer.

24. And be it further enacted and declared, That nothing herein contained shall extend or be construed to extend to prevent any such employer from advancing to any such artificer any money to be by him contributed to any friendly society or bank for savings duly established according to law, nor from advancing to any such artificer any money for his relief in sickness, or for the education of any child or children of such artificer, nor from deducting or contracting to deduct any sum or sums of money from the wages of such artificers for the education of any such child or children of such artificer.

[See now sections 7, 8, and 9 of Truck Act, 1887.]

25. And be it further enacted and declared, That in the meaning and for the purposes of this Act, any agreement, understanding, device, contrivance, collusion, or arrangement whatsoever on the subject of wages, whether written or oral, whether direct or indirect, to which the employer and artificer are parties or are assenting, or by which they are mutually bound to each other, or whereby either of them shall have endeavoured to impose an obligation on the other of them, shall be and be deemed a " contract."

26. [Commencement of Act.]

27. The provisions of this Act extend over Great Britain and Ireland.

[The schedules to the Act have been repealed by the Truck Act, 1887 (50 & 51 Vict., c. 46).]

II. TRUCK AMENDMENT ACT, 1887.

(50 & 51 VICT. Cap. 46.)

1. This Act may be cited as the Truck Amendment Act, 1887. The Act of the session of the first and second years of the reign of King William the Fourth, chapter thirty-seven, intituled " An Act to prohibit the payment in certain trades of wages in goods or otherwise than in the current coin of the realm " (in this Act referred to as the principal Act), may be cited as the Truck Act, 1831, and that Act and this Act may be cited together as the Truck Acts, 1831 and 1887, and shall be construed together as one Act.

2. The provisions of the principal Act shall extend to, apply to, and include any workman as defined in the Employers and Workmen Act, 1875, section ten, and the expression " artificer " in the principal Act shall be construed to include every workman to whom the principal Act is extended and applied by this Act, and all provisions and enactments in the principal Act inconsistent herewith are hereby repealed.

3. Whenever by agreement, custom, or otherwise a workman is entitled to receive in anticipation of the regular period of the payment of his wages an advance as part or on account thereof, it shall not be lawful for the employer to withhold such advance or make any deduction in respect of such advance on account of poundage, discount, or interest, or any similar charge.

4. Nothing in the principal Act or this Act shall render illegal a contract with a servant in husbandry for giving him food, drink, not being intoxicating, a cottage, or other allowances or privileges, in addition to money wages as a remuneration for his services.

5. In any action brought by a workman for the recovery of his wages, the employer shall not be entitled to any set off or counter-claim in respect of any goods supplied to the workman by any person under any order or direction of the employer, or any agent of the employer, and the employer of a workman or any agent of the employer, or any person supplying goods to the workman under any order or direction of such employer or agent, shall not be entitled to sue the workman for or in respect of any goods supplied by such employer or agent, or under such order or direction, as the case may be.

Provided that nothing in this section shall apply to anything excepted by section twenty-three of the principal Act.

6. No employer shall, directly or indirectly, by himself or his agent, impose as a condition, express or implied, in or for the employment of any workman any terms as to the place at which, or the manner in which, or the person with whom, any wages or portion of wages paid to the workman are or is to be expended, and no employer shall by himself or his agent dismiss any workman from his employment for or on account of the place at which, or the manner in which, or the person with whom, any wages or portion of wages paid by the employer to such workman are or is expended or fail to be expended.

7. Where any deduction is made by an employer from a workman's wages for education, such workman on sending his child to any state-inspected school selected by the workman shall be entitled to have the school fees of his child at that school paid by the employer at the same rate and to the same extent as the other workmen from whose wages the like deduction is made by such employer.

In this section " state-inspected school " means any elementary school inspected under the direction of the Education Department in England or Scotland or of the Board of National Education in Ireland.

8. No deduction shall be made from a workman's wages for sharpening or repairing tools, except by agreement not forming part of the condition of hiring.

9. Where deductions are made from the wages of any workmen for the education of children or in respect of medicine, medical attendance, or tools, once at least in every year the employer shall, by himself or his agent, make out a correct account of the receipts and expenditure in respect of such deductions, and submit the same to be audited by two auditors appointed by the said workmen, and shall produce to the auditors all such books, vouchers, and documents, and afford them all such other facilities as are required for such audit.

10. Where articles are made by a person at his own home, or otherwise, without the employment of any person under him except a member of his own family, the principal Act and this Act shall apply as if he were a workman, and the shopkeeper, dealer, trader, or other person buying the articles in the way of trade were his employer, and the provisions of this Act with respect to the payment of wages shall apply as if the price of an article were wages earned during the seven days next preceding the date at which any article is received from the workman by the employer.

This section shall apply only to articles under the value of £5, knitted or otherwise, manufactured of wool, worsted, yarn, stuff, jersey, linen, fustian, cloth, serge, cotton, leather, fur, hemp, flax, mohair, or silk, or of any combination thereof, or made or prepared of bone, thread, silk, or cotton lace, or of lace made of any mixed materials. Where it is made to appear to her Majesty the Queen in Council that, in the interests of persons making articles to which this section applies in any county or place in the United Kingdom, it is expedient so to do, it shall be lawful for her Majesty, by Order in Council, to suspend the operation of this section in such county or place, and the same shall accordingly be suspended, either wholly or in part, and either with or without any limitations or exceptions, according as is provided by the Order.

11. If any employer or his agent contravenes or fails to comply with any of the foregoing provisions of this Act, such employer or agent, as the case may be, shall be guilty of an offence against the principal Act, and shall be liable to the penalties imposed by section nine of that Act as if the offence were such an offence as in that section mentioned.

12.—(1.) Where an offence for which an employer is, by virtue of the principal Act or this Act, liable to a penalty has in fact been committed by some agent of the employer or other person, such agent or other person shall be liable to the same penalty as if he were the employer.

(2.) Where an employer is charged with an offence against the principal Act or this Act he shall be entitled, upon information duly laid by him, to have any other person whom he charges as the actual offender brought before the court at the time appointed for hearing the charge, and if, after the commission of the offence has been proved the employer proves to the satisfaction of the court that he had used due diligence to enforce the execution of the said Acts, and that the said other person had committed the offence in question without his knowledge, consent, or connivance, the said other person shall be summarily convicted of such offence, and the employer shall be exempt from any penalty.

When it is made to appear to the satisfaction of an inspector of factories or mines, or in Scotland a procurator fiscal, at the time of discovering the offence, that the employer had used due diligence to enforce the execution of the said Acts, and also by what person such offence had been committed, and also that it had been committed without the knowledge, consent, or connivance of the employer, then the inspector or procurator fiscal shall proceed against the person whom he believes to be the actual offender in the first instance without first proceeding against the employer.

13.—(1.) Any offence against the principal Act or this Act may be prosecuted, and any penalty therefore recovered in manner provided by the Summary Jurisdiction Acts, so, however, that no penalty shall be imposed on summary conviction exceeding that prescribed by the principal Act for a second offence.

(2.) It shall be the duty of the inspectors of factories and the inspectors of mines to enforce the provisions of the principal Act and this Act within their districts so far as respects factories, workshops, and mines inspected by them respectively, and such inspectors shall for this purpose have the same powers and authorities as they respectively have for the purpose of enforcing the provisions of any Acts relating to factories, workshops, or mines, and all expenses incurred by them under this section shall be defrayed out of moneys provided by Parliament.

(3.) In England all penalties recovered under the principal Act and this Act shall be paid into the receipt of her Majesty's Exchequer, and be carried to the Consolidated Fund.

(4.) In Scotland—

(*a.*) The procurators fiscal of the sheriff court shall, as part of their official duty, investigate and prosecute offences against the principal Act or this Act, and such prosecution may also be instituted in the sheriff court at the instance of any inspector of factories or inspector of mines ;

(*b.*) All offences against the said Acts shall be prosecuted in the sheriff court.

14. In this Act, unless the context otherwise requires,—

The expression " Summary Jurisdiction Acts " means, as respects England, the Summary Jurisdiction Acts as defined by the Summary Jurisdiction Act, 1879 ; and, as respects Scotland, means the Summary Jurisdiction (Scotland) Acts, 1864 and 1881, and any Acts amending the same :

Other expressions have the same meaning as in the principal Act.

15. So much of the principal Act as disqualifies any justice from acting as such under the principal Act is hereby repealed.

A person engaged in the same trade or occupation as an employer charged with an offence against the principal Act or this Act shall not act as a justice of the peace in hearing and determining such charge.

16. The provisions of the principal Act conferring powers on any overseers or overseer of the poor shall be deemed to confer those powers in the case of England on the guardians of a union, and in the case of Scotland on the inspectors of the poor.

17. The Acts mentioned in the schedule to this Act are hereby repealed to the extent in the third column of the said schedule mentioned, without prejudice to anything heretofore done or suffered in respect thereof.

18. The principal Act, so far as it is not hereby repealed, and this Act shall extend to Ireland, subject to the following provisions :

(1.) Any offence against the principal Act or this Act may be prosecuted and any penalty therefor may be recovered in the manner provided by the Summary Jurisdiction (Ireland) Acts ; (that is to say) within the Dublin Metropolitan Police District the Acts regulating the powers and duties of justices of the peace and of the police of that district, and elsewhere in Ireland the Petty Sessions (Ireland) Act, 1851, and the Acts amending the same ;

(2.) Penalties recovered under the principal Act or this Act shall be applied in the manner directed by the Fines (Ireland) Act, 1851, and the Acts amending the same.

SCHEDULE.

Session and Chapter.	Title of Act.	Extent of Repeal.
12 Geo. 1. c. 34.	An Act to prevent unlawful combinations of workmen employed in the woollen manufactures, and for better payment of their wages.	Section three, and so much of section eight as applies to section three.
22 Geo. 2. c. 27.	An Act, the title of which begins with "An Act for the more effectual preventing of frauds," and ends with the words "and for the better payment of their wages."	So much of section twelve as applies to any enactment repealed by this Act.
30 Geo. 2. c. 12.	An Act, the title of which begins with the words "An Act to amend an Act," and ends with the words "payment of the workmen's wages in any other manner than in money."	Sections two and three.
57 Geo. 3. c. 115.	An Act, the title of which begins with the words "An Act to extend the provisions of an Act," and ends with the words "articles of cutlery."	The whole Act.
57 Geo. 3. c. 122.	An Act, the title of which begins with the words "An Act to extend the provisions," and ends with the words "extending the provisions of the said Acts to Scotland and Ireland."	The whole Act.
1 & 2 Will. 4. c. 37.	An Act to prohibit the payment in certain trades of wages in goods or otherwise than in the current coin of the realm.	Section ten, down to "be produced to the court and jury" inclusive; section eleven, section twelve, section fifteen, section sixteen, section eighteen, section nineteen, in section twenty the words "or servant in hus-

SCHEDULE (*continued*).

Session and Chapter.	Title of Act.	Extent of Repeal.
1 & 2 Will. 4 c. 37 (*continued*).	An Act to prohibit the payment, &c. (*continued*).	bandry " ; section twenty-one, section twenty-two, section twenty-four from "and unless the agreement" inclusive to end of section, and section twenty-five from "all workmen" to "purposes aforesaid" both inclusive, and the schedules.

III. THE INFANTS' RELIEF ACT, 1874.

(37 & 38 VIC. CAP. 62.)

1. All contracts, whether by speciality or by simple contract, henceforth entered into by infants for the repayment of money lent or to be lent, or for goods supplied or to be supplied, other than contracts for necessaries, and all accounts stated with infants shall be absolutely void. This enactment will not invalidate any contract into which an infant may, by any existing or future statute, or by the rules of the common law or equity enter except such as now by law are voidable.

2. No action shall be brought whereby to charge any person upon any promise made after full age to pay any debt contracted during infancy, or upon any ratification made after full age of any promise or contract made during infancy whether there shall or shall not be any new consideration for such promise or ratification after full age.

IV. EMPLOYERS AND WORKMEN ACT, 1875.

(38 & 39 VIC. CAP. 90.)

Preliminary.

1. This Act may be cited as the Employers and Workmen Act, 1875.

2. This Act, except so far as it authorises any rules to be made or other thing to be done at any time after the passing of this Act, shall come into operation on the first day of September one thousand eight hundred and seventy-five.

PART I.

Jurisdiction—Jurisdiction of County Court.

3. In any proceeding before a county court in relation to any dispute between an employer and a workman arising out of or incidental to their relation as such (which dispute is hereinafter referred to as a dispute under this Act) the court may, in addition to any jurisdiction it might have exercised if this Act had not passed, exercise all or any of the following powers ; that is to say,

(1.) It may adjust and set off the one against the other all such claims on the part either of the employer or of the workman arising out of or incidental to the relation between them, as the court may find to be subsisting, whether such claims are liquidated or unliquidated, and are for wages, damages, or otherwise ; and,

(2.) If, having regard to all the circumstances of the case, it thinks it just to do so, it may rescind any contract between the employer and the workman upon such terms as to the apportionment of wages or other sums due thereunder, and as to the payment of wages or damages, or other sums due, as it thinks just ; and,

(3.) Where the court might otherwise award damages for any breach of contract it may, if the defendant be willing to give security to the satisfaction of the court for the performance by him of so much of his contract as remains unperformed, with the consent of the plaintiff, accept such security, and order performance of the contract accordingly, in place either of the whole of the damages which would otherwise have been awarded, or some part of such damages.

The security shall be an undertaking by the defendant and one or more surety or sureties that the defendant will perform his contract, subject on non-performance to the payment of a sum to be specified in the undertaking.

Any sum paid by a surety on behalf of a defendant in respect of a security under this Act, together with all costs incurred by such surety in respect of such security, shall be deemed to be a debt due to him from the defendant ; and where such security has been given in or under the direction of a court of summary jurisdiction, that court may order payment to the surety of the sum which has so become due to him from the defendant.

Court of Summary Jurisdiction.

4. A dispute under this Act between an employer and a workman may be heard and determined by a court of summary jurisdiction, and such court, for the purposes of this Act, shall be deemed to be a court of civil jurisdiction, and in a proceeding in relation to any such dis-

pute the court may order payment of any sum which it may find to be due as wages, or damages, or otherwise, and may exercise all or any of the powers by this Act conferred on a county court : Provided that in any proceeding in relation to any such dispute the court of summary jurisdiction—

(1.) Shall not exercise any jurisdiction where the amount claimed exceeds ten pounds ; and

(2.) Shall not make an order for the payment of any sum exceeding ten pounds, exclusive of the costs incurred in the case, and

(3.) Shall not require security to an amount exceeding ten pounds from any defendant or his surety or sureties.

5. Any dispute between an apprentice to whom this Act applies and his master, arising out of or incidental to their relation as such (which dispute is hereinafter referred to as a dispute under this Act) may be heard and determined by a court of summary jurisdiction.

6. In a proceeding before a court of summary jurisdiction in relation to a dispute under this Act between a master and an apprentice, the court shall have the same powers as if the dispute were between an employer and a workman, and the master were the employer and the apprentice the workman, and the instrument of apprenticeship a contract between an employer and a workman, and shall also have the following powers :

(1.) It may make an order directing the apprentice to perform his duties under the apprenticeship ; and,

(2.) If it rescinds the instrument of apprenticeship it may, if it thinks it just so to do, order the whole or any part of the premium paid on the binding of the apprentice to be repaid.

Where an order is made directing an apprentice to perform his duties under the apprenticeship, the court may from time to time, if satisfied after the expiration of not less than one month from the date of the order that the apprentice has failed to comply therewith, order him to be imprisoned for a period not exceeding fourteen days.

7. In a proceeding before a court of summary jurisdiction in relation to a dispute under this Act between a master and an apprentice, if there is any person liable, under the instrument of apprenticeship, for the good conduct of the apprentice, that person may, if the court so direct, be summoned in 'like manner as if he were the defendant in such proceeding to attend on the hearing of the proceeding, and the court may, in addition to or in substitution for any order which the court is authorised to make against the apprentice, order the person so summoned to pay damages for any breach of the contract of apprenticeship to an amount not exceeding the limit (if any) to which he is liable under the instrument of apprenticeship.

The court may, if the person so summoned, or any other person, is willing to give security to the satisfaction of the court for the performance by the apprentice of his contract of apprenticeship, accept such security instead of or in mitigation of any punishment which it is authorised to inflict upon the apprentice.

PART II.

Procedure.

8. A person may give security under this Act in a county court or court of summary jurisdiction by an oral or written acknowledgment in or under the direction of the court of the undertaking or condition by which and the sum for which he is bound, in such manner and form as may be prescribed by any rule for the time being in force, and in any case where security is so given, the court in or under the direction of which it is given may order payment of any sum which may become due in pursuance of such security.

The Lord Chancellor may at any time after the passing of this Act, and from time to time make, and when made, rescind, alter, and add to, rules with respect to giving security under this Act.

9. Any dispute or matter in respect of which jurisdiction is given by this Act to a court of summary jurisdiction shall be deemed to be a matter on which that court has authority by law to make an order on complaint in pursuance of the Summary Jurisdiction Act, but shall not be deemed to be a criminal proceeding ; and all powers by this Act conferred on a court of summary jurisdiction shall be deemed to be in addition to and not in derogation of any powers conferred on it by the Summary Jurisdiction Act, except that a warrant shall not be issued under that Act for apprehending any person other than an apprentice for failing to appear to answer a complaint in any proceeding under this Act, and that an order made by a court of summary jurisdiction under this Act for the payment of any money shall not be enforced by imprisonment except in the manner and under the conditions by this Act provided ; and no goods or chattels shall be taken under a distress ordered by a court of summary jurisdiction which might not be taken under an execution issued by a county court.

A court of summary jurisdiction may direct any sum of money, for the payment of which it makes an order under this Act, to be paid by instalments, and may from time to time rescind or vary such order.

Any sum payable by any person under the order of a court of summary jurisdiction in pursuance of this Act, shall be deemed to be a debt due from him in pursuance of a judgment of a competent court within the meaning of the fifth section of the Debtors Act, 1869, and may be enforced accordingly ; and as regards any such debt a court of summary jurisdiction shall be deemed to be a court within the meaning of the said section.

The Lord Chancellor may at any time after the passing of this Act, and from time to time make, and when made, rescind, alter, and add to, rules for carrying into effect the jurisdiction by this Act given to a court of summary jurisdiction, and in particular for the purpose of regulating the costs of any proceedings in a court of summary jurisdiction, with power to provide that the same shall not exceed the costs which would in a similar case be incurred in a county court, and any rules so made in so far as they relate to the exercise of jurisdiction under the said fifth section of the Debtors Act, 1869, shall be deemed to be prescribed rules within the meaning of the said section.

Part III.

Definitions and Miscellaneous.

Definitions.

10. In this Act—

The expression "workman" does not include a domestic or menial servant, but save as aforesaid, means any person who, being a labourer, servant in husbandry, journeyman, artificer, handicraftsman, miner, or otherwise engaged in manual labour, whether under the age of twenty-one years or above that age, has entered into or works under a contract with an employer, whether the contract be made before or after the passing of this Act, be express or implied, oral or in writing, and be a contract of service or a contract personally to execute any work or labour.

The expression "the Summary Jurisdiction Act" means the Act of the session of the eleventh and twelfth years of the reign of her present Majesty, chapter forty-three, intituled "an Act to facilitate the performance of the duties of Justices of the Peace out of sessions within England and Wales with respect to summary convictions and orders," inclusive of any Acts amending the same.

The expression "court of summary jurisdiction" means—

(1.) As respects the city of London, the Lord Mayor or any alderman of the said city sitting at the Mansion House or Guildhall justice room ; and

(2.) As respects any police court division in the metropolitan police district, any metropolitan police magistrate sitting at the police court for that division ; and

(3.) As respects any city, town, liberty, borough, place, or district for which a stipendiary magistrate is for the time being acting, such stipendiary magistrate sitting at a police court or other place appointed in that behalf ; and

(4.) Elsewhere any justice or justices of the peace to whom jurisdiction is given by the Summary Jurisdiction Act : Provided that, as respects any case within the cognizance of such justice or justices as last aforesaid, a complaint under this Act shall be heard and determined and an order for imprisonment made by two or more justices of the peace in petty sessions sitting at some place appointed for holding petty sessions.

Nothing in this section contained shall restrict the jurisdiction of the Lord Mayor or any alderman of the city of London, or of any metropolitan police or stipendiary magistrate in respect of any act or jurisdiction which may now be done or exercised by him out of court.

11. In the case of a child, young person, or woman subject to the provisions of the Factory Acts, 1833 to 1874, any forfeiture on the ground of absence or leaving work shall not be deducted from or set off against a claim for wages or other sum due for work done before such absence or leaving work, except to the amount of the damage (if any) which the employer may have sustained by reason of such absence or leaving work.

Application.

12. This Act in so far as it relates to apprentices shall apply only to an apprentice to the business of a workman as defined by this Act upon whose binding either no premium is paid, or the premium (if any) paid does not exceed twenty-five pounds, and to an apprentice bound under the provisions of the Acts relating to the relief of the poor.

Saving Clause.

13. Nothing in this Act shall take away or abridge any local or special jurisdiction touching apprentices.

This Act shall not apply to seamen or to apprentices to the sea service.

Part IV.

Application of Act to Scotland.

14. This Act shall extend to Scotland, with the modifications following ; that is to say,

In this Act with respect to Scotland—

The expression " county court " means the ordinary sheriff court of the county :

The expression " the court of summary jurisdiction " means the small debt court of the sheriff of the county :

The expression " sheriff " includes sheriff substitute :

The expression " instrument of apprenticeship " means indenture :

The expression " plaintiff " or " complainant " means pursuer or complainer :

The expression " defendant " includes defender or respondent :

The expression " the Summary Jurisdiction Act " means the Act of the seventh year of the reign of His Majesty King William the Fourth and the first year of the reign of Her present Majesty, chapter forty-one, intituled " An Act for the more effectual recovery of small debts in the Sheriff Courts, and for regulating the establishment of circuit courts for the trial of small debt causes by the sheriffs in Scotland," and the Acts amending the same.

The expression " surety " means cautioner :

This Act shall be read and construed, as if for the expression " the Lord Chancellor," wherever it occurs therein, the expression " the Court of Session by act of sederunt " were substituted.

All jurisdictions, powers, and authorities necessary for the purposes of this Act are hereby conferred on sheriffs in their ordinary or small debt courts, as the case may be, who shall have full power to make any order on any summons, petition, complaint, or other proceeding under this Act, that any county court or court of summary jurisdiction is empowered to make on any complaint or other proceeding under this Act.

Any decree or order pronounced or made by a sheriff under this Act shall be enforced in the same manner and under the same conditions in and under which a decree or order pronounced or made by him in his ordinary or small debt court, as the case may be, is enforced.

PART V.

Application of Act to Ireland.

15. This Act shall extend to Ireland, with the modifications following ; that is to say,

The expression "county court" shall be construed to mean civil bill court ;

The expression "Lord Chancellor" shall be construed to mean the Lord Chancellor of Ireland :

The expression "The Summary Jurisdiction Act" shall be construed to mean, as regards the police district of Dublin metropolis, the Acts regulating the powers and duties of justices of the peace for such district, and elsewhere in Ireland, the Petty Sessions (Ireland) Act, 1851, and any Acts amending the same :

The expression "court of summary jurisdiction" shall be construed to mean any justice or justices of the peace or other magistrate to whom jurisdiction is given by the Summary Jurisdiction Act :

The court of summary jurisdiction, when hearing and determining complaints under this Act, shall in the police district of Dublin metropolis be constituted of one or more of the divisional justices of the said district, and elsewhere in Ireland of two or more justices of the peace in petty sessions sitting at a place appointed for holding petty sessions :

The expression "fifth section of the Debtors Act, 1869," shall be construed to mean "sixth section of Debtors Act (Ireland), 1872."

V. TRADE UNION ACT AMENDMENT ACT, 1876.

(39 & 40 VICT. CAP. 22.)

---

1. This Act and the Trade Union Act, 1871, hereafter termed the principal Act, shall be construed as one Act and may be cited together as the "Trade Union Acts, 1871 and 1876," and this Act may be cited separately as the "Trade Union Act Amendment Act, 1876."

2. Notwithstanding anything in section five of the principal Act contained, a trade union, whether registered or unregistered, which insures or pays money on the death of a child under ten years of age shall be deemed to be within the provisions of section twenty-eight of the Friendly Societies Act, 1875.

3. Whereas by section eight of the principal Act it is enacted that "the real or personal estate of any branch of a trade union shall be vested in the trustees of such branch," the said section shall be read and construed as if immediately after the hereinbefore recited words there were inserted the words "or of the trustees of the trade union if the rules of the trade union so provide."

4. When any person being or having been a trustee of a trade union or of any branch of a trade union, and, whether appointed before or after the legal establishment thereof in whose name any stock belonging to such union or branch, transferrable at the Bank of England or Bank of Ireland is standing, either jointly with another or others, or solely, is absent from Great Britain or Ireland respectively, or becomes bankrupt, or files any petition or executes any deed for liquidation of his affairs by assignment or arrangement or for composition with his creditors, or become a lunatic, or is dead, or has been removed from his office of trustee, or if it be unknown whether such person is living or dead, the registrar, on the application in writing from the secretary and three members of the union or branch, and on proof satisfactory to him, may direct the transfer of the stock into the names of any other persons as trustees for the union or branch, and such transfer shall be made by the surviving or continuing trustees, and if there be no such trustee or if such trustee refuse, or be unable to make such transfer and the registrar so direct, then by the Accountant-General or Deputy, or Assistant Accountant-General of the Bank of England or Bank of Ireland as the case may be, and the Governors and Companies of the Bank of England and Bank of Ireland respectively are hereby indemnified for anything done by them or any of their officers in pursuance of this provision against any claim or demand of any persons injuriously affected thereby.

5. The jurisdiction conferred in the case of certain offences by section twelve of the principal Act, upon the court of summary jurisdiction for the place in which the registered office of a trade union is situate may be exercised either by that court or by the court of summary jurisdiction for the place where the offence has been committed.

6. Trade unions carrying on or intending to carry on business in more than one country, shall be registered in the country in which their registered office is situate ; but copies of the rules of such unions and of all amendments of the same shall, when registered, be sent to the registrar of each of the other countries to be recorded by him and until such rules be so recorded, the union shall not be entitled to any of the privileges of this Act or the principal Act in the country in which such rules have not been recorded, and until such amendments of rules be recorded, the same shall not take effect in such country. In this section "country" means England, Scotland, or Ireland.

7. Whereas by the "Life Assurance Companies Act, 1870," it is provided that the said Act shall not apply to societies registered under the Acts relating to Friendly Societies : The said Acts (or the amending Acts) shall not apply or be deemed to have applied to trade unions registered, or to be registered under the principal Act.

8. No certificate of registration of a trade union shall be withdrawn or cancelled otherwise than by the Chief Registrar of Friendly Societies; or, in the case of trade unions registered and doing business exclusively in Scotland or Ireland, by the Assistant Registrar for Scotland or Ireland ; and in the following cases—

    (1.) At the request of the trade union, to be evinced in such manner as such Chief or Assistant Registrar shall from time to time direct ;

(2.) On proof to his satisfaction that a certificate of registration has been obtained by fraud, or mistake, or that the registration of the trade union has become void under section six of the Trade Union Act, 1871, or that such trade union wilfully, and after notice from a registrar whom it may concern, violated any of the provisions of the Trade Union Acts, or has ceased to exist. Not less than two months' previous notice in writing specifying briefly the ground of any proposed withdrawal or cancelling of certificate (unless where the same is shown to have become void as aforesaid, in which case it shall be the duty of the Chief or Assistant Registrar to cancel the same forthwith), shall be given by the Chief or Assistant Registrar to a trade union before the certificate of registration of the same can be withdrawn or cancelled (except at its request). A trade union whose certificate of registration has been withdrawn or cancelled, shall from the time of such withdrawal or cancelling absolutely cease to enjoy as such the privileges of a registered trade union, but without prejudice to any liability actually incurred by such trade union, which may be enforced against the same as if such withdrawal or cancelling had not taken place.

9. A person under the age of twenty-one but above the age of sixteen may be a member of a trade union, unless provision be made in the rules thereof to the contrary, and may, subject to the rules of the trade union, enjoy all the rights of a member except as herein provided, and execute all instruments and give all acquittances necessary to be executed or given under the rules, but shall not be a member of the committee of management, trustee, or treasurer of the trade union.

10. A member of a trade union not being under the age of sixteen years may, by writing under his hand, delivered at or sent to the registered office of the trade union, nominate any person not being an officer or servant of the trade union (unless such officer or servant is the husband, wife, father, mother, child, brother, sister, nephew or niece of the nominator) to whom any moneys payable on the death of such member not exceeding £50 shall be paid at his decease, and may from time to time revoke or vary such nomination by a writing under his hand similarly sent or delivered; and on receiving satisfactory proof of the death of the nominator, the trade union shall pay to the nominee the amount due to the deceased member not exceeding the sum aforesaid.

11. A trade union may with the approval in writing of the Chief Registrar of Friendly Societies, or in the case of trade unions registered and doing business exclusively in Scotland or Ireland, of the Assistant Registrar for Scotland or Ireland respectively, change its name by the consent of not less than two-thirds of the total number of members. No change of name shall affect any right or obligation of the trade union or of any member thereof, and any pending legal proceedings may be continued by or against the trustees of the trade union or any other officer who may sue or be sued on behalf of such trade union notwithstanding its new name.

12. Any two or more trade unions may by the consent of not less than two-thirds of the members of each or every such trade union

become amalgamated together as one trade union with or without any dissolution or division of the funds of such trade unions or either or any of them; but no amalgamation shall prejudice any right of a creditor of either or any union party thereto.

13. Notice in writing of every change of name or amalgamation signed, in the case of a change of name, by seven members and countersigned by the secretary of the trade union changing its name, and accompanied by a statutory declaration by such secretary that the provisions of this Act in respect of changes of name have been complied with; and in the case of an amalgamation, signed by seven members and countersigned by the secretary of each or every union party thereto, and accompanied by a statutory declaration by each or every such secretary that the provisions of this Act in respect of amalgamation have been complied with, shall be sent to the Central Office established by the Friendly Societies Act, 1875, and registered there; and until such change of name or amalgamation is so registered the same shall not take effect.

14. The rules of every trade union shall provide for the manner of dissolving the same, and notice of every dissolution of a trade union under the hand of the secretary and seven members of the same shall be sent within fourteen days thereafter to the Central Office hereinbefore mentioned; or in the case of trade unions registered and doing business exclusively in Scotland or Ireland, to the Assistant-Registrar for Scotland or Ireland respectively, and shall be registered by them: Provided, that the rules of any trade union registered before the passing of this Act shall not be invalidated by the absence of a provision for dissolution.

15. A trade union which fails to give any notice or send any document which it is required by this Act to give or send, and every officer or other person bound by the rules thereof to give or send the same, or if there be no such officer, then every member of the committee of management of the union, unless proved to have been ignorant of or to have attempted to prevent the omission to give or send the same, is liable to a penalty of not less than one pound and not more than five pounds, recoverable at the suit of the Chief or any Assistant Registrar of Friendly Societies, or of any person aggrieved, and to an additional penalty of the like amount for each week during which the omission continues.

16. So much of section twenty-three of the principal Act as defines the term "trade union," except the proviso qualifying such definition, is hereby repealed, and in lieu thereof be it enacted as follows: The term "trade union" means any combination, whether temporary or permanent, for regulating the relations between workmen and masters, or between workmen and workmen, or between masters and masters, or for imposing restrictive conditions on the conduct of any trade or business, whether such combination would or would not if the principal Act had not been passed have been deemed to have been an unlawful combination by reason of some one or more of its purposes being in restraint of trade.

VI. FACTORY AND WORKSHOP ACT, 1878.

(41 VIC. CAP. 16.)

Preliminary.

1. This Act may be cited as the Factory and Workshop Act, 1878.

2. This Act shall come into operation on the first day of January, one thousand eight hundred and seventy-nine, which day is in this Act referred to as the commencement of this Act: Provided that at any time after the passing of this Act, any appointment, regulation, or order may be made, any notice issued, form prescribed, and act done which appears to a Secretary of State necessary or proper to be made, issued, prescribed, or done for the purpose of bringing this Act into operation at the commencement thereof.

PART I.

GENERAL LAW RELATING TO FACTORIES AND WORKSHOPS.

(1.) *Sanitary Provisions.*

3. A factory and a workshop shall be kept in a cleanly state and free from effluvia arising from any drain, privy, or other nuisance.

A factory or workshop shall not be so overcrowded while work is carried on therein as to be injurious to the health of the persons employed therein, and shall be ventilated in such a manner as to render harmless, so far as is practicable, all the gases, vapours, dust, or other impurities generated in the course of the manufacturing process or handicraft carried on therein that may be injurious to health.

A factory or workshop in which there is a contravention of this section shall be deemed not to be kept in conformity with this Act.

4. Where it appears to an inspector under this Act that any act, neglect, or default in relation to any drain, watercloset, earthcloset, privy, ashpit, water-supply, nuisance, or other matter in a factory or workshop is punishable or remediable under the law relating to public health, but not under this Act, that inspector shall give notice in writing of such act, neglect, or default to the sanitary authority in whose district the factory or workshop is situate, and it shall be the duty of the sanitary authority to make such inquiry into the subject of the notice, and take such action thereon, as to that authority may seem proper for the purpose of enforcing the law.

An inspector under this Act may, for the purposes of this section, take with him into a factory or a workshop a medical officer of health, inspector of nuisances, or other officer of the sanitary authority.

[See now Factory and Workshop Act, 1891 (54 & 55 Vic. c. 75), sections 1, 2, 3, and 4 *infra*].

(2.) *Safety.*

5. With respect to the fencing of machinery in a factory the following provisions shall have effect:

(1.) Every hoist or teagle near to which any person is liable to pass or to be employed, and every fly-wheel directly connected with the steam or water or other mechanical power, whether in the engine house or not, and every part of a steam engine and water wheel, shall be securely fenced [see now section 6 of 54 & 55 Vic. c. 75, *infra*]; and

(2.) Every wheel-race not otherwise secured shall be securely fenced close to the edge of the wheel-race; and

(3.) Every part of the mill gearing shall either be securely fenced or be in such position or of such construction as to be equally safe to every person employed in the factory as it would be if it were securely fenced; and

(4.) All fencing shall be constantly maintained in an efficient state while the parts required to be fenced are in motion or use for the purpose of any manufacturing process. [See now section 6 of 54 & 55 Vic. c. 75, *infra*.]

A factory in which there is a contravention of this section shall be deemed not to be kept in conformity with this Act.

[Sections 6, 7, and 8 of 41 Vic. c. 16, relating to fencing machinery, vats, pans, and fixing of grindstones have been repealed by 54 & 55 Vic. c. 75.

See *infra* as to escape from fire, section 7 of 54 & 55 Vic. c. 75; and as to special rules and regulations, sections 8, 9, 10, 11, and 12 of same Act.]

9. A child shall not be allowed to clean any part of the machinery in a factory while the same is in motion by the aid of steam, water, or other mechanical power.

A young person or woman shall not be allowed to clean such part of the machinery in a factory as is mill-gearing while the same is in motion for the purpose of propelling any part of the manufacturing machinery.

A child, young person, or woman shall not be allowed to work between the fixed and traversing part of any self-acting machine while the machine is in motion by the action of steam, water, or other mechanical power.

A child, young person, or woman allowed to clean or to work in contravention of this section shall be deemed to be employed contrary to the provisions of this Act.

[See now section 17 of 54 & 55 Vic. c. 75, *infra*.]

(3.) *Employment and Meal Hours.*

10. A child, young person, or woman shall not be employed in a factory or a workshop except during the period of employment hereinafter mentioned.

11. With respect to the employment of young persons and women in a textile factory the following regulations shall be observed:

(1.) The period of employment, except on Saturday, shall either begin at six o'clock in the morning and end at six o'clock in the evening, or begin at seven o'clock in the morning and end at seven o'clock in the evening; and

(2.) The period of employment on Saturday shall begin either at six o'clock or at seven o'clock in the morning; and

(3.) Where the period of employment on Saturday begins at six o'clock in the morning, that period—

(*a.*) If not less than one hour is allowed for meals, shall end at one o'clock in the afternoon as regards employment in any manufacturing process, and at half-past one o'clock in the afternoon as regards employment for any purpose whatever ; and

(*b.*) If less than one hour is allowed for meals, shall end at half-an-hour after noon as regards employment in any manufacturing process, and at one o'clock in the afternoon as regards employment for any purpose whatever; and

(4.) Where the period of employment on Saturday begins at seven o'clock in the morning, that period shall end at half-past one o'clock in the afternoon as regards any manufacturing process, and at two o'clock in the afternoon as regards employment for any purpose whatever ; and

(5.) There shall be allowed for meals during the said period of employment in the factory—

(*a.*) on every day except Saturday not less than two hours, of which one hour at the least, either at the same time or at different times, shall be before three o'clock in the afternoon ; and

(*b.*) on Saturday not less than half-an-hour ; and

(6.) A young person or woman shall not be employed continuously for more than four hours and a half, without an interval of at least half-an-hour for a meal.

12. With respect to the employment of children in a textile factory the following regulations shall be observed :

(1.) Children shall not be employed except on the system either of employment in morning and afternoon sets, or of employment on alternate days only ; and

(2.) The period of employment for a child in a morning set shall, except on Saturday, begin at the same hour as if the child were a young person, and end at one o'clock in the afternoon, or, if the dinner time begins before one o'clock, at the beginning of dinner time ; and

(3.) The period of employment for a child in an afternoon set shall, except on Saturday, begin at one o'clock in the afternoon, or at any later hour at which the dinner time terminates, and end at the same hour as if the child were a young person ; and

(4.) The period of employment for any child on Saturday shall begin and end at the same hour as if the child were a young person ; and

(5.) A child shall not be employed in two successive periods of seven days in a morning set, nor in two successive periods of seven days in an afternoon set, and a child shall not be employed on two successive Saturdays, nor on Saturday in any week if on any other day in the same week his period of employment has exceeded five hours and a half ; and

(6.) When a child is employed on the alternate day system the period of employment for such child and the time allowed for meals shall be the same as if the child were a young person, but the child shall not be employed on two successive days, and shall not be employed on the same day of the week in two successive weeks ; and

(7.) A child shall not on either system be employed continuously for any longer period than he could be if he were a young person without an interval of at least half-an-hour for a meal.

13. With respect to the employment of young persons and women in a non-textile factory, and of young persons in a workshop, the following regulations shall be observed :

(1.) The period of employment, except on Saturday, shall (save as is in this Act specially excepted) either begin at six o'clock in the morning and end at six o'clock in the evening, or begin at seven o'clock in the morning and end at seven o'clock in the evening ; and

(2.) The period of employment on Saturday shall (save as is in this Act specially excepted) begin at six o'clock in the morning or at seven o'clock in the morning, and end at two o'clock in the afternoon ; and

(3.) There shall be allowed for meals during the said period of employment in the factory or workshop—

(a.) on every day except Saturday not less than one hour and a half, of which one hour at the least, either at the same time or at different times, shall be before three o'clock in the afternoon ; and

(b.) on Saturday not less than half-an-hour ; and

(4.) A young person or a woman in a non-textile factory and a young person in a workshop shall not be employed continuously for more than five hours without an interval of at least half-an-hour for a meal.

14. With respect to the employment of children in a non-textile factory and a workshop the following regulations shall be observed :

(1.) Children shall not be employed except either on the system of employment in morning and afternoon sets, or (in a factory or workshop in which not less than two hours are allowed for meals on every day except Saturday) on the system of employment on alternate days only ; and

(2.) The period of employment for a child in the morning set on every day, including Saturday, shall begin at six or seven o'clock in the morning and end at one o'clock in the afternoon, or, if the dinner time begins before one o'clock, at the beginning of dinner time ; and

(3.) The period of employment for a child in an afternoon set on every day, including Saturday, shall begin at one o'clock in the afternoon, or at any hour later than half-past twelve o'clock at which the dinner time terminates, and end on Saturday at two o'clock in the afternoon, and on any other day at six or seven o'clock in the evening, according as the period of employment for children in the morning set began at six or seven o'clock in the morning ; and

(4.) A child shall not be employed in two successive periods of seven days in a morning set, nor in two successive periods of seven days in an afternoon set, and a child shall not be employed on Saturday in any week in the same set in which he has been employed on any other day of the same week ; and

(5.) When a child is employed on the alternate day system—

(*a.*) The period of employment for such child shall, except on Saturday, either begin at six o'clock in the morning and end at six o'clock in the evening, or begin at seven o'clock in the morning and end at seven o'clock in the evening ; and

(*b.*) The period of employment for such child shall on Saturday begin at six or seven o'clock in the morning, and end at two o'clock in the afternoon ; and

(*c.*) There shall be allowed to such child for meals during the said period of employment not less, on any day except Saturday, than two hours, and on Saturday than half an hour ; but

(*d.*) The child shall not be employed in any manner on two successive days, and shall not be employed on the same day of the week in two successive weeks ; and

(6.) A child shall not on either system be employed continuously for more than five hours without an interval of at least half-an-hour for a meal.

15. With respect to the employment of women in workshops, the following regulations shall be observed :

(1.) In a workshop which is conducted on the system of employing therein children and young persons, or either of them, a woman shall not be employed except during the same period and subject to the same restrictions as if she were a young person ; and the regulations of this Act with respect to the employment of young persons in a workshop shall apply accordingly to the employment of women in that workshop.

[See now section 13 of 54 & 55 Vic. c. 75, *infra.*]

A workshop shall not be deemed to be conducted on the system of not employing therein either children or young persons until the occupier has served on an inspector notice of his intention to conduct his workshop on that system.

16. Where persons are employed at home, that is to say, in a private house, room, or place which, though used as a dwelling, is by reason of the work carried on there a factory or workshop within the meaning of this Act, and in which neither steam, water, nor other mechanical power is used in aid of the manufacturing process carried on there, and in which the only persons employed are members of the same family dwelling there, the foregoing regulations of this Act with respect to the employment of children, young persons, and women shall not apply to such factory or workshop, and in lieu thereof the following regulations shall be observed therein :

(1.) A child or young person shall not be employed in the factory or workshop except during the period of employment hereinafter mentioned ; and

(2.) The period of employment for a young person shall, except on Saturday, begin at six o'clock in the morning and end at nine o'clock in the evening, and shall on Saturday begin at six o'clock in the morning and end at four o'clock in the afternoon ; and

(3.) There shall be allowed to every young person for meals and absence from work during the period of employment not less, except on Saturday, than four hours and a half, and on Saturday than two hours and a half ; and

(4.) The period of employment for a child on every day either shall begin at six o'clock in the morning and end at one o'clock in the afternoon, or shall begin at one o'clock in the afternoon and end at eight o'clock in the evening or on Saturday at four o'clock in the afternoon ; and for the purpose of the provisions of this Act respecting education such child shall be deemed, according to circumstances, to be employed in a morning or afternoon set ; and

(5.) A child shall not be employed before the hour of one in the afternoon in the two successive periods of seven days, nor after that hour in two successive periods of seven days, and a child shall not be employed on Saturday in any week before the hour of one in the afternoon, if on any other day in the same week he has been employed before that hour, nor after that hour if on any other day of the same week he has been employed after that hour ; and

(6.) A child shall not be employed continuously for more than five hours without an interval of at least half-an-hour for a meal.

17. With respect to meals the following regulations shall (save as is in this Act specially excepted) be observed in a factory and workshop :

(1.) All children, young persons, and women employed therein shall have the times allowed for meals at the same hour of the day ; and

(2.) A child, young person, or woman shall not during any part of the times allowed for meals in the factory or workshop, be employed in the factory or the workshop, or be allowed to remain in a room in which a manufacturing process or handicraft is then being carried on.

[For section 18 now read section 15 of 54 & 55 Vic. c. 75, *infra*.]

19. The occupier of a factory or workshop may from time to time fix within the limits allowed by this Act, and shall (save as is in this Act specially excepted) specify in a notice affixed in the factory or workshop, the period of employment, the times allowed for meals, and whether the children are employed on the system of morning and afternoon sets or of alternate days.

The period of employment and the times allowed for meals in the factory or workshop shall be deemed to be the period and the times specified in the notice affixed in the factory or workshop ; and all the children in the factory or workshop shall be employed either on the system of morning and afternoon sets or on the system of alternate days according to the system for the time being specified in such notice :

Provided that a change in such period or times or system of employment shall not be made until after the occupier has served on an inspector and affixed in the factory or workshop notice of his intention to make such change, and shall not be made oftener than once a quarter, unless for special cause allowed in writing by an inspector.

20. A child under the age of ten years shall not be employed in a factory or workshop. [See, however, section 18 of 54 & 55 Vic. c. 75, *infra*.]

21. A child, young person, or woman shall not (save as is in this Act specially excepted) be employed on Sunday in a factory or workshop.

(4.) *Holidays.*

22. The occupier of a factory or of a workshop shall (save as is in this Act specially excepted) allow to every child, young person, and woman employed therein the following holidays; that is to say,

(1.) The whole of Christmas Day, and the whole either of Good Friday or, if it is so specified by the occupier in the notice affixed in the factory or workshop, of the next public holiday under the Holidays Extension Act, 1875; and in addition

(2.) Eight half holidays in every year, but a whole holiday may be allowed in lieu of two such half holidays; and

(3.) At least half of the said half holidays or whole holidays shall be allowed between the fifteenth day of March and the first day of October in every year; and

[For sub-section 4 now read section 16 (4) of 54 & 55 Vic. c. 75, *infra*.]

(5.) A half holiday shall comprise at least one half of the period of employment for young persons and women on some day other than Saturday.

A child, young person, or woman who—

(*a.*) On a whole holiday fixed by or in pursuance of this section for a factory or workshop is employed in the factory or workshop, or

(*b.*) On a half holiday fixed in pursuance of this section for a factory or workshop is employed in the factory or workshop during the portion of the period of employment assigned for such half holiday,

shall be deemed to be employed contrary to the provisions of this Act.

If in a factory or workshop such whole holidays or half holidays as required by this section are not fixed in conformity therewith, the occupier of the factory or workshop shall be liable to a fine not exceeding five pounds.

[See, further, sections 33 and 34 of 54 & 55 Vic. c. 75, *infra*.]

(5.) *Education of Children.*

23. The parent of a child employed in a factory or in a workshop shall cause that child to attend some recognised efficient school (which school may be selected by such parent), as follows:

(1.) The child, when employed in a morning or afternoon set, shall in every week, during any part of which he is so employed, be caused to attend on each work day for at least one attendance; and

(2.) The child, when employed on the alternate day system, shall on each work day preceding each day of employment in the factory or workshop be caused to attend for at least two attendances;

(3.) An attendance for the purposes of this section shall be an attendance as defined for the time being by a Secretary of State with the consent of the Education Department, and be between the hours of eight in the morning and six in the evening:

Provided that—

(a.) A child shall not be required by this Act to attend school on Saturday or on any holiday or half holiday allowed under this Act in the factory or workshop in which the child is employed; and

(b.) The non-attendance of the child shall be excused on every day on which he is certified by the teacher of the school to have been prevented from attending by sickness or other unavoidable cause, also when the school is closed during the ordinary holidays or for any other temporary cause; and

(c.) Where there is not within the distance of two miles, measured according to the nearest road, from the residence of the child a recognised efficient school which the child can attend, attendance at a school temporarily approved in writing by an inspector under this Act, although not a recognised efficient school, shall for the purposes of this Act be deemed attendance at a recognised efficient school until such recognised efficient school as aforesaid is established, and with a view to such establishment the inspector shall immediately report to the Education Department every case of the approval of a school by him under this section.

A child who has not in any week attended school for all the attendances required by this section shall not be employed in the following week until he has attended school for the deficient number of attendances.

The Education Department shall from time to time, by the publication of lists or by notices or otherwise as they think expedient, provide for giving to all persons interested information of the schools in each school district which are recognised efficient schools.

24. The occupier of a factory or workshop in which a child is employed shall on Monday in every week (after the first week in which such child began to work therein), or on some other day appointed for that purpose by an inspector, obtain from the teacher of the recognised efficient school attended by the child, a certificate (according to the prescribed form and directions) respecting the attendance of such child at school in accordance with this Act.

The employment of a child without obtaining such certificate as is required by this section shall be deemed to be employment of a child contrary to the provisions of this Act.

The occupier shall keep every such certificate for two months after the date thereof, if the child so long continues to be employed in his factory or his workshop, and shall produce the same to an inspector when required during that period.

25. The board authority or persons who manage a recognised efficient school attended by a child employed in a factory or workshop,

or some person authorised by such board authority or person, may apply in writing to the occupier of the factory or workshop to pay a weekly sum specified in the application, not exceeding threepence and not exceeding one twelfth part of the wages of the child, and after that application the occupier, so long as he employs the child, shall be liable to pay to the applicants, while the child attends their school, the said weekly sum, and the sum may be recovered as a debt, and the occupier may deduct the sum so paid by him from the wages payable for the services of the child.

26. When a child of the age of thirteen years has obtained from a person authorised by the Education Department a certificate of having attained such standard of proficiency in reading, writing, and arithmetic, or such standard of previous due attendance at a certified efficient school, as hereinafter mentioned, that child shall be deemed to be a young person for the purposes of this Act.

The standards of proficiency and due attendance for the purposes of this section shall be such as may be from time to time fixed for the purposes of this Act by a Secretary of State, with the consent of the Education Department, and the standards so fixed shall be published in the London Gazette, and shall not have effect until the expiration of at least six months after such publication.

Attendance at a certified day industrial school shall be deemed for the purposes of this section to be attendance at a certified efficient school.

(6.) *Certificates of Fitness for Employment.*

27. In a factory a child or a young person under the age of sixteen years shall not be employed for more than seven, or if the certifying surgeon for the district resides more than three miles from the factory thirteen, work days, unless the occupier of the factory has obtained a certificate, in the prescribed form, of the fitness of such child or young person for employment in that factory.

A certificate of fitness for employment for the purposes of this Act shall be granted by the certifying surgeon for the district, and shall be to the effect that he is satisfied, by the production of a certificate of birth or other sufficient evidence, that the person named in the certificate of fitness is of the age therein specified, and has been personally examined by him, and is not incapacitated by disease or bodily infirmity for working daily for the time allowed by law in the factory named in the certificate.

28. In order to enable occupiers of workshops to better secure the observance of this Act, and prevent the employment in their workshops of children and young persons under the age of sixteen years who are unfitted for that employment, an occupier of a workshop is hereby authorised to obtain, if he thinks fit, from the certifying surgeon for the district, certificates of the fitness of children and of young persons under the age of sixteen years for employment in his workshop, in like manner as if that workshop were a factory, and the certifying surgeon shall examine the children and young persons, and grant certificates accordingly.

29. Where an inspector is of opinion that a child or a young person under the age of sixteen years is by disease or bodily infirmity incapacitated for working daily for the time allowed by law in the factory or workshop in which he is employed, he may serve written

notice thereof on the occupier of the factory or workshop requiring that the employment of such child or young person be discontinued from the period named therein, not being less than one nor more than seven days after the service of such notice, and the occupier shall not continue after the period named in such notice to employ such child or young person (notwithstanding a certificate of fitness has been previously obtained for such child or young person), unless the certifying surgeon for the district has, after the service of the notice, personally examined such child or young person, and has certified that such child or young person is not so incapacitated as aforesaid.

30. All factories and workshops in the occupation of the same occupier, and in the district of the same certifying surgeon, or any of them, may be named in the certificate of fitness for employment, if the surgeon is of opinion that he can truly give the certificate for employment therein.

The certificate of birth (which may be produced to a certifying surgeon) shall either be a certified copy of the entry in the register of births, kept in pursuance of the Acts relating to the registration of births, of the birth of the child or young person (whether such copy be obtained in pursuance of the Elementary Education Act, 1876, or otherwise), or be a certificate from a local authority within the meaning of the Elementary Education Act, 1876, to the effect that it appears from the returns transmitted to such authority in pursuance of the said Act by the registrar of births and deaths that the child was born at the date named in the certificate.

Where a certificate of fitness for employment is to the effect that the certifying surgeon has been satisfied of the age of a child or young person by evidence other than the production of a certificate of birth, an inspector may, by notice in writing, annul the surgeon's certificate, if he has reasonable cause to believe that the real age of the child or young person named in it is less than that mentioned in the certificate, and thereupon that certificate shall be of no avail for the purposes of this Act.

When a child becomes a young person a fresh certificate of fitness must be obtained.

The occupier shall, when required, produce to an inspector at the factory or workshop in which a child or young person is employed, the certificate of fitness of such child or young person for employment, which he is required to obtain under this Act.

[See as to certificates of birth, section 30 of 54 & 55 Vic. c. 75, *infra.*]

(7.) *Accidents.*

31. Where there occurs in a factory or a workshop any accident which either—

(*a.*) causes loss of life to a person employed in the factory or in the workshop, or

(*b.*) causes bodily injury to a person employed in the factory or in the workshop, and is produced either by machinery moved by steam, water, or other mechanical power, or through a vat, pan, or other structure filled with hot liquid or molten metal or other substance, or by explosion, or by escape of gas, steam, or metal, and is of such a nature as to prevent the person injured by it from returning to his work in the factory or workshop within forty-eight hours after · the occurrence of the accident,

written notice of the accident shall forthwith be sent to the inspector and to the certifying surgeon for the district, stating the residence of the person killed or injured, or the place to which he may have been removed, and if any such notice is not sent the occupier of the factory or workshop shall be liable to a fine not exceeding five pounds.

If any such accident as aforesaid occurs to a person employed in an iron mill or blast furnace, or other factory or workshop where the occupier is not the actual employer of the person killed or injured, the actual employer shall immediately report the same to the occupier, and in default shall be liable to a fine not exceeding five pounds.

A notice of an accident, of which notice is required by section sixty-three of the Explosives Act, 1875, to be sent to a government inspector, need not be sent to the certifying surgeon in pursuance of this section.

32. Where a certifying surgeon receives in pursuance of this Act notice of an accident in a factory or a workshop, he shall with the least possible delay proceed to the factory or workshop, and make a full investigation as to the nature and cause of the death or injury caused by that accident, and within the next twenty-four hours send to the inspector a report thereof.

The certifying surgeon, for the purpose only of an investigation under this section, shall have the same powers as an inspector, and shall also have power to enter any room in a building to which the person killed or injured has been removed.

There shall be paid to the said surgeon for the investigation such fee, not exceeding ten or less than three shillings, as a Secretary of State considers reasonable, which fee shall be paid as expenses incurred by a Secretary of State in the execution of this Act.

[As to other regulations on accidents, see section twenty-two of 54 & 55 Vic. c. 75, *infra;* and as to Scotland, section thirty-three, *infra.*]

PART II.

Special Provisions relating to Particular Classes of Factories and Workshops.

(1.) *Special Provisions for Health in Certain Factories and Workshops.*

33. For the purpose of securing the observance of the requirements of this Act as to cleanliness in every factory and workshop, all the inside walls of the rooms of a factory or workshop, and all the ceilings or tops of such rooms (whether such walls, ceilings, or tops be plastered or not), and all the passages and staircases of a factory or workshop, if they have not been painted with oil or varnished once at least within seven years, shall be limewashed once at least within every fourteen months, to date from the period when last limewashed; and if they have been so painted or varnished shall be washed with hot water and soap once at least within every fourteen months, to date from the period when last washed.

A factory or workshop in which there is a contravention of this section shall be deemed not to be kept in conformity with this Act.

Where it appears to a Secretary of State that in any class of factories or workshops, or parts thereof, the regulations in this section are not required for the purpose of securing therein the observance of the requirements of this Act as to cleanliness, or are by reason of special circumstances inapplicable, he may, if he thinks fit, by order made under this part of this Act, grant to such class of factories or workshops, or parts thereof, a special exception that the regulations in this section shall not apply thereto.

34. Where a bakehouse is situate in any city, town, or place containing, according to the last published Census for the time being, a population of more than five thousand persons, all the inside walls of the rooms of such bakehouse, and all the ceilings or tops of such rooms (whether such walls, ceilings, or tops be plastered or not), and all the passages and staircases of such bakehouse, shall either be painted with oil or varnished or be limewashed, or be partly painted or varnished and partly limewashed; where painted with oil or varnished there shall be three coats of paint or varnish, and the paint or varnish shall be renewed once at least in every seven years, and shall be washed with hot water and soap once at least in every six months; where limewashed the limewashing shall be renewed once at least in every six months.

A bakehouse in which there is any contravention of this section shall be deemed not to be kept in conformity with this Act.

35. Where a bakehouse is situate in any city, town, or place containing, according to the last published Census for the time being, a population of more than five thousand persons, a place on the same level with the bakehouse, and forming part of the same building, shall not be used as a sleeping place, unless it is constructed as follows; that is to say,

> unless it is effectually separated from the bakehouse by a partition extending from the floor to the ceiling; and

> unless there be an external glazed window of at least nine superficial feet in area, of which at the least four and a half superficial feet are made to open for ventilation.

Any person who lets or occupies or continues to let or knowingly suffers to be occupied any place contrary to this section shall be liable to a fine not exceeding, for the first offence, twenty shillings, and for every subsequent offence five pounds.

36. If in a factory or workshop where grinding, glazing, or polishing on a wheel, or any process is carried on, by which dust is generated and inhaled by the workers to an injurious extent, it appears to an inspector that such inhalation could be to a great extent prevented by the use of a fan or other mechanical means, the inspector may direct a fan or other mechanical means of a proper construction for preventing such inhalation to be provided within a reasonable time; and if the same is not provided, maintained, and used, the factory or workshop shall be deemed not to be kept in conformity with this Act.

37. A child, young person, or woman shall not be employed in any part of a factory in which wet-spinning is carried on, unless sufficient means be employed and continued for protecting the workers from being wetted, and, where hot water is used, for preventing the escape of steam into the room occupied by the workers.

A factory in which there is a contravention of this section shall be deemed not to be kept in conformity with this Act.

(2.) *Special Restrictions as to Employment, Meals, and Certificates of Fitness.*

38. A child or young person shall not, to the extent mentioned in the First Schedule to this Act, be employed in the factories or workshops or parts thereof named in that schedule.

Notice of the prohibition in this section shall be affixed in a factory or workshop to which it applies.

39. A child, young person, or woman shall not be allowed to take a meal or to remain during the times allowed for meals in the parts of factories or workshops to which this section applies; and a child, young person, or woman allowed to take a meal or to remain in contravention of this section shall be deemed to be employed contrary to the provisions of this Act.

Notice of the prohibition in this section shall be affixed in a factory or workshop to which it applies.

This section applies to the parts of factories or workshops named in the Second Schedule to this Act.

Where it appears to a Secretary of State that by reason of the nature of the process in any class of factories or workshops or parts thereof not named in the said schedule, the taking of meals therein is specially injurious to health, he may, if he thinks fit, by order made under this part of this Act, extend the prohibition in this section to the said class of factories or workshops or parts thereof.

If the prohibition in this section is proved to the satisfaction of a Secretary of State to be no longer necessary for the protection of the health of children, young persons, and women in any class of factories or workshops or parts thereof to which the prohibition has been extended by an order, he may, by an order made under this part of this Act, rescind the order of extension, without prejudice nevertheless to the subsequent making of another order.

40. In print works and bleaching and dyeing works the period of employment for a child, young person, and woman, and the times allowed for meals, shall be the same as if the said works were a textile factory, and the regulations of this Act with respect to the employment of children, young persons, and women in a textile factory shall apply accordingly, as if print works and bleaching and dyeing works were textile factories; save that nothing in this section shall prevent the continuous employment of a child, young person, or woman in the said works without an interval of half an hour for a meal, for the period allowed by this Act in a non-textile factory.

41. Where it appears to a Secretary of State that by reason of special circumstances affecting any class of workshops it is expedient for protecting the health of the children and of the young persons under the age of sixteen years employed therein, to extend thereto the prohibition in this section mentioned, he may, by order made under this part of this Act, extend to such class of workshops the prohibition in this Act of the employment of children and young persons under the age of sixteen years without a certificate of the fitness of such child or young person for employment, and thereupon the provisions of this Act with respect to certificates of fitness for employment shall apply to the class of workshops named in the order in like manner as if they were factories.

If the prohibition is proved to the satisfaction of the Secretary of State to be no longer necessary for the protection of the health of the children and the young persons under the age of sixteen years employed in any class of workshops to which it has been extended under this section, he may by order made under this part of this Act rescind the order of extension, without prejudice nevertheless to the subsequent making of another order.

(3.) *Special Exceptions relaxing General Law in certain Factories and Workshops.*

(a.) *Period of Employment.*

42. In the factories and workshops or parts thereof to which this exception applies the period of employment for young persons and women, if so fixed by the occupier and specified in the notice, may, except on Saturday, begin at eight o'clock in the morning and end at eight o'clock in the evening, and on Saturday may begin at eight o'clock in the morning and end at four o'clock in the afternoon, or where it begins at seven o'clock in the morning may end at three o'clock in the afternoon; and the period of employment for a child in a morning set may begin at the same hour, and the period of employment for a child in an afternoon set may end at the same hour.

This exception applies to the factories and workshops and parts thereof specified in Part One of the Third Schedule to this Act.

Where it is proved to the satisfaction of a Secretary of State that the customs or exigencies of the trade carried on in any class of non-textile factories or workshops or part thereof, either generally or when situate in any particular locality, require the extension thereto of this exception, and that the extension can be made without injury to the health of the children, young persons, and women affected thereby, he may by order made under this part of this Act extend this exception accordingly.

43. Where it is proved to the satisfaction of a Secretary of State that the customs or exigencies of the trade carried on in any class of non-textile factories or workshops or parts thereof, either generally or when situate in any particular locality, require that the special exception hereafter in this section mentioned should be granted, and that such grant can be made without injury to the health of the children, young persons, and women affected thereby, he may by order made under this part of this Act grant to such class of factories or workshops or parts thereof a special exception, that the period of employment for young persons and women therein, if so fixed by the occupier and specified in the notice, may on any day except Saturday begin at nine o'clock in the morning and end at nine o'clock in the evening, and in such case the period of employment for a child in a morning set shall begin at nine o'clock in the morning, and the period of employment for a child in an afternoon set shall end at eight o'clock in the evening.

44. The regulations of this Act with respect to the employment of young persons in textile factories shall not prevent the employment,

O

in the part of a textile factory in which a machine for the manufacture of lace is moved by steam, water, or other mechanical power, of any male young person above the age of sixteen years between four o'clock in the morning and ten o'clock in the evening, if he is employed in accordance with the following conditions; namely,

    (*a*.) Where such young person is employed on any day before the beginning or after the end of the ordinary period of employment in the factory, there shall be allowed him for meals and absence from work between the above-mentioned hours of four in the morning and ten in the evening not less than nine hours ; and

    (*b*.) Where such young person is employed on any day before the beginning of the ordinary period of employment in the factory, he shall not be employed on the same day after the end of that period ; and

    (*c*.) Where such young person is employed on any day after the end of the ordinary period of employment in the factory, he shall not be employed next morning before the beginning of the ordinary period of employment.

For the purpose of this exception the ordinary period of employment in the factory means the period of employment for young persons under the age of sixteen years or women in the factory, or if none are employed means such period as can under this Act be fixed for the employment of such young persons and women in the factory, and notice of such period shall be affixed in the factory.

45. The regulations of this Act with respect to the employment of young persons in non-textile factories or workshops shall not prevent the employment, in the part of a bakehouse in which the process of baking bread is carried on, of any male young person above the age of sixteen years between five o'clock in the morning and nine o'clock in the evening, if he is employed in accordance with the following conditions ; namely,

    (*a*.) Where such young person is employed on any day before the beginning or after the end of the ordinary period of employment in the bakehouse, there shall be allowed him for meals and absence from work between the above-mentioned hours of five in the morning and nine in the evening not less than seven hours ; and

    (*b*.) Where such young person is employed on any day before the beginning of the ordinary period of employment in the bakehouse, he shall not be employed after the end of that period on the same day ; and

    (*c*.) Where such young person is employed on any day after the end of the ordinary period of employment in the bakehouse, he shall not be employed next morning before the beginning of the ordinary period of employment.

For the purpose of this exception the ordinary period of employment in the bakehouse means the period of employment for young persons under the age of sixteen years or women in the bakehouse, or if none are employed, means such period as can under this Act be fixed for the employment of such young persons and women in the bakehouse, and notice of such period shall be affixed in the bakehouse.

Where it is proved to the satisfaction of the Secretary of State that the exigencies of the trade carried on in bakehouses, either generally or when situate in any particular locality, require that the special exception hereafter in this section mentioned should be granted, and that such grant can be made without injury to the health of the male young persons affected thereby, he may by order made under this part of this Act grant to bakehouses, or to bakehouses situate in the said locality, a special exception permitting the employment of male young persons of sixteen years of age and upwards as if they were no longer young persons.

46. Where it is proved to the satisfaction of a Secretary of State that the customs or exigencies of the trade carried on in any class of non-textile factories or workshops, either generally or when situate in any particular locality, require some other day in the week to be substituted for Saturday as regards the hour at which the period of employment for children, young persons, and women is required by this Act to end on Saturday, he may by order made under this part of this Act grant to such class of factories or workshops a special exception, authorising the occupier of every such factory or workshop to substitute by a notice affixed in his factory or workshop some other day for Saturday, and in such case this Act shall apply in such factory or workshop in like manner as if the substituted day were Saturday, and Saturday were an ordinary work day.

47. In the process of Turkey red dyeing, nothing in Part One of this Act shall prevent the employment of young persons and women on Saturday until half-past four o'clock in the afternoon, but the additional number of hours so worked shall be computed as part of the week's limit of work, which shall in no case be exceeded.

48. In any of the textile factories to which this exception applies, if the period of employment for young persons and women, as fixed by the occupier and specified in the notice, begins at the hour of seven in the morning, and the whole time between that hour and eight o'clock is allowed for meals, the regulations of this Act with respect to the employment of children, young persons, and women shall not prevent a child, young person, or woman, between the first day of November and the last day of March next following, being employed continuously, without an interval of at least half an hour for a meal, for the same period as if the factory were a non-textile factory.

This exception applies to the textile factories specified in Part Seven of the Third Schedule to this Act.

Where it is proved to the satisfaction of a Secretary of State that in any class of textile factories, either generally or when situate in any particular locality, the customary habits of the persons employed therein require the extension thereto of this exception, and that the manufacturing process carried on therein is of a healthy character, and the extension can be made without injury to the health of the children, young persons, and women affected thereby, he may by order made under this part of this Act extend this exception accordingly.

49. Where it is proved to the satisfaction of a Secretary of State that the customs or exigencies of the trade carried on in any class of non-textile factories or workshops, either generally or when situate in any particular locality, require that the special exception hereafter in this section mentioned should be granted, he may by order made under this part of this Act grant to such class of factories or work-

shops a special exception, authorising the occupier of any such factory or workshop to allow all or any of the half holidays, or whole holidays in lieu of them, on different days to any of the children, young persons, and women employed in his factory or workshop, or to any sets of such children, young persons, and women, and not on the same days.

50. Where the occupier of a factory or workshop is a person of the Jewish religion, the regulations of this Act with respect to the employment of young persons and women shall not prevent him—

> (1.) If he keeps his factory or workshop closed on Saturday until sunset, from employing young persons and women on Saturday from after sunset until nine o'clock in the evening ; or
>
> (2.) If he keeps his factory or workshop closed on Saturday both before and after sunset, from employing young persons and women one hour on every other day in the week (not being Sunday), in addition to the hours allowed by this Act, so that such hour be at the beginning or end of the period of employment, and be not before six o'clock in the morning or after nine o'clock in the evening ; or
>
> (3.) If all the children, young persons, and women in his factory or workshop are of the Jewish religion, from giving them, if so specified in a notice affixed in the factory or workshop as by this Act provided, any two public holidays under the Holidays Extension Act, 1875, in lieu of Christmas Day and Good Friday, but in that case such factory or workshop shall not be open for traffic on Christmas Day or Good Friday.

51. No penalty shall be incurred by any person in respect of any work done on Sunday in a factory or workshop by a young person or woman of the Jewish religion, subject to the following conditions :

> (1.) The occupier of the factory or workshop shall be of the Jewish religion ; and
>
> (2.) The factory or workshop shall be closed on Saturday and shall not be open for traffic on Sunday ; and
>
> (3.) The occupier shall not avail himself of the exception authorising the employment of young persons and women on Saturday evening, or for an additional hour during any other day of the week.

Where the occupier avails himself of this exception, this Act shall apply to the factory or workshop in like manner as if in the provisions thereof respecting Sunday the word Saturday were substituted for Sunday, and in the provisions thereof respecting Saturday the word Sunday, or, if the occupier so specify in the notice, the word Friday were substituted for Saturday.

(b.) *Meal Hours.*

52. The provisions of this Act which require that all the children, young persons, and women employed in a factory or workshop shall have the times allowed for meals at the same hour of the day shall not apply in the cases mentioned in Part Two of the Third Schedule to this Act.

The provisions of this Act which require that a child, young person, and woman shall not, during any part of the times allowed for meals in a factory or workshop, be employed in a factory or the workshop, or be allowed to remain in a room in which a manufacturing process or handicraft is being carried on, shall not apply in the cases and to the extent mentioned in Part Two of the Third Schedule to this Act.

Where it is proved to the satisfaction of a Secretary of State that in any class of factories or workshops or parts thereof it is necessary, by reason of the continuous nature of the process, or of special circumstances affecting such class, to extend thereto the exceptions in this section or either of them, and that such extension can be made without injury to the health of the children, young persons, and women affected thereby, he may by order made under this part of this Act extend the same accordingly.

(c.) *Overtime.*

53. The regulations of this Act with respect to the employment of young persons and women shall not prevent the employment in the factories and workshops or parts thereof to which this exception applies of young persons and of women during a period of employment beginning at six o'clock in the morning and ending at eight o'clock in the evening, or beginning at seven o'clock in the morning and ending at nine o'clock in the evening, or beginning at eight o'clock in the morning and ending at ten o'clock in the evening, if they are employed in accordance with the following conditions ; namely,

(1.) There shall be allowed to every such young person and woman for meals during the period of employment not less than two hours, of which half an hour shall be after five o'clock in the evening ; and

(2.) Any such young person or woman shall not be so employed on the whole for more than five days in any one week, nor for more than forty-eight days in any twelve months.

This exception applies to the factories and workshops and parts thereof specified in Part Three of the Third Schedule to this Act.

Where it is proved to the satisfaction of a Secretary of State that in any class of non-textile factories or workshops or parts thereof it is necessary, by reason of the material which is the subject of the manufacturing process or handicraft therein being liable to be spoiled by the weather, or by reason of press of work arising at certain recurring seasons of the year, or by reason of the liability of the business to a sudden press of orders arising from unforeseen events, to employ young persons and women in manner authorised by this exception, and that such employment will not injure the health of the young persons and women affected thereby, he may by order made under this part of this Act extend this exception to such factories or workshops or parts thereof.

54. If in any factory or workshop or part thereof to which this exception applies, the process in which a child, young person, or woman is employed is in an incomplete state at the end of the period of employment of such child, young person, or woman, the provisions of this Act with respect to the period of employment shall not prevent

such child, young person, or woman from being employed for a
further period not exceeding thirty minutes :

Provided that such further periods when added to the total number
of hours of the periods of employment of such child, young person, or
woman in that week, do not raise that total above the number otherwise allowed under this Act.

This exception applies to the factories and workshops specified in
Part Four of the Third Schedule to this Act.

Where it is proved to the satisfaction of a Secretary of State that
in any class of non-textile factories or workshops or parts thereof
the time for the completion of a process cannot by reason of the
nature thereof be accurately fixed, and that the extension to such
class of factories or workshops or parts thereof of this exception can
be made without injury to the health of the children, young persons,
and women affected thereby, he may by order made under this part
of this Act, extend this exception accordingly.

55. Nothing in this Act shall prevent the employment of young
persons and women so far as is necessary for the purpose only of
preventing any damage which may arise from spontaneous combustion in the process of Turkey red dyeing, or from any extraordinary
atmospheric influence in the process of open-air bleaching. [See also
section 32 of 54 & 55 Vic., c. 75, *infra.*]

56. The regulations of this Act with respect to the employment of
young persons and women shall not prevent the employment, in the
factories and workshops and parts thereof to which this exception
applies, of women during a period of employment beginning at six
o'clock in the morning and ending at eight o'clock in the evening, or
beginning at seven o'clock in the morning and ending at nine o'clock
in the evening, if they are employed in accordance with the following
conditions ; namely,

    (1.) There shall be allowed to every such woman for meals
        during the period of employment not less than two hours,
        of which half an hour shall be after five o'clock in the
        evening ; and

    (2.) Any such woman shall not be so employed on the whole for
        more than five days in any one week, nor for more than
        ninety-six days in any twelve months.

This exception applies to the factories and workshops and parts
thereof specified in Part Five of the Third Schedule to this Act.

Where it is proved to the satisfaction of a Secretary of State that
in any class of non-textile factories or workshops or parts thereof
it is necessary, by reason of the perishable nature of the articles or
materials which are the subject of the manufacturing process or
handicraft, to employ women in manner authorised by this exception, and that such employment will not injure the health of the
women employed, he may by order made under this part of this
Act extend this exception to such factories or workshops or parts
thereof.

57. Where it appears to a Secretary of State that factories driven
by water power are liable to be stopped by drought or flood, he may,
by order made under this part of this Act, grant to such factories a
special exception permitting the employment of young persons and
women during a period of employment from six o'clock in the morning
until seven o'clock in the afternoon, on such conditions as he may

think proper, but so as that no person shall be deprived of the meal hours by this Act provided, nor be so employed on Saturday, and that as regards factories liable to be stopped by drought, such special exception shall not extend to more than ninety-six days in any period of twelve months, and as regards factories liable to be stopped by floods, such special exception shall not extend to more than forty-eight days in any period of twelve months. This overtime shall not extend in any case beyond the time already lost during the previous twelve months.

(d.) *Nightwork.*

58. Nothing in this Act shall prevent the employment, in factories and workshops to which this exception applies, of male young persons during the night, if they are employed in accordance with the following conditions :

    (1.) The period of employment shall not exceed twelve consecutive hours, and shall begin and end at the hours specified in the notice in this Act mentioned ; and

    (2.) The provisions of Part One of this Act with respect to the allowance of time for meals to young persons during the period of employment shall be observed with the necessary modifications as to the hour at which the times allowed for meals are fixed ; and

    (3.) A male young person employed during any part of the night shall not be employed during any part of the twelve hours preceding or succeeding the period of employment ; and

    (4.) A male young person shall not be employed on more than six nights, or in the case of blast furnaces or paper mills seven nights, in any two weeks.

The provisions of this Act with respect to the period of employment on Saturday, and with respect to the allowance to young persons of eight half holidays in every year or of whole holidays in lieu of them, shall not apply to a male young person employed in day and night turns in pursuance of this exception.

This exception applies to the factories and workshops specified in Part Six of the Third Schedule to this Act.

Where it is proved to the satisfaction of a Secretary of State that in any class of non-textile factories or workshops or parts thereof it is necessary, by reason of the nature of the business requiring the process to be carried on throughout the night, to employ male young persons of sixteen years of age or upwards at night, and that such employment will not injure the health of the male young persons employed, he may by order made under this part of this Act extend this exception to such factories or workshops or parts thereof, so far as regards young persons of the age of sixteen years or upwards.

59. In a factory or workshop in which the process of printing newspapers is carried on on not more than two nights in the week, nothing in this Act shall prevent the employment of a male young person of sixteen years of age and upwards at night during not more than two nights in a week, as if he were no longer a young person.

60. In glass works nothing in this Act shall prevent any male young person from working according to the accustomed hours of the works, if he is employed in accordance with the following conditions; namely,

(1.) The total number of hours of the periods of employment shall not exceed sixty in any one week ; and

(2.) The periods of employment for any such young person shall not exceed fourteen hours in four separate turns per week, or twelve hours in five separate turns per week, or ten hours in six separate turns per week, or any less number of hours in the accustomed number of separate turns per week, so that such number of turns do not exceed nine ; and,

(3.) Such young person shall not work in any turn without an interval of time not less than one full turn ; and,

(4.) There shall be allowed to [such young person during each turn (so far as is practicable) the like times for meals as are required by this Act to be allowed in any other non-textile factory or workshop.

(4.) *Special Exception for Domestic and certain other Factories and Workshops.*

61. The provisions of this Act which relate—

(1.) To the cleanliness (including limewashing, painting, varnishing, and washing) or to the freedom from effluvia, or to the overcrowding, or ventilation of a factory or workshop ; or

(2.) To all children, young persons, and women employed in a factory or workshop having the times allowed for meals at the same hour of the day, or during any part of the times allowed for meals in a factory or workshop being employed in the factory or workshop or being allowed to remain in any room ; or

(3.) To the affixing of any notice or abstract in a factory or workshop ; or specifying any matter in the notice so affixed ; or

(4.) To the allowance of any holidays to a child, young person, or woman; or

(5.) To the sending notice of accidents ;

shall not apply—

(*a*.) Where persons are employed at home, that is to say, to a private house, room, or place which, though used as a dwelling, is by reason of the work carried on there a factory or workshop within the meaning of this Act, and in which neither steam, water, nor other mechanical power is used, and in which the only persons employed are members of the same family dwelling there. [See 54 & 55 Vict., c. 75, *infra*.]

And the provisions of this Act with respect to certificates of fitness for employment shall apply to any such private house, room, or place as aforesaid, which by reason of the nature of the work carried on there is a factory, as if the same were a workshop within the meaning of this Act, and not a factory.

Where the occupier of a workshop has served on an inspector

notice of his intention to conduct that workshop on the system of not employing children or young persons therein, the workshop shall be deemed for all the purposes of this Act to be conducted on the said system until the occupier changes it, and no change shall be made until the occupier has served on the inspector notice of his intention to change the system, and until the change a child or young person employed in the workshop shall be deemed to be employed contrary to the provisions of this Act. A change in the said system shall not be made oftener than once a quarter, unless for special cause allowed in writing by an inspector.

Nothing in this section shall exempt a bakehouse from the provisions of this Act with respect to cleanliness (including limewashing, painting, varnishing, and washing), or to freedom from effluvia.

62. The regulations of this Act with respect to the employment of women shall not apply to flax scutch mills which are conducted on the system of not employing either children or young persons therein, and which are worked intermittently, and for periods only which do not exceed in the whole six months in any year. A flax scutch mill shall not be deemed to be conducted on the system of not employing therein either children or young persons until the occupier has served on an inspector notice of his intention to conduct such mill on that system.

(5.) *Supplemental as to Special Provisions.*

63. Where it appears to a Secretary of State that the adoption of any special means or provision for the cleanliness or ventilation of a factory or workshop is required for the protection of the health of any child, young person, or woman employed, in pursuance of an exception under this part of this Act, either for a longer period than is otherwise allowed by this Act, or at night, he may by order made under this part of this Act direct that the adoption of such means or provision shall be a condition of such employment; and if it appears to a Secretary of State that the adoption of any such means or provision is no longer required, or is, having regard to all the circumstances, inexpedient, he may, by order made under this part of this Act, rescind the order directing such adoption without prejudice to the subsequent making of another order.

64. Where an exception has been granted or extended under this part of this Act by an order of a Secretary of State, and it appears to a Secretary of State that such exception is injurious to the health of the children, young persons, or women employed in, or is no longer necessary for the carrying on of the business in, the class of factories or workshops or parts thereof to which the said exception was so granted or extended, he may by an order made under this part of this Act rescind the grant or extension, without prejudice to the subsequent making of another order.

65. Where a Secretary of State has power to make an order under this part of this Act, the following provisions shall apply to that order :

(1.) The order shall be under the hand of the Secretary of State and shall be published in the London Gazette, and shall come into operation at the date of such publication in the London Gazette, or at any later date mentioned in the order :

o 3

(2.) The order may be temporary or permanent, conditional or
unconditional, and whether extending a prohibition or
exception, granting an exception, directing the adoption of
any means or provisions, or rescinding a previous order,
or effecting any other thing, may do so either wholly or
partly:

(3.) The order shall be laid as soon as may be before both Houses
of Parliament, and if either House of Parliament, within
the next forty days after the same has been so laid before
such House, resolve that such order ought to be annulled,
the same shall after the date of such resolution be of no
effect, without prejudice to the validity of anything done
in the meantime under such order or to the making of any
new order:

(4.) The order, while it is in force, shall, so far as is consistent
with the tenor thereof, apply as if it formed part of the
enactment which provides for the extension or grant or
otherwise for making the order.

66. An occupier of a factory or workshop, not less than seven days
before he avails himself of any special exception under this part of
this Act, shall serve on an inspector, and (except in the case of a
factory or workshop to which the provisions of this Act with respect
to the affixing of notices do not apply) affix in his factory or workshop
notice of his intention so to avail himself, and whilst he avails himself
of the exception shall keep the notice so affixed.

Before the service of such notice on the inspector the special exception shall not be deemed to apply to the factory or workshop, and
after the service of such notice on the inspector it shall not be competent in any proceeding under this Act for the occupier to prove that
such special exception does not apply to his factory or workshop,
unless he has previously served on an inspector notice that he no
longer intends to avail himself of such special exception.

The notice so served and affixed shall specify the hours for the
beginning and end of the period of employment, and the times to be
allowed for meals to every child, young person, and woman where
they differ from the ordinary hours or times.

An occupier of a factory or workshop shall enter in the prescribed
register, and report to an inspector, the prescribed particulars respecting the employment of a child, young person, or woman in pursuance
of an exception, but such entry and report need not be made in the
case of a factory or workshop to which the provisions of this Act with
respect to the affixing of notices do not apply, except so far as may be
from time to time prescribed by a Secretary of State.

Where the occupier of a factory or workshop avails himself of an
exception under this part of this Act, and a condition for availing
himself of such exception (whether specified in this part of this Act,
or in an order of a Secretary of State made under this part of this
Act) is not observed in that factory or workshop, then

(1.) If such condition relates to the cleanliness, ventilation, or
overcrowding of the factory or workshop, the factory or
workshop shall be deemed not to be kept in conformity
with this Act; and

(2.) In any other case a child, young person, or woman employed
in the factory or workshop, in alleged pursuance of the

said exception, shall be deemed to be employed contrary to the provisions of this Act.

[See further section 14 of 54 & 55 Vic., c. 75, *infra*.]

PART III.

ADMINISTRATION, PENALTIES, AND LEGAL PROCEEDINGS.

(1.) *Inspection.*

67. A Secretary of State from time to time, with the approval of the Treasury as to numbers and salaries, may appoint such inspectors (under whatever title he may from time to time fix) and such clerks and servants as he may think necessary for the execution of this Act, and may assign to them their duties and award them their salaries, and may constitute a principal inspector with an office in London, and may regulate the cases and manner in which the inspectors, or any of them, are to execute and perform the powers and duties of inspectors under this Act, and may remove such inspectors, clerks, and servants.

The salaries of the inspectors, clerks, and servants, and the expenses incurred by them or by a Secretary of State in the execution of this Act, shall be paid out of moneys provided by Parliament.

Notice of the appointment of every such inspector shall be published in the London Gazette.

A person who is the occupier of a factory or workshop, or is directly or indirectly interested therein or in any process or business carried on therein, or in a patent connected therewith, or is employed in or about a factory or workshop, shall not act as an inspector under this Act.

An inspector under this Act shall not be liable to serve in any parochial or municipal office.

Such annual report of the proceedings of the inspectors as the Secretary of State from time to time directs shall be laid before both Houses of Parliament.

A reference in this Act to an inspector refers, unless it is otherwise expressed, to an inspector appointed in pursuance of this section, and a notice or other document required by this Act to be sent to an inspector shall be sent to such inspector as a Secretary of State from time to time directs, by declaration published in the London Gazette or otherwise as he thinks expedient for making the same known to all persons interested.

68. An inspector under this Act shall for the purpose of the execution of this Act have power to do all or any of the following things ; namely,

> (1.) To enter, inspect, and examine at all reasonable times by day and night a factory and a workshop and every part thereof when he has reasonable cause to believe that any person is employed therein, and to enter by day any place which he has reasonable cause to believe to be a factory or workshop ; and
>
> (2.) To take with him in either case a constable into a factory in which he has reasonable cause to apprehend any serious obstruction in the execution of his duty ; and

(3.) To require the production of the registers, certificates, notices, and documents kept in pursuance of this Act, and to inspect, examine, and copy the same ; and

(4.) To make such examination and inquiry as may be necessary to ascertain whether the enactments for the time being in force relating to public health and the enactments of this Act are complied with, so far as respects the factory or workshop and the persons employed therein ; and

(5.) To enter any school in which he has reasonable cause to believe that children employed in a factory or workshop are for the time being educated ; and

(6.) To examine either alone or in the presence of any other person, as he thinks fit, with respect to matters under this Act, every person whom he finds in a factory or workshop, or such a school as aforesaid, or whom he has reasonable cause to believe to be or to have been within the preceding two months employed in a factory or workshop, and to require such person to be so examined and to sign a declaration of the truth of the matters respecting which he is so examined ; and

(7.) To exercise such other powers as may be necessary for carrying this Act into effect.

[See further sections 8 and 28 of 54 & 55 Vic., c. 75, *infra*.]

The occupier of every factory and workshop, his agents and servants, shall furnish the means required by an inspector as necessary for an entry, inspection, examination, inquiry, or the exercise of his powers under this Act in relation to such factory and workshop.

Every person who wilfully delays an inspector in the exercise of any power under this section, or who fails to comply with a requisition of an inspector in pursuance of this section, or to produce any certificate or document which he is required by or in pursuance of this Act to produce, or who conceals or prevents a child, young person, or woman from appearing before or being examined by an inspector, or attempts so to conceal or prevent a child, young person, or woman, shall be deemed to obstruct an inspector in the execution of his duties under this Act : Provided always, that no one shall be required under this section to answer any question or to give any evidence tending to criminate himself.

Where an inspector is obstructed in the execution of his duties under this Act, the person obstructing him shall be liable to a fine not exceeding five pounds ; and where an inspector is so obstructed in a factory or workshop, the occupier of that factory or workshop shall be liable to a fine not exceeding five, or where the offence is committed at night, twenty pounds ; and where an inspector is so obstructed in a factory or workshop within the meaning of section sixteen of this Act, the occupier shall be liable to a fine not exceeding one, or where the offence is committed at night, five pounds.

[For section 69 now read section 25 of 54 & 55 Vic., c. 75, *infra*.]

70. Every inspector under this Act shall be furnished with the prescribed certificate of his appointment, and on applying for admission to a factory or workshop shall, if required, produce to the occupier the said certificate.

Every person who forges or counterfeits any such certificate, or makes use of any forged, counterfeited, or false certificate, or personates the inspector named in any such certificate, or falsely pretends to be an inspector under this Act, shall be liable to be imprisoned for a period not exceeding three months with or without hard labour.

(2.) *Certifying Surgeons.*

71. Where there is no certifying surgeon resident within three miles of a factory or workshop, the poor law medical officer shall be for the time being the certifying surgeon under this Act for such factory or workshop.

72. Subject to such regulations as may be from time to time made by a Secretary of State, an inspector may from time to time appoint a sufficient number of duly registered medical practitioners to be certifying surgeons for the purposes of this Act, and may from time to time revoke any such appointment.

Every appointment and revocation of appointment of a certifying surgeon may be annulled by a Secretary of State upon appeal to him for that purpose.

A surgeon who is the occupier of a factory or workshop, or is directly or indirectly interested therein or in any process or business carried on therein or in a patent connected therewith, shall not be a certifying surgeon for that factory or workshop.

A Secretary of State may from time to time make rules for the guidance of certifying surgeons, and for the particulars to be registered respecting their visits, and for the forms of certificates and other documents to be used by them.

[See further section 19 of 54 & 55 Vict. c. 75, *infra.*]

73. A certificate of fitness for employment shall not be granted for the purposes of this Act, except upon personal examination of the person named therein.

A certifying surgeon shall not examine a child or young person for the purposes of a certificate of fitness for employment, or sign any such certificate, elsewhere than at the factory or workshop where such child or young person is or is about to be employed, unless the number of children and young persons employed in that factory or workshop are less than five, or unless for some special reason allowed in writing by an inspector.

If a certifying surgeon refuses to grant for any person examined by him a certificate of fitness for employment, he shall when required give in writing and sign the reasons for such refusal.

74. With respect to the fees to be paid to certifying surgeons in respect of the examination of, and grant of certificates of fitness for employment for, children and young persons in factories or workshops, the following provisions shall have effect:

    (1.) The occupier may agree with the certifying surgeon as to the amount of such fees:

    (2.) In the absence of any such agreement the fees shall be those named in the following scale:—

When the examination is at a factory or workshop not exceeding one mile from the surgeon's residence,	2s. 6d. for each visit and 6d. for each person after the first five examined at that visit.

When the examination is at a factory or workshop more than one mile from the surgeon's residence,	The above fees and an additional 6d. for each complete half mile over and above the mile.
When the examination is not at the factory or workshop, but at the residence of the surgeon, or at some place appointed by the surgeon for the purpose, and which place, as well as the day and hour, appointed for the purpose shall be published in the prescribed manner,	6d. for each person examined.

(3.) The occupier shall pay the fees on the completion of the examination, or if any certificates are granted at the time at which the surgeon signs the certificates, or at any other time directed by an inspector:

(4.) The occupier may deduct the fee or any part thereof, not exceeding in any case threepence, from the wages of the person for whom the certificate was granted:

(5.) A Secretary of State may from time to time, if he think it expedient, alter any fees fixed by this section.

(3.) *Miscellaneous.*

75. Every person shall, within one month after he begins to occupy a factory, serve on an inspector a written notice containing the name of the factory, the place where it is situate, the address to which he desires his letters to be addressed, the nature of the work, the nature and amount of the moving power therein, and the name of the firm under which the business of the factory is to be carried on, and in default shall be liable to a fine not exceeding five pounds.

[See as to Workshops, section 26 of 54 & 55 Vict. c. 75, *infra.*]

76. Where an inspector, by notice in writing, names a public clock, or some other clock open to public view, for the purpose of regulating the period of employment in a factory or workshop, the period of employment and times allowed for meals for children, young persons, and women in that factory or workshop shall be regulated by that clock, which shall be specified in the notice affixed in the factory or workshop.

77. The occupier of every factory and workshop to which this section applies shall keep in the prescribed form and with the prescribed particulars registers of the children and young persons employed in that factory or workshop, and of their employment, and of other matters under this Act.

The occupier of a factory or workshop shall send to an inspector such extracts from any register kept in pursuance of this Act as the inspector from time to time requires for the execution of his duties under this Act.

This section applies to every factory and workshop in which a child or young person under the age of sixteen years is, for the time being, prohibited under this Act from being employed without a certificate of fitness for employment.

Where by reason of the number of children and young persons employed in a factory or workshop to which this section does not for the time being apply, or otherwise, it seems expedient to a Secretary of State so to do, he may order the occupier of that factory or workshop to keep a register under this section, with power to rescind such order, and while such order is in force this section shall apply to that factory or workshop.

In the event of a contravention of this section in a factory or workshop, the occupier of the factory or workshop shall be liable to a fine not exceeding forty shillings.

[As to outworkers, see section 27 of 54 & 55 Vict. c. 75, *infra*.]

78. There shall be affixed at the entrance of a factory and a workshop, and in such other parts thereof as an inspector for the time being directs, and be constantly kept so affixed in the prescribed form and in such position as to be easily read by the persons employed in the factory or workshop,—

(1.) The prescribed abstract of this Act; and

(2.) A notice of the name and address of the prescribed inspector; and

(3.) A notice of the name and address of the certifying surgeon for the district; and

(4.) A notice of the clock (if any) by which the period of employment and times for meals in the factory or workshop are regulated; and

(5.) Every notice and document required by this Act to be affixed in the factory or workshop.

In the event of a contravention of this section in a factory or workshop, the occupier of the factory or workshop shall be liable to a fine not exceeding forty shillings.

[See further as to particulars, section 24 of 54 & 55 Vict. c. 75, *infra*.]

79. Any notice, order, requisition, summons, and document under this Act may be in writing or print, or partly in writing and partly in print.

Any notice, order, requisition, summons, and document required or authorised to be served or sent for the purposes of this Act may be served and sent by delivering the same to or at the residence of the person on or to whom it is to be served or sent, or, where that person is the occupier of a factory or workshop, by delivering the same or a true copy thereof to his agent or to some person in such factory or workshop; it may also be served or sent by post by a pre-paid letter, and if served or sent by post shall be deemed to have been served and received respectively at the time when the letter containing the same would be delivered in the ordinary course of post, and in proving such service or sending it shall be sufficient to prove that it was properly addressed and put into the post; and where it is required to be served on or sent to the occupier of a factory or workshop, it shall be deemed to be properly addressed if addressed to the occupier of such factory or workshop at the factory or workshop, with the addition of the proper postal address, but without naming the person who is the occupier.

80. Any Act for the time being in force relating to weights and measures shall extend to weights, measures, scales, balances, steel-yards, and weighing machines used in a factory or workshop in checking or ascertaining the wages of any person employed therein, in like manner as if they were used in the sale of goods, and as if such factory or workshop were a place where goods are kept for sale, and such Act shall apply accordingly, and every inspector of, or other person authorised to inspect or examine, weights and measures, shall inspect, stamp, mark, search for, and examine the said weights and measures, scales, balances, steelyards, and weighing machines accordingly, and for that purpose shall have the same powers and duties as he has in relation to weights, measures, scales, balances, steelyards, and weighing machines used in the sale of goods.

(4.) *Fines.*

81. If a factory or workshop is not kept in conformity with this Act, the occupier thereof shall be liable to a fine not exceeding ten pounds.

The court of summary jurisdiction, in addition to or instead of inflicting such fine, may order certain means to be adopted by the occupier, within the time named in the order, for the purpose of bringing his factory or workshop into conformity with this Act ; the court may, upon application, enlarge the time so named, but if, after the expiration of the time as originally named or enlarged by subsequent order, the order is not complied with, the occupier shall be liable to a fine not exceeding one pound for every day that such non-compliance continues. [See also section 28 of 54 & 55 Vict. c 75, *infra.*]

82. If any person is killed or suffers any bodily injury in consequence of the occupier of a factory having neglected to fence any machinery required by or in pursuance of this Act to be securely fenced, or having neglected to maintain such fencing, or in consequence of the occupier of a factory or workshop having neglected to fence any vat, pan, or other structure required by or in pursuance of this Act to be securely fenced, or having neglected to maintain such fencing, the occupier of the factory or workshop shall be liable to a fine not exceeding one hundred pounds, the whole or any part of which may be applied for the benefit of the injured person or his family, or otherwise as a Secretary of State determines :

Provided that the occupier of a factory shall not be liable to a fine under this section if an information against him for not fencing the part of the machinery, or the vat, pan, or other structure, by which the death or bodily injury was inflicted, has been heard and dismissed previous to the time when the death or bodily injury was inflicted. [See also section 28 of 54 & 55 Vict. c. 75, *infra.*]

83. Where a child, young person, or woman is employed in a factory or workshop contrary to the provisions of this Act, the occupier of the factory or workshop shall be liable to a fine not exceeding three, or if the offence was committed during the night, five pounds for each child, young person, or woman so employed ; and where a child, young person, or woman is so employed in a factory or workshop within the meaning of section sixteen of this Act, the occupier shall be liable to a fine not exceeding one, or if the offence was committed during the night, two pounds for each child, young person, or woman so employed.

A child, young person, or woman who is not allowed times for meals and absence from work as required by this Act, or during any part of the 'times allowed for meals and absence from work is, in contravention of the provisions of this Act, employed in the factory or workshop or allowed to remain in any room, shall be deemed to be employed contrary to the provisions of this Act. [See also section 28 of 54 & 55 Vict. c. 75, *infra.*]

84. The parent of a child or young person shall,—

(1.) If such child or young person is employed in a factory or workshop contrary to the provisions of this Act, be liable to a fine not exceeding twenty shillings for each offence, unless it appears to the court that such offence was committed without the consent, connivance, or wilful default of such parent; and

(2.) If he neglects to cause such child to attend school in accordance with this Act, be liable to a fine not exceeding twenty shillings for each offence.

85. Every person who forges or counterfeits any certificate for the purposes of this Act (for the forging or counterfeiting of which no other punishment is provided), or who gives or signs any such certificate knowing the same to be false in any material particular, or who knowingly utters or makes use of any certificate so forged, counterfeited or false as aforesaid, or who knowingly utters or makes use of as applying to any person a certificate which does not so apply, or who personates any person named in a certificate, or who wilfully connives at the forging, counterfeiting, giving, signing, uttering, making use, or personating as aforesaid, shall be liable to a fine not exceeding twenty pounds, or to imprisonment for a term not exceeding three months with or without hard labour.

Every person who wilfully makes a false entry in any register, notice, certificate, or document required by this Act to be kept or served or sent, or who wilfully makes or signs a false declaration under this Act, or who knowingly makes use of any such false entry or declaration, shall be liable to a fine not exceeding twenty pounds, or to imprisonment for a term not exceeding three months with or without hard labour.

86. Where an offence for which the occupier of a factory or workshop is liable under this Act to a fine, has in fact been committed by some agent, servant, workman, or other person, such agent, servant, workman, or other person shall be liable to the same fine as if he were the occupier.

87. Where the occupier of a factory or workshop is charged with an offence against this Act, he shall be entitled upon information duly laid by him to have any other person whom he charges as the actual offender brought before the court at the time appointed for hearing the charge; and if, after 'the commission of the offence has been proved, the occupier of the factory or workshop proves to the satisfaction of the court that he had used due diligence to enforce the execution of the Act, and that the said other person had committed the offence in question without his knowledge, consent, or connivance, the said other person shall be summarily convicted of such offence, and the occupier shall be exempt from any fine.

When it is made to appear to the satisfaction of an inspector at the time of discovering the offence, that the occupier of the factory or workshop had used all due diligence to enforce the execution of this Act, and also by what person such offence had been committed, and also that it had been committed without the knowledge, consent, or connivance of the occupier and in contravention of his orders, then the inspector shall proceed against the person whom he believes to be the actual offender in the first instance, without first proceeding against the occupier of the factory or workshop.

88. A person shall not be liable in respect of a repetition of the same kind of offence from day to day to any larger amount of fines than the highest fine fixed by this Act for the offence, except—

(a.) where the repetition of the offence occurs after an information has been laid for the previous offence ; or

(b.) where the offence is one of employing two or more children, young persons, or women contrary to the provisions of this Act.

(5) *Legal Proceedings.*

89. All offences under this Act shall be prosecuted, and all fines under this Act shall be recovered, on summary conviction before a court of summary jurisdiction in manner provided by the Summary Jurisdiction Acts.

A summary order may be made for the purposes of this Act by a court of summary jurisdiction in manner provided by the Summary Jurisdiction Acts.

All fines imposed in pursuance of this Act shall, save as otherwise expressly provided by this Act, be paid into the Exchequer.

The court of summary jurisdiction, when hearing and determining a case arising under this Act, shall be constituted either of two or more justices of the peace sitting at some court or public place at which justices are for the time being accustomed to assemble for the purpose of holding petty sessions or of some magistrate or officer sitting alone or with others at some court or other place appointed for the public administration of justice, and for the time being empowered by law to do alone any act authorised to be done by more than one justice of the peace.

Where a proceeding is taken before a court of summary jurisdiction with respect to an offence against this Act alleged to be committed in or with reference to a factory or workshop, the occupier of that factory or workshop, and the father, son, or brother of such occupier, shall not be qualified to act as a member of such court.

90. If any person feels aggrieved by a conviction or order made by a court of summary jurisdiction on determining an information or complaint under this Act, he may appeal therefrom ; subject, in England, to the conditions and regulations following :

(1) The appeal shall be made to the next practicable court of general or quarter sessions having jurisdiction in the county or place in which the decision of the court was given, holden not less than twenty-one days after the day on which such decision was given ; and

[See now section 4 of 47 & 48 Vict. c. 43, and Schedule].

91. The following provisions shall have effect with respect to summary proceedings for offences and fines under this Act :

(1.) [See section 29 of 54 & 55 Vict. c. 75, *infra.*]

(2.) and (3.) [See section 4 of 47 & 48 Vict. c. 43, and Schedule.]

(4.) It shall be sufficient to allege that a factory or workshop is a factory or workshop within the meaning of this Act, without more :

(5.) It shall be sufficient to state the name of the ostensible occupier of the factory or workshop or title of the firm by which the occupier employing persons in the factory or workshop is usually known :

(6.) A conviction or order made in any matter arising under this Act, either originally or on appeal, shall not be quashed for want of form, and a conviction or order made by a court of summary jurisdiction against which a person is authorised by this Act to appeal shall not be removed by certiorari or otherwise, either at the instance of the Crown or of any private person, into a superior court except for the purpose of the hearing and determination of a special case. [See however 47 & 48 Vict. c. 43.]

92. If a person is found in a factory, except at meal times, or while all the machinery of the factory is stopped, or for the sole purpose of bringing food to the persons employed in the factory between the hours of four and five o'clock in the afternoon, such person shall, until the contrary is proved, be deemed for the purposes of this Act to have been then employed in the factory :

Provided that yards, playgrounds, and places open to the public view, school rooms, waiting rooms, and other rooms belonging to the factory in which no machinery is used or manufacturing process carried on, shall not be taken to be any part of the factory within the meaning of this enactment; and this enactment shall not apply to a factory or workshop to which the provisions of this Act with respect to the affixing of notices do not apply.

Where a child or young person is, in the opinion of the court, apparently of the age alleged by the informant, it shall lie on the defendant to prove that the child or young person is not of that age.

A declaration in writing by a certifying surgeon for the district that he has personally examined a person employed in a factory or workshop in that district, and believes him to be under the age set forth in the declaration, shall be admissible in evidence of the age of that person.

A copy of a conviction for an offence against this Act purporting to be certified under the hand of the clerk of the peace having the custody of such conviction to be a true copy shall be receivable as evidence, and every such clerk of the peace shall, upon the written request of an inspector and payment of a fee of one shilling, deliver to him a copy of the conviction so certified. [Section 30 of 54 & 55 Vict. c. 75, extends this to workshops.]

PART IV.
DEFINITIONS, SAVINGS, APPLICATION TO SCOTLAND AND IRELAND, AND REPEAL.

(1.) *Definitions.*

93. The expression " textile factory " in this Act means—
any premises wherein or within the close or curtilage of which steam, water, or other mechanical power is used to move or

work any machinery employed in preparing, manufacturing, or finishing, or in any process incident to the manufacture of, cotton, wool, hair, silk, flax, hemp, jute, tow, china-grass, cocoa-nut fibre, or other like material, either separately or mixed together, or mixed with any other material, or any fabric made thereof :

Provided that print works, bleaching and dyeing works, lace warehouses, paper mills, flax scutch mills, rope works, and hat works shall not be deemed to be textile factories.

The expression "non-textile factory" in this Act means—

(1.) any works, warehouses, furnaces, mills, foundries, or places named in Part One of the Fourth Schedule to this Act.

(2.) also any premises or places named in Part Two of the said schedule wherein, or within the close or curtilage or precincts of which, steam, water, or other mechanical power is used in aid of the manufacturing process carried on there.

(3.) also any premises wherein, or within the close or curtilage or precincts of which, any manual labour is exercised by way of trade or for purposes of gain in or incidental to the following purposes, or any of them; that is to say,

(a.) in or incidental to the making of any article or of part of any article, or

(b.) in or incidental to the altering, repairing, ornamenting, or finishing of any article, or

(c.) in or incidental to the adapting for sale of any article,

and wherein, or within the close or curtilage or precincts of which, steam, water, or other mechanical power is used in aid of the manufacturing process carried on there.

The expression "factory" in this Act means textile factory and non-textile factory, or either of such descriptions of factories.

The expression "workshop" in this Act means—

(1.) any premises or places named in Part Two of the Fourth Schedule to this Act, which are not a factory within the meaning of this Act,

(2.) also any premises, room, or place not being a factory within the meaning of this Act, in which premises, room, or place, or within the close or curtilage or precincts of which premises, any manual labour is exercised by way of trade or for purposes of gain in or incidental to the following purposes or any of them; that is to say,

(a.) in or incidental to the making of any article or of part of any article, or

(b.) in or incidental to the altering, repairing, ornamenting, or finishing of any article, or

(c.) in or incidental to the adapting for sale of any article,

and to which or over which premises, room, or place the employer of the persons working therein has the right of access or control.

A part of a factory or workshop may for the purposes of this Act be taken to be a separate factory or workshop; and a place solely used as a dwelling shall not be deemed to form part of the factory or work-shop for the purposes of this Act.

[See, however, section 31 of 54 & 55 Vict. c. 75, *infra*.]

Where a place situate within the close, curtilage, or precincts forming a factory or workshop is solely used for some purpose other than the manufacturing process or handicraft carried on in the factory or workshop, such place shall not be deemed to form part of that factory or workshop for the purposes of this Act, but shall, if other-wise it would be a factory or workshop, be deemed to be a separate factory or workshop, and be regulated accordingly.

Any premises or place shall not be excluded from the definition of a factory or workshop by reason only that such premises or place are or is in the open air.

This Act shall not apply to such workshops, other than bake-houses, as are conducted on the system of not employing any child, young person, or woman therein, but save as aforesaid applies to all fac-tories and workshops as before defined, inclusive of factories and workshops belonging to the Crown; provided that in case of any public emergency a Secretary of State may exempt a factory or work-shop belonging to the Crown from this Act to the extent and during the period named by him.

The exercise by any child or young person in any recognised efficient school during a portion of the school hours of any manual labour for the purpose of instructing such child or young person in any art or handicraft, shall not be deemed to be an exercise of manual labour for the purpose of gain within the meaning of this Act.

94. A child, young person, or woman who works in a factory or workshop, whether for wages or not, either in a manufacturing pro-cess or handicraft, or in cleaning any part of the factory or workshop used for any manufacturing process or handicraft, or in cleaning or oiling any part of the machinery, or in any other kind of work what-soever incidental to or connected with the manufacturing process or handicraft, or connected with the article made or otherwise the sub-ject of the manufacturing process or handicraft therein, shall, save as is otherwise provided by this Act, be deemed to be employed therein within the meaning of this Act.

For the purposes of this Act an apprentice shall be deemed to work for hire.

95. The expression "certified efficient school" in this Act means a public elementary school within the meaning of the Elementary Education Acts, 1870 and 1873, and any workhouse school in Eng-land certified to be efficient by the Local Government Board, and also any elementary school which is not conducted for private profit and is open at all reasonable times to the inspection of Her Majesty's in-spectors of schools, and requires the like attendance from its scholars as is required in a public elementary school, and keeps such registers of those attendances as may be for the time being required by the Education Department, and is certified by the Education Department to be an efficient school; and the expression "recognised efficient school" means a certified efficient school as above defined, and also any school which the Education Department have not refused to take into consideration under the Elementary Education Act, 1870, as a school giving efficient elementary education to and suitable for the children of a school district, and which is recognised for the time being by an inspector under this Act as giving efficient elementary education, and the inspector shall immediately report to the Education Department every school so recognised by him.

96. In this Act, unless the context otherwise requires,—

The expression "child" means a person under the age of fourteen years :

The expression "young person" means a person of the age of fourteen years and under the age of eighteen years :

The expression "woman" means a woman of eighteen years of age and upwards :

The expression "parent" means a parent or guardian of, or person having the legal custody of, or the control over, or having direct benefit from the wages of a child or young person :

The expression "Treasury" means the Commissioners of Her Majesty's Treasury :

The expression "Secretary of State" means one of Her Majesty's Principal Secretaries of State :

The expression "Education Department" means the Lords of the Committee of the Privy Council on Education :

The expression "sanitary authority" means an urban or rural sanitary authority within the meaning of the Public Health Act, 1875, and any commissions, board, or vestry in the metropolis having the like powers as such urban sanitary authority :

The expression "person" includes a body of persons corporate or unincorporate :

The expression "week" means the period between midnight on Saturday night and midnight on the succeeding Saturday night :

The expression "night" means the period between nine o'clock in the evening and six o'clock in the succeeding morning :

The expression "prescribed" means prescribed for the time being by a Secretary of State :

The expression "Summary Jurisdiction Acts" means the Act of the session of the eleventh and twelfth years of the reign of her present Majesty, chapter forty-three, intituled "An Act to facilitate the performance of the duties of justices of the peace out of sessions within England and Wales with respect to summary convictions and orders," and any Acts amending the same :

The expression "court of summary jurisdiction" means any justice or justices of the peace, metropolitan police magistrate, stipendiary or other magistrate, or officer, by whatever name called, to whom jurisdiction is given by the Summary Jurisdiction Acts or any Acts therein referred thereto :

The expression "mill-gearing" comprehends every shaft, whether upright, oblique, or horizontal, and every wheel, drum, or pulley by which the motion of the first moving power is communicated to any machine appertaining to a manufacturing process.

The factories and workshops named in the Fourth Schedule to this Act are in this Act referred to by the names therein assigned to them.

Special Exemption of certain Trades.

97. The exercise in a private house or private room by the family dwelling therein, or by any of them, of manual labour by way of trade or for purposes of gain in or incidental to any of the handicrafts specified in the Fifth Schedule to this Act, shall not of itself constitute such house or room a workshop within the meaning of this Act.

When it is proved to the satisfaction of a Secretary of State that by reason of the light character of the handicraft carried on in any private house or private room by the family dwelling therein, or by any of them, it is expedient to extend this section to that handicraft, he may by order extend the same.

The order shall be made in manner provided by Part Two of this Act, and that part shall apply so far as circumstances admit as if the order were an order extending an exception.

98. The exercise in a private house or private room by the family dwelling therein, or by any of them, of manual labour for the purposes of gain in or incidental to some of the purposes in this Act in that behalf mentioned, shall not of itself constitute such house or room a workshop where the labour is exercised at irregular intervals, and does not furnish the whole or principal means of living to such family.

(2.) Savings.

99. Where in a factory the owner or hirer of a machine or implement moved by steam, water, or other mechanical power, in or about or in connection with which machine or implement children, young persons, or women are employed, is some person other than the occupier of a factory, and such children, young persons, or women are in the employment and pay of the owner or hirer of such machine or implement, in any such case such owner or hirer shall, so far as respects any offence against this Act which may be committed in relation to such children, young persons, or women, be deemed to be the occupier of the factory.

100. Nothing in this Act shall extend—

    (1.) To any young person, being a mechanic, artisan, or labourer, working only in repairing either the machinery in or any part of a factory or workshop; or

    (2.) To the process of gutting, salting, and packing fish immediately upon its arrival in the fishing boats.

101. The provisions of section ninety-one of the Public Health Act, 1875, with respect to a factory, workshop, or workplace not kept in a cleanly state or not ventilated or overcrowded, shall not apply to a factory or workshop which is subject to the provisions of this Act relating to cleanliness, ventilation and overcrowding, but shall apply to every other factory, workshop, and workplace.

It is hereby declared that the Public Health Act, 1875, shall apply to buildings in which persons are employed, whatever their number may be, in like manner as it applies to buildings where more than twenty are employed.

102. Any enactment or document referring to the Acts repealed by this Act, or any of them, or to any enactment thereof, shall be construed to refer to this Act and to the corresponding enactment thereof.

(3.) *Application of Act to Scotland and Ireland.*

103. [This clause is now obsolete.]

104· Where the age of any child is required to be ascertained or proved for the purposes of this Act, or for any purpose connected with the elementary education or employment in labour of such child, any person, on presenting a written requisition in such form and containing such particulars as may be from time to time prescribed by a Secretary of State, and on payment of such fee, not exceeding one shilling, as a Secretary of State from time to time fixes, shall be entitled to obtain—

(1.) In Scotland an extract under the hand of the registrar under the Act of the seventeenth and eighteenth years of her present Majesty, chapter eighty, and any Acts amending the same, of the entry in the register kept under those Acts ; and

(2.) In Ireland a certified copy under the hand of the registrar or superintendent registrar under the Registration of Births and Deaths (Ireland) Act of the entry in the register under that Act of the birth of the child named in the requisition.

[See now section 35 of 54 & 56 Vict. c. 75, *infra*.]

105. In the application of this Act to Scotland—

(1.) The expression "certified efficient school" means any public or other elementary school under Government inspection :

[For (2) now read section 33 (4) of 54 & 55 Vict. c. 75, *infra*.]

(3.) The expression "sanitary authority" means the local authority under the Public Health (Scotland) Act, 1867 :

(4.) The expression "medical officer of health" means the medical officer under the Public Health (Scotland) Act, 1867, or where no such officer has been appointed, the medical officer appointed by the parochial board :

The expression "poor law medical officer" means the medical officer appointed by the parochial board :

(5.) The expression "Companies Clauses Consolidation Act, 1845," means the Companies Clauses Consolidation (Scotland) Act, 1845 :

(6.) The expression "Summary Jurisdiction Acts" means the Summary Procedure Act, 1864, and any Acts amending the same :

(7.) The expression "court of summary jurisdiction" means the sheriff of the county or any of his substitutes :

(8.) The expression "Education Department" means the Lords of the Committee of the Privy Council appointed by Her Majesty on Education in Scotland :

(9.) The expression "county court" means the sheriff court :

(10.) All matters required by this Act to be published in the London Gazette shall (if they relate exclusively to Scotland), instead of being published in the London Gazette, be published in the Edinburgh Gazette only :

(11.) The expression "information" means petition or complaint :

(12.) The expression "informant" means petitioner, pursuer, or complainer :

(13.) The expression "defendant" means defender or respondent :

(14.) The expression "clerk of the peace" means sheriff clerk:

(15.) All offences under this Act shall be prosecuted and all penalties under this Act shall be recovered under the provisions of the Summary Jurisdiction Acts at the instance of the procurator fiscal or of an inspector under this Act:

(16.) The court may make, and may also from time to time alter or vary, summary orders under this Act on petition by such procurator fiscal or inspector presented in common form:

(17.) All fines under this Act in default of payment, and all orders made under this Act failing compliance, may be enforced by imprisonment for a term to be specified in the order or conviction, but not exceeding three months:

(18.) It shall be no objection to the competency of an inspector to give evidence as a witness in any prosecution for offences under this Act, that such prosecution is brought at the instance of such inspector:

(19.) Every person convicted of an offence under this Act shall be liable in the reasonable costs and charges of such conviction:

(20.) All penalties imposed and recovered under this Act shall be paid to the clerk of the court, and by him accounted for and paid to the Queen's and Lord Treasurer's Remembrancer, on behalf of her Majesty's Exchequer, and shall be carried to the Consolidated Fund:

(21.) All jurisdictions, powers, and authorities necessary for the purposes of this section are conferred on the sheriffs and their substitutes:

(22.) Any person may appeal from any order or conviction under this Act to the Court of Justiciary, under and in terms of the Act of the twentieth year of the reign of his Majesty King George the Second, chapter forty-three, or under any enactment amending that Act, or applying or incorporating its provisions, or any of them, with regard to appeals, or to the Court of Justiciary at Edinburgh under and in terms of the Summary Prosecutions Appeal (Scotland) Act, 1875.

[See further section 33 of 54 & 55 Vict. c. 75, *infra*.]

106. In the application of this Act to Ireland—

(1.) The expression "certified efficient school" means any national school, or any school recognised by the Lord Lieutenant and Privy Council as affording sufficient means of literary education for the purposes of this Act:

[For (2) now read section 34 of 54 & 55 Vict. c. 75, *infra*.]

(3) The expression "sanitary authority" means an urban or rural sanitary authority within the meaning of the Public Health (Ireland) Act, 1874, and any Act amending the same:

(4.) The expression "medical officer of health" means the medical sanitary officer of the sanitary district:
The expression "poor law medical officer" means the dispensary doctor:

(5.) Any act authorised to be done or consent required to be given by the Education Department under this Act shall

P

be done and given by the Lord Lieutenant or Lords Justices of Ireland, acting by and with the advice of the Privy Council in Ireland :

(6.) The expression " county court " means the civil bill court :

(7.) The expression "Summary Jurisdiction Acts" means, within the police district of Dublin metropolis, the Acts regulating the powers and duties of justices of the peace for such districts, or of the police of such district, and elsewhere in Ireland the Petty Sessions (Ireland) Act, 1851, and any Act amending the same :

(8.) A court of summary jurisdiction when hearing and determining an information or complaint in any matter arising under this Act shall be constituted within the police district of Dublin metropolis of one of the divisional justices of that district sitting at a police court within the district, and elsewhere of a stipendiary magistrate sitting alone, or with others, or of two or more justices of the peace sitting in petty sessions at a place appointed for holding petty sessions :

(9.) Appeals from a court of summary jurisdiction shall lie in the manner and subject to the conditions and regulations prescribed in the twenty-fourth section of the Petty Sessions (Ireland) Act, 1851, and any Acts amending the same :

(10.) All fines imposed under this Act shall, save as is otherwise expressly provided by this Act, be applied in the manner directed by the Fines Act (Ireland), 1851, and any Act amending the same :

(11.) The provisions of section nineteen of the Public Health Act, 1866, or of any enactment substituted for that section with respect to any factory, workshop, or workplace not kept in a cleanly state, or not ventilated, or overcrowded, shall not apply to any factory or workshop which is subject to the provisions of this Act with respect to cleanliness, ventilation, and overcrowding, but shall apply to every other factory, workshop, and workplace :

It is hereby declared that the Sanitary Acts within the meaning of the Public Health (Ireland) Act, 1874, shall apply to buildings in which persons are employed, whatever their number may be, in like manner as they apply to buildings where more than twenty persons are employed :

(12.) All matters required by this Act to be published in the London Gazette shall, if they relate exclusively to Ireland, instead of being published in the London Gazette, be published in the Dublin Gazette only.

(4.) *Repeal.*

107. The Acts specified in the Sixth Schedule to this Act are hereby repealed from and after the commencement of this Act to the extent in the third column of that schedule mentioned :

Provided that—

(1.) All notices affixed in the factory in pursuance of the Acts hereby repealed shall, so far as they are in accordance with the provisions of this Act, be deemed to have been affixed in pursuance of this Act ; and

(2.) All inspectors, sub-inspectors, officers, clerks, and servants appointed in pursuance of the Acts hereby repealed shall continue in office and shall be subject to removal and have the same powers and duties as if they had been appointed in pursuance of this Act; and

(3.) All certifying surgeons appointed in pursuance of any Act hereby repealed shall be deemed to have been appointed in pursuance of this Act; and

(4.) All surgical certificates granted in pursuance of any Act hereby repealed shall have effect as certificates of fitness for employment granted in pursuance of this Act, and all registers kept in pursuance of any Act hereby repealed shall, until otherwise directed by a Secretary of State, be deemed to be the registers required by this Act; and

(5.) Any order made by a Secretary of State in pursuance of any enactment hereby repealed for granting any permission or relaxation to any factories or workshops may, if the Secretary of State so direct, continue in force for a period not exceeding three months after the commencement of this Act; and

(6.) The standard of proficiency fixed by the Education Department in pursuance of any enactment hereby repealed shall be deemed to have been fixed in pursuance of this Act; and

(7.) [Now obsolete.]

(8.) This repeal shall not affect—

    (a.) Anything duly done or suffered under any enactment hereby repealed; or

    (b.) Any obligation or liability incurred under any enactment hereby repealed; or

    (c.) Any penalty or punishment incurred in respect of any offence committed against an enactment hereby repealed; or

    (d.) Any legal proceeding or remedy in respect of any such obligation, liability, penalty, or punishment as aforesaid, and any such legal proceeding and remedy may be carried on as if this Act had not passed.

SCHEDULES.

FIRST SCHEDULE.

SPECIAL PROVISIONS FOR HEALTH.

Factories and Workshops in which the Employment of Young Persons and Children is restricted.

1. In a part of a factory or workshop in which there is carried on—

    the process of silvering of mirrors by the mercurial process; or

    the process of making white lead,

a young person or child shall not be employed.

2. In the part of a factory in which the process of melting or annealing glass is carried on a child or female young person shall not be employed.

3. In a factory or workshop in which there is carried on—

(*a.*) the making or finishing of bricks or tiles not being ornamental tiles : or

(*b.*) the making or finishing of salt,

a girl under the age of sixteen years shall not be employed.

4. In a part of a factory or workshop in which there is carried on—

(*a.*) Any dry grinding in the metal trade, or

(*b.*) the dipping of lucifer matches,

a child shall not be employed.

5. In any grinding in the metal trades other than dry grinding or in fustian cutting a child under the age of eleven years shall not be employed.

SECOND SCHEDULE.

SPECIAL RESTRICTIONS.

Places forbidden for Meals.

The prohibition on a child, young person, or woman taking a meal or remaining during the times allowed for meals in certain parts of factories or workshops applies to the parts of factories and workshops following ; that is to say,

(1.) In the case of glass works, to any part in which the materials are mixed ; and

(2.) In the case of glass works where flint glass is made, to any part in which the work of grinding, cutting, or polishing is carried on ; and

(3.) In the case of lucifer-match works, to any part in which any manufacturing process or handicraft (except that of cutting the wood) is usually carried on ; and

(4.) In the case of earthenware works, to any part known or used as dippers house, dippers drying room, or china scouring room.

THIRD SCHEDULE.

SPECIAL EXCEPTIONS.

PART I.

Period of Employment.

The exception respecting the employment of children, young persons, and women between the hours of eight in the morning and eight in the evening, and on Saturday between the hours of eight in the morning and four in the afternoon or between the hours of seven in the morning and three in the afternoon, applies to any factory or workshop or part thereof in which any of the following manufacturing processes or handicrafts are carried on ; that is to say,

(*a.*) Lithographic printing :

(*b.*) Turkey red dyeing :

(c.) The making of any article of wearing apparel :
(d.) The making of furniture hangings :
(e.) Artificial flower making :
(f.) Bon-bon and Christmas present making .
(g.) Valentine making :
(h.) Fancy box making :
(i.) Envelope making :
(k.) Almanac making :
(l.) Playing card making :
(m.) Machine ruling :
(n.) Biscuit making :
(o.) Firewood cutting :
(p.) Job dyeing : or
(q.) Aërated water making : and also to
(r.) Bookbinding works :
(s.) Letter-press printing works : and
(t.) A part of a factory or workshop which is a warehouse not used for any manufacturing process or handicraft, and in which persons are solely employed in polishing, cleaning, wrapping, or packing up goods.

PART II.

Meal Hours.

The cases in which the provisions of this Act as to meal times being allowed at the same hour of the day are not to apply are—
(1.) The case of children, young persons, and women employed in the following factories ; that is to say,
> Blast furnaces,
> Iron mills,
> Paper mills,
> Glass works, and
> Letter-press printing works ; and
(2.) The cases of male young persons employed in that part of any print works or bleaching and dyeing works in which the process of dyeing or open-air bleaching is carried on.

The cases in which and the extent to which the provisions of this Act as to a child, young person or woman. during the times allowed for meals being employed or being allowed to remain in a room in which a manufacturing process or handicraft is being carried on, are not to apply are—
(1.) The case of children, young persons, and women employed in the following factories ; that is to say,
> Iron mills,
> Paper mills,
> Glass works (save as otherwise provided by this Act), and
> Letter-press printing works; and
(2.) The case of a male young person employed in that part of any print works or bleaching and dyeing works in which the process of dyeing or open-air bleaching is carried on, to this extent, that the said provisions shall not prevent him, during the times allowed for meals to any other young person or to any child or woman, from being em-

ployed or being allowed to remain in any room in which any manufacturing process is carried on, and shall not prevent, during the times allowed for meals to such male young person, any other young person or any child or woman from being employed in the factory or allowed to remain in any room in which any manufacturing process is carried on.

PART III.

Overtime.

The exception with respect to the employment of young persons and women for forty-eight days in any twelve months during a period of employment, beginning at six or seven o'clock in the morning and ending at eight or nine o'clock in the evening, or beginning at eight o'clock in the morning and ending at ten o'clock in the evening, applies to each of the factories and workshops, and parts thereof, following ; that is to say,

(1.) Where the material which is the subject of the manufacturing process or handicraft is liable to be spoiled by weather ; namely,

 (*a*.) Flax scutch mills ; and

 (*b*.) A factory or workshop or part thereof in which is carried on the making or finishing of bricks or tiles not being ornamental tiles ; and

 (*c*.) The part of rope works in which is carried on the open-air process ; and

 (*d*.) The part of bleaching and dyeing works in which is carried on open-air bleaching or Turkey red dyeing ; and

 (*e*.) A factory or workshop or part thereof in which is carried on glue making ; and

(2.) Where press of work arises at certain recurring seasons of the year ; namely,

 (*f*.) Letter-press printing works ;

 (*g*.) Bookbinding works ; and

a factory, workshop, or part thereof in which is carried on the manufacturing process or handicraft of—

 (*h*.) Lithographic printing ; or

 (*i*.) Machine ruling ; or

 (*k*.) Firewood-cutting ; or

 (*l*.) Bon-bon and Christmas present making ; or

 (*m*.) Almanac making ; or

 (*n*.) Valentine making ; or

 (*o*.) Envelope making ; or

 (*p*.) Aërated water making ; or

 (*q*.) Playing card making ; and

(3.) Where the business is liable to sudden press of orders arising from unforeseen events ; namely,

A factory or workshop, or part thereof, in which is carried on the manufacturing process or handicraft of—

 (*r*.) The making up of any article of wearing apparel ; or

 (*s*.) The making up of furniture hangings ; or

 (*t*.) Artificial flower making ; or

  (*u.*) Fancy box making ; or

  (*v.*) Biscuit making ; or

  (*w.*) Job dyeing ; and also,

  (*x.*) A part of a factory or workshop which is a warehouse not used for any manufacturing process or handicraft, and in which persons are solely employed in polishing, cleaning, wrapping, or packing up goods.

Provided that the said exception shall not apply—

  (*a.*) Where persons are employed at home, that is to say, to a private house, room, or place which, though used as a dwelling, is by reason of the work carried on there a factory or workshop within the meaning of this Act, and in which neither steam, water, nor other mechanical power is used, and in which the only persons employed are members of the same family dwelling there ; or

  (*b.*) To a workshop or part thereof which is conducted on the system of not employing any child or young person therein.

PART IV.

Additional Half Hour.

The exception with respect to the employment of a child, young person, or woman for a further period of thirty minutes where the process is in an incomplete state applies to the factories following ; (that is to say),

  (*a.*) Bleaching and dyeing works ;

  (*b.*) Print works ;

  (*c.*) Iron mills in which male young persons are not employed during any part of the night ;

  (*d.*) Foundries in which male young persons are not employed during any part of the night ; and

  (*e.*) Paper mills in which male young persons are not employed during any part of the night.

PART V.

Overtime for Perishable Articles.

The exception with respect to the employment of women for ninety-six days in any twelve months during a period of employment beginning at six or seven o'clock in the morning and ending at eight or nine o'clock in the evening applies to a factory or workshop or part thereof in which any of the following processes is carried on ; namely,

The process of making preserves from fruit,

The process of preserving or curing fish, or

The process of making condensed milk.

PART VI.

Night Work.

The exception with respect to the employment of male young persons during the night applies to the factories following (that is to say),

(*a.*) Blast furnaces,
(*b.*) Iron mills,
(*c.*) Letter-press printing works, and
(*d.*) Paper mills.

PART VII.

Spell.

The exception respecting the continuous employment in certain textile factories during the winter months of children, young persons, and women without an interval of at least half an hour for a meal for the same period as in a non-textile factory, applies to textile factories solely used for—

(*a.*) The making of elastic web ; or
(*b.*) The making of ribbon ; or
(*c.*) The making of trimming.

FOURTH SCHEDULE.

LIST OF FACTORIES AND WORKSHOPS.

PART I.

Non-Textile Factories.

(1.) "Print works," that is to say, any premises in which any persons are employed to print figures, patterns, or designs upon any cotton, linen, woollen, worsted, or silken yarn, or upon any woven or felted fabric not being paper ;

(2.) "Bleaching and dyeing works," that is to say, any premises in which the processes of bleaching, beetling, dyeing, [calendering, finishing, hooking, lapping, and making up and packing any yarn or cloth of any material, or the dressing or finishing of lace, or any one or more of such processes, or any process incidental thereto, are or is carried on ;

(3.) "Earthenware works," that is to say, any place in which persons work for hire in making or assisting in making, finishing, or assisting in finishing, earthenware of any description, except bricks and tiles not being ornamental tiles. [See now section 38 of 54 & 55 Vict. c. 75, *infra.*]

(4.) "Lucifer-match works," that is to say, any place in which persons work for hire in making lucifer-matches, or in mixing the chemical materials for making them, or in any process incidental to making lucifer matches, except the cutting of the wood ;

(5.) "Percussion-cap works," that is to say, any place in which persons work for hire in making percussion caps, or in mixing or storing the chemical materials for making them, or in any process incidental to making percussion caps ;

(6.) "Cartridge works," that is to say, any place in which persons work for hire in making cartridges, or in any process incidental to making cartridges, except the manufacture of the paper or other material that is used in making the cases of the cartridges ;

(7.) "Paper-staining works," that is to say, any place in which persons work for hire in printing a pattern in colours upon sheets of paper, either by blocks applied by hand, or by rollers worked by steam, water, or other mechanical power ;

(8.) " Fustian-cutting works," that is to say, any place in which persons work for hire in fustian-cutting ;

(9.) " Blast furnaces," that is to say, any blast furnace or other furnace or premises in or on which the process of smelting or otherwise obtaining any metal from the ores is carried on ;

(10.) " Copper mills " ;

(11.) " Iron mills," that is to say, any mill, forge, or other premises in or on which any process is carried on for converting iron into malleable iron, steel, or tin plate, or for otherwise making or converting steel ;

(12.) " Foundries," that is to say, iron foundries, copper foundries, brass foundries, and other premises or places in which the process of founding or casting any metal is carried on; except any premises or places in which such process is carried on by not more than five persons and as subsidiary to the repair or completion of some other work ;

(13.) " Metal and india-rubber works," that is to say, any premises in which steam, water, or other mechanical power is used for moving machinery employed in the manufacture of machinery, or in the manufacture of any article of metal not being machinery, or in the manufacture of india-rubber or gutta-percha, or of articles made wholly or partially of india-rubber or gutta-percha ;

(14.) " Paper mills," that is to say, any premises in which the manufacture of paper is carried on ;

(15.) " Glass works," that is to say, any premises in which the manufacture of glass is carried on ;

(16.) " Tobacco factories," that is to say, any premises in which the manufacture of tobacco is carried on ;

(17.) " Letter-press printing works," that is to say, any premises in which the process of letter-press printing is carried on ;

(18.) " Bookbinding works," that is to say, any premises in which the process of bookbinding is carried on ;

(19.) Flax scutch mills.

Part II.

Non-Textile Factories and Workshops.

(20.) " Hat works," that is to say, any premises in which the manufacture of hats or any process incidental to their manufacture is carried on ;

(21.) " Rope works," that is to say, any premises being a ropery, ropewalk, or rope work, in which is carried on the laying or twisting or other process of preparing or finishing the lines, twines, cords, or ropes, and in which machinery moved by steam, water, or other mechanical power is not used for drawing or spinning the fibres of flax, hemp, jute, or tow, and which has no internal communication with any buildings or premises joining or forming part of a textile factory, except such communication as is necessary for the transmission of power ;

(22.) " Bakehouses," that is to say, any places in which are baked bread, biscuits, or confectionery from the baking or selling of which a profit is derived ;

(23.) " Lace warehouses," that is to say, any premises, room, or place not included in bleaching and dyeing works as hereinbefore defined, in which persons are employed upon any manufacturing process or handicraft in relation to lace, subsequent to the making of lace upon a lace machine moved by steam, water, or other mechanical power ;

(24.) ''Shipbuilding yards,'' that is to say, any premises in which any ships, boats, or vessels used in navigation are made, finished, or repaired ;

(25.) '' Quarries,'' that is to say, any place, not being a mine, in which persons work in getting slate, stone, coprolites, or other minerals ;

(26.) ''Pit-banks,'' that is to say, any place above ground adjacent to a shaft of a mine, in which place the employment of women is not regulated by the Coal Mines Regulation Act, 1872, or the Metalliferous Mines Regulation Act, 1872, whether such place does or does not form part of the mine within the meaning of those Acts.

FIFTH SCHEDULE.

Special Exemptions.

Straw plaiting.
Pillow-lace making.
Glove making.

SIXTH SCHEDULE.

Acts Repealed.

Session and Chapter.	Title of Act.	Extent of Repeal.
42 Geo. 3. c. 73.	An Act for the preservation of the health and morals of apprentices and others employed in cotton and other mills and cotton and other factories.	The whole Act.
3 & 4 Will. 4. c. 103.	An Act to regulate the labour of children and young persons in the mills and factories of the United Kingdom.	The whole Act.
7 & 8 Vict. c. 15.	An Act to amend the Laws relating to labour in factories.	The whole Act.
9 & 10 Vict. c. 40.	An Act to declare certain ropeworks not within the operation of the Factory Acts.	The whole Act.
13 & 14 Vict. c. 54.	An Act to amend the Acts relating to labour in factories.	The whole Act.

SIXTH SCHEDULE (*continued*).

Session and Chapter.	Title of Act.	Extent of Repeal.
16 & 17 Vict. c. 104.	An Act further to regulate the employment of children in factories.	The whole Act.
19 & 20 Vict. c. 38.	The Factory Act, 1856.	The whole Act.
24 & 25 Vict. c. 119.	An Act to place the employment of women, young persons, youths, and children in lace factories under the regulations of the Factories Acts.	The whole Act.
26 & 27 Vict. c. 40.	The Bakehouse Regulation Act, 1863.	The whole Act.
27 & 28 Vict. c. 48.	The Factory Acts Extension Act, 1864.	The whole Act.
29 & 30 Vict. c. 90.	The Sanitary Act, 1866.	The following words (so far as unrepealed) in section nineteen, "not already under the operation of any general Act for the regulation of factories or bakehouses."
30 & 31 Vict. c. 103.	The Factories Acts Extension Act, 1867.	The whole Act.
30 & 31 Vict. c. 146.	The Workshop Regulation Act, 1867.	The whole Act.
33 & 34 Vict. c. 62.	The Factory and Workshop Act, 1870.	The whole Act.
34 & 35 Vict. c. 19.	An Act for exempting persons professing the Jewish religion from penalties in respect of young persons and females professing the said religion working on Sundays.	The whole Act.
34 & 35 Vict. c. 104.	The Factory and Workshop Act, 1871.	The whole Act.
37 & 38 Vict. c. 44.	The Factory Act, 1874.	The whole Act.
38 & 39 Vict. c. 55.	The Public Health Act, 1875.	The following words in section four, "more than twenty," and the words "at one time," and the following

Session and Chapter.	Title of Act.	Extent of Repeal.
38 & 39 Vict. c. 55 (*continued*).	The Public Health Act, 1875 (*continued*).	words in section ninety-one, "not already under the operation of any general Act for the regulation of factories or bakehouses."
39 & 40 Vict. c. 79.	The Elementary Education Act, 1876.	Section eight and the following words in section forty-eight, "the Factory Acts, 1833 to 1874, as amended by this Act, and includes the Workshop Acts, 1867 to 1871, as amended by this Act, and ".

VII. FACTORY AND WORKSHOP ACT, 1891.

(54 & 55 VICT. CAP. 75.)

Sanitary Provisions.

1.—(1.) If the Secretary of State is satisfied that the provisions of the law relating to public health as to effluvia arising from any drain, privy, or other nuisance, or with respect to cleanliness, ventilation, overcrowding, or limewashing are not observed in any workshops or class of workshops (including workshops conducted on the system of not employing any child, young person, or woman therein) or laundries, he may, if he thinks fit, by order, authorise and direct an inspector or inspectors under the principal Act to take, during such period as may be mentioned in the order, such steps as appear necessary or proper for enforcing the said provisions.

(2.) An inspector authorised in pursuance of this section shall, for the purpose of his duties, have the same powers with respect to workshops and laundries to which this section applies, as he has under the principal Act as amended by this Act with respect to factories, and may for the same purpose take the like proceedings for punishing or remedying any default in compliance with the said provisions of the law relating to public health as might be taken by the sanitary authority of the district in which the workshops or laundries are situate, and shall be entitled to recover from that sanitary authority all such expenses in and about any proceedings in respect of such workshops or laundries as he may incur and are not recovered from any other person, and have not been incurred in any unsuccessful proceedings.

2.—(1.) Section four of the principal Act shall apply to workshops conducted on the system of not employing any child, young person, or woman therein, and to laundries.

(2.) Where notice of an act, neglect, or default is given by an inspector under the said section four, as amended by this Act, to a sanitary authority, and proceedings are not taken within a reasonable time for punishing or remedying the act, neglect, or default, the inspector may take the like proceedings for punishing or remedying the same as the sanitary authority might have taken, and shall be entitled to recover from the sanitary authority all such expenses in and about the proceedings as the inspector incurs and are not recovered from any other person, and have not been incurred in any unsuccessful proceedings.

3.—(1.) Sections three and thirty-three of the Factory and Workshop Act, 1878 (which relate to cleanliness, ventilation, and overcrowding in, and limewashing of, factories and workshops), shall cease to apply to workshops.

(2.) For the purpose of their duties with respect to workshops (not being workshops to which the Public Health (London) Act, 1891, applies), a sanitary authority and their officers shall, without prejudice to their other powers, have all such powers of entry, inspection, taking legal proceedings or otherwise, as an inspector under the principal Act.

(3.) If any child, young person, or woman, is employed in a workshop, and the medical officer of the sanitary authority becomes aware thereof, he shall forthwith give written notice thereof to the factory inspector of the district.

4.—(1.) Every workshop as defined by the principal Act (including any workshop conducted on the system of not employing any child, young person, or woman therein), and every workplace within the meaning of the Public Health Act, 1875, shall be kept free from effluvia arising from any drain, water closet, earth closet, privy, urinal, or other nuisance, and unless so kept shall be deemed to be a nuisance liable to be dealt with summarily under the law relating to public health.

(2.) Where on the certificate of a medical officer of health or inspector of nuisances it appears to any sanitary authority that the limewashing, cleansing, or purifying of any such workshop, or of any part thereof, is necessary for the health of the persons employed therein, the sanitary authority shall give notice in writing to the owner or occupier of the workshop to limewash, cleanse, or purify the same or part thereof, as the case may require.

(3.) If the person to whom notice is so given fails to comply therewith within the time therein specified, he shall be liable to a fine not exceeding ten shillings for every day during which he continues to make default, and the sanitary authority may, if they think fit, cause the workshop or part to be limewashed, cleansed, or purified, and may recover in a summary manner the expenses incurred by them in so doing from the person in default.

(4.) This section shall not apply to any workshop or workplace to which the Public Health (London) Act, 1891, applies.

5.—In section three of the principal Act, for the word "privy," shall be substituted the words "water closet, earth closet, privy, urinal," and for the words "injurious to the health of the persons employed therein" shall be substituted the words "dangerous or injurious to the health of the persons employed therein."

Safety.

6.—(1.) The words "near to which any person is liable to pass or to be employed" in sub-section (1) of section five of the principal Act are hereby repealed.

(2.) In sub-section three of the same section before the word "every part" shall be inserted the words "all dangerous parts of the machinery and."

7.—(1.) Every factory of which the construction is commenced after the first day of January one thousand eight hundred and ninety-two, and in which more than forty persons are employed, shall be furnished with a certificate from the sanitary authority of the district in which the factory is situate that the factory is provided on the storeys above the ground floor with such means of escape in case of fire for the persons employed therein as can reasonably be required under the circumstances of each case, and a factory not so furnished shall be deemed not to be kept in conformity with the principal Act, and it shall be the duty of the sanitary authority to examine every such factory, and on being satisfied that the factory is so provided to give such a certificate as aforesaid.

(2.) With respect to all factories to which the foregoing provisions of this section do not apply, and in which more than forty persons are employed, it shall be the duty of the sanitary authority of every district, as soon as may be after the passing of this Act, and afterwards from time to time, to ascertain whether all such factories within their district are provided with such means of escape as aforesaid, and, in the case of any factory which is not so provided, to serve on the person being within the meaning of the Public Health Act, 1875, the owner of the factory a notice in writing specifying the measures necessary for providing such means of escape as aforesaid, and requiring him to carry out the same before a specified date, and thereupon such owner shall, notwithstanding any agreement with the occupier, have power to take such steps as are necessary for complying with the requirements, and, unless such requirements are so complied with, such owner shall be liable to a fine not exceeding one pound for every day that such non-compliance continues. In case of a difference of opinion between the owner of the factory and the sanitary authority, the difference shall, on the application of either party, be referred to arbitration, and thereupon the provisions of the First Schedule to this Act shall have effect, except that the parties to the arbitration shall be the sanitary authority on the one hand and the owner on the other, and the award on the arbitration shall be binding on the parties thereto. If the owner alleges that the occupier of the factory ought to bear or contribute to the expenses of complying with the require-ment, he may apply to the county court having jurisdiction where the factory is situate, and thereupon the county court, after hearing the occupier, may make such order as appears to the court just and equitable under all the circumstances of the case.

(3.) All expenses incurred by a sanitary authority in the execution of this section shall be defrayed—

(a.) in the case of an authority of an urban district, as part of their expenses of the general execution of the Public Health Act, 1875 ; and

(b.) in the case of an authority of a rural district, as special expenses incurred in the execution of the Public Health Act, 1875 ; and such expenses shall be charged to the contributory place in which the factory is situate.

(4.) In the application of this section to the administrative county of London, the London County Council shall take the place of the sanitary authority, and their expenses in the execution of this section shall be defrayed as part of their expenses in the management of the Metropolitan Building Act, 1855, and the Acts amending the same.

Special Rules and Requirements.

8.—(1.) Where the Secretary of State certifies that in his opinion any machinery or process or particular description of manual labour used in a factory or workshop (other than a domestic workshop) is dangerous or injurious to health or dangerous to life or limb, either generally or in the case of women, children, or any other class of persons, or that the provision for the admission of fresh air is not sufficient, or that the quantity of dust generated or inhaled in any factory or workshop is dangerous or injurious to health, the chief inspector may serve on the occupier of the factory or workshop a notice in writing, either proposing such special rules or requiring the adoption of such special measures as appear to the chief inspector to be reasonably practicable and to meet the necessities of the case.

(2.) Unless within twenty-one days after receipt of the notice the occupier serves on the chief inspector a notice in writing that he objects to the rules or requirements, the rules shall be established, or, as the case may be, the requirement shall be observed.

(3.) If the notice of objection suggests any modification of the rules or requirement, the Secretary of State shall consider the suggestion and may assent thereto with or without any further modification which may be agreed on between the Secretary of State and the occupier, and thereupon the rules shall be established, or, as the case may be, the requirement shall be observed, subject to such modification.

(4.) If the Secretary of State does not assent to any objection or modification suggested as aforesaid by the occupier, the matter in difference between the Secretary of State and the occupier shall be referred to arbitration under this Act, and the date of the receipt of the notice of objection by the Secretary of State shall be deemed to be the date of the reference, and the rules shall be established, or the requisition shall have effect, as settled by an award on arbitration.

(5.) Any notice under this section may be served by post.

(6.) With respect to arbitrations under this Act the provisions in the First Schedule to this Act shall have effect.

(7.) No person shall be precluded by any agreement from doing, or be liable under any agreement to any penalty or forfeiture for doing, such acts as may be necessary in order to comply with the provisions of this section.

9.—(1.) If any person who is bound to observe any special rules established for any factory or workshop under this Act acts in contravention of, or fails to comply with, any such special rule, he shall be liable on summary conviction to a fine not exceeding two pounds; and the occupier of the factory or workshop shall also be liable on summary conviction to a fine not exceeding ten pounds, unless he proves that he had taken all reasonable means, by publishing, and to the best of his power enforcing, the rules to prevent the contravention or noncompliance.

(2.) A factory or workshop in which there is a contravention of any requirement made under this Act shall be deemed not to be kept in conformity with the principal Act.

10.—(1.) After special rules are established under this Act in any factory or workshop, the Secretary of State may from time to time propose to the occupier of the factory or workshop any amendment of the rules or any new rules; and the provisions of this Act with respect to the original rules shall apply to all such amendments and new rules in like manner, as nearly as may be, as they apply to the original rules.

(2.) The occupier of any factory or workshop in which special rules are established may from time to time propose in writing to the chief inspector, with the approval of the Secretary of State, any amendment of the rules or any new rules, and the provisions of this Act with respect to a suggestion of an occupier for modifying the special rules proposed by a chief inspector shall apply to all such amendments and new rules in like manner, as nearly as may be, as they apply to such a suggestion.

11.—(1.) Printed copies of all special rules for the time being in force under this Act in any factory or workshop shall be kept posted up in legible characters in conspicuous places in the factory or workshop where they may be conveniently read by the persons employed. In a factory or workshop in Wales or Monmouthshire the rules shall be posted up in the Welsh language also.

(2.) A printed copy of all such rules shall be given by the occupier to any person affected thereby on his or her application.

(3.) If the occupier of any factory or workshop fails to comply with any provision of this section, he shall be liable on summary conviction to a fine not exceeding ten pounds.

(4.) Every person who pulls down, injures, or defaces any special rules when posted up in pursuance of this Act, or any notice posted up in pursuance of the special rules, shall be liable on summary conviction to a fine not exceeding five pounds.

12. An inspector shall, when required, certify a copy which is shown to his satisfaction to be a true copy of any special rules for the time being established under this Act for any factory or workshop, and a copy so certified shall be evidence (but not to the exclusion of other proof) of those special rules, and of the fact that they are duly established under this Act.

Period of Employment.

13.—(1.) For subsection (2) of section fifteen of the principal Act the following subsection shall be substituted, namely :—

(2.) In a workshop which is conducted on the system of not employing therein either children or young persons, and the occupier of which has served on an inspector notice of his intention to conduct his workshop on that system—

(*a*.) The period of employment for a woman shall, except on Saturday, be a specified period of twelve hours taken between six o'clock in the morning and ten o'clock in the evening, and shall on Saturday be a specified period of eight hours, taken between six o'clock in the morning and four o'clock in the afternoon ; and

(*b*.) There shall be allowed to a woman for meals and absence from work during the period of employment, a specified period not less, except on Saturday, than one hour and a half, and on Saturday than half an hour.

14.—(1.) The report required by section sixty-six of the principal Act respecting the employment of a child, young person, or woman in pursuance of an exception relating to employment overtime, must be sent to an inspector not later than eight o'clock in the evening on which the child, young person, or woman is employed in pursuance of the exception.

(2.) Where, under the said section sixty-six, the occupier of a factory or workshop is required to make an entry and report respecting the employment overtime of a child, young person, or woman in the factory or workshop, he shall cause a note containing the prescribed particulars respecting the employment to be kept affixed in the factory or workshop during the prescribed time, and in default of so doing shall be liable, on summary conviction, to a fine not exceeding five pounds.

15. For section eighteen of the principal Act the following section shall be substituted, namely,—

In a non-textile factory or workshop where a young person or woman has not been actually employed for more than eight hours on any day in a week, and notice of such non-employment has been affixed in the factory or workshop and served on the inspector, the period of employment on Saturday in that week for that young person or woman may be from six o'clock in the morning to four o'clock in the afternoon, with an interval of not less than two hours for meals.

Holidays.

16. For subsection (4) of section twenty-two of the principal Act the following subsection shall be substituted, namely :—

(4.) Cessation from work shall not be deemed to be a half holiday or whole holiday, unless a notice of the half holiday or whole holiday has been affixed in the factory or workshop during the first week in January, and a copy thereof has on the same day been forwarded to the inspector of the district : Provided that any such notice may be changed by a subsequent notice affixed and sent in like manner not less than fourteen days before the holiday or half holiday to which it applies.

Conditions of Employment.

17. An occupier of a factory or workshop shall not knowingly allow a woman to be employed therein within four weeks after she has given birth to a child.

18. On and after the first day of January one thousand eight hundred and ninety-three no child under the age of eleven years shall be employed in a factory or workshop.

Provided always, that any child lawfully employed under the principal Act, or any Act relating to the employment of children, at the time that the provisions of this section come into operation shall be exempt from its provisions.

19. Every certifying surgeon acting under this or the principal Act shall in each year make at the prescribed time a report in the prescribed form to the Secretary of State as to the persons inspected during the year, and the results of the inspection.

20. Where the age of any child or young person under the age of sixteen years is required to be ascertained or proved for the purposes of this Act, or for any purpose connected with the elementary education or employment in labour of such child or young person, any person shall, on presenting a written requisition, in such form, and containing such particulars as may be from time to time prescribed by the Local Government Board, and on payment of a fee of sixpence, be entitled to obtain a certified copy under the hand of a registrar or superintendent registrar of the entry in the register, under the Births and Deaths Registration Acts, 1836 to 1874, of the birth of that child or young person; and such form of requisition shall on request be supplied without charge by every superintendent registrar and registrar of births, deaths, and marriages.

21. There shall be repealed so much of section sixty-one of the principal Act as enacts that the provisions therein mentioned shall not apply to a workshop which is conducted on the system of not employing children or young persons therein, and the occupier of which has served on an inspector notice of his intention to conduct his workshop on that system.

Miscellaneous.

22.—(1.) In section thirty-one of the principal Act for the words " and is of such a nature as to prevent the person injured by it from " returning to his work in the factory or workshop within forty-eight " hours after the occurrence of the accident," shall be substituted the words " and is of such a nature as to prevent the person injured by " it from returning to his work in the factory or workshop and doing " five hours' work on any day during the next three days after the " occurrence of the accident."

(2.) The notice required under that section shall, where the person killed or injured is not removed to his own residence, state both his residence and the place to which he has been removed.

(3.) Where a death has occurred by accident in any factory or workshop, the coroner shall forthwith advise the district inspector under this Act of the time and place of the holding of the inquest, and at such inquest any relative of any person whose death may have been caused by the accident with respect to which the inquest is being held, and any inspector under the principal Act, and the occupier of the factory or workshop in which the accident occurred, and any person appointed by the order in writing of the majority of the workpeople employed in the said factory or workshop shall be at liberty to attend and examine any witness either in person or by his counsel, solicitor, or agent, subject nevertheless to the order of the coroner.

23. In the appointment of inspectors of factories in Wales and Monmouthshire, among candidates otherwise equally qualified, persons having a knowledge of the Welsh language shall be preferred.

24. Every person who is engaged as a weaver in the cotton, worsted, or woollen, or linen or jute trade, or as a winder, weaver, or reeler in the cotton trade, and is paid by the piece, in or in connection with any factory or workshop, shall have supplied to him with his work sufficient particulars to enable him to ascertain the rate of wages at which he is entitled to be paid for the work, and the occupier of the factory or workshop shall supply him with such particulars accordingly.

If the occupier of any factory or workshop fails to supply such particulars then, unless he proves that he has given the best information in his power with respect to such particulars, he shall be liable -for each offence to a fine not exceeding ten pounds, and in the case of a second or subsequent conviction for the same offence within two years from the last conviction for that offence not less than one pound.

Provided always, that in the event of anyone who is engaged as an operative in any factory or workshop receiving such particulars, and subsequently disclosing the same with a fraudulent object or for the purpose of gain, whether they be furnished directly to him or to a fellow workman, he shall be liable for each offence to a fine not exceeding ten pounds.

Provided also, that anyone who shall solicit or procure a person so engaged in any factory to disclose such particulars with the object or purpose aforesaid, or shall pay or reward such person, or shall cause such person to be paid or rewarded, for so disclosing such particulars, shall be guilty of an offence, and shall be liable for each offence to a fine not exceeding ten pounds.

25. The powers of entry conferred by section sixty-eight of the principal Act on an inspector under that Act may be exercised without the authority or warrant required in certain cases by section sixty-nine of that Act.

26.—(1.) Section seventy-five of the principal Act (which requires notice to be given of the occupation of a factory) shall apply to a workshop (including any workshop conducted on the system of not employing any child, young person, or woman therein) in like manner as it applies to a factory.

(2.) Where an inspector receives notice in pursuance of this section with respect to a workshop, he shall forthwith forward the notice to the sanitary authority of the district in which the workshop is situate.

27.—(1.) The occupier of every factory and workshop (including any workshop conducted on the system of not employing any child, young person, or woman therein) and every contractor employed by any such occupier in the business of the factory or workshop shall, if so required by the Secretary of State by an order made in accordance with section sixty-five of the principal Act, and subject to any exceptions mentioned in the order, keep in the prescribed form and with the prescribed particulars lists showing the names of all persons directly employed by him, either as workman or as contractor, in the business of the factory or workshop, outside the factory or workshop, and the places where they are employed, and every such list shall be open to inspection by any inspector under the principal Act or by any officer of a sanitary authority.

(2.) In the event of a contravention of this section by the occupier of a factory or workshop, or by a contractor, the occupier or contractor shall be liable to a fine not exceeding forty shillings.

28. The fine imposed on a conviction under sections sixty-eight, eighty-one, eighty-two, or eighty-three of the principal Act, for any offence in relation to a factory, shall, in case of a second or subsequent conviction for the same offence within two years from the last conviction for that offence, be not less than one pound for each offence.

29. In summary proceedings for offences and fines under the principal Act as amended by any subsequent Act, an information may be laid within three months after the date at which the offence comes to the knowledge of a factory inspector, or in case of an inquest being held in relation to the offence, then within two months after the conclusion of the inquest, so, however, that it shall not be laid after the expiration of six months from the commission of the offence.

30. Section ninety-two of the principal Act shall apply to a workshop in like manner as it applies to a factory.

31. In section ninety-three of the principal Act for the words " a place solely used as a dwelling shall not be deemed to form part of the factory or workshop for the purposes of this Act," shall be substituted the words " a room solely used for the purpose of sleeping therein shall not be deemed to form part of the factory or workshop for the purposes of this Act."

32. Nothing in the principal Act as amended by this Act shall apply to the process of cleaning and preparing fruit so far as is necessary to prevent the spoiling of the fruit on its arrival at a factory or workshop during the months of June, July, August, and September.

33. In the application of this Act to Scotland, the following modifications shall be made, namely—

(1.) The expression " Births and Deaths Registration Acts, 1836 to 1874," shall mean the Acts relating to the registration of births, deaths, and marriages in Scotland :

(2.) The expression " Public Health Act, 1875," where it occurs in section seven of this Act shall mean the Public Health (Scotland) Act, 1867, and the Acts amending the same :

(3.) The Board of Supervision shall be substituted for the Local Government Board :

(4.) In lieu of Christmas Day, and either Good Friday or the next public holiday under the Holidays Extension Act, 1875, there shall be allowed as a holiday to every child, young person, and woman employed in a factory or workshop within a burgh or police burgh, the two days in each year set apart by the Church of Scotland for the observance of the sacramental fast in the parish in which the factory or workshop is situate, and in such burghs or police burghs where such fast days have been abolished or discontinued there shall be allowed as a holiday to every child, young person, and woman employed in a factory or workshop in such burghs or police burghs such two whole days in each year, separated by an interval of not less than three months, as shall be fixed by the magistrates or police commissioners in such burghs or police burghs, and such magistrates or police commissioners, as the case may be, are hereby required to fix, and from time to time, if it shall seem expedient to them to do so, to alter such holidays, and give public notice thereof fourteen days before the date at any time fixed.

(5.) Where a death has occurred by accident in any factory or workshop a public inquiry in open court shall be held by the sheriff, upon the petition of any party interested, and the sheriff shall forthwith advise the district inspector under this Act of the time and place of the holding of the inquiry, and at such inquiry any relative of any person whose death has been caused by the accident with respect to which the inquiry is being held, and the occupier or manager of the factory or workshop in which the accident occurred, and any person appointed by the order in writing of the majority of the workpeople employed in the said factory or workshop, shall be at liberty to attend and examine any witness, either in person, or by his counsel, solicitor, or agent, subject nevertheless to the order of the sheriff.

34. For subsection (2) of section one hundred and six of the principal Act, the following subsection shall be substituted :—

(2.) In lieu of any two half-holidays allowed under the provisions of subsection (2) of section twenty-two of this Act, there shall be allowed as a holiday to every child, young person, and woman employed in a factory or workshop the whole of the seventeenth day of March, when that day does not fall on a Sunday, or at the option of the occupier of the factory or workshop, either Good Friday (unless that day is otherwise fixed as a holiday) or Easter Tuesday.

35. The fee to be charged in pursuance of section one hundred and four of the principal Act shall not exceed sixpence, and that section shall apply in the case of a young person under the age of sixteen years in like manner as it applies in the case of a child.

36. The expression "retail bakehouse" in the Factory and Workshops Act, 1883, shall not include any place which is a factory within the meaning of the principal Act.

37.—(1.) For the purposes of the principal Act and this Act the expression "machinery" shall include any driving strap or band, and the expression "process" shall include the use of any locomotive.

(2.) In this Act the expression "domestic workshop" means a workshop to which section sixteen of the principal Act applies.

38. There shall be added in line three, subsection (3), of the Fourth Schedule of the principal Act, after "earthenware," the words "or china."

39. The enactments specified in the Second Schedule to this Act are hereby repealed to the extent mentioned in the third column of that schedule.

Provided that any special rules or requirements made under any enactment repealed by this Act shall continue to have effect as if made under this Act, and the provisions of this Act shall apply thereto accordingly.

40. This Act shall, except where it is otherwise expressed, come into operation on the first day of January one thousand eight hundred and ninety-two:

41.—(1.) This Act may be cited as the Factory and Workshop Act, 1891, and shall be construed as one with the Factory and Workshop Act, 1878.

(2.) The Factory and Workshop Act, 1878, the Factory and Workshop Act, 1883, and the Cotton Cloth Factories Act, 1889, may, together with this Act, be cited collectively as the Factory and Workshops Acts, 1878 to 1891.

SCHEDULES.

FIRST SCHEDULE.
REFERRING TO SECTIONS 7 AND 8.

1. The parties to the arbitration are in this schedule deemed to be the occupiers of the factory or workshop on the one hand and the chief inspector, on behalf of the Secretary of State, on the other.

2. Each of the parties to the arbitration may, within fourteen days after the date of the reference, appoint an arbitrator.

3. No person shall act as arbitrator or umpire under this Act who is employed in, or in the management of, or is interested in, the factory or workshop to which the arbitration relates.

4. The appointment of an arbitrator under this section shall be in writing, and notice of the appointment shall be forthwith sent to the other party to the arbitration, and shall not be revoked without the consent of that party.

5. The death or removal of, or other change in, any of the parties to the arbitration shall not affect the proceedings under this schedule.

6. If within the said fourteen days either of the parties fails to appoint an arbitrator, the arbitrator appointed by the other party may proceed to hear and determine the matter in difference, and in that case the award of the single arbitrator shall be final.

7. If before an award has been made any arbitrator appointed by either party dies or becomes incapable to act, or for seven days refuses or neglects to act, the party by whom that arbitrator was appointed may appoint some other to act in his place; and if he fails to do so within seven days after notice in writing from the other party for that purpose, the remaining arbitrator may proceed to hear and determine the matter in difference, and in that case the award of the single arbitrator shall be final.

8. In either of the foregoing cases where an arbitrator is empowered to act singly, on one of the parties failing to appoint, the party so failing may, before the single arbitrator has actually proceeded in the arbitration, appoint an arbitrator, who shall then act as if no failure had occurred.

9. If the arbitrators fail to make their award within twenty-one days after the day on which the last of them was appointed, or within such extended time (if any) as may have been appointed for that purpose by both arbitrators under their hands, the matter in difference shall be determined by the umpire appointed as hereinafter mentioned.

10. The arbitrators, before they enter on the matter referred to them, shall appoint by writing under their hands an umpire to decide on points on which they may differ.

11. If the umpire dies or becomes incapable of acting before he has

made his award, or refuses to make his award within a reasonable time after the matter has been brought within his cognizance, the persons or person who appointed such umpire shall forthwith appoint another umpire in his place.

12. If the arbitrators refuse or fail, or for seven days after the request of either party neglect, to appoint an umpire, then on the application of either party an umpire may be appointed by the chairman of the quarter sessions within the jurisdiction of which the factory or workshop is situate.

13. The decision of every umpire on the matters referred to him shall be final.

14. If a single arbitrator fails to make his award within twenty-one days after the day on which he was appointed, the party who appointed him may appoint another arbitrator to act in his place.

15. Arrangements shall, whenever practicable, be made for the matters in difference being heard at the same time before the arbitrators and the umpire.

16. The arbitrators and the umpire, or any of them, may examine the parties and their witnesses on oath, and may also consult any counsel, engineer, or scientific person whom they may think it expedient to consult.

17. The payment, if any, to be made to any arbitrator or umpire for his services shall be fixed by the Secretary of State, and together with the costs of the arbitration and award shall be paid by the parties, or one of them, according as the award may direct. Such costs may be taxed by a master of the Supreme Court, or, in Scotland, by the auditor of the Court of Session, and the taxing officer shall, on the written application of either of the parties, ascertain and certify the proper amount thereof. The amount, if any, payable by the Secretary of State shall be paid as part of the expenses of inspectors under the principal Act. The amount, if any, payable by the occupier of the factory or workshop may in the event of nonpayment be recovered in the same manner as fines under the principal Act.

SECOND SCHEDULE.
Referring to Section 39.
Enactments Repealed.

Session and Chapter.	Title or Short Title.	Extent of Repeal.
41 & 42 Vict. c. 16.	The Factory and Workshop Act, 1878.	In section three, the words "and a workshop" and "or workshop" wherever they occur. In section five, subsection (1), the words "near to which any person is liable to pass or to be employed." Sections six, seven, and eight. Section fifteen, from "and" at the end of subsection (1) to the end of the section.

SECOND SCHEDULE *(continued)*—

Session and Chapter.	Title or Short Title.	Extent of Repeal.
41 & 42 Vict. c. 16 *(continued)*.	The Factory and Workshop Act, 1878 *(continued)*.	In section twenty-two, subsection (4).
		In section thirty-one the words " and is of such a nature as to prevent the person injured by it from returning to his work in the factory or workshop within forty-eight hours after the occurrence of the accident."
		In section thirty-three the words " and workshop," " or workshop," and " or workshops," wherever they respectively occur.
		Section sixty-one, from "or" at the end of the paragraph marked (*a*) to the words "workshop on that system."
		Section sixty-nine.
		Section ninety-one, from "(1.) The information shall be laid" to "commission of the offence."
		In section one hundred and one, the words " or workshop."
46 & 47 Vict. c. 53.	The Factory and Workshop Act, 1883.	Sections seven to twelve and subsections (2) and (3) of section seventeen.
51 & 52 Vict. c. 22.	The Factory and Workshop Amendment (Scotland) Act, 1888.	The whole Act.
52 & 53 Vict. c. 62.	The Cotton Cloth Factories Act, 1889.	Section twelve.

VIII. EMPLOYERS' LIABILITY ACT, 1880.

(43 & 44 VICT. CAP. 42.)

---

1. By this Act where personal injury is caused to a workman
(1.) By reason of any defect in the condition of the ways, works, machinery, or plant connected with or used in the business of the employer; or

(2.) By reason of the negligence of any person in the service of the employer who has any superintendence intrusted to him whilst in the exercise of such superintendence ; or

(3.) By reason of any person in the service of the employer to whose orders or directions the workman at the time of the injury was bound to conform, and did conform where such injury resulted from his having so conformed ; or

(4.) By reason of the act or omission of any person in the service of the employer done or made in obedience to the rules or bye-laws of the employer or in obedience to the particular instructions given by any person delegated with the authority of the employer in that behalf ; or

(5.) By reason of the negligence of any person in the service of the employer who has the charge or control of any signal, points, locomotive engine, or train upon a railway, the workman, or in case the injury resulted in death, the legal personal representatives of the workman, and any person entitled in case of death shall have the same right of compensation and remedies against the employer as if the workman had not been a workman of, nor in the service of, the employer, nor engaged in his work.

2. A workman is not entitled to any right of compensation or remedy against the employer in any of the following cases ; that is to say—

(1.) Under subsection one of section one unless the defect therein mentioned arose from or had not been discovered or remedied owing to the negligence of the employer or of some person in the service of the employer and entrusted with the duty of seeing that the ways, works, machinery, or plant were in proper order or condition.

(2.) Under subsection four of section one, unless the injury resulted from some impropriety or defect in the rules, bye-laws, or instructions therein mentioned, provided that where a rule or bye-law has been approved or has been accepted as a proper rule or bye-law by one of her Majesty's principal Secretaries of State, or by the Board of Trade or any other department of the Government under or by virtue of any Act of Parliament, it shall not be deemed for the purposes of this Act to be an improper or defective rule or bye-law.

(3.) In any case where the workman knew of the defect or negligence which caused his injury and failed within a reasonable time to give, or cause to be given, information thereof to the employer or some person superior to himself in the service of the employer, unless he was aware that the employer or such superior already knew of the said defect or negligence.

3. The amount of compensation recoverable is not to exceed such sum as may be found to be equivalent to the estimated earnings during the three years preceding the injury of a person in the same grade employed during those years in the like employment and in the district in which the workman is employed at the time of the injury.

4. An action for the recovery of compensation for an injury is not maintainable unless notice that injury has been sustained is given within six weeks and the action is commenced within six months from the occurrence of the accident causing the injury, or in case of death, within twelve months from the time of death. Provided always that in case of death the want of such notice is no bar to the maintenance of such action if the judge shall be of opinion that there was reasonable excuse for such want of notice.

5. There will be deducted from any compensation awarded to any workman, or representatives of a workman, or persons claiming by or under or through a workman in respect of any cause of action arising hereunder, any penalty or part of a penalty which may have been made in pursuance of any other Act of Parliament to such workman, representatives, or persons in respect of the same cause of action, and where an action has been brought under this Act by any workman or the representatives of any workman, or any persons claiming by, under, or through such workman for compensation in respect of any cause of action arising under this Act, and payment has not previously been made of any penalty, or part of a penalty, under any other Act of Parliament in respect of the same cause of action such workman, representatives, or person shall not be entitled thereafter to receive any penalty, or part of a penalty, under any other Act of Parliament in respect of the same cause of action.

6.—(1.) Every action for recovery of compensation under this Act must be brought in a County Court, but may upon the application of either plaintiff or defendant be removed into a superior court in like manner and upon the same conditions as an action commenced in a County Court may by law be removed.

(2.) Upon the trial of any such action in a County Court before the judge without a jury, one or more assessors may be appointed for the purpose of ascertaining the amount of compensation.

7. Notice in respect of an injury hereunder must give the name and address of the person injured, and shall state in ordinary language the cause of the injury, and the date at which it was sustained, and shall be served on the employer, or if there is more than one employer, upon one of such employers. The notice may be served by delivering the same to or at the residence or place of business of the person on whom it is to be served. The notice may also be served by post by a registered letter addressed to the person on·whom it is to be served at his last known place of residence or place of business; and if served by post shall be deemed to have been served at the time when a letter containing the same would be delivered in the ordinary course of post; and in proving the service of such notice, it shall be sufficient to prove that the notice was properly addressed and registered. Where the employer is a body of persons corporate or unincorporate, the notice shall be served by delivering the same at, or by sending it by post in a registered letter addressed to the office, or if there be more than one office, any one of the body of such offices. A notice under this section will not be deemed invalid by reason of any defect or inaccuracy therein, unless the judge who tries the action arising from the injury mentioned in the notice shall be of opinion that the defendant in the action is prejudiced in his defence by such defect or inaccuracy, and that the defect or inaccuracy was for the purpose of misleading.

8. For the purposes of this Act, unless the context otherwise requires, the expression " person who has superintendence entrusted to

him," means a person whose sole or principal duty is that of super-intendence, and who is not ordinarily engaged in manual labour. The expression "employer" includes a body of persons, corporate or incorporate. The expression "workman" means a railway servant and any person to whom the Employers and Workmen Act, 1875, applies.

IX. PAYMENT OF WAGES IN PUBLIC-HOUSES PROHIBITION ACT, 1883.

(46 & 47 VICT. Cap. 31.)

Whereas by the Coal Mines Regulation Act, 1872, and the Metal-liferous Mines Regulation Act, 1882, the payment in public-houses, beershops, or other places in the said Acts mentioned of wages to persons employed in or about any mines to which the said Acts apply, is prohibited, and it is expedient to extend such prohibition to the payment in public-houses, beer-shops, and other places in England and Scotland of wages to all workmen as defined by this Act.

1. This Act may be cited as "The Payment of Wages in Public-houses Prohibition Act, 1883."

2. In this Act the expression "workman" means any person who is a labourer, servant in husbandry, journeyman, artificer, handi-craftsman, or is otherwise engaged in manual labour, whether under the age of twenty-one years or above that age, but does not include a domestic or menial servant, nor any person employed in or about any mine to which the Coal Mines Regulation Act, 1872, or the Metal-liferous Mines Regulation Act, 1882, applies.

3. From and after the passing of this Act no wages shall be paid to any workman at or within any public-house, beershop, or place for the sale of any spirits, wine, cider, or other spirituous or fermented liquor, or any office, garden, or place belonging thereto or occupied therewith, save and except such wages as are paid by the resident owner or occupier of such public-house, beershop, or place to any workman bona-fide employed by him.

Every person who contravenes or fails to comply with or permits any person to contravene or fail to comply with this Act shall be guilty of an offence against this Act.

And in the event of any wages being paid by any person in con-travention of the provisions of this Act, for or on behalf of any employer, such employer shall himself be guilty of an offence against this Act, unless he prove that he had taken all reasonable means in his power for enforcing the provisions of this Act and to prevent such contravention.

4. Every person who is guilty of an offence against this Act shall be liable to a penalty not exceeding ten pounds for each offence ; and all offences against this Act may be prosecuted and all penalties under this Act may be recovered by any person summarily in England in the manner provided by the Summary Jurisdiction Acts, and in Scotland in the manner provided by the Summary Jurisdiction (Scot-land) Acts, 1864 and 1881.

This Act shall not apply to Ireland.

X. SHOP HOURS ACT, 1892.

(55 & 56 VICT. CAP. 62.)

Whereas the health of many young persons employed in shops and warehouses is seriously injured by reason of the length of the period of employment :

Be it therefore enacted by the Queen's most Excellent Majesty, by and with the advice and consent of the Lords Spiritual and Temporal, and Commons, in this present Parliament assembled, and by the authority of the same, as follows :

1. This Act may be cited as the Shop Hours Act, 1892.

2. This Act shall come into operation on the first day of September one thousand eight hundred and ninety-two.

3.—(1.) No young person shall be employed in or about a shop for a longer period than seventy-four hours, including meal times, in any one week.

(2.) No young person shall to the knowledge of his employer be employed in or about a shop having been previously on the same day employed in any factory or workshop, as defined by the Factory and Workshop Act, 1878, for the number of hours permitted by the said Act or for a longer period than will together with the time during which he has been so previously employed complete such number of hours.

4. In every shop in which a young person is employed a notice shall be kept exhibited by the employer in a conspicuous place referring to the provisions of this Act and stating the number of hours in the week during which a young person may lawfully be employed in that shop.

5. Where any young person is employed in or about a shop contrary to the provisions of this Act, the employer shall be liable to a fine not exceeding one pound for each person so employed.

6. Where the employer of any young person is charged with an offence against this Act, he shall be entitled upon information duly laid by him to have any other person whom he charges as the actual offender brought before the court at the time appointed for hearing the charge ; and if, after the commission of the offence has been proved, the said employer proves to the satisfaction of the court that he has used due diligence to enforce the execution of the Act, and that the said other person has committed the offence in question without his knowledge, consent, or connivance, the said other person shall be summarily convicted of such offence, and the occupier shall be exempt from any fine.

7. All offences under this Act shall be prosecuted, and all fines under this Act shall be recovered, in like manner as offences and fines are prosecuted and recovered under the Factory and Workshop Act, 1878, and sections eighty-eight, eighty-nine, ninety, and ninety-one of the said Act, and so much of section ninety-two thereof as relates to evidence respecting the age of any person, and the provisions relating to the application of the said Act to Scotland and Ireland, so far as those provisions are applicable, shall have effect as if re-enacted in this Act and in terms made applicable thereto.

8. The council of any county or borough, and in the city of London the common council, may appoint such inspectors as they may think necessary for the execution of this Act within the areas of their

respective jurisdictions, and sections sixty-eight and seventy of the Factory and Workshop Act, 1878, shall apply in the case of any such inspector as if he were appointed under that Act, and as if the expression workshop as used in those sections included any shop within the meaning of this Act.

The powers conferred by this section may be exercised in Ireland by the council of any municipal borough and by the commissioners of any town or township.

9. In this Act, unless the context otherwise requires—

"Shop" means retail and wholesale shops, markets, stalls, and warehouses in which assistants are employed for hire, and includes licensed public-houses and refreshment houses of any kind :

"Young person" means a person under the age of eighteen years: Other words and expressions have the same meanings respectively as in the Factory and Workshop Act, 1878.

10. Nothing in this Act shall apply to a shop where the only persons employed are members of the same family, dwelling in the building of which the shop forms part or to which the shop is attached, or to members of the employer's family so dwelling, or to any person wholly employed as a domestic servant.

XI. MASTER AND SERVANT ACT, 1889.

(52 & 53 VICT. Cap. 24.)

Whereas certain statutes relating to master and servant in particular manufactures have, partly by reason of changes in the methods of manufacture and in the conditions of employment, and partly by reason of improvements in the general law, either ceased to be put in force or become unnecessary, and it is expedient with a view to the revision of the statute law, and particularly to the improvement of the revised edition of the statutes, to expressly and specifically repeal the same :

Be it therefore enacted by the Queen's most Excellent Majesty, by and with the advice and consent of the Lords Spiritual and Temporal, and Commons, in this present Parliament assembled, and by the authority of the same, as follows :—

1. This Act may be cited as the Master and Servant Act, 1889.

2. The enactments described in the schedule to this Act are hereby repealed :

Provided that where any enactment not comprised in the schedule has been repealed, confirmed, revived, or perpetuated by any enactment hereby repealed, such repeal, confirmation, revivor, or perpetuation shall not be affected by the repeal effected by this Act :

And the repeal by this Act of any enactment shall not affect any enactment in which such enactment has been applied, incorporated, or referred to :

And this Act shall not affect the validity, invalidity, effect or consequences of anything already done or suffered,—or any existing status or capacity,—or any right, title, obligation, or liability already acquired, accrued, or incurred, or any remedy or proceeding in respect thereof,—or any release or discharge of or from any debt, penalty, obligation, liability, claim or demand,—or any indemnity,—or the proof of any past act or thing :

And this Act shall not extend to repeal any enactment so far as the same may be in force in any part of her Majesty's dominions out of the United Kingdom.

SCHEDULE.

ENACTMENTS which have been already REPEALED are in some instances INCLUDED in this SCHEDULE, in order to avoid the necessity of reference to PREVIOUS STATUTES.

Session and Chapter.	Title of Act.
* Ann. stat. 2. c. 22.	An Act for the more effectual preventing the Abuses and Frauds of persons employed in the working up the Woollen, Linen, Fustian, Cotton, and Iron Manufactures of this Kingdom.
2 Geo. 1. c. 17 . . Irish.	An Act to empower Justices of the Peace to determine disputes about Servants, Artificers, Day Labourers, Wages, and other small Demands, and to oblige Masters to pay the same, and to punish Idle and Disorderly Servants. in part; namely, sections two, nine, and sixteen.
9 Geo. 1. c. 27 . .	An Act for preventing Journeymen Shoemakers selling, exchanging, or pawning Boots, Shoes, Slippers, Cut Leather, or other Materials for making Boots, Shoes, or Slippers, and for better regulating the said Journeymen.
12 Geo. 1. c. 34 . .	An Act to prevent unlawful Combinations of Workmen imployed in the Woollen Manufactures, and for better Payment of their Wages.
13 Geo. 1. c. 26 .	An Act for better Regulation of the Linen and Hempen Manufactures in that Part of Great Britain called Scotland. in part; namely, except section eighteen.
13 Geo. 2. c. 8 . .	An Act to explain and amend an Act made in the First Year of the Reign of Her late Majesty Queen Anne, intituled "An Act for "the more effectual preventing the Abuses "and Frauds of Persons employed in the "working up the Woollen, Linen, Fustian, "Cotton, and Iron Manufactures of this "Kingdom"; and for extending the said Act to the Manufactures of Leather.
15 Geo. 2. c. 27 . .	An Act for the more effectual preventing any Cloth or Woollen Goods remaining upon the Rack or Tenters, or any Woollen Yarn or wooll left out to dry, from being stolen or taken away in the Night-time.

* These references are to the Statutes Revised.

SCHEDULE (*continued*).

Session and Chapter.	Title of Act.
25 Geo. 2. c. 8 . . Irish.	An Act for the better adjusting and more easy recovery of the Wages of certain Servants, and for the better regulation of such Servants and of certain Apprentices; and for the punishment of all such Owners of Coal and their Agents as shall knowingly employ and set at Work Persons retained in the service of other Coal-owners; and also that Mutual Debts between Party and Party be set one against the other.
	in part; namely, sections two and seven.
27 Geo. 2. c. 7 . .	An Act for the more effectual preventing of Frauds and Abuses committed by Persons employed in the Manufacture of Clocks and Watches.
29 Geo. 2. c. 12 . Irish.	An Act to prevent unlawful combinations of Tenants, Colliers, Miners, and others; and the sending of threatening Letters without Names, or with Fictitious Names subscribed thereto; and the malicious destruction of Carriages; and for the more effectual Punishment of wicked Persons who shall maliciously set fire to Houses or Out-houses, or to Stacks of Hay, Corn, Straw, or Turf, or to Ships or Boats.
	in part; namely, sections nine, ten, eleven, and twelve.
30 Geo. 2. c. 12 .	An Act to amend an Act made in the Twenty-ninth year of the Reign of His present Majesty, intituled "An Act to render more effectual an " Act passed in the Twelfth Year of the Reign " of His late Majesty King George, to prevent " unlawful Combinations of Workmen em- " ployed in the Woollen Manufactures, and " for better Payment of their Wages; and " also an Act passed in the Thirteenth Year of " the Reign of His said late Majesty, for the " better Regulation of the Woollen Manufac- " ture, and for preventing Disputes among " the Persons concerned therein; and for " limiting a Time for prosecuting for the " Forfeiture appointed by the aforesaid " Act in case of Payment of the Workman's " Wages in any other Manner than in " Money."
5 Geo. 3. c. 51 . .	An Act for repealing several Laws relating to the Manufacture of Woollen Cloth in the County of York, and also so much of several

SCHEDULE (*continued*).

Session and Chapter.	Title of Act.
5 Geo. 3. c. 51 (*continued*).	other Laws as prescribes particular Standards of Width and Length of such Woollen Cloths; and for substituting other Regulations of the Cloth Trade within the West Riding of the said county, for preventing Frauds in certifying the Contents of the Cloth, and for preserving the Credit of the said Manufacture at the Foreign market.
6 Geo. 3. c. 23.	An Act to amend an Act made in the last Session of Parliament, intituled "An Act for repeal- " ing several Laws relating to the Manufac- " ture of Woollen Cloth in the County of York, " and also so much of several other Laws as " prescribes particular Standards of Width " and Length of such Woollen Cloths; and " for substituting other Regulations of the " Cloth Trade within the West Riding of the " said County, for preventing Frauds in cer- " tifying the Contents of the Cloth, and for " preserving the Credit of the said Manufac- " ture at the Foreign Market."
14 Geo. 3. c 25.	An Act for the more effectual preventing Frauds and Embezzlements by Persons employed in the Woollen Manufactory.
14 Geo. 3. c. 44.	An Act to amend an Act made in the Twenty-second Year of the Reign of His late Majesty King George the Second, intituled "An Act " for the more effectual preventing of Frauds " and Abuses committed by Persons employed " in the Manufacture of Hats, and in the " Woollen, Linen, Fustian, Cotton, Iron, " Leather, Fur, Hemp, Flax, Mohair, and " Silk Manufactures; and for preventing un- " lawful Combinations of Journeymen Dyers " and Journeymen Hot Pressers, and of all " Persons employed in the said several Manu- " factures; and for the better Payment of " their Wages."
17 Geo. 3. c. 55	An Act for the better regulating the Hat Manu-factory.
23 Geo. 3. c. 15	An Act for rendering more effectual the Pro-visions contained in an Act of the Thirteenth Year of King George the First for preventing Frauds and Abuses in the Dyeing Trade. in part; namely, sections five to twelve, and section thirteen from "directed to any con-stable" to end of section.

SCHEDULE (*continued*).

Session and Chapter.	Title of Act.
24 Geo. 3. Sess. 2. c. 3.	An Act for more effectually preventing Frauds and Abuses committed by Persons employed in the Manufactures of combing Wool, Worsted Yarn, and Goods made from Worsted in the County of Suffolk.
25 Geo. 3. c. 40	An Act for more effectually preventing Frauds and Abuses committed by Persons employed in the Manufactures of Combing Wool, Worsted Yarn, and Goods made from Worsted, in the Counties of Bedford, Huntingdon, Northampton, Leicester, Rutland, and Lincoln, and the Isle of Ely.
28 Geo. 3. c. 55	An Act for the better and more effectual Protection of Stocking Frames, and the Machines or Engines annexed thereto or used therewith, and for the Punishment of Persons destroying or injuring of such Stocking Frames, Machines, or Engines, and the Framework, Knitted Pieces, Stockings, and other Articles and Goods used and made in the Hosiery or Framework-knitted Manufactory, or breaking or destroying any Machinery contained in any Mill or Mills used or any way employed in preparing or spinning of Wool or Cotton for the Use of the Stocking Frame.
31 Geo. 3. c. 56	An Act more effectually to prevent Abuses and Frauds committed by Persons employed in the Manufactures of Combing Wool and Worsted Yarn in the County of Norfolk and City of Norwich and County of the said City.
51 Geo. 3. c. 41	An Act to repeal so much of an Act passed in the Eighteenth Year of the Reign of King George the Second, intituled " An Act for the " more effectual preventing the stealing of " Linen, Fustian, and Cotton Goods and " Wares in Buildings, Fields, Grounds, and " other Places used for printing, whitening, " bleaching, or drying the same," as takes away the Benefit of Clergy from Persons stealing Cloth in Places therein mentioned ; and for more effectually preventing such Felonies.

XII. MERCHANT SHIPPING ACT, 1889.

(52 & 53 VICT. Cap. 46.)

1. Every master of a ship, and every person acting lawfully as master of a ship by reason of the decease or incapacity from illness of the master of the ship, shall, so far as the case permits, have the same rights, liens, and remedies for the recovery of disbursements properly made by him on account of the ship and for liabilities properly incurred by him on account of the ship as a master now has for the recovery of his wages; and if in any proceedings in any Court of Admiralty or Vice-Admiralty, or in any County Court having Admiralty jurisdiction, touching the claim of a master, or any person lawfully acting as master, to wages or such disbursements or liabilities as aforesaid any right of set off or counterclaim is set up, it shall be lawful for the court to enter into and adjudicate upon all, and to settle all accounts then arising or outstanding and unsettled between the parties to the proceeding, and to direct payment of any balance which is found to be due.

2.—(i.) Any agreement with a seaman made under section 149 of the Merchant Shipping Act, 1854 (17 & 18 Vict. c. 104), may contain a stipulation for payment to or on behalf of the seaman conditionally on his going to sea in pursuance of the agreement of a sum not exceeding the amount of one month's wages, payable to the seaman under the agreement.

(ii.) Save as authorised by this section any agreement by or on behalf of the employer of a seaman for the payment of money to or on behalf of the seaman conditionally on his going to sea from any port in the United Kingdom shall be void, and no money paid in satisfaction or in respect of any such agreement shall be deducted from the seaman's wages, and no person shall have any right of action, suit, or set off against the seaman or his assignee in respect of any money so paid or purporting to have been so paid.

(iii.) Nothing herein shall affect any allotment made under the Merchant Shipping Act, 1854, or the Acts amending the same.

(iv.) Section 2 of the Merchant Seamen (Payment of Wages and Rating) Act, 1880 (43 & 44 Vict. c. 16) is hereby repealed.

3. Every superintendent of a mercantile marine office shall keep at his office a list of the seamen who, to the best of his knowledge and belief, have deserted or failed to join their ships after signing an agreement to proceed therein, and shall on request show this list to any master of a ship. A superintendent of a mercantile office shall not be liable in respect of any entry made in good faith in the list so kept.

4. Where a seaman has agreed with the master of a British ship for payment of his wages in British sterling or any other money, any payment of or on account of his wages, if made in any other currency than that stated in the agreement, shall notwithstanding anything in the agreement be made at the rate of exchange for the money stated

in the agreement for the time current at the place where the payment is made.

5. The provisions of the Merchant Shipping Act, 1854, and the Acts amending the same with respect to steam-ships shall apply to ships propelled by electricity or other mechanical power, with such modification as the Board of Trade may from time to time prescribe for purposes of adaptation.

6.—(i.) This Act may be cited as "The Merchant Shipping Act, 1889."

(ii.) This Act shall be construed as one with the Merchant Shipping Act, 1854, and the Acts amending the same, and this Act and those Acts may be cited collectively as "The Merchant Shipping Acts, 1854 to 1889."

XIII. ARBITRATION ACT, 1889.

(52 & 53 VICT. CAP. 49.)

References by Consent out of Court.

1. A submission, unless a contrary intention is expressed therein, shall be irrevocable, except by leave of the Court or a judge, and shall have the same effect in all respects as if it had been made an order of Court.

2. A submission, unless a contrary intention is expressed therein, shall be deemed to include the provisions set forth in the First Schedule to this Act, so far as they are applicable to the reference under the submission.

3. Where a submission provides that the reference shall be to an official referee, any official referee to whom application is made shall, subject to any order of the Court or a judge as to transfer or otherwise, hear and determine the matters agreed to be referred.

4. If any party to a submission, or any person claiming through or under him, commences any legal proceedings in any Court against any other party to the submission, or any person claiming through or under him, in respect of any matter agreed to be referred, any party to such legal proceedings may at any time after appearance, and before delivering any pleadings or taking any other steps in the proceedings, apply to that Court to stay the proceedings, and that Court or a judge thereof, if satisfied that there is no sufficient reason why the matter should not be referred in accordance with the submission, and that the applicant was, at the time when the proceedings were commenced, and still remains, ready and willing to do all things necessary to the proper conduct of the arbitration, may make an order staying the proceedings.

5. In any of the following cases:

(a) Where a submission provides that the reference shall be to a single arbitrator, and all the parties do not after differences have arisen concur in the appointment of an arbitrator:

(b) If an appointed arbitrator refuses to act, or is incapable of acting, or dies, and the submission does not show that it was intended that the vacancy should not be supplied, and the parties do not supply the vacancy :

(c) Where the parties or two arbitrators are at liberty to appoint an umpire or third arbitrator and do not appoint him :

(d) Where an appointed umpire or third arbitrator refuses to act, or is incapable of acting, or dies, and the submission does not show that it was intended that the vacancy should not be supplied, and the parties or arbitrators do not supply the vacancy :

any party may serve the other parties or the arbitrators, as the case may be, with a written notice to appoint an arbitrator, umpire, or third arbitrator.

If the appointment is not made within seven clear days after the service of the notice, the Court or a judge may, on application by the party who gave the notice, appoint an arbitrator, umpire, or third arbitrator, who shall have the like powers to act in the reference and make an award as if he had been appointed by consent of all parties.

6. Where a submission provides that the reference shall be to two arbitrators, one to be appointed by each party, then, unless the submission expresses a contrary intention—

(a) If either of the appointed arbitrators refuses to act, or is incapable of acting, or dies, the party who appointed him may appoint a new arbitrator in his place ;

(b) If, on such a reference, one party fails to appoint an arbitrator, either originally or by way of substitution as aforesaid, for seven clear days after the other party, having appointed his arbitrator, has served the party making default with notice to make the appointment, the party who has appointed an arbitrator may appoint that arbitrator to act as sole arbitrator in the reference, and his award shall be binding on both parties as if he had been appointed by consent :

Provided that the Court or a judge may set aside any appointment made in pursuance of this section.

7. The arbitrators or umpire acting under a submission shall, unless the submission expresses a contrary intention, have power—

(a.) to administer oaths to or take the affirmations of the parties and witnesses appearing ; and

(b.) to state an award as to the whole or part thereof in the form of a special case for the opinion of the Court ; and

(c.) to correct in an award any clerical mistake or error arising from any accidental slip or omission.

8. Any party to a submission may sue out a writ of subpœna ad testificandum, or a writ of subpœna duces tecum, but no person shall be compelled under any such writ to produce any document which he could not be compelled to produce on the trial of an action.

9. The time for making an award may from time to time be enlarged by order of the Court or a judge, whether the time for making the award has expired or not.

10.—(1.) In all cases of reference to arbitration the Court or a judge may from time to time remit the matters referred, or any of them, to the reconsideration of the arbitrators or umpire.

(2.) Where an award is remitted, the arbitrators or umpire shall, unless the order otherwise directs, make their award within three months after the date of the order.

11.—(1.) Where an arbitrator or umpire has misconducted himself, the Court may remove him.

(2.) Where an arbitrator or umpire has misconducted himself, or an arbitration or award has been improperly procured, the Court may set the award aside.

12. An award on a submission may, by leave of the Court or a judge, be enforced in the same manner as a judgment or order to the same effect.

References under Order of Court.

13.—(1.) Subject to Rules of Court and to any right to have particular cases tried by a jury, the Court or a judge may refer any question arising in any cause or matter (other than a criminal proceeding by the Crown) for inquiry or report to any official or special referee.

(2.) The report of an official or special referee may be adopted wholly or partially by the Court or a judge, and if so adopted may be enforced as a judgment or order to the same effect.

14. In any cause or matter (other than a criminal proceeding by the Crown),—

(*a.*) If all the parties interested who are not under disability consent ; or,

(*b.*) If the cause or matter requires any prolonged examination of documents or any scientific or local investigation which cannot in the opinion of the Court or a judge conveniently be made before a jury or conducted by the Court through its other ordinary officers ; or,

(*c.*) If the question in dispute consists wholly or in part of matters of account;

the Court or a judge may at any time order the whole cause or matter, or any question or issue of fact arising therein, to be tried before a special referee or arbitrator respectively agreed on by the parties, or before an official referee or officer of the Court.

15.—(1.) In all cases of reference to an official or special referee or arbitrator under an order of the Court or a judge in any cause or matter, the official or special referee or arbitrator shall be deemed to be an officer of the Court, and shall have such authority, and shall conduct the reference in such manner, as may be prescribed by Rules of Court, and subject thereto as the Court or a judge may direct.

(2.) The report or award of any official or special referee or arbitrator on any such reference shall, unless set aside by the Court or a judge, be equivalent to the verdict of a jury.

(3.) The remuneration to be paid to any special referee or arbitrator to whom any matter is referred under order of the Court or a judge shall be determined by the Court or a judge.

16. The Court or a judge shall, as to references under order of the Court or a judge, have all the powers which are by this Act conferred on the Court or a judge as to references by consent out of Court.

17. Her Majesty's Court of Appeal shall have all the powers conferred by this Act on the Court or a judge thereof under the provisions relating to references under order of the Court.

General.

18.—(1.) The Court or a judge may order that a writ of subpœna ad testificandum or of subpœna duces tecum shall issue to compel the attendance before an official or special referee, or before any arbitrator or umpire, of a witness wherever he may be within the United Kingdom.

(2.) The Court or a judge may also order that a writ of habeas corpus ad testificandum shall issue to bring up a prisoner for examination before an official or special referee, or before any arbitrator or umpire.

19. Any referee, arbitrator, or umpire may at any stage of the proceedings under a reference, and shall, if so directed by the Court or a judge, state in the form of a special case for the opinion of the Court any question of law arising in the course of the reference.

20. Any order made under this Act may be made on such terms as to costs, or otherwise, as the authority making the order thinks just.

21. Provision may from time to time be made by Rules of Court for conferring on any master, or other officer of the Supreme Court, all or any of the jurisdiction conferred by this Act on the Court or a judge.

22. Any person who wilfully and corruptly gives false evidence before any referee, arbitrator, or umpire shall be guilty of perjury, as if the evidence had been given in open court, and may be dealt with, prosecuted, and punished accordingly.

23. This Act shall, except as in this Act expressly mentioned, apply to any arbitration to which Her Majesty the Queen, either in right of the Crown, or of the Duchy of Lancaster or otherwise, or the Duke of Cornwall, is a party, but nothing in this Act shall empower the Court or a judge to order any proceedings to which Her Majesty or the Duke of Cornwall is a party, or any question or issue in any such proceedings, to be tried before any referee, arbitrator, or officer without the consent of Her Majesty or the Duke of Cornwall, as the case may be, or shall affect the law as to costs payable by the Crown.

24. This Act shall apply to every arbitration under any Act passed before or after the commencement of this Act as if the arbitration were pursuant to a submission, except in so far as this Act is inconsistent with the Act regulating the arbitration or with any rules or procedure authorised or recognised by that Act.

25. This Act shall not affect any arbitration pending at the commencement of this Act, but shall apply to any arbitration commenced after the commencement of this Act under any agreement or order made before the commencement of this Act.

26.—(1.) The enactments described in the Second Schedule to this Act are hereby repealed to the extent therein mentioned, but this repeal shall not affect anything done or suffered, or any right acquired or duty imposed or liability incurred, before the commencement of this Act, or the institution or prosecution to its termination of any legal proceeding or other remedy for ascertaining or enforcing any such liability.

(2.) Any enactment or instrument referring to any enactment repealed by this Act shall be construed as referring to this Act.

27. In this Act, unless the contrary intention appears,—

" Submission " means a written agreement to submit present or future differences to arbitration, whether an arbitrator is named therein or not.

" Court " means Her Majesty's High Court of Justice.

"Judge" means a judge of Her Majesty's High Court of Justice.

" Rules of Court " means the Rules of the Supreme Court made by the proper authority under the Judicature Acts.

28. This Act shall not extend to Scotland or Ireland.

29. This Act shall commence and come into operation on the first day of January one thousand eight hundred and ninety.

30. This Act may be cited as the Arbitration Act, 1889.

SCHEDULES.

THE FIRST SCHEDULE.

Provisions to be implied in Submissions.

a. If no other mode of reference is provided, the reference shall be to a single arbitrator.

b. If the reference is to two arbitrators, the two arbitrators may appoint an umpire at any time within the period during which they have power to make an award.

c. The arbitrators shall make their award in writing within three months after entering on the reference, or after having been called on to act by notice in writing from any party to the submission, or on or before any later day to which the arbitrators, by any writing signed by them, may from time to time enlarge the time for making the award.

d. If the arbitrators have allowed their time or extended time to expire without making an award, or have delivered to any party to the submission, or to the umpire a notice in writing, stating that they cannot agree, the umpire may forthwith enter on the reference in lieu of the arbitrators.

e. The umpire shall make his award within one month after the original or extended time appointed for making the award of the arbitrators has expired, or on or before any later day to which the umpire by any writing signed by him may from time to time enlarge the time for making his award.

f. The parties to the reference, and all persons claiming through them respectively, shall, subject to any legal objection, submit to be examined by the arbitrators or umpire, on oath or affirmation, in relation to the matters in dispute, and shall, subject as aforesaid, produce before the arbitrators or umpire, all books, deeds, papers, accounts, writings, and documents within their possession or power respectively which may be required or called for, and do all other things which during the proceedings on the reference the arbitrators or umpire may require.

g. The witnesses on the reference shall, if the arbitrators or umpire thinks fit, be examined on oath or affirmation.

h. The award to be made by the arbitrators or umpire shall be final and binding on the parties and the persons claiming under them respectively.

i. The costs of the reference and award shall be in the discretion of the arbitrators or umpire, who may direct to and by whom and in what manner those costs or any part thereof shall be paid, and may tax or settle the amount of costs to be so paid or any part thereof, and may award costs to be paid as between solicitor and client.

THE SECOND SCHEDULE.

Enactments Repealed.

Session and Chapter.	Title or Short Title.	Extent of Repeal.
9 Will. 3. c. 15 .	An Act for determining differences by arbitration.	The whole Act.
3 & 4 Will. 4. c. 42	An Act for the further amendment of the law and the better advancement of justice.	Sections thirty-nine to forty-one, both inclusive.
17 & 18 Vict. c.125	The Common Law Procedure Act, 1854.	Sections three to seventeen, both inclusive.
36 & 37 Vict. c. 66	The Supreme Court of Judicature Act, 1873.	Section fifty-six, from "Subject to any Rules of Court" down to "as a judgment by the Court," both inclusive, and the words "special referees or." Sections fifty-seven to fifty-nine, both inclusive.
47 & 48 Vict. c. 61	The Supreme Court of Judicature Act, 1884.	Sections nine to eleven, both inclusive.

XIV. AN ACT TO DECLARE AND AMEND THE LAW OF PARTNERSHIP, 1890.

(53 & 54 VICT. CAP. 39.)

Nature of Partnership.

1.—(1.) Partnership is the relation which subsists between persons carrying on a business in common with a view of profit.

(2.) But the relation between members of any company or association which is—

(*a.*) Registered as a company under the Companies Act, 1862, or any other Act of Parliament for the time being in force and relating to the registration of joint stock companies; or

(*b.*) Formed or incorporated by or in pursuance of any other Act of Parliament or letters patent, or Royal Charter; or

(*c.*) A company engaged in working mines within and subject to the jurisdiction of the Stannaries:

is not a partnership within the meaning of this Act.

2. In determining whether a partnership does or does not exist, regard shall be had to the following rules:—

(1.) Joint tenancy, tenancy in common, joint property, common property, or part ownership does not of itself create a partnership as to anything so held or owned, whether the tenants or owners do or do not share any profits made by the use thereof.

(2.) The sharing of gross returns does not of itself create a partnership, whether the persons sharing such returns have or have not a joint or common right or interest in any property from which or from the use of which the returns are derived.

(3.) The receipt by a person of the share of the profits of a business is *prima facie* evidence that he is a partner in the business, but the receipt of such a share, or of a payment contingent on or varying with the profits of a business, does not of itself make him a partner in the business; and in particular:—

(*a.*) The receipt by a person of a debt or other liquidated amount by instalments or otherwise out of the accruing profits of a business does not of itself make him a partner in the business or liable as such;

(*b.*) A contract for the remuneration of a servant or agent of a person engaged in a business by a share of the profits of the business does not of itself make the servant or agent a partner in the business or liable as such;

(*c.*) A person being the widow or child of a deceased partner, receiving by way of annuity a portion of the profits made in the business in which the deceased person was a partner is not by reason only of such receipt a partner in the business or liable as such;

(*d*.) The advance of money by way of loan to a person engaged or about to engage in any business on a contract with that person that the lender shall receive a rate of interest varying with the profits, or shall receive a share of the profits arising from carrying on the business does not of itself make the lender a partner with the person or persons carrying on the business or liable as such provided that the contract is in writing and signed by or on behalf of all the parties thereto ;

(*e*.) A person receiving by way of annuity or otherwise a portion of the profits of a business in consideration of the sale by him of the good-will of the business is not by reason only of such receipt a partner in the business or liable as such.

3. In the event of any person to whom money has been advanced by way of loan upon such a contract as is mentioned in the last foregoing section, or of any buyer of a good-will in consideration of a share of the profits of the business, being adjudged a bankrupt, entering into an arrangement to pay his creditors less than twenty shillings in the pound, or dying in insolvent circumstances, the lender of the loan shall not be entitled to recover anything in respect of his loan, and the seller of the good-will shall not be entitled to recover anything in respect of the share of profits contracted for, until the claims of the other creditors of the borrower or buyer for valuable consideration in money or money's worth have been satisfied.

4.—(1). Persons who have entered into partnership with one another are for the purposes of this Act called collectively a firm, and the name under which their business is carried on is called the firm-name.

(2.) In Scotland a firm is a legal person distinct from the partners of whom it is composed, but an individual partner may be charged on a decree of diligence directed against the firm, and on payment of the debts is entitled to relief *pro ratâ* from the firm and its other members.

Relations of Partners to persons dealing with them.

5. Every partner is an agent of the firm and his other partners for the purposes of the business of the partnership ; and the acts of every partner who does any act for carrying on in the usual way business of the kind carried on by the firm of which he is a member bind the firm and his partners, unless the partner so acting has in fact no authority to act for the firm in the particular matter, and the person with whom he is dealing either knows that he has no authority, or does not know or believe him to be a partner.

6. An act or instrument relating to the business of the firm and done or executed in the firm-name, or in any other manner showing an intention to bind the firm, by any person thereto authorised, whether a partner or not, is binding on the firm and all its partners.

Provided that this section shall not affect any general rule of law relating to the execution of deeds or negotiable instruments.

7. Where one partner pledges the credit of a firm for a purpose apparently not connected with the firm's ordinary course of business, the firm is not bound, unless he is in fact specially authorised by the

other partners ; but this section does not affect any personal liability incurred by an individual partner.

8. If it has been agreed between the partners that any restriction shall be placed on the power of any one or more of them to bind the firm, no act done in contravention of the agreement is binding on the firm with respect to persons having notice of the agreement.

9. Every partner in a firm is liable jointly with the other partners, and in Scotland severally also, for all debts and obligations of the firm incurred while he is a partner ; and after his death his estate is also severally liable in a due course of administration for such debts and obligations, so far as they remain unsatisfied, but subject in England or Ireland to the prior payment of his separate debts.

10. Where, by any wrongful act or omission of any partner acting in the ordinary course of the business of the firm, or with the authority of his co-partners, loss or injury is caused to any person not being a partner in the firm, or any penalty is incurred, the firm is liable therefor to the same extent as the partner so acting or omitting to act.

11. In the following cases ; namely—

(*a.*) Where one partner acting within the scope of his apparent authority receives the money or property of a third person and misapplies it ; and

(*b.*) Where a firm in the course of its business receives money or property of a third person, and the money or property so received is misapplied by one or more of the partners while it is in the custody of the firm ;

the firm is liable to make good the loss.

12. Every partner is liable jointly with his co-partners and also severally for everything for which the firm while he is a partner therein becomes liable under either of the two last preceding sections.

13. If a partner, being a trustee, improperly employs trust-property in the business or on the account of the partnership, no other partner is liable for the trust-property to the persons beneficially interested therein :

Provided as follows :—

(1.) This section shall not affect any liability incurred by any partner by reason of his having notice of a breach of trust; and

(2.) Nothing in this section shall prevent trust money from being followed and recovered from the firm if still in its possession or under its control.

14.—(1.) Every one who by words spoken or written or by conduct represents himself, or who knowingly suffers himself to be represented, as a partner in a particular firm, is liable as a partner to any one who has on the faith of any such representation given credit to the firm, whether the representation has or has not been made or communicated to the person so giving credit by or with the knowledge of the apparent partner making the representation or suffering it to be made.

(2.) Provided that where after a partner's death the partnership business is continued in the old firm-name, the continued use of that name or of the deceased partner's name as part thereof shall not of itself make his executors or administrators' estate or effects liable for any partnership debts contracted after his death.

15. An admission or representation made by any partner concerning the partnership affairs, and in the ordinary course of its business, is evidence against the firm.

16. Notice to any partner who habitually acts in the partnership business of any matter relating to partnership affairs operates as notice to the firm, except in the case of a fraud on the firm committed by or with the consent of that partner.

17.—(1.) A person who is admitted as a partner into an existing firm does not thereby become liable to the creditors of the firm for anything done before he became a partner.

(2.) A partner who retires from a firm does not thereby cease to be liable for partnership debts or obligations incurred before his retirement.

(3.) A retiring partner may be discharged from any existing liabilities, by an agreement to that effect between himself and the members of the firm as newly constituted and the creditors, and this agreement may be either expressed or inferred as a fact from the course of dealing between the creditors and the firm as newly constituted.

18. A continuing guaranty or cautionary obligation given either to a firm or to a third person in respect of the transactions of a firm is, in the absence of agreement to the contrary, revoked as to future transactions by any change in the constitution of the firm to which, or of the firm in respect of the transactions of which, the guaranty or obligation was given.

Relations of Partners to one another.

19. The mutual rights and duties of partners, whether ascertained by agreement or defined by this Act, may be varied by the consent of all the partners, and such consent may be either expressed or inferred from a course of dealing.

20.—(1.) All property and rights and interests in property originally brought into the partnership stock or acquired, whether by purchase or otherwise, on account of the firm, or for the purposes and in the course of the partnership business, are called in this Act partnership property, and must be held and applied by the partners exclusively for the purposes of the partnership and in accordance with the partnership agreement.

(2.) Provided that the legal estate or interest in any land, or in Scotland the title to and interest in any heritable estate, which belongs to the partnership shall devolve according to the nature and tenure thereof, and the general rules of law thereto applicable, but in trust, so far as necessary, for the persons beneficially interested in the land under this section.

(3.) Where co-owners of an estate or interest in any land, or in Scotland of any heritable estate, not being itself partnership property, are partners as to profits made by the use of that land or estate, and purchase other land or estate out of the profits to be used in like manner, the land or estate so purchased belongs to them, in the absence of an agreement to the contrary, not as partners, but as co-owners for the same respective estates and interests as are held by them in the land or estate first mentioned at the date of the purchase.

21. Unless the contrary intention appears, property bought with money belonging to the firm is deemed to have been bought on account of the firm.

22. Where land or any heritable interest therein has become partnership property, it shall, unless the contrary intention appears, be treated as between the partners (including the representatives of a deceased partner), and also as between the heirs of a deceased partner and his executors or administrators, as personal or moveable and not real or heritable estate.

23.—(1.) After the commencement of this Act a writ of execution shall not issue against any partnership property except on a judgment against the firm.

(2.) The High Court, or a judge thereof, or the Chancery Court of the County Palatine of Lancaster, or a county court, may, on the application by summons of any judgment creditor of a partner, make an order charging that partner's interest in the partnership property and profits with payment of the amount of the judgment debt and interest thereon, and may by the same or a subsequent order appoint a receiver of that partner's share of profits (whether already declared or accruing), and of any other money which may be coming to him in respect of the partnership, and direct all accounts and inquiries, and give all other orders and directions which might have been directed or given if the charge had been made in favour of the judgment creditor by the partner, or which the circumstances of the case may require.

(3.) The other partner or partners shall be at liberty at any time to redeem the interest charged, or in case of a sale being directed, to purchase the same.

(4.) This section shall apply in the case of a cost-book company as if the company were a partnership within the meaning of this Act.

(5.) This section shall not apply to Scotland.

24. The interests of partners in the partnership property and their rights and duties in relation to the partnership shall be determined, subject to any agreement express or implied between the partners, by the following rules:

(1.) All the partners are entitled to share equally in the capital and profits of the business, and must contribute equally towards the losses whether of capital or otherwise sustained by the firm.

(2.) The firm must indemnify every partner in respect of payments made and personal liabilities incurred by him—

(a.) In the ordinary and proper conduct of the business of the firm; or

(b.) In or about anything necessarily done for the preservation of the business or property of the firm.

(3.) A partner making, for the purpose of the partnership, any actual payment or advance beyond the amount of capital which he has agreed to subscribe, is entitled to interest at the rate of five per cent. per annum from the date of the payment or advance.

(4.) A partner is not entitled, before the ascertainment of profits, to interest on the capital subscribed by him.

(5.) Every partner may take part in the management of the partnership business.

(6.) No partner shall be entitled to remuneration for acting in the partnership business.

(7.) No person may be introduced as a partner without the consent of all existing partners.

(8.) Any difference arising as to ordinary matters connected with the partnership business may be decided by a majority of the partners, but no change may be made in the nature of the partnership business without the consent of all existing partners.

(9.) The partnership books are to be kept at the place of business of the partnership (or the principal place, if there is more than one), and every partner may, when he thinks fit, have access to and inspect and copy any of them.

25. No majority of the partners can expel any partner unless a power to do so has been conferred by express agreement between the partners.

26.—(1.) Where no fixed term has been agreed upon for the duration of the partnership, any partner may determine the partnership at any time on giving notice of his intention so to do to all the other partners.

(2.) Where the partnership has originally been constituted by deed, a notice in writing, signed by the partner giving it, shall be sufficient for this purpose.

27.—(1.) Where a partnership entered into for a fixed term is continued after the term has expired, and without any express new agreement, the rights and duties of the partners remain the same as they were at the expiration of the term, so far as is consistent with the incidents of a partnership at will.

(2.) A continuance of the business by the partners or such of them as habitually acted therein during the term, without any settlement or liquidation of the partnership affairs, is presumed to be a continuance of the partnership.

28. Partners are bound to render true accounts and full information of all things affecting the partnership to any partner or his legal representatives.

29.—(1). Every partner must account to the firm for any benefit derived by him without the consent of the other partners from any transaction concerning the partnership, or from any use by him of the partnership property name or business connexion.

(2.) This section applies also to transactions undertaken after a partnership has been dissolved by the death of a partner, and before the affairs thereof have been completely wound up, either by any surviving partner or by the representatives of the deceased partner.

30. If a partner, without the consent of the other partners, carries on any business of the same nature as and competing with that of the firm, he must account for and pay over to the firm all profits made by him in that business.

31.—(1.) An assignment by any partner of his share in the partnership, either absolute or by way of mortgage or redeemable charge, does not, as against the other partners, entitle the assignee, during the continuance of the partnership, to interfere in the management or administration of the partnership business or affairs, or to require any accounts of the partnership transactions, or to inspect the partnership books, but entitles the assignee only to receive the share of profits to which the assigning partner would otherwise be entitled, and the assignee must accept the account of profits agreed to by the partners.

(2.) In case of a dissolution of the partnership, whether as respects all the partners or as respects the assigning partner, the assignee is entitled to receive the share of the partnership assets to which the assigning partner is entitled as between himself and the other partners, and, for the purpose of ascertaining that share, to an account as from the date of the dissolution.

Dissolution of Partnership, and its consequences.

32. Subject to any agreement between the partners, a partnership is dissolved—

    (*a.*) If entered into for a fixed term, by the expiration of that term : .

    (*b.*) If entered into for a single adventure or undertaking, by the termination of that adventure or undertaking :

    (*c.*) If entered into for an undefined time, by any partner giving notice to the other or others of his intention to dissolve the partnership.

In the last-mentioned case the partnership is dissolved as from the date mentioned in the notice as the date of dissolution, or, if no date is so mentioned, as from the date of the communication of the notice.

33.—(1.) Subject to any agreement between the partners, every partnership is dissolved as regards all the partners by the death or bankruptcy of any partner.

(2.) A partnership may, at the option of the other partners, be dissolved if any partner suffers his share of the partnership property to be charged under this Act for his separate debt.

34. A partnership is in every case dissolved by the happening of any event which makes it unlawful for the business of the firm to be carried on or for the members of the firm to carry it on in partnership.

35. On application by a partner the Court may decree a dissolution of the partnership in any of the following cases :

    (*a.*) When a partner is found lunatic by inquisition, or in Scotland by cognition, or is shown to the satisfaction of the Court to be of permanently unsound mind, in either of which cases the application may be made as well on behalf of that partner by his committee or next friend or person having title to intervene as by any other partner :

    (*b.*) When a partner, other than the partner suing, becomes in any other way permanently incapable of performing his part of the partnership contract :

    (*c.*) When a partner, other than the partner suing, has been guilty of such conduct as, in the opinion of the Court, regard being had to the nature of the business, is calculated to prejudicially affect the carrying on of the business :

    (*d.*) When a partner, other than the partner suing, wilfully or persistently commits a breach of the partnership agreement, or otherwise so conducts himself in matters relating to the partnership business that it is not reasonably practicable for the other partner or partners to carry on the business in partnership with him :

    (*e.*) When the business of the partnership can only be carried on at a loss :

    (*f.*) Whenever in any case circumstances have arisen which, in the opinion of the Court, render it just and equitable that the partnership be dissolved.

36.—(1.) Where a person deals with a firm after a change in its constitution he is entitled to treat all apparent members of the old firm as still being members of the firm until he has notice of the change.

(2.) An advertisement in the London Gazette as to a firm whose principal place of business is in England or Wales, in the Edinburgh Gazette as to a firm whose principal place of business is in Scotland, and in the Dublin Gazette as to a firm whose principal place of business is in Ireland, shall be notice as to persons who had not dealings with the firm before the date of the dissolution or change so advertised.

(3.) The estate of a partner who dies, or who becomes bankrupt, or of a partner who, not having been known to the person dealing with the firm to be a partner, retires from the firm, is not liable for partnership debts contracted after the date of the death, bankruptcy, or retirement respectively.

37. On the dissolution of a partnership or retirement of a partner any partner may publicly notify the same, and may require the other partner or partners to concur for that purpose in all necessary or proper acts, if any, which cannot be done without his or their concurrence.

38. After the dissolution of a partnership the authority of each partner to bind the firm, and the other rights and obligations of the partners, continue notwithstanding the dissolution so far as may be necessary to wind up the affairs of the partnership, and to complete transactions begun but unfinished at the time of the dissolution, but not otherwise.

Provided that the firm is in no case bound by the acts of a partner who has become bankrupt; but this proviso does not affect the liability of any person who has after the bankruptcy represented himself or knowingly suffered himself to be represented as a partner of the bankrupt.

39. On the dissolution of a partnership every partner is entitled, as against the other partners in the firm, and all persons claiming through them in respect of their interests as partners, to have the property of the partnership applied in payment of the debts and liabilities of the firm, and to have the surplus assets after such payment applied in payment of what may be due to the partners respectively after deducting what may be due from them as partners to the firm; and for that purpose any partner or his representatives may on the termination of the partnership apply to the Court to wind up the business and affairs of the firm.

40. Where one partner has paid a premium to another on entering into a partnership for a fixed term, and the partnership is dissolved before the expiration of that term otherwise than by the death of a partner, the Court may order the repayment of the premium, or of such part thereof as it thinks just, having regard to the terms of the partnership contract and to the length of time during which the partnership has continued; unless

(a.) the dissolution is, in the judgment of the Court, wholly or chiefly due to the misconduct of the partner who paid the premium, or

(b.) the partnership has been dissolved by an agreement containing no provision for a return of any part of the premium.

41. Where a partnership contract is rescinded on the ground of the fraud or misrepresentation of one of the parties thereto, the party entitled to rescind is, without prejudice to any other right, entitled—

(a.) to a lien on, or right of retention of, the surplus of the partnership assets, after satisfying the partnership liabilities, for any sum of money paid by him for the purchase of a share in the partnership and for any capital contributed by him, and is

(b.) to stand in the place of the creditors of the firm for any payments made by him in respect of the partnership liabilities, and

(c.) to be indemnified by the person guilty of the fraud or making the representation against all the debts and liabilities of the firm.

42.—(1.) Where any member of a firm has died or otherwise ceased to be a partner, and the surviving or continuing partners carry on the business of the firm with its capital or assets without any final settlement of accounts as between the firm and the outgoing partner or his estate, then, in the absence of any agreement to the contrary, the outgoing partner or his estate is entitled at the option of himself or his representatives to such share of the profits made since the dissolution as the Court may find to be attributable to the use of his share of the partnership assets, or to interest at the rate of five per cent. per annum on the amount of his share of the partnership assets.

(2.) Provided that where by the partnership contract an option is given to surviving or continuing partners to purchase the interest of a deceased or outgoing partner, and that option is duly exercised, the estate of the deceased partner, or the outgoing partner or his estate, as the case may be, is not entitled to any further or other share of profits ; but if any partner assuming to act in exercise of the option does not in all material respects comply with the terms thereof, he is liable to account under the foregoing provisions of this section.

43. Subject to any agreement between the partners, the amount due from surviving or continuing partners to an outgoing partner or the representatives of a deceased partner in respect of the outgoing or deceased partner's share is a debt accruing at the date of the dissolution or death.

44. In settling accounts between the partners after a dissolution of partnership, the following rules shall, subject to any agreement, be observed :

(a.) Losses, including losses and deficiencies of capital, shall be paid first out of profits, next out of capital, and lastly, if necessary, by the partners individually in the proportion in which they were entitled to share profits :

(b.) The assets of the firm including the sums, if any, contributed by the partners to make up losses or deficiencies of capital, shall be applied in the following manner and order :

1. In paying the debts and liabilities of the firm to persons who are not partners therein :

2. In paying to each partner rateably what is due from the firm to him for advances as distinguished from capital :

3. In paying to each partner rateably what is due from the firm to him in respect of capital :

R

4. The ultimate residue, if any, shall be divided among the partners in the proportion in which profits are divisible.

Supplemental.

45. In this Act, unless the contrary intention appears,—

The expression "court" includes every court and judge having jurisdiction in the case:

The expression "business" includes every trade, occupation, or profession.

46. The rules of equity and of common law applicable to partnership shall continue in force except so far as they are inconsistent with the express provisions of this Act.

47. (1.) In the application of this Act to Scotland the bankruptcy of a firm or of an individual shall mean sequestration under the Bankruptcy (Scotland) Acts, and also in the case of an individual the issue against him of a decree of cessio bonorum.

(2.) Nothing in this Act shall alter the rules of the law of Scotland relating to the bankruptcy of a firm or of the individual partners thereof.

48. The Acts mentioned in the schedule to this Act are hereby repealed to the extent mentioned in the third column of that schedule.

49. This Act shall come into operation on the first day of January one thousand eight hundred and ninety one.

50. This Act may be cited as the Partnership Act, 1890.

SCHEDULE.

Enactments Repealed.

Session and Chapter.	Title or Short Title.	Extent of Repeal.
19 & 20 Vict. c. 60	The Mercantile Law Amendment (Scotland) Act, 1856.	Section seven.
19 & 20 Vict. c. 97	The Mercantile Law Amendment Act, 1856.	Section four.
28 & 29 Vict. c. 86	An Act to amend the law of partnership.	The whole Act.

INDEX.

288

being
of stea
A fa
deeme

(2.)

38.
the I
shop
N
or w
3!
a m
fac
you
tra
to

or

tl

r
t

PRINTED BY J. S. VIRTUE AND CO., LIMITED, CITY R

7, STATIONERS' HALL COURT, LONDON, E.C.

February, 1892.

A

CATALOGUE OF BOOKS

INCLUDING NEW AND STANDARD WORKS IN

ENGINEERING: CIVIL, MECHANICAL, AND MARINE, MINING AND METALLURGY, ELECTRICITY AND ELECTRICAL ENGINEERING, ARCHITECTURE AND BUILDING, INDUSTRIAL AND DECORATIVE ARTS, SCIENCE, TRADE AGRICULTURE, GARDENING, LAND AND ESTATE MANAGEMENT, LAW, &c.

PUBLISHED BY

CROSBY LOCKWOOD & SON.

MECHANICAL ENGINEERING, etc.

New Pocket-Book for Mechanical Engineers.

THE MECHANICAL ENGINEER'S POCKET-BOOK OF TABLES, FORMULÆ, RULES AND DATA. A Handy Book of Reference for Daily Use in Engineering Practice. By D. KINNEAR CLARK, M.Inst.C.E., Author of "Railway Machinery," "Tramways," &c. &c. Small 8vo, nearly 700 pages. With Illustrations. Rounded edges, cloth limp, 7s. 6d.; or leather, gilt edges, 9s. [*Just published.*

New Manual for Practical Engineers.

THE PRACTICAL ENGINEER'S HAND-BOOK. Comprising a Treatise on Modern Engines and Boilers: Marine, Locomotive and Stationary. And containing a large collection of Rules and Practical Data relating to recent Practice in Designing and Constructing all kinds of Engines, Boilers, and other Engineering work. The whole constituting a comprehensive Key to the Board of Trade and other Examinations for Certificates of Competency in Modern Mechanical Engineering. By WALTER S. HUTTON, Civil and Mechanical Engineer, Author of "The Works' Manager's Handbook for Engineers," &c. With upwards of 370 Illustrations. Fourth Edition, Revised, with Additions. Medium 8vo, nearly 500 pp., price 18s. Strongly bound. [*Just published.*

☞ *This work is designed as a companion to the Author's* "WORKS' MANAGER'S HAND-BOOK." *It possesses many new and original features, and contains, like its predecessor, a quantity of matter not originally intended for publication, but collected by the author for his own use in the construction of a great variety of modern engineering work.*

*** OPINIONS OF THE PRESS.

" A thoroughly good practical handbook, which no engineer can go through without learning something that will be of service to him."—*Marine Engineer.*

" An excellent book of reference for engineers, and a valuable text-book for students of engineering."—*Scotsman.*

" This valuable manual embodies the results and experience of the leading authorities on mechanical engineering."—*Building News.*

" The author has collected together a surprising quantity of rules and practical data, and has shown much judgment in the selections he has made. . . . There is no doubt that this book is one of the most useful of its kind published, and will be a very popular compendium."—*Engineer.*

" A mass of information, set down in simple language, and in such a form that it can be easily referred to at any time. The matter is uniformly good and well chosen, and is greatly elucidated by the illustrations. The book will find its way on to most engineers' shelves, where it will rank as one of the most useful books of reference."—*Practical Engineer.*

" Should be found on the office shelf of all practical engineers."—*English Mechanic.*

Handbook for Works' Managers.

THE WORKS' MANAGER'S HANDBOOK OF MODERN RULES, TABLES, AND DATA. For Engineers, Millwrights, and Boiler Makers; Tool Makers, Machinists, and Metal Workers; Iron and Brass Founders, &c. By W. S. HUTTON, C.E., Author of "The Practical Engineer's Handbook." Fourth Edition, carefully Revised, and partly Re-written. In One handsome Volume, medium 8vo, 15s. strongly bound. [*Just published.*

☞ *The Author having compiled Rules and Data for his own use in a great variety of modern engineering work, and having found his notes extremely useful, decided to publish them—revised to date—believing that a practical work, suited to the* DAILY REQUIREMENTS OF MODERN ENGINEERS, *would be favourably received.*
In the Third Edition, the following among other additions have been made, viz.: Rules for the Proportions of Riveted Joints in Soft Steel Plates, the Results of Experiments by PROFESSOR KENNEDY *for the Institution of Mechanical Engineers—Rules for the Proportions of Turbines—Rules for the Strength of Hollow Shafts of Whitworth's Compressed Steel, &c.*

*** OPINIONS OF THE PRESS.

"The author treats every subject from the point of view of one who has collected workshop notes for application in workshop practice, rather than from the theoretical or literary aspect. The volume contains a great deal of that kind of information which is gained only by practical experience, and is seldom written in books."—*Engineer.*
"The volume is an exceedingly useful one, brimful with engineers' notes, memoranda, and rules, and well worthy of being on every mechanical engineer's bookshelf."—*Mechanical World.*
"The information is precisely that likely to be required in practice. . . . The work forms a desirable addition to the library not only of the works manager, but of anyone connected with general engineering."—*Mining Journal.*
"A formidable mass of facts and figures, readily accessible through an elaborate index . . . . . Such a volume will be found absolutely necessary as a book of reference in all sorts of 'works' connected with the metal trades."—*Ryland's Iron Trades Circular.*
"Brimful of useful information, stated in a concise form, Mr. Hutton's books have met a pressing want among engineers. The book must prove extremely useful to every practical man possessing a copy."—*Practical Engineer.*

Practical Treatise on Modern Steam-Boilers.

STEAM-BOILER CONSTRUCTION. A Practical Handbook for Engineers, Boiler-Makers, and Steam Users. Containing a large Collection of Rules and Data relating to the Design, Construction, and Working of Modern Stationary, Locomotive, and Marine Steam-Boilers. By WALTER S. HUTTON, C.E., Author of "The Works' Manager's Handbook," &c. With upwards of 300 Illustrations. Medium 8vo, 18s. cloth. [*Just published.*

"Every detail, both in boiler design and management, is clearly laid before the reader. The volume shows that boiler construction has been reduced to the condition of one of the most exact sciences; and such a book is of the utmost value to the *fin de siècle* Engineer and Works' Manager."—*Marine Engineer.*
"There has long been room for a modern handbook on steam boilers; there is not that room now, because Mr. Hutton has filled it. It is a thoroughly practical book for those who are occupied in the construction, design, se'ection, or use of boilers."—*Engineer.*

"The Modernised Templeton."

THE PRACTICAL MECHANIC'S WORKSHOP COMPANION. Comprising a great variety of the most useful Rules and Formulæ in Mechanical Science, with numerous Tables of Practical Data and Calculated Results for Facilitating Mechanical Operations. By WILLIAM TEMPLETON, Author of "The Engineer's Practical Assistant," &c. &c. Sixteenth Edition, Revised, Modernised, and considerably Enlarged by WALTER S. HUTTON, C.E., Author of "The Works' Manager's Handbook," "The Practical Engineer's Handbook," &c. Fcap. 8vo, nearly 500 pp., with Eight Plates and upwards of 250 Illustrative Diagrams, 6s., strongly bound for workshop or pocket wear and tear. [*Just published.*

*** OPINIONS OF THE PRESS.

"In its modernised form Hutton's 'Templeton' should have a wide sale, for it contains much valuable information which the mechanic will often find of use, and not a few tables and notes which he might look for in vain in other works. This modernised edition wi be appreciated by all who have learned to value the original editions of 'Templeton.'"—*English Mechanic.*
"It has met with great success in the engineering workshop, as we can testify; and there are a great many men who, in a great measure, owe their rise in life to this little book."—*Building News.*
"This familiar text-book—well known to all mechanics and engineers—is of essential service to the every-day requirements of engineers, millwrights, and the various trades connected with engineering and building. The new modernised edition is worth its weight in gold."—*Building News.* (Second Notice.)
"This well-known and largely used book contains information, brought up to date, of the sort so useful to the foreman and draughtsman. So much fresh information has been introduced as to constitute it practically a new book. It will be largely used in the office and workshop."—*Mechanical World.*

Stone-working Machinery.

STONE-WORKING MACHINERY, and the Rapid and Economical Conversion of Stone. With Hints on the Arrangement and Management of Stone Works. By M. POWIS BALE, M.I.M.E. With Illusts. Crown 8vo, 9s.

"Should be in the hands of every mason or student of stone-work."—Colliery Guardian.
"A capital handbook for all who manipulate stone for building or ornamental purposes."—Machinery Market.

Pump Construction and Management.

PUMPS AND PUMPING : A Handbook for Pump Users. Being Notes on Selection, Construction and Management. By M. POWIS BALE, M.I.M.E., Author of "Woodworking Machinery," &c. Crown 8vo, 2s. 6d.

"The matter is set forth as concisely as possible. In fact, condensation rather than diffuseness has been the author's aim throughout; yet he does not seem to have omitted anything likely to be of use."—Journal of Gas Lighting.

Milling Machinery, etc.

MILLING MACHINES AND PROCESSES : A Practical Treatise on Shaping Metals by Rotary Cutters, including Information on Making and Grinding the Cutters. By PAUL N. HASLUCK, Author of " Lathework." With upwards of 300 Engravings. Large crown 8vo, 12s. 6d. cloth.

[Just published.

Turning.

LATHE-WORK : A Practical Treatise on the Tools, Appliances, and Processes employed in the Art of Turning. By PAUL N. HASLUCK. Fourth Edition, Revised and Enlarged. Cr. 8vo, 5s. cloth.

"Written by a man who knows, not only how work ought to be done, but who also knows how to do it, and how to convey his knowledge to others. To all turners this book would be valuable."—Engineering.

"We can safely recommend the work to young engineers. To the amateur it will simply be invaluable. To the student it will convey a great deal of useful information."—Engineer.

Screw-Cutting.

SCREW THREADS : And Methods of Producing Them. With Numerous Tables, and complete directions for using Screw-Cutting Lathes. By PAUL N. HASLUCK, Author of " Lathe-Work," &c. With Fifty Illustrations. Third Edition, Enlarged. Waistcoat-pocket size, 1s. 6d. cloth.

"Full of useful information, hints and practical criticism. Taps, dies and screwing-tools generally are illustrated and their action described."—Mechanical World.

"It is a complete compendium of all the details of the screw cutting lathe; in fact a multum-in-parvo on all the subjects it treats upon."—Carpenter and Builder.

Smith's Tables for Mechanics, etc.

TABLES, MEMORANDA, AND CALCULATED RESULTS, FOR MECHANICS, ENGINEERS, ARCHITECTS, BUILDERS, etc. Selected and Arranged by FRANCIS SMITH. Fifth Edition, thoroughly Revised and Enlarged, with a New Section of ELECTRICAL TABLES, FORMULÆ, and MEMORANDA. Waistcoat-pocket size, 1s. 6d. limp leather. [Just published.

"It would, perhaps, be as difficult to make a small pocket-book selection of notes and formulæ to suit ALL engineers as it would be to make a universal medicine; but Mr. Smith's waistcoat-pocket collection may be looked upon as a successful attempt."—Engineer.

"The best example we have ever seen of 250 pages of useful matter packed into the dimensions of a card-case."—Building News. "A veritable pocket treasury of knowledge."—Iron.

Engineer's and Machinist's Assistant.

THE ENGINEER'S, MILLWRIGHT'S, and MACHINIST'S PRACTICAL ASSISTANT. A collection of Useful Tables, Rules and Data. By WILLIAM TEMPLETON. 7th Edition, with Additions. 18mo, 2s. 6d. cloth.

"Occupies a foremost place among books of this kind. A more suitable present to an apprentice to any of the mechanical trades could not possibly be made."—Building News.

"A deservedly popular work, it should be in the 'drawer' of every mechanic."—English Mechanic.

Iron and Steel.

"IRON AND STEEL" : A Work for the Forge, Foundry, Factory, and Office. Containing ready, useful, and trustworthy Information for Iron-masters; Managers of Bar, Rail, Plate, and Sheet Rolling Mills; Iron and Metal Founders; Iron Ship and Bridge Builders; Mechanical, Mining, and Consulting Engineers; Contractors, Builders, &c. By CHARLES HOARE. Eighth Edition, Revised and considerably Enlarged. 32mo, 6s. leather.

"One of the best of the pocket books."—English Mechanic.

"We cordially recommend this book to those engaged in considering the details of all kinds of Iron and steel works."—Naval Science.

Engineering Construction.

PATTERN-MAKING : A Practical Treatise, embracing the Main Types of Engineering Construction, and including Gearing, both Hand and Machine made, Engine Work, Sheaves and Pulleys, Pipes and Columns, Screws, Machine Parts, Pumps and Cocks, the Moulding of Patterns in Loam and Greensand, &c., together with the methods of Estimating the weight of Castings; to which is added an Appendix of Tables for Workshop Reference. By a FOREMAN PATTERN MAKER. With upwards of Three Hundred and Seventy Illustrations. Crown 8vo, 7s. 6d. cloth.

"A well-written technical guide, evidently written by a man who understands and has practised what he has written about. . . . We c rdially recommend it to engineering students, young journeymen, and others desirous of being initiated into the mysteries of pattern-making."—*Builder.*
"We can confidently recommend this comprehensive treatise.'—*Building News.*
" Likely to prove a welcome guide to many workmen, especially to draughtsmen who have lacked a training in the shops, pupils pursuing their practical studies in our factories, and to employers and managers in engineering works."—*Hardware Trade Journal.*
"More than 370 illustrations help to explain the text, which is, however, always clear and explicit- thus rendering the work an excellent *vade mecum* for the apprentice who desires to become mast 'c of his trade.'—*English Mechanic.*

Dictionary of Mechanical Engineering Terms.

LOCKWOOD'S DICTIONARY OF TERMS USED IN THE PRACTICE OF MECHANICAL ENGINEERING, embracing those current in the Drawing Office, Pattern Shop, Foundry, Fitting, Turning, Smith's and Boiler Shops, &c. &c. Comprising upwards of 6,000 Definitions. Edited by A FOREMAN PATTERN-MAKER, Author of " Pattern Making." Crown 8vo, 7s. 6d. cloth.

"Just the sort of handy dictionary required by the various trades engaged in mechanical engineering. The practical engineering pupil will find the book of great value in his studies, and every foreman engineer and mechanic should have a copy."—*Building News.*
"After a careful examination of the book, and trying all manner of words, we think that the engineer will here find all he is likely to require. It will be largely used."—*Practical Engineer.*
"One of the most useful books which can be presented to a mechanic or student."—*English Mechanic.*
"Not merely a dictionary, but, to a certain extent, also a most valuable guide. It strikes us as a happy idea to combine with a definition of the phrase useful information on the subject of which it treats."—*Machinery Market.*
"No word having connection with any branch of constructive engineering seems to be omitted. No more comprehensive work has been, so far, issued. —*Knowledge.*
"We strongly commend this useful and reliable adviser to our friends in the workshop, and to students everywhere."—*Colliery Guardian.*

Steam Boilers.

A TREATISE ON STEAM BOILERS: Their Strength, Construction, and Economical Working. By ROBERT WILSON, C.E. Fifth Edition. 12mo, 6s. cloth.

"The best treatise that has ever been published on steam boilers."—*Engineer.*
"The author shows himself perfect master of his subject, and we heartily recommend all employing steam power to possess themselves of the work."—*Ryland's Iron Trade Circular.*

Boiler Chimneys.

BOILER AND FACTORY CHIMNEYS; Their Draught-Power and Stability. With a Chapter on *Lightning Conductors.* By ROBERT WILSON, A.I.C.E., Author of "A Treatise on Steam Boilers," &c. Second Edition. Crown 8vo, 3s. 6d. cloth.

"Full of useful information, definite in statement, and thoroughly practical in treatment. — *The Local Government Chronicle.*
" A valuable contribution to the iterature of scientific building."—*The Builder.*

Boiler Making.

THE BOILER-MAKER'S READY RECKONER & ASSISTANT. With Examples of Practical Geometry and Templating, for the Use of Platers, Smiths and Riveters. By JOHN COURTNEY, Edited by D. K. CLARK, M.I.C.E. Third Edition, 480 pp., with 140 Illusts. Fcap. 8vo, 7s. half-bound.

" No workman or apprentice should be without this book."—*Iron Trade Circular.*
" Boiler-makers will readily recognise the value of this volume. . . . The tables are clearly printed, and so arranged that they can be referred to with the greatest facility, so that it cannot be doubted that they will be generally appreciated and much used."—*Mining Journal.*

Warming.

HEATING BY HOT WATER; with Information and Suggestions on the best Methods of Heating Public, Private and Horticultural Buildings. By WALTER JONES. With Illustrations, crown 8vo, 2s. cloth.

" We confidently recommend all interested in heating by hot water to secure a copy of thi valuable little treatise."—*The Plumber and Decorator.*

Steam Engine.

TEXT-BOOK ON THE STEAM ENGINE. With a Supplement on Gas Engines, and PART II. ON HEAT ENGINES. By T. M. GOODEVE, M.A., Barrister-at-Law. Professor of Mechanics at the Normal School of Science and the Royal School of Mines; Author of "The Principles of Mechanics," "The Elements of Mechanism," &c. Eleventh Edition, Enlarged. With numerous Illustrations. Crown 8vo, 6s. c'oth.

"Professor Goodeve has given us a treatise on the steam engine which will bear comparison with anything written by Huxley or Maxwell, and we can award it no higher praise."—*Engineer.*
" Mr. Goodeve's text-book is a work of which every young engineer should possess himself.'
—*Mining Journal.*

Gas Engines.

ON GAS-ENGINES. Being a Reprint, with some Additions, of the Supplement to the *Text-book on the Steam Engine,* by T. M. GOODEVE, M.A. Crown 8vo, 2s. 6d. cloth.

" Like all Mr. Goodeve's writings, the present is no exception in point of general excellence. It is a valuable little volume."—*Mechanical World.*

Steam.

THE SAFE USE OF STEAM. Containing Rules for Unprofessional Steam-users. By an ENGINEER. Sixth Edition. Sewed, 6d.

" If steam-users would but learn this little book by heart boiler explosions would become sensations by their rarity."—*English Mechanic.*

Reference Book for Mechanical Engineers.

THE MECHANICAL ENGINEER'S REFERENCE BOOK, for Machine and Boiler Construction. In Two Parts. Part I. GENERAL ENGINEERING DATA. Part II. BOILER CONSTRUCTION. With 51 Plates and numerous Illustrations. By NELSON FOLEY, M.I.N.A. Folio, £5 5s. halfbound. [*Just published.*

Coal and Speed Tables.

A POCKET BOOK OF COAL AND SPEED TABLES, for Engineers and Steam-users. By NELSON FOLEY, Author of " Boiler Construction." Pocket-size, 3s. 6d. cloth ; 4s. leather.

" These tables are designed to meet the requirements of every-day use ; and may be commended to engineers and users of steam."—*Iron.*
" This pocket-book well merits the attention of the practical engineer. Mr. Foley has compiled a very useful set of tables, the information contained in which is frequently required by engineers, coal consumers and users of steam."—*Iron and Coal Trades Review.*

Fire Engineering.

FIRES, FIRE-ENGINES, AND FIRE-BRIGADES. With a History of Fire-Engines, their Construction, Use, and Management; Remarks on Fire-Proof Buildings, and the Preservation of Life from Fire ; Foreign Fire Systems, &c. By C. F. T. YOUNG, C.E. With numerous Illustrations, 544 pp., demy 8vo, £1 4s. cloth.

" To such of our readers as are interested in the subject of fires and fire apparatus, we can most heartily commend this book."—*Engineering.*
" It displays much evidence of careful research ; and Mr. Young has put his facts neatly together. It is evident enough that his acquaintance with the practical details of the construction of steam fire engines is accurate and full."—*Engineer.*

Estimating for Engineering Work, &c.

ENGINEERING ESTIMATES, COSTS AND ACCOUNTS : A Guide to Commercial Engineering. With numerous Examples of Estimates and Costs of Millwright Work, Miscellaneous Productions, Steam Engines and Steam Boilers; and a Section on the Preparation of Costs Accounts. By A GENERAL MANAGER. Demy 8vo, 12s. cloth.

" This is an excellent and very useful book, covering subject-matter in constant requisition in every factory and workshop. . . . The book is invaluable, not only to the young engineer, but also to the estimate department of every works."—*Builder.*
" We accord the work unqualified praise. The information is given in a plain, straightforward manner, and bears throughout evidence of the intimate practical acquaintance of the author with every phrase of commercial engineering."—*Mechanical World.*

Elementary Mechanics.

CONDENSED MECHANICS. A Selection of Formulæ, Rules, Tables, and Data for the Use of Engineering Students, Science Classes, &c. In Accordance with the Requirements of the Science and Art Department By W. G. CRAWFORD HUGHES, A.M.I.C.E. Crown 8vo, 2s. 6d. cloth.
[*Just published.*

THE POPULAR WORKS OF MICHAEL REYNOLDS
("The Engine Driver's Friend ").

Locomotive-Engine Driving.

LOCOMOTIVE-ENGINE DRIVING : A Practical Manual for Engineers in charge of Locomotive Engines. By Michael Reynolds, Member of the Society of Engineers, formerly Locomotive Inspector L. B. and S. C. R. Eighth Edition. Including a Key to the Locomotive Engine. With Illustrations and Portrait of Author. Crown 8vo, 4s. 6d. cloth.

"Mr. Reynolds has supplied a want, and has supplied it well. We can confidently recommend the book, not only to the practical driver, but to everyone who takes an interest in the performance of locomotive engines."—*The Engineer.*

"Mr. Reynolds has opened a new chapter in the literature of the day. This admirable practical treatise, of the practical utility of which we have to speak in terms of warm commendation."—*Athenæum.*

"Evidently the work of one who knows his subject thoroughly."—*Railway Service Gazette.*

"Were the cautions and rules given in the book to become part of the every-day working of our engine-drivers, we might have fewer distressing accidents to deplore."—*Scotsman.*

Stationary Engine Driving.

STATIONARY ENGINE DRIVING : A Practical Manual for Engineers in charge of Stationary Engines. By Michael Reynolds. Fourth Edition, Enlarged. With Plates and Woodcuts. Crown 8vo, 4s. 6d. cloth.

"The author is thoroughly acquainted with his subjects, and his advice on the various points treated is clear and practical. . . . He has produced a manual which is an exceedingly useful one for the class for whom it is specially intended."—*Engineering.*

"Our author leaves no stone unturned. He is determined that his readers shall not only know something about the stationary engine, but all about it."—*Engineer.*

"An engineman who has mastered the contents of Mr. Reynolds's book will require but little actual experience with boilers and engines before he can be trusted to look after them."—*English Mechanic.*

The Engineer, Fireman, and Engine-Boy.

THE MODEL LOCOMOTIVE ENGINEER, FIREMAN, and ENGINE-BOY. Comprising a Historical Notice of the Pioneer Locomotive Engines and their Inventors. By Michael Reynolds. With numerous Illustrations and a fine Portrait of George Stephenson. Crown 8vo, 4s. 6d. cloth.

"From the technical knowledge of the author it will appeal to the railway man of to-day more forcibly than anything written by Dr. Smiles. . . . The volume contains information of a technical kind, and facts that every driver should be familiar with."—*English Mechanic.*

"We should be glad to see this book in the possession of everyone in the kingdom who has ever laid, or is to lay, hands on a locomotive engine."—*Iron.*

Continuous Railway Brakes.

CONTINUOUS RAILWAY BRAKES : A Practical Treatise on the several Systems in Use in the United Kingdom ; their Construction and Performance. With copious Illustrations and numerous Tables. By Michael Reynolds. Large crown 8vo, 9s. cloth.

"A popular explanation of the different brakes. It will be of great assistance in forming public opinion, and will be studied with benefit by those who take an interest in the brake."—*English Mechanic.*

"Written with sufficient technical detail to enable the principle and relative connection of the various parts of each particular brake to be readily grasped."—*Mechanical World.*

Engine-Driving Life.

ENGINE-DRIVING LIFE : Stirring Adventures and Incidents in the Lives of Locomotive-Engine Drivers. By Michael Reynolds. Second Edition, with Additional Chapters. Crown 8vo, 2s. cloth.

"From first to last perfectly fascinating. Wilkie Collins's most thrilling conceptions are thrown into the shade by true incidents, endless in their variety, related in every page.'—*North British Mail.*

"Anyone who wishes to get a real insight into railway life cannot do better than read 'Engine-Driving Life' for himself; and if he once take it up he will find that the author's enthusiasm and real love of the engine-driving profession will carry him on till he has read every page."—*Saturday Review.*

Pocket Companion for Enginemen.

THE ENGINEMAN'S POCKET COMPANION AND PRACTICAL EDUCATOR FOR ENGINEMEN, BOILER ATTENDANTS, AND MECHANICS. By Michael Reynolds. With Forty-five Illustrations and numerous Diagrams. Second Edition, Revised. Royal 18mo, 3s. 6d., strongly bound for pocket wear.

"This admirable work is well suited to accomplish its object, being the honest workmanship of a competent engineer."—*Glasgow Herald.*

"A most meritorious work, giving in a succinct and practical form all the information an engine-minder desirous of mastering the scientific principles of his daily calling would require.'—*Miller.*

"A boon to those who are striving to become efficient mechanics."—*Daily Chronicle.*

French-English Glossary for Engineers, etc.

A POCKET GLOSSARY of TECHNICAL TERMS: ENGLISH-FRENCH, FRENCH-ENGLISH; with Tables suitable for the Architectural, Engineering, Manufacturing and Nautical Professions. By JOHN JAMES FLETCHER, Engineer and Surveyor. 200 pp. Waistcoat-pocket size, 1s. 6d., limp leather.

"It ought certainly to be in the waistcoat-pocket of every professional man."—*Iron.*

"It is a very great advantage for readers and correspondents in France and England to have so large a number of the words relating to engineering and manufacturers collected in a liliputian volume. The little book will be useful both to students and travellers.'—*Architect.*

"The glossary of terms is very complete, and many of the tables are new and well arranged. We cordially commend the book."—*Mechanical World.*

Portable Engines.

THE PORTABLE ENGINE; ITS CONSTRUCTION AND MANAGEMENT. A Practical Manual for Owners and Users of Steam Engines generally. By WILLIAM DYSON WANSBROUGH. With 90 Illustrations. Crown 8vo, 3s. 6d. cloth.

"This is a work of value to those who use steam machinery. . . . Should be read by every-one who has a steam engine, on a farm or elsewhere."—*Mark Lane Express.*

"We cordially commend this work to buyers and owners of steam engines, and to those who have to do with their construction or use."—*Timber Trades Journal.*

"Such a general knowledge of the steam engine as Mr. Wansbrough furnishes to the reader should be acquired by all intelligent owners and others who use the steam engine."—*Building News.*

"An excellent text-book of this useful form of engine, which describes with all necessary minuteness the details of the various devices. . . ' The Hints to Purchasers contain a good deal of commonsense and practical wisdom."—*English Mechanic.*

CIVIL ENGINEERING, SURVEYING, etc.

MR. HUMBER'S IMPORTANT ENGINEERING BOOKS.

The Water Supply of Cities and Towns.

A COMPREHENSIVE TREATISE on the WATER-SUPPLY OF CITIES AND TOWNS. By WILLIAM HUMBER, A-M.Inst.C.E., and M. Inst. M.E., Author of "Cast and Wrought Iron Bridge Construction," &c. &c. Illustrated with 50 Double Plates, 1 Single Plate, Coloured Frontispiece, and upwards of 250 Woodcuts, and containing 400 pages of Text. Imp. 4to, £6 6s. elegantly and substantially half-bound in morocco,

List of Contents.

I. Historical Sketch of some of the means that have been adopted for the Supply of Water to Cities and Towns.—II. Water and the Foreign Matter usually associated with it.—III. Rainfall and Evaporation.—IV. Springs and the water-bearing formations of various districts.—V. Measurement and Estimation of the flow of Water—VI. On the Selection of the Source of Supply.—VII. Wells.—VIII. Reservoirs,—IX. The Purification of Water.—X. Pumps. — XI. Pumping Machinery. — XII. Conduits.—XIII. Distribution of Water.—XIV. Meters, Service Pipes, and House Fittings.—XV. The Law and Economy of Water Works. XVI. Constant and Intermittent Supply.—XVII. Description of Plates. — Appendices, giving Tables of Rates of Supply, Velocities, &c. &c., together with Specifications of several Works illustrated, among which will be found: Aberdeen, Bideford, Canterbury, Dundee, Halifax, Lambeth, Rotherham, Dublin, and others.

"The most systematic and valuable work upon water supply hitherto produced in English, or in any other language. . . . Mr. Humber's work is characterised almost throughout by an exhaustiveness much more distinctive of French and German than of English technical treatises."—*Engineer.*

"We can congratulate Mr. Humber on having been able to give so large an amount of information on a subject so important as the water supply of cities and towns. The plates, fifty in number, are mostly drawings of executed works, and alone would have commanded the attention of every engineer whose practice may lie in this branch of the profession."—*Builder.*

Cast and Wrought Iron Bridge Construction.

A COMPLETE AND PRACTICAL TREATISE ON CAST AND WROUGHT IRON BRIDGE CONSTRUCTION, including Iron Foundations. In Three Parts—Theoretical, Practical, and Descriptive. By WILLIAM HUMBER, A.M.Inst.C.E., and M.Inst.M.E. Third Edition, Revised and much improved, with 115 Double Plates (20 of which now first appear in this edition), and numerous Additions to the Text. In Two Vols., imp. 4to, £6 16s. 6d. half-bound in morocco.

"A very valuable contribution to the standard literature of civil engineering. In addition to elevations, plans and sections, large scale details are given which very much enhance the instructive worth of those illustrations."—*Civil Engineer and Architect's Journal.*

"Mr. Humber's stately volumes, lately issued—in which the most important bridges erected during the last five years, under the direction of the late Mr. Brunel, Sir W. Cubitt, Mr. Hawkshaw, Mr. Page, Mr. Fowler, Mr. Hemans, and others among our most eminent engineers, are drawn and specified in great detail."—*Engineer.*

MR. HUMBER'S GREAT WORK ON MODERN ENGINEERING.

Complete in Four Volumes, imperial 4to, price £12 12s., half-morocco. Each Volume sold separately as follows:—

A RECORD OF THE PROGRESS OF MODERN ENGINEER-

ING. FIRST SERIES. Comprising Civil, Mechanical, Marine, Hydraulic, Railway, Bridge, and other Engineering Works, &c. By WILLIAM HUMBER, A-M.Inst.C.E., &c. Imp. 4to, with 36 Double Plates, drawn to a large scale, Photographic Portrait of John Hawkshaw, C.E., F.R.S., &c., and copious descriptive Letterpress, Specifications, &c., £3 3s. half-morocco.

List of the Plates and Diagrams.

Victoria Station and Roof, L. B. & S. C. R. (8 plates); Southport Pier (2 plates); Victoria Station and Roof, L. C. & D. and G. W. R. (6 plates); Roof of Cremorne Music Hall; Bridge over G. N. Railway; Roof of Station, Dutch Rhenish Rail (2 plates); Bridge over the Thames, West London Extension Railway (5 plates); Armour Plates: Suspension Bridge, Thames (4 plates); The Allen Engine; Suspension Bridge, Avon (3 plates); Underground Railway (3 plates).

"Handsomely lithographed and printed. It will find favour with many who desire to preserve in a permanent form copies of the plans and specifications prepared for the guidance of the contractors for many important engineering works."—*Engineer.*

HUMBER'S RECORD OF MODERN ENGINEERING. SECOND

SERIES. Imp. 4to, with 36 Double Plates, Photographic Portrait of Robert Stephenson, C.E., M.P., F.R.S., &c., and copious descriptive Letterpress, Specifications, &c., £3 3s. half-morocco.

List of the Plates and Diagrams.

Birkenhead Docks, Low Water Basin (15 plates); Charing Cross Station Roof, C. C. Railway (3 plates); Digswell Viaduct, Great Northern Railway; Robbery Wood Viaduct, Great Northern Railway; Iron Permanent Way; Clydach Viaduct, Merthyr, Tredegar, and Abergavenny Railway; Ebbw Viaduct, Merthyr, Tredegar, and Abergavenny Railway; College Wood Viaduct, Cornwall Railway; Dublin Winter Palace Roof (3 plates); Bridge over the Thames, L. C. & D. Railway (6 plates); Albert Harbour, Greenock (4 plates).

"Mr. Humber has done the profession good and true service, by the fine collection of examples he has here brought before the profession and the public."—*Practical Mechanic's Journal.*

HUMBER'S RECORD OF MODERN ENGINEERING. THIRD

SERIES. Imp. 4to, with 40 Double Plates, Photographic Portrait of J. R. M'Clean, late Pres. Inst. C.E., and copious descriptive Letterpress, Specifications, &c., £3 3s. half-morocco.

List of the Plates and Diagrams.

MAIN DRAINAGE, METROPOLIS.—*North Side.*—Map showing Interception of Sewers; Middle Level Sewer (2 plates); Outfall Sewer, Bridge over River Lea (3 plates); Outfall Sewer, Bridge over Marsh Lane, North Woolwich Railway, and Bow and Barking Railway Junction; Outfall Sewer, Bridge over Bow and Barking Railway (3 plates); Outfall Sewer, Bridge over East London Waterworks' Feeder (2 plates); Outfall Sewer, Reservoir (2 plates); Outfall Sewer, Tumbling Bay and Outlet; Outfall Sewer, Penstocks. *South Side.*—Outfall Sewer, Bermondsey Branch (2 plates); Outfall Sewer, Reservoir and Outlet (4 plates); Outfall Sewer, Filth Hoist; Sections of Sewers (North and South Sides). THAMES EMBANKMENT.—Section of River Wall; Steamboat Pier, Westminster (2 plates); Landing Stairs between Charing Cross and Waterloo Bridges; York Gate (2 plates); Overflow and Outlet at Savoy Street Sewer (3 plates); Steamboat Pier, Waterloo Bridge (3 plates); Junction of Sewers, Plans and Sections; Gullies, Plans and Sections; Rolling Stock; Granite and Iron Forts.

"The drawings have a constantly increasing value, and whoever desires to possess clear representations of the two great works carried out by our Metropolitan Board will obtain Mr. Humber's volume."—*Engineer.*

HUMBER'S RECORD OF MODERN ENGINEERING. FOURTH

SERIES. Imp. 4to, with 36 Double Plates, Photographic Portrait of John Fowler, late Pres. Inst. C.E., and copious descriptive Letterpress, Specifications, &c., £3 3s. half-morocco.

List of the Plates and Diagrams.

Abbey Mills Pumping Station, Main Drainage, Metropolis (4 plates); Barrow Docks (5 plates); Manquis Viaduct, Santiago and Valparaiso Railway (2 plates); Adam's Locomotive, St. Helen's Canal Railway (2 plates); Cannon Street Station Roof, Charing Cross Railway (3 plates); Road Bridge over the River Moka (2 plates); Telegraphic Apparatus for Mesopotamia; Viaduct over the River Wye, Midland Railway (3 plates); St. Germans Viaduct, Cornwall Railway (2 plates); Wrought-Iron Cylinder for Diving Bell; Millwall Docks (6 plates); Milroy's Patent Excavator; Metropolitan District Railway (6 plates); Harbours, Ports, and Breakwaters (3 plates).

"We gladly welcome another year's issue of this valuable publication from the able pen of Mr. Humber. The accuracy and general excellence of this work are well known, while its usefulness in giving the measurements and details of some of the latest examples of engineering, as carried out by the most eminent men in the profession, cannot be too highly prized."—*Artisan.*

Strains, Calculation of.

A HANDY BOOK FOR THE CALCULATION OF STRAINS
IN GIRDERS AND SIMILAR STRUCTURES, AND THEIR STRENGTH.
Consisting of Formulæ and Corresponding Diagrams, with numerous details
for Practical Application, &c. By WILLIAM HUMBER, A-M.Inst.C.E., &c.
Fifth Edition. Crown 8vo, nearly 100 Woodcuts and 3 Plates, 7s. 6d. cloth
" The formulæ are neatly expressed, and the diagrams good."—*Athenæum.*
" We heartily commend this really *handy* book to our engineer and architect readers."—*English Mechanic.*

Barlow's Strength of Materials, enlarged by Humber

A TREATISE ON THE STRENGTH OF MATERIALS;
with Rules for Application in Architecture, the Construction of Suspension
Bridges, Railways, &c. By PETER BARLOW, F.R.S. A New Edition, revised
by his Sons, P. W. BARLOW, F.R.S., and W. H. BARLOW, F.R.S.; to which
are added, Experiments by HODGKINSON, FAIRBAIRN, and KIRKALDY; and
Formulæ for Calculating Girders, &c. Arranged and Edited by W. HUMBER,
A-M.Inst.C.E. Demy 8vo, 400 pp., with 19 large Plates and numerous Woodcuts, 18s. cloth.

" Valuable alike to the student, tyro, and the experienced practitioner, it will always rank in
future, as it has hitherto done, as the standard treatise on that particular subject."—*Engineer.*
" There is no greater authority than Barlow."—*Building News.*
" As a scientific work of the first class. it deserves a foremost place on the bookshelves of every
civil engineer and practical mechanic."—*English Mechanic.*

Trigonometrical Surveying.

AN OUTLINE OF THE METHOD OF CONDUCTING A
TRIGONOMETRICAL SURVEY, for the Formation of Geographical and
Topographical Maps and Plans, Military Reconnaissance, Levelling, &c., with
Useful Problems, Formulæ, and Tables. By Lieut.-General FROME, R.E.
Fourth Edition, Revised and partly Re-written by Major General Sir CHARLES
WARREN, G.C.M.G., R.E. With 19 Plates and 115 Woodcuts, royal 8vo, 16s.
cloth.

" The simple fact that a fourth edition has been called for is the best testimony to its merits.
No words of praise from us can strengthen the position so well and so steadily maintained by this
work. Sir Charles Warren has revised the entire work, and made such additions as were necessary
to bring every portion of the contents up to the present date."—*Broad Arrow.*

Field Fortification.

A TREATISE ON FIELD FORTIFICATION, THE ATTACK
OF FORTRESSES, MILITARY MINING, AND RECONNOITRING. By
Colonel I. S. MACAULAY, late Professor of Fortification in the R.M.A., Wool-
wich. Sixth Edition, crown 8vo, cloth, with separate Atlas of 12 Plates, 12s.

Oblique Bridges.

A PRACTICAL AND THEORETICAL ESSAY ON OBLIQUE
BRIDGES. With 13 large Plates. By the late GEORGE WATSON BUCK,
M.I.C.E. Third Edition, revised by his Son, J. H. WATSON BUCK, M.I.C.E.;
and with the addition of Description to Diagrams for Facilitating the Construction of Oblique Bridges, by W. H. BARLOW, M.I.C.E. Royal 8vo, 12s.
cloth.

" The standard text-book for all engineers regarding skew arches is Mr. Buck's treatise, and
would be impossible to consult a better."—*Engineer.*
"Mr. Buck's treatise is recognised as a standard text-book, and his treatment has divested the
subject of many of the intricacies supposed to belong to it. As a guide to the engineer and architect, on a confessedly difficult subject, Mr. Buck's work is unsurpassed."—*Building News.*

Water Storage, Conveyance and Utilisation.

WATER ENGINEERING : A Practical Treatise on the Measurement, Storage, Conveyance and Utilisation of Water for the Supply of Towns,
for Mill Power, and for other Purposes. By CHARLES SLAGG, Water and
Drainage Engineer, A.M.Inst.C.E., Author of " Sanitary Work in the Smaller
Towns, and in Villages," &c. With numerous Illusts. Cr. 8vo. 7s. 6d. cloth.

" As a small practical treatise on the water supply of towns, and on some applications of
water-power, the work is in many respects excellent."—*Engineering.*
" The author has collated the results deduced from the experiments of the most eminent
authorities, and has presented them in a compact and practical form, accompanied by very clear
and detailed explanations. . . . The application of water as a motive power is treated very
carefully and exhaustively."—*Builder.*
" For anyone who desires to begin the study of hydraulics with a consideration of the practical
applications of the science there is no better guide."—*Architect.*

Statics, Graphic and Analytic.

GRAPHIC AND ANALYTIC STATICS, in their Practical Application to the Treatment of Stresses in Roofs, Solid Girders, Lattice, Bowstring and Suspension Bridges, Braced Iron Arches and Piers, and other Frameworks. By R. Hudson Graham, C.E. Containing Diagrams and Plates to Scale. With numerous Examples, many taken from existing Structures. Specially arranged for Class-work in Colleges and Universities. Second Edition, Revised and Enlarged. 8vo, 16s. cloth.

"Mr. Graham's book will find a place wherever graphic and analytic statics are used or studied." —*Engineer.*

"The work is excellent from a practical point of view, and has evidently been prepared with much care. The directions for working are ample, and are illustrated by an abundance of well-selected examples. It is an excellent text-book for the practical draughtsman."—*Athenæum.*

Student's Text-Book on Surveying.

PRACTICAL SURVEYING : A Text-Book for Students preparing for Examination or for Survey-work in the Colonies. By George W. Usill, A.M.I.C.E., Author of "The Statistics of the Water Supply of Great Britain." With Four Lithographic Plates and upwards of 330 Illustrations. Second Edition, Revised. Crown 8vo, 7s. 6d. cloth.

"The best forms of instruments are described as to their construction, uses and modes of employment, and there are innumerable hints on work and equipment such as the author, in his experience as surveyor, draughtsman and teacher, has found necessary, and which the student in his inexperience will find most serviceable."—*Engineer.*

"The latest treatise in the English language on surveying, and we have no hesitation in saying that the student will find it a better guide than any of its predecessors . . . . Deserves to be recognised as the first book which should be put in the hands of a pupil of Civil Engineering, and every gentleman of education who sets out for the Colonies would find it well to have a copy."—*Architect.*

"A very useful, practical handbook on field practice. Clear, accurate and not too condensed."—*Journal of Education.*

Survey Practice.

AID TO SURVEY PRACTICE, for Reference in Surveying, Levelling, and Setting-out ; and in Route Surveys of Travellers by Land and Sea. With Tables, Illustrations, and Records. By Lowis D'A. Jackson, A.M.I.C.E., Author of "Hydraulic Manual," "Modern Metrology," &c. Second Edition, Enlarged. Large crown 8vo, 12s. 6d. cloth.

"Mr. Jackson has produced a valuable *vade-mecum* for the surveyor. We can recommend this book as containing an admirable supplement to the teaching of the accomplished surveyor."—*Athenæum.*

"As a text-book we should advise all surveyors to place it in their libraries, and study well the matured instructions afforded in its pages."—*Colliery Guardian.*

"The author brings to his work a fortunate union of theory and practical experience which, aided by a clear and lucid style of writing, renders the book a very useful one."—*Builder.*

Surveying, Land and Marine.

LAND AND MARINE SURVEYING, in Reference to the Preparation of Plans for Roads and Railways; Canals, Rivers, Towns' Water Supplies; Docks and Harbours. With Description and Use of Surveying Instruments. By W. D. Haskoll, C.E., Author of "Bridge and Viaduct Construction," &c. Second Edition, Revised, with Additions. Large cr. 8vo, 9s. cl.

"This book must prove of great value to the student. We have no hesitation in recommending it, feeling assured that it will more than repay a careful study."—*Mechanical World.*

"A most useful and well arranged book for the aid of a student. We can strongly recommend it as a carefully-written and valuable text-book. It enjoys a well-deserved repute among surveyors." —*Builder.*

"This volume cannot fail to prove of the utmost practical utility. It may be safely recommended to all students who aspire to become clean and expert surveyors."—*Mining Journal.*

Tunnelling.

PRACTICAL TUNNELLING. Explaining in detail the Setting-out of the works, Shaft-sinking and Heading-driving, Ranging the Lines and Levelling underground, Sub-Excavating, Timbering, and the Construction of the Brickwork of Tunnels, with the amount of Labour required for, and the Cost of, the various portions of the work. By Frederick W. Simms, F.G.S., M.Inst.C.E. Third Edition, Revised and Extended by D. Kinnear Clark, M.Inst.C.E. Imperial 8vo, with 21 Folding Plates and numerous Wood Engravings, 30s. cloth.

"The estimation in which Mr. Simms's book on tunnelling has been held for over thirty years cannot be more truly expressed than in the words of the late Prof. Rankine:—'The best source of information on the subject of tunnels is Mr. F. W. Simms's work on Practical Tunnelling.'"—*Architect.*

"It has been regarded from the first as a text book of the subject. . . . Mr. Clarke has added immensely to the value of the book."—*Engineer.*

Levelling.

A TREATISE ON THE PRINCIPLES AND PRACTICE OF LEVELLING. Showing its Application to purposes of Railway and Civil Engineering, in the Construction of Roads; with Mr. TELFORD'S Rules for the same. By FREDERICK W. SIMMS, F.G.S., M.Inst.C.E. Seventh Edition, with the addition of LAW's Practical Examples for Setting-out Railway Curves, and TRAUTWINE'S Field Practice of Laying-out Circular Curves. With 7 Plates and numerous Woodcuts, 8vo, 8s. 6d. cloth. **** TRAUTWINE on Curves may be had separate, 5s.

"The text-book on levelling in most of our engineering schools and colleges."—*Engineer.*
"The publishers have rendered a substantial service to the profession, especially to the younger members, by bringing out the present edition of Mr. Simms's useful work."—*Engineering.*

Heat, Expansion by.

EXPANSION OF STRUCTURES BY HEAT. By JOHN KEILY, C.E., late of the Indian Public Works and Victorian Railway Departments. Crown 8vo, 3s. 6d. cloth.

SUMMARY OF CONTENTS.

Section I. FORMULAS AND DATA.
Section II. METAL BARS.
Section III. SIMPLE FRAMES.
Section IV. COMPLEX FRAMES AND PLATES.
Section V. THERMAL CONDUCTIVITY.
Section VI. MECHANICAL FORCE OF HEAT.
Section VII. WORK OF EXPANSION AND CONTRACTION.
Section VIII. SUSPENSION BRIDGES.
Section IX. MASONRY STRUCTURES.

"The aim the author has set before him, viz., to show the effects of heat upon metallic and other structures, is a laudable one, for this is a branch of physics upon which the engineer or architect can find but little reliable and comprehensive data in books."—*Builder.*
"Whoever is concerned to know the effect of changes of temperature on such structures as suspension bridges and the like, could not do better than consult Mr. Keily's valuable and handy exposition of the geometrical principles involved in these changes."—*Scotsman.*

Practical Mathematics.

MATHEMATICS FOR PRACTICAL MEN: Being a Commonplace Book of Pure and Mixed Mathematics. Designed chiefly for the use of Civil Engineers, Architects and Surveyors. By OLINTHUS GREGORY, LL.D., F.R.A.S., Enlarged by HENRY LAW, C.E. 4th Edition, carefully Revised by J. R. YOUNG, formerly Professor of Mathematics, Belfast College. With 13 Plates, 8vo, £1 1s. cloth.

"The engineer or architect will here find ready to his hand rules for solving nearly every mathematical difficulty that may arise in his practice The rules are in all cases explained by means of examples, in which every step of the process is clearly worked out."—*Builder.*
"One of the most serviceable books for practical mechanics. . . It is an instructive book for the student, and a text-book for him who, having once mastered the subjects it treats of, needs occasionally to refresh his memory upon them."—*Building News.*

Hydraulic Tables.

HYDRAULIC TABLES, CO-EFFICIENTS, and FORMULÆ for finding the Discharge of Water from Orifices, Notches, Weirs, Pipes, and Rivers. With New Formulæ, Tables, and General Information on Rainfall, Catchment-Basins, Drainage, Sewerage, Water Supply for Towns and Mill Power. By JOHN NEVILLE, Civil Engineer, M.R.I.A. Third Ed., carefully Revised, with considerable Additions. Numerous Illusts. Cr. 8vo, 14s. cloth.

"Alike valuable to students and engineers in practice; its study will prevent the annoyance of avoidable failures, and assist them to select the readiest means of successfully carrying out any given work connected with hydraulic engineering."—*Mining Journal.*
"It is, of all English books on the subject, the one nearest to completeness. . . . From the good arrangement of the matter, the clear explanations, and abundance of formulæ, the carefully calculated tables, and, above all, the thorough, acquaintance with both theory and construction, which is displayed from first to last, the book w be found to be an acquisition."—*Architect.*

Hydraulics.

HYDRAULIC MANUAL. Consisting of Working Tables and Explanatory Text. Intended as a Guide in Hydraulic Calculations and Field Operations. By LOWIS D'A. JACKSON, Author of "Aid to Survey Practice," "Modern Metrology," &c. Fourth Edition, Enlarged. Large cr. 8vo, 16s. cl.

"The author has had a wide experience in hydraulic engineering and has been a careful observer of the facts which have come under his notice, and from the great mass of material at his command he has constructed a manual which may be accepted as a trustworthy guide to this branch of the engineer's profession. We can heartily recommend this volume to all who desire to be acquainted with the latest development of this important subject."—*Engineering.*
"The standard-work in this department of mechnnics.'—*Scotsman.*
"The most useful feature of this work is its freedom from what is superannuated, and its thorough adoption of recent experiments; the text is, in fact, in great part a short account of the great modern experiments."—*Nature.*

Drainage.

ON THE DRAINAGE OF LANDS, TOWNS AND BUILD-
INGS. By G. D. DEMPSEY, C.E., Author of "The Practical Railway En-
gineer," &c. Revised, with large Additions on RECENT PRACTICE IN
DRAINAGE ENGINEERING, by D. KINNEAR CLARK, M.Inst.C.E. Author of
"Tramways," "A Manual of Rules, Tables, and Data for Engineers," &c.
Second Edition. 12mo, 5s. cloth.

"The new matter added to Mr. Dempsey's excellent work is characterised by the comprehen-
sive grasp and accuracy of detail for which the name of Mr. D. K. Clark is a sufficient voucher."—
Athenæum.
"As a work on recent practice in drainage engineering, the book is to be commended to all
who are making that branch of engineering science their special study."—Iron.
"A comprehensive manual on drainage engineering, and a useful introduction to the student."
Building News.

Tramways and their Working.

TRAMWAYS : THEIR CONSTRUCTION AND WORKING.
Embracing a Comprehensive History of the System ; with an exhaustive
Analysis of the various Modes of Traction, including Horse-Power, Steam,
Heated Water, and Compressed Air ; a Description of the Varieties of Rolling
Stock ; and ample Details of Cost and Working Expenses: the Progress
recently made in Tramway Construction, &c. &c.   By D. KINNEAR CLARK,
M.Inst.C.E.   With over 200 Wood Engravings, and 13 Folding Plates.   Two
Vols., large crown 8vo, 30s. cloth.

"All interested in tramways must refer to it, as all railway engineers have turned to the author's
work 'Railway Machinery.'"—Engineer.
"An exhaustive and practical work on tramways, in which the history of this kind of locomotion, and a description and cost of the various modes of laying tramways, are to be found."—
Building News.
"The best form of rails, the best mode of construction, and the best mechanical appliances
are so fairly indicated in the work under review, that any engineer about to construct a tramway
will be enabled at once to obtain the practical information which will be of most service to him.'—
Athenæum.

Oblique Arches.

A PRACTICAL TREATISE ON THE CONSTRUCTION OF
OBLIQUE ARCHES. By JOHN HART. Third Edition, with Plates. Imperial 8vo, 8s. cloth.

Curves, Tables for Setting-out.

TABLES OF TANGENTIAL ANGLES AND MULTIPLES
for Setting-out Curves from 5 to 200 Radius. By ALEXANDER BEAZELEY,
M.Inst.C.E. Third Edition. Printed on 48 Cards, and sold in a cloth box,
waistcoat-pocket size, 3s. 6d.

"Each table is printed on a small card, which, being placed on the theodolite, leaves the hands
free to manipulate the instrument—no small advantage as regards the rapidity of work."—Engineer.
"Very handy ; a man may know that all his day's work must fa on two of these cards, which
he puts into his own card-case, and leaves the rest behind."—Athenæum.

Earthwork.

EARTHWORK TABLES. Showing the Contents in Cubic
Yards of Embankments, Cuttings, &c., of Heights or Depths up to an average
of 80 feet. By JOSEPH BROADBENT, C.E., and FRANCIS CAMPIN, C.E. Crown
8vo, 5s. cloth.

"The way in which accuracy is attained, by a simple division of each cross section into three
elements, two in which are constant and one variable, is ingenious."—Athenæum.

Tunnel Shafts.

THE CONSTRUCTION OF LARGE TUNNEL SHAFTS : A
Practical and Theoretical Essay.   By J. H. WATSON BUCK, M.Inst.C.E.,
Resident Engineer, London and North-Western Railway.   Illustrated with
Folding Plates, royal 8vo, 12s. cloth.

"Many of the methods given are of extreme practical value to the mason ; and the observations
on the form of arch, the rules for ordering the stone, and the construction of the templates will be
found of considerable use. We commend the book to the engineering profession."—Building News.
"Will be regarded by civil engineers as of the utmost value, and calculated to save much time
and obviate many mistakes."—Colliery Guardian.

Girders, Strength of.

GRAPHIC TABLE FOR FACILITATING THE COMPUTA-
TION OF THE WEIGHTS OF WROUGHT IRON AND STEEL
GIRDERS, etc., for Parliamentary and other Estimates. By J. H. WATSON
BUCK, M.Inst.C.E. On a Sheet, 2s.6d.

River Engineering.

RIVER BARS: The Causes of their Formation, and their Treatment by "Induced Tidal Scour;" with a Description of the Successful Reduction by this Method of the Bar at Dublin. By I. J. MANN, Assist. Eng. to the Dublin Port and Docks Board. Royal 8vo, 7s. 6d. cloth.

"We recommend all interested in harbour works—and, indeed, those concerned in the improvements of rivers generally—to read Mr. Mann's interesting work on the treatment of river bars."—*Engineer.*

Trusses.

TRUSSES OF WOOD AND IRON. Practical Applications of Science in Determining the Stresses, Breaking Weights, Safe Loads, Scantlings, and Details of Construction, with Complete Working Drawings. By WILLIAM GRIFFITHS, Surveyor, Assistant Master, Tranmere School of Science and Art. Oblong 8vo, 4s. 6d. cloth.

"This handy little book enters so minutely into every detail connected with the construction of roof trusses, that no student need be ignorant of these matters."—*Practical Engineer.*

Railway Working.

SAFE RAILWAY WORKING. A Treatise on Railway Accidents: Their Cause and Prevention; with a Description of Modern Appliances and Systems. By CLEMENT E. STRETTON, C.E., Vice-President and Consulting Engineer, Amalgamated Society of Railway Servants. With Illustrations and Coloured Plates. Second Edition, Enlarged. Crown 8vo, 3s. 6d. cloth. [*Just published.*

"A book for the engineer, the directors, the managers; and, in short, all who wish for information on railway matters will find a perfect encyclopædia in 'Safe Railway Working.'"—*Railway Review.*

"We commend the remarks on railway signalling to all railway managers, especially where a uniform code and practice is advocated."—*Herepath's Railway Journal.*

"The author may be congratulated on having collected, in a very convenient form, much valuable information on the principal questions affecting the safe working of railways."—*Railway Engineer.*

Field-Book for Engineers.

THE ENGINEER'S, MINING SURVEYOR'S, AND CONTRACTOR'S FIELD-BOOK. Consisting of a Series of Tables, with Rules, Explanations of Systems, and use of Theodolite for Traverse Surveying and Plotting the Work with minute accuracy by means of Straight Edge and Set Square only; Levelling with the Theodolite, Casting-out and Reducing Levels to Datum, and Plotting Sections in the ordinary manner; setting-out Curves with the Theodolite by Tangential Angles and Multiples, with Right and Left-hand Readings of the Instrument: Setting-out Curves without Theodolite, on the System of Tangential Angles by sets of Tangents and Offsets; and Earthwork Tables to 80 feet deep, calculated for every 6 inches in depth. By W. DAVIS HASKOLL, C.E. With numerous Woodcuts. Fourth Edition, Enlarged. Crown 8vo, 12s. cloth.

"The book is very handy; the separate tables of sines and tangents to every minute will make it useful for many other purposes, the genuine traverse tables existing all the same."—*Athenæum.*

"Every person engaged in engineering field operations will estimate the importance of such a work and the amount of valuable time which will be saved by reference to a set of reliable tables prepared with the accuracy and fulness of those given in this volume."—*Railway News.*

Earthwork, Measurement of.

A MANUAL ON EARTHWORK. By ALEX. J. S. GRAHAM, C.E. With numerous Diagrams. Second Edition. 18mo, 2s. 6d. cloth

"A great amount of practical information, very admirably arranged, and available for rough estimates, as well as for the more exact calculations required in the engineer's and contractor's offices."—*Artisan.*

Strains in Ironwork.

THE STRAINS ON STRUCTURES OF IRONWORK; with Practical Remarks on Iron Construction. By F. W. SHEILDS, M.Inst.C.E. Second Edition, with 5 Plates. Royal 8vo, 5s. cloth.

"The student cannot find a better little book on this subject."—*Engineer.*

Cast Iron and other Metals, Strength of.

A PRACTICAL ESSAY ON THE STRENGTH OF CAST IRON AND OTHER METALS. By THOMAS TREDGOLD, C.E. Fifth Edition, including HODGKINSON'S Experimental Researches. 8vo, 12s. cloth.

ARCHITECTURE, BUILDING, etc.

Construction.
THE SCIENCE OF BUILDING : An Elementary Treatise on the Principles of Construction. By E. WYNDHAM TARN, M.A., Architect. Third Edition, Enlarged, with 59 Engravings. Fcap. 8vo, 4s. cloth.
" A very valuable book, which we strongly recommend to all students."—*Builder.*
" No architectural student should be without this handbook."—*Architect.*

Villa Architecture.
A HANDY BOOK OF VILLA ARCHITECTURE : Being a Series of Designs for Villa Residences in various Styles. With Outline Specifications and Estimates. By C. WICKES, Author of "The Spires and Towers of England," &c. 61 Plates, 4to, £1 11s. 6d. half-morocco, gilt edges.
" The whole of the designs bear evidence of their being the work of an artistic architect, and they will prove very valuable and suggestive."—*Building News.*

Text-Book for Architects.
THE ARCHITECT'S GUIDE: Being a Text-Book of Useful Information for Architects, Engineers, Surveyors, Contractors, Clerks of Works, &c. &c. By FREDERICK ROGERS, Architect, Author of "Specifications for Practical Architecture," &c. Second Edition, Revised and Enlarged. With numerous Illustrations. Crown 8vo, 6s. cloth.
" As a text-book of useful information for architects, engineers, surveyors, &c., it would be hard to find a handier or more complete little volume."—*Standard.*
" A young architect could hardly have a better guide-book."—*Timber Trades Journal.*

Taylor and Cresy's Rome.
THE ARCHITECTURAL ANTIQUITIES OF ROME. By the late G. L. TAYLOR, Esq., F.R.I.B.A., and EDWARD CRESY, Esq. New Edition, thoroughly Revised by the Rev. ALEXANDER TAYLOR, M.A. (son of the late G. L. Taylor, Esq.), Fellow of Queen's College, Oxford, and Chaplain of Gray's Inn. Large folio, with 130 Plates, half-bound, £3 3s.
" Taylor and Cresy's work has from its first publication been ranked among those professional books which cannot be bettered. . . . It would be difficult to find examples of drawings, even among those of the most painstaking students of Gothic, more thoroughly worked out than are the one hundred and thirty plates in this volume."—*Architect.*

Linear Perspective.
ARCHITECTURAL PERSPECTIVE : The whole Course and Operations of the Draughtsman in Drawing a Large House in Linear Perspective. Illustrated by 39 Folding Plates. By F. O. FERGUSON. Demy 8vo, 3s. 6d. boards.   [*Just published.*

Architectural Drawing.
PRACTICAL RULES ON DRAWING, for the Operative Builder and Young Student in Architecture. By GEORGE PYNE. With 14 Plates, 4to, 7s. 6d. boards.

Sir Wm. Chambers on Civil Architecture.
THE DECORATIVE PART OF CIVIL ARCHITECTURE. By Sir WILLIAM CHAMBERS, F.R.S. With Portrait, Illustrations, Notes, and an Examination of Grecian Architecture, by JOSEPH GWILT, F.S.A. Revised and Edited by W. H. LEEDS, with a Memoir of the Author. 66 Plates, 4to, 21s. cloth.

House Building and Repairing.
THE HOUSE-OWNER'S ESTIMATOR ; or, What will it Cost to Build, Alter, or Repair? A Price Book adapted to the Use of Unprofessional People, as well as for the Architectural Surveyor and Builder. By JAMES D. SIMON, A.R.I.B.A. Edited and Revised by FRANCIS T. W. MILLER, A.R.I.B.A. With numerous Illustrations. Fourth Edition, Revised. Crown 8vo, 3s. 6d. cloth.
"In two years it will repay its cost a hundred times over."—*Field.*

Cottages and Villas.
COUNTRY AND SUBURBAN COTTAGES AND VILLAS How to Plan and Build Them. Containing 33 Plates, with Introduction, General Explanations, and Description of each Plate. By JAMES W. BOGUE, Architect, Author of "Domestic Architecture," &c. 4to, 10s. 6d. cloth.

The New Builder's Price Book, 1892.

LOCKWOOD'S BUILDER'S PRICE BOOK FOR 1892. A Comprehensive Handbook of the Latest Prices and Data for Builders, Architects, Engineers and Contractors. *Re-constructed, Re-written and Further Enlarged.* By FRANCIS T. W. MILLER. 700 closely-printed pages, crown 8vo, 4s. cloth. · [*Just published.*

" This book is a very useful one, and should find a place in every English office connected with the building and engineering professions."—*Industries.*

"This Price Book has been set up in new type. . . . Advantage has been taken of the transformation to add much additional information, and the volume is now an excellent book of reference."—*Architect.*

" In its new and revised form this Price Book is what a work of this kind should be—comprehensive, reliable, well arranged, legible and well b_u_id.'—*British Architect.*

" A work of established reputation."—*Athenæum.*

" This very useful handbook is well written, exceedingly clear in its explanations and great care has evidently been taken to ensure accuracy."—*Morning Advertiser.*

Designing, Measuring, and Valuing.

THE STUDENT'S GUIDE to the PRACTICE of MEASUR-ING AND VALUING ARTIFICERS' WORKS. Containing Directions for taking Dimensions, Abstracting the same, and bringing the Quantities into Bill, with Tables of Constants for Valuation of Labour, and for the Calculation of Areas and Solidities. Originally edited by EDWARD DOBSON, Architect. With Additions on Mensuration and Construction, and a New Chapter on Dilapidations, Repairs, and Contracts, by E. WYNDHAM TARN, M.A. Sixth Edition, including a Complete Form of a Bill of Quantities. With 8 Plates and 63 Woodcuts. Crown 8vo, 7s. 6d. cloth.

" Well fulfils the promise of its title-page, and we can thoroughly recommend it to the class for whose use it has been compiled. Mr. Tarn's additions and revisions have much increased the usefulness of the work, and have especially augmented its value to students."—*Engineering.*

" This edition will be found the most complete treatise on the principles of measuring and valuing artificers' work that has yet been published."—*Building News.*

Pocket Estimator and Technical Guide.

THE POCKET TECHNICAL GUIDE, MEASURER AND ESTIMATOR FOR BUILDERS AND SURVEYORS. Containing Technical Directions for Measuring Work in all the Building Trades, Complete Specifications for Houses, Roads, and Drains, and an easy Method of Estimating the parts of a Building collectively. By A. C. BEATON, Author of "Quantities and Measurements," &c. Sixth Edition, Revised. With 53 Woodcuts, waistcoat-pocket size, 1s. 6d. gilt edges. [*Just published.*

" No builder, architect, surveyor, or valuer should be without his ' Beaton.'"—*Building News.*

" Contains an extraordinary amount of information in daily requisition in measuring and estimating. Its presence in the pocket will save valuable time and trouble."—*Building World.*

Donaldson on Specifications.

THE HANDBOOK OF SPECIFICATIONS; or, Practical Guide to the Architect, Engineer, Surveyor, and Builder, in drawing up Specifications and Contracts for Works and Constructions. Illustrated by Precedents of Buildings actually executed by eminent Architects and Engineers. By Professor T. L. DONALDSON, P.R.I.B.A., &c. New Edition, in One large Vol., 8vo, with upwards of 1,000 pages of Text, and 33 Plates, £1 11s. 6d. cloth.

" In this work forty-four specifications of executed works are given, including the specifications for parts of the new Houses of Parliament, by Sir Charles Barry, and for the new Royal Exchange, by Mr. Tite, M.P. The latter, in particular, is a very complete and remarkable document. It embodies, to a great extent, as Mr. Donaldson mentions, 'the bill of quantities with the description of the works.' . . . It is valuable as a record, and more valuable still as a book of precedents. . . . Suffice it to say that Donaldson's 'Handbook of Specifications must be bought by all architects."—*Builder.*

Bartholomew and Rogers' Specifications.

SPECIFICATIONS FOR PRACTICAL ARCHITECTURE. A Guide to the Architect, Engineer, Surveyor, and Builder. With an Essay on the Structure and Science of Modern Buildings. Upon the Basis of the Work by ALFRED BARTHOLOMEW, thoroughly Revised, Corrected, and greatly added to by FREDERICK ROGERS, Architect. Second Edition, Revised, with Additions. With numerous Illustrations, medium 8vo, 15s. cloth.

" The collection of specifications prepared by Mr. Rogers on the basis of Bartholomew's work is too well known to need any recommendation from us. It is one of the books with which every young architect must be equipped ; for time has shown that the specifications cannot be set aside through any defect in them."—*Architect.*

Building; Civil and Ecclesiastical.

A BOOK ON BUILDING, Civil and Ecclesiastical, including Church Restoration ; with the Theory of Domes and the Great Pyramid, &c. By Sir EDMUND BECKETT, Bart., LL.D., F.R.A.S., Author of "Clocks and Watches, and Bells," &c. Second Edition, Enlarged. Fcap. 8vo, 5s. cloth.
"A book which is always amusing and nearly always instructive. The style throughout is in the highest degree condensed and epigrammatic."—*Times.*

Ventilation of Buildings.

VENTILATION. *A Text Book to the Practice of the Art of Ventilating Buildings.* With a Chapter upon Air Testing. By W. P. BUCHAN, R.P., Sanitary and Ventilating Engineer, Author of " Plumbing," &c. With 170 Illustrations. 12mo, 4s. cloth boards.   [*Just published.*

The Art of Plumbing.

PLUMBING. *A Text Book to the Practice of the Art or Craft of the Plumber, with Supplementary Chapters on House Drainage, embodying the latest Improvements.* By WILLIAM PATON BUCHAN, R.P., Sanitary Engineer and Practical Plumber. Sixth Edition, Enlarged to 370 pages, and 380 Illustrations. 12mo, 4s. cloth boards.
"A text book which may be safely put in the hands of every young plumber, and which will also be found useful by architects and medical professors."—*Builder.*
" A valuable text book, and the only treatise which can be regarded as a really reliable manual of the plumber's art."—*Building News.*

Geometry for the Architect, Engineer, etc.

PRACTICAL GEOMETRY, *for the Architect, Engineer and Mechanic.* Giving Rules for the Delineation and Application of various Geometrical Lines, Figures and Curves. By E. W. TARN, M.A., Architect, Author of "The Science of Building," &c. Second Edition. With 172 Illustrations, demy 8vo, 9s. cloth.
" No book with the same objects in view has ever been published in which the clearness of the rules laid down and the illustrative diagrams have been so satisfactory."—*Scotsman.*

The Science of Geometry.

THE GEOMETRY OF COMPASSES; *or, Problems Resolved by the mere Description of Circles, and the use of Coloured Diagrams and Symbols.* By OLIVER BYRNE. Coloured Plates. Crown 8vo, 3s. 6d. cloth.
" The treatise is a good one, and remarkable—like all Mr. Byrne's contributions to the science of geometry—for the lucid character of its teaching."—*Building News.*

DECORATIVE ARTS, etc.

Woods and Marbles (Imitation of).

SCHOOL OF PAINTING FOR THE IMITATION OF WOODS AND MARBLES, as Taught and Practised by A. R. VAN DER BURG and P. VAN DER BURG, Directors of the Rotterdam Painting Institution. Royal folio, 18½ by 12½ in., Illustrated with 24 full-size Coloured Plates; also 12 plain Plates, comprising 154 Figures. Second and Cheaper Edition. Price £1 11s. 6d.

List of Plates.

1. Various Tools required for Wood Painting—2, 3. Walnut : Preliminary Stages of Graining and Finished Specimen—4. Tools used for Marble Painting and Method of Manipulation—5,6. St. Remi Marble: Earlier Operations and Finished Specimen—7. Methods of Sketching different Grains, Knots, &c.—8, 9. Ash: Preliminary Stages and Finished Specimen—10. Methods of Sketching Marble Grains—11, 12. Breche Marble: Preliminary Stages of Working and Finished Specimen—13. Maple: Methods of Producing the different Grains—14, 15. Bird's-eye Maple: Preliminary Stages and Finished Specimen—16. Methods of Sketching the different Species of White Marble—17, 18. White Marble: Preliminary Stages of Process and Finished Specimen—19. Mahogany: Specimens of various Grains and Methods of Manipulation—20, 21. Mahogany: Earlier Stages and Finished Specimen—22, 23, 24. Sienna Marble: Varieties of Grain, Preliminary Stages and Finished Specimen—25, 26, 27. Juniper Wood: Methods of producing Grain, &c.: Preliminary Stages and Finished Specimen—28, 29, 30. Vert de Mer Marble: Varieties of Grain and Methods of Working Unfinished and Finished Specimens—31, 32. 33. Oak: Varieties of Grain, Tools Employed, and Methods of Manipulation, Preliminary Stages and Finished Specimen—34, 35, 36. Waulsort Marble: Varieties of Grain, Unfinished and Finished Specimens.

⁎⁎⁎ OPINIONS OF THE PRESS.
" Those who desire to attain skill in the art of painting woods and marbles will find advantage in consulting this book. . . . Some of the Working Men's Clubs should give their young men the opportunity to study it."—*Builder.*
" A comprehensive guide to the art. The explanations of the processes, the manipulation and management of the colours, and the beautifully executed plates will not be the least valuable to the student who aims at making his work a faithful transcript of nature."—*Building News.*

House Decoration.

ELEMENTARY DECORATION. A Guide to the Simpler Forms of Everyday Art, as applied to the Interior and Exterior Decoration of Dwelling Houses, &c. By JAMES W. FACEY, Jun. With 68 Cuts. 12mo, 2s. cloth limp.

PRACTICAL HOUSE DECORATION : A Guide to the Art of Ornamental Painting, the Arrangement of Colours in Apartments, and the principles of Decorative Design. With some Remarks upon the Nature and Properties of Pigments. By JAMES WILLIAM FACEY, Author of " Elementary Decoration," &c. With numerous Illustrations. 12mo, 2s. 6d. cloth limp.

N.B.—The above Two Works together in One Vol., strongly half-bound, 5s.

Colour.

A GRAMMAR OF COLOURING. Applied to Decorative Painting and the Arts. By GEORGE FIELD. New Edition, Revised, Enlarged, and adapted to the use of the Ornamental Painter and Designer. By ELLIS A. DAVIDSON. With New Coloured Diagrams and Engravings. 12mo, 3s. 6d. cloth boards.

"The book is a most useful *resume* of the properties of pigments."—*Builder.*

House Painting, Graining, etc.

HOUSE PAINTING, GRAINING, MARBLING, AND SIGN WRITING, A Practical Manual of. By ELLIS A. DAVIDSON. Sixth Edition. With Coloured Plates and Wood Engravings. 12mo, 6s. cloth boards.

" A mass of information, of use to the amateur and of value to the practical man."—*English Mechanic.*
"Simply invaluable to the youngster entering upon this particular calling, and highly serviceable to the man who is practising it."—*Furniture Gazette.*

Decorators, Receipts for.

THE DECORATOR'S ASSISTANT : A Modern Guide to Decorative Artists and Amateurs, Painters, Writers, Gilders, &c. Containing upwards of 600 Receipts, Rules and Instructions ; with a variety of Information for General Work connected with every Class of Interior and Exterior Decorations, &c. Fourth Edition, Revised. 152 pp., crown 8vo, 1s. in wrapper.

" Full of receipts of value to decorators, painters, gilders, &c. The book contains the gist of larger treatises on colour and technical processes. It would be difficult to meet with a work so full of varied information on the painter's art."—*Building News.*
" We recommend the work to all who, whether for pleasure or profit, require a guide to decoration."—*Plumber and Decorator.*

Moyr Smith on Interior Decoration.

ORNAMENTAL INTERIORS, ANCIENT AND MODERN. By J. MOYR SMITH. Super-royal 8vo, with 32 full-page Plates and numerous smaller Illustrations, handsomely bound in cloth, gilt top, price 18s.

' The book is well illustrated and handsomely got up, and contains some true criticism and a good many good examples of decorative treatment."—*The Builder.*
' This is the most elaborate and beautiful work on the artistic decoration of interiors that we have seen. . . . The scrolls, panels and other designs from the author's own pen are very beautiful and chaste ; but he takes care that the designs of other men shall figure even more than his own."—*Liverpool Albion.*
" To all who take an interest in elaborate domestic ornament this handsome volume will be welcome."—*Graphic.*

British and Foreign Marbles.

MARBLE DECORATION and the Terminology of British and Foreign Marbles. A Handbook for Students. By GEORGE H. BLAGROVE, Author of " Shoring and its Application," &c. With 28 Illustrations. Crown 8vo, 3s. 6d. cloth.

" This most useful and much wanted handbook should be in the hands of every architect and builder."—*Building World.*
" It is an excellent manual for students, and interesting to artistic readers generally."—*Saturday Review.*
" A carefully and usefully written treatise ; the work is essentially practical."—*Scotsman.*

Marble Working, etc.

MARBLE AND MARBLE WORKERS : A Handbook for Architects, Artists, Masons and Students. By ARTHUR LEE, Author of " A Visit to Carrara," " The Working of Marble," &c. Small crown 8vo, 2s. cloth.

" A really valuable addition to the technical literature of architects and masons.'—*Building News.*

C

DELAMOTTE'S WORKS ON ILLUMINATION AND ALPHABETS.

A PRIMER OF THE ART OF ILLUMINATION, for the Use of Beginners: with a Rudimentary Treatise on the Art, Practical Directions for its exercise, and Examples taken from Illuminated MSS., printed in Gold and Colours. By F. DELAMOTTE. New and Cheaper Edition. Small 4to, 6s. ornamental boards.

"The examples of ancient MSS. recommended to the student, which, with much good sense, the author chooses from collections accessible to all, are selected with judgment and knowledge, as well as taste."—*Athenæum.*

ORNAMENTAL ALPHABETS, Ancient and Mediæval, from the Eighth Century, with Numerals; including Gothic, Church-Text, large and small, German, Italian, Arabesque, Initials for Illumination, Monograms, Crosses, &c. &c., for the use of Architectural and Engineering Draughtsmen, Missal Painters, Masons, Decorative Painters, Lithographers, Engravers, Carvers, &c. &c. Collected and Engraved by F. DELAMOTTE, and printed in Colours. New and Cheaper Edition. Royal 8vo, oblong, 2s. 6d. ornamental boards.

"For those who insert enamelled sentences round gilded chalices, who blazon shop legends over shop-doors, who letter church walls with pithy sentences from the Decalogue, this book will be useful."—*Athenæum.*

EXAMPLES OF MODERN ALPHABETS, Plain and Ornamental; including German, Old English, Saxon, Italic, Perspective, Greek, Hebrew, Court Hand, Engrossing, Tuscan, Riband, Gothic, Rustic, and Arabesque; with several Original Designs, and an Analysis of the Roman and Old English Alphabets, large and small, and Numerals, for the use of Draughtsmen, Surveyors, Masons, Decorative Painters, Lithographers, Engravers, Carvers, &c. Collected and Engraved by F. DELAMOTTE, and printed in Colours. New and Cheaper Edition. Royal 8vo, oblong, 2s. 6d. ornamental boards.

"There is comprised in it every possible shape into which the letters of the alphabet and numerals can be formed, and the talent which has been expended in the conception of the various plain and ornamental letters is wonderful."—*Standard.*

MEDIÆVAL ALPHABETS AND INITIALS FOR ILLUMI-NATORS. By F. G. DELAMOTTE. Containing 21 Plates and Illuminated Title, printed in Gold and Colours. With an Introduction by J. WILLIS BROOKS. Fourth and Cheaper Edition. Small 4to, 4s. ornamental boards.

"A volume in which the letters of the alphabet come forth glorified in gilding and all the colours of the prism interwoven and intertwined and intermingled."—*Sun.*

THE EMBROIDERER'S BOOK OF DESIGN. Containing Initials, Emblems, Cyphers, Monograms, Ornamental Borders, Ecclesiastical Devices, Mediæval and Modern Alphabets, and National Emblems. Collected by F. DELAMOTTE, and printed in Colours. Oblong royal 8vo, 1s. 6d. ornamental wrapper.

"The book will be of great assistance to ladies and young children who are endowed with the art of plying the needle in this most ornamental and useful pretty work."—*East Anglian Times.*

Wood Carving.

INSTRUCTIONS IN WOOD-CARVING, for Amateurs; with Hints on Design. By A LADY. With Ten Plates. New and Cheaper Edition. Crown 8vo, 2s. in emblematic wrapper.

"The handicraft of the wood-carver, so well as a book can impart it, may be learnt from 'A Lady's' publication."—*Athenæum.*
"The directions given are plain and easily understood."—*English Mechanic.*

Glass Painting.

GLASS STAINING AND THE ART OF PAINTING ON GLASS. From the German of Dr. GESSERT and EMANUEL OTTO FROMBERG. With an Appendix on THE ART OF ENAMELLING. 12mo, 2s. 6d. cloth limp.

Letter Painting.

THE ART OF LETTER PAINTING MADE EASY. By JAMES GREIG BADENOCH. With 12 full-page Engravings of Examples, 1s. 6d. cloth limp.

"The system is a simple one, but quite original, and well worth the careful attention of letter painters. It can be easily mastered and remembered."—*Building News.*

CARPENTRY, TIMBER, etc.

Tredgold's Carpentry, Revised & Enlarged by Tarn.

THE ELEMENTARY PRINCIPLES OF CARPENTRY. A Treatise on the Pressure and Equilibrium of Timber Framing, the Resistance of Timber, and the Construction of Floors, Arches, Bridges, Roofs, Uniting Iron and Stone with Timber, &c. To which is added an Essay on the Nature and Properties of Timber, &c., with Descriptions of the kinds of Wood used in Building; also numerous Tables of the Scantlings of Timber for different purposes, the Specific Gravities of Materials, &c. By THOMAS TREDGOLD, C.E. With an Appendix of Specimens of Various Roofs of Iron and Stone, Illustrated. Seventh Edition, thoroughly revised and considerably enlarged by E. WYNDHAM TARN, M.A., Author of "The Science of Building," &c. With 61 Plates, Portrait of the Author, and several Woodcuts. In one large vol., 4to, price £1 5s. cloth.

"Ought to be in every architect's and every builder's library."—*Builder.*

" A work whose monumental excellence must commend it wherever skilful carpentry is concerned. The author's principles are rather confirmed than impaired by time. The additional plates are of great intrinsic value."—*Building News.*

Woodworking Machinery.

WOODWORKING MACHINERY : Its Rise, Progress, and Construction. With Hints on the Management of Saw Mills and the Economical Conversion of Timber. Illustrated with Examples of Recent Designs by leading English, French, and American Engineers. By M. POWIS BALE, A.M.Inst.C.E., M.I.M.E. Large crown 8vo, 12s. 6d. cloth.

"Mr. Bale is evidently an expert on the subject and he has collected so much information that his book is all-sufficient for builders and others engaged in the conversion of timber."—*Architect.*

"The most comprehensive compendium of wood-working machinery we have seen. The author is a thorough master of his subject."—*Building News.*

" The appearance of this book at the present time will, we should think, give a considerable impetus to the onward march of the machinist engaged in the designing and manufacture of wood-working machines. It should be in the office of every wood-working factory."—*English Mechanic.*

Saw Mills.

SAW MILLS : Their Arrangement and Management, and the Economical Conversion of Timber. (A Companion Volume to " Woodworking Machinery.") By M. POWIS BALE. With numerous Illustrations. Crow 8vo, 10s. 6d. cloth.

" The *administration* of a large sawing establishment is discussed, and the subject examined from a financial standpoint. We could not desire a more complete or practical treatise."—*Builder.*

" We highly recommend Mr. Bale's work to the attention and perusal of all those who are engaged in the art of wood conversion, or who are about building or remodelling saw-mills on improved principles."—*Building News.*

Carpentering.

THE CARPENTER'S NEW GUIDE ; or, Book of Lines for Carpenters; comprising all the Elementary Principles essential for acquiring a knowledge of Carpentry. Founded on the late PETER NICHOLSON's Standard Work. A New Edition, Revised by ARTHUR ASHPITEL, F.S.A. Together with Practical Rules on Drawing, by GEORGE PYNE. With 74 Plates, 4to, £1 1s. cloth.

Handrailing and Stairbuilding.

A PRACTICAL TREATISE ON HANDRAILING : Showing New and Simple Methods for Finding the Pitch of the Plank, Drawing the Moulds, Bevelling, Jointing-up, and Squaring the Wreath. By GEORGE COLLINGS. Second Edition, Revised and Enlarged, to which is added A TREATISE ON STAIRBUILDING. With Plates and Diagrams. 12mo, 2s. 6d. cloth limp.

" Will be found of practical utility in the execution of this difficult branch of joinery."—*Builder.*

" Almost every difficult phase of this somewhat intricate branch of joinery is elucidated by the aid of plates and explanatory letterpress."—*Furniture Gazette.*

Circular Work.

CIRCULAR WORK IN CARPENTRY AND JOINERY : A Practical Treatise on Circular Work of Single and Double Curvature. By GEORGE COLLINGS, Author of " A Practical Treatise on Handrailing." Illustrated with numerous Diagrams. Second Edition. 12mo, 2s. 6d. cloth limp.

" An excellent example of what a book of this kind should be. Cheap in price, clear in definition and practical in the examples selected."—*Builder.*

Timber Merchant's Companion.

THE TIMBER MERCHANT'S AND BUILDER'S COM-PANION. Containing New and Copious Tables of the Reduced Weight and Measurement of Deals and Battens, of all sizes, from One to a Thousand Pieces, and the relative Price that each size bears per Lineal Foot to any given Price per Petersburg Standard Hundred; the Price per Cube Foot of Square Timber to any given Price per Load of 50 Feet; the proportionate Value of Deals and Battens by the Standard, to Square Timber by the Load of 50 Feet; the readiest mode of ascertaining the Price of Scantling per Lineal Foot of any size, to any given Figure per Cube Foot, &c. &c.   By WILLIAM DOWSING. Fourth Edition, Revised and Corrected. Cr. 8vo, 3s. cl.

"We are glad to see a fourth edition of these admirable tables, which for correctness and simplicity of arrangement leave nothing to be desired."—*Timber Trades Journal.*

"An exceedingly well-arranged, clear, and concise manual of tables for the use of all who buy or sell timber."—*Journal of Forestry.*

Practical Timber Merchant.

THE PRACTICAL TIMBER MERCHANT. Being a Guide for the use of Building Contractors, Surveyors, Builders, &c., comprising useful Tables for all purposes connected with the Timber Trade, Marks of Wood, Essay on the Strength of Timber, Remarks on the Growth of Timber, &c.   By W. RICHARDSON. Fcap. 8vo, 3s. 6d. cloth.

"This handy manual contains much valuable information for the use of timber merchants, builders, foresters, and all others connected with the growth, sale, and manufacture of timber."—*Journal of Forestry.*

Timber Freight Book.

THE TIMBER MERCHANT'S, SAW MILLER'S, AND IMPORTER'S FREIGHT BOOK AND ASSISTANT. Comprising Rules, Tables, and Memoranda relating to the Timber Trade. By WILLIAM RICHARDSON, Timber Broker; together with a Chapter on "SPEEDS OF SAW MILL MACHINERY," by M. POWIS BALE, M.I.M.E., &c. 12mo, 3s. 6d. cl. boards.

"A very useful manual of rules, tables, and memoranda relating to the timber trade. We recommend it as a compendium of calculation to all timber measurers and merchants, and as supplying a real want in the trade."—*Building News.*

Packing-Case Makers, Tables for.

PACKING-CASE TABLES; showing the number of Super-ficial Feet in Boxes or Packing-Cases, from six inches square and upwards. By W. RICHARDSON, Timber-Broker. Third Edition. Oblong 4to, 3s. 6d. cl.

"Invaluable labour-saving tables."—*Ironmonger.*

"Will save much labour and calculation."—*Grocer.*

Superficial Measurement.

THE TRADESMAN'S GUIDE TO SUPERFICIAL MEA-SUREMENT. Tables calculated from 1 to 200 inches in length, by 1 to 108 inches in breadth. For the use of Architects, Surveyors, Engineers, Timber Merchants, Builders, &c. By JAMES HAWKINGS. Third Edition. Fcap., 3s. 6d. cloth.

"A useful collection of tables to facilitate rapid calculation of surfaces. The exact area of any surface of which the limits have been ascertained can be instantly determined. The book will be found of the greatest utility to all engaged in building operations."—*Scotsman.*

"These tables will be found of great assistance to all who require to make calculations in super-ficial measurement."—*English Mechanic.*

Forestry.

THE ELEMENTS OF FORESTRY. Designed to afford In-formation concerning the Planting and Care of Forest Trees for Ornament or Profit, with Suggestions upon the Creation and Care of Woodlands. By F. B. HOUGH. Large crown 8vo, 10s. cloth.

Timber Importer's Guide.

THE TIMBER IMPORTER'S, TIMBER MERCHANT'S AND BUILDER'S STANDARD GUIDE. By RICHARD E. GRANDY. Compris-ing an Analysis of Deal Standards, Home and Foreign, with Comparative Values and Tabular Arrangements for fixing Nett Landed Cost on Baltic and North American Deals, including all intermediate Expenses, Freight, Insurance, &c. &c. Together with copious Information for the Retailer and Builder. Third Edition, Revised. 12mo, 2s. cloth limp.

"Everything it pretends to be: built up gradually, it leads one from a forest to a treenall, and throws in, as a makeweight, a host of material concerning bricks, columns, cisterns, &c."—*English Mechanic.*

MARINE ENGINEERING, NAVIGATION, etc.

Chain Cables.

CHAIN CABLES AND CHAINS. Comprising Sizes and Curves of Links, Studs, &c., Iron for Cables and Chains, Chain Cable and Chain Making, Forming and Welding Links, Strength of Cables and Chains, Certificates for Cables, Marking Cables, Prices of Chain Cables and Chains, Historical Notes, Acts of Parliament, Statutory Tests, Charges for Testing, List of Manufacturers of Cables, &c. &c. By THOMAS W. TRAILL, F.E.R.N., M. Inst. C.E., Engineer Surveyor in Chief, Board of Trade, Inspector of Chain Cable and Anchor Proving Establishments, and General Superintendent, Lloyd's Committee on Proving Establishments. With numerous Tables, Illustrations and Lithographic Drawings. Folio, £2 2s. cloth, bevelled boards.

"It contains a vast amount of valuable information. Nothing seems to be wanting to make it a complete and standard work of reference on the subject."—*Nautical Magazine*.

Marine Engineering.

MARINE ENGINES AND STEAM VESSELS (A Treatise on). By ROBERT MURRAY, C.E. Eighth Edition, thoroughly Revised, with considerable Additions by the Author and by GEORGE CARLISLE, C.E., Senior Surveyor to the Board of Trade at Liverpool. 12mo, 5s. cloth boards.

" Well adapted to give the young steamship engineer or marine engine and boiler maker a general introduction into his practical work."—*Mechanical World*.

" We feel sure that this thoroughly revised edition will continue to be as popular in the future as it has been in the past, as, for its size, it contains more useful information than any similar treatise."—*Industries*.

The information given is both sound and sensible, and well qualified to direct young seagoing hands on the straight road to the extra chief's certificate. Most useful to surveyors, inspectors, draughtsmen, and all young engineers who take an interest in their profession."—*Glasgow Herald*.

"An indispensable manual for the student of marine engineering."—*Liverpool Mercury*.

Pocket-Book for Naval Architects and Shipbuilders.

THE NAVAL ARCHITECT'S AND SHIPBUILDER'S POCKET-BOOK of Formulæ, Rules, and Tables, and MARINE ENGINEER'S AND SURVEYOR'S Handy Book of Reference. By CLEMENT MACKROW, Member of the Institution of Naval Architects, Naval Draughtsman. Fourth Edition, Revised. With numerous Diagrams, &c. Fcap., 12s. 6d. strongly bound in leather.

"Will be found to contain the most useful tables and formulæ required by shipbuilders, carefully collected from the best authorities, and put together in a popular and simple form."—*Engineer*.

" The professional shipbuilder has now, in a convenient and accessible form, reliable data for solving many of the numerous problems that present themselves in the course of his work."—*Iron*.

"There is scarcely a subject on which a naval architect or shipbuilder can require to refresh his memory which will not be found within the covers of Mr. Mackrow's book."—*English Mechanic*.

Pocket-Book for Marine Engineers.

A POCKET-BOOK OF USEFUL TABLES AND FORMULÆ FOR MARINE ENGINEERS. By FRANK PROCTOR, A.I.N.A. Third Edition. Royal 32mo, leather, gilt edges, with strap, 4s.

"We recommend it to our readers as going far to supply a long-felt want."—*Naval Science*.

"A most useful companion to all marine engineers."—*United Service Gazette*.

Introduction to Marine Engineering.

ELEMENTARY ENGINEERING : A Manual for Young Marine Engineers and Apprentices. In the Form of Questions and Answers on Metals, Alloys, Strength of Materials, Construction and Management of Marine Engines and Boilers, Geometry, &c. &c. With an Appendix of Useful Tables. By JOHN SHERREN BREWER, Government Marine Surveyor, Hongkong. Small crown 8vo, 2s. cloth.

" Contains much valuable information for the class for whom it is intended, especially in the chapters on the management of boilers and engines."—*Nautical Magazine*.

" A useful introduction to the more elaborate text books."—*Scotsman*.

" To a student who has the requisite desire and resolve to attain a thorough knowledge, Mr. Brewer offers decidedly useful help."—*Athenæum*.

Navigation.

PRACTICAL NAVIGATION. Consisting of THE SAILOR'S SEA-BOOK, by JAMES GREENWOOD and W. H. ROSSER; together with the requisite Mathematical and Nautical Tables for the Working of the Problems, by HENRY LAW, C.E., and Professor J. R. YOUNG. Illustrated. 12mo, 7s. strongly half-bound.

MINING AND METALLURGY.

Metalliferous Mining in the United Kingdom.

BRITISH MINING: A Treatise on the History, Discovery, Practical Development, and Future Prospects of Metalliferous Mines in the United Kingdom. By ROBERT HUNT, F.R.S., Keeper of Mining Records; Editor of "Ure's Dictionary of Arts, Manufactures, and Mines," &c. Upwards of 950 pp., with 230 Illustrations. Second Edition, Revised. Super-royal 8vo, £2 2s. cloth.

"One of the most valuable works of reference of modern times. Mr. Hunt, as keeper of mining records of the United Kingdom, has had opportunities for such a task not enjoyed by anyone else, and has evidently made the most of them. . . . The language and style adopted are good, and the treatment of the various subjects laborious, conscientious, and scientific."—*Engineering*.

"The book is, in fact, a treasure-house of statistical information on mining subjects, and we know of no other work embodying so great a mass of matter of this kind. Were this the only merit of Mr. Hunt s volume, it would be sufficient to render it indispensable in this library of everyone interested in the development of the mining and metallurgical industries of this country."—*Athenæum*.

"A mass of information not elsewhere available, and of the greatest value to those who may be interested in our great mineral industries."—*Engineer*.

"A sound, business-like collection of interesting facts. . . . The amount of information Mr. Hunt has brought together is enormous. . . . The volume appears likely to convey more instruction upon the subject than any work hitherto published."—*Mining Journal*.

Colliery Management.

THE COLLIERY MANAGER'S HANDBOOK: A Comprehensive Treatise on the Laying-out and Working of Collieries, Designed as a Book of Reference for Colliery Managers, and for the Use of Coal-Mining Students preparing for First-class Certificates. By CALEB PAMELY, Mining Engineer and Surveyor; Member of the North of England Institute of Mining and Mechanical Engineers; and Member of the South Wales Institute of Mining Engineers. With nearly 500 Plans, Diagrams, and other Illustrations. Medium 8vo, about 600 pages. Price £1 5s. strongly bound.

[Just published.

Coal and Iron.

THE COAL AND IRON INDUSTRIES OF THE UNITED KINGDOM. Comprising a Description of the Coal Fields, and of the Principal Seams of Coal, with Returns of their Produce and its Distribution, and Analyses of Special Varieties. Also an Account of the occurrence of Iron Ores in Veins or Seams; Analyses of each Variety; and a History of the Rise and Progress of Pig Iron Manufacture. By RICHARD MEADE, Assistant Keeper of Mining Records. With Maps. 8vo, £1 8s. cloth.

"The book is one which must find a place on the shelves of all interested in coal and iron production, and in the iron, steel, and other metallurgical industries."—*Engineer*.

"Of this book we may unreservedly say that it is the best of its class which we have ever met. . . A book of reference which no one engaged in the iron or coal trades should omit from his library."—*Iron and Coal Trades Review*.

Prospecting for Gold and other Metals.

THE PROSPECTOR'S HANDBOOK: A Guide for the Prospector and Traveller in Search of Metal-Bearing or other Valuable Minerals. By J. W. ANDERSON, M.A. (Camb.), F.R.G.S., Author of "Fiji and New Caledonia." Fifth Edition, thoroughly Revised and Enlarged. Small crown 8vo, 3s. 6d. cloth.

"Will supply a much felt want, especially among Colonists, in whose way are so often thrown many mineralogical specimens the value of which it is difficult to determine."—*Engineer*.

"How to find commercial minerals, and how to identify them when they are found, are the leading points to which attention is directed. The author has managed to pack as much practical detail into his pages as would supply material for a book three times its size."—*Mining Journal*.

Mining Notes and Formulæ.

NOTES AND FORMULÆ FOR MINING STUDENTS. By JOHN HERMAN MERIVALE, M.A., Certificated Colliery Manager, Professor of Mining in the Durham College of Science, Newcastle-upon-Tyne. Third Edition, Revised and Enlarged. Small crown 8vo, 2s. 6d. cloth.

"Invaluable to anyone who is working up for an examination on mining subjects."—*Coal and Iron Trades Review*.

"The author has done his work in an exceedingly creditable manner, and has produced a book that will be of service to students, and those who are practically engaged in mining operations."—*Engineer*.

"A vast amount of technical matter of the utmost value to mining engineers, and of considerable interest to students."—*Schoolmaster*.

Explosives.

A HANDBOOK ON MODERN EXPLOSIVES. Being a Practical Treatise on the Manufacture and Application of Dynamite, Gun-Cotton, Nitro-Glycerine and other Explosive Compounds. Including the Manufacture of Collodion-Cotton. By M. EISSLER, Mining Engineer and Metallurgical Chemist, Author of "The Metallurgy of Gold," &c. With about 100 Illustrations. Crown 8vo, 10s. 6d. cloth.

"Useful not only to the miner, but also to officers of both services to whom blasting and the use of explosives generally may at any time become a necessary auxiliary."—*Nature.*

"A veritable mine of information on the subject of explosives employed for military, mining and blasting purposes."—*Army and Navy Gazette.*

"The book is clearly written. Taken as a whole, we consider it an excellent little book and one that should be found of great service to miners and others who are engaged in work requiring the use of explosives."—*Athenæum.*

Gold, Metallurgy of.

THE METALLURGY OF GOLD : A Practical Treatise on the Metallurgical Treatment of Gold-bearing Ores. Including the Processes of Concentration and Chlorination, and the Assaying, Melting and Refining of Gold. By M. EISSLER, Mining Engineer and Metallurgical Chemist, formerly Assistant Assayer of the U. S. Mint, San Francisco. Third Edition, Revised and greatly Enlarged. With 187 Illustrations. Crown 8vo, 12s. 6d. cloth.

"This book thoroughly deserves its title of a 'Practical Treatise.' The whole process of gold milling, from the breaking of the quartz to the assay of the bullion, is described in clear and orderly narrative and with much, but not too much, fulness of detail."—*Saturday Review.*

"The work is a storehouse of information and valuable data, and we strongly recommend it to all professional men engaged in the gold-mining industry."—*Mining Journal*

Silver, Metallurgy of.

THE METALLURGY OF SILVER : A Practical Treatise on the Amalgamation, Roasting and Lixiviation of Silver Ores, Including the Assaying, Melting and Refining of Silver Bullion. By M. EISSLER, Author of "The Metallurgy of Gold" Second Edition, Enlarged. With 150 Illustrations. Crown 8vo, 10s. 6d. cloth. [*Just published.*

"A practical treatise, and a technical work which we are convinced will supply a long-felt want amongst practical men, and at the same time be of value to students and others indirectly connected with the industries."—*Mining Journal.*

"From first to last the book is thoroughly sound and reliable."—*Colliery Guardian.*

"For chemists, practical miners, assayers and investors alike, we do not know of any work on the subject so handy and yet so comprehensive."—*Glasgow Herald.*

Silver-Lead, Metallurgy of.

THE METALLURGY OF ARGENTIFEROUS LEAD : A Practical Treatise on the Smelting of Silver-Lead Ores and the Refining of Lead Bullion. Including Reports on various Smelting Establishments and Descriptions of Modern Furnaces and Plants in Europe and America. By M. EISSLER, M.E., Author of "The Metallurgy of Gold," &c. Crown 8vo. 400 pp., with numerous Illustrations, 12s. 6d. cloth. [*Just published.*

Metalliferous Minerals and Mining.

TREATISE ON METALLIFEROUS MINERALS AND MINING. By D. C. DAVIES, F.G.S., Mining Engineer, &c., Author of "A Treatise on Slate and Slate Quarrying." Illustrated with numerous Wood Engravings. Fourth Edition, carefully Revised. Crown 8vo, 12s. 6d. cloth.

"Neither the practical miner nor the general reader interested in mines can have a better book for his companion and his guide."—*Mining Journal.* [*Mining World.*

"We are doing our readers a service in calling their attention to this valuable work."—

"As a history of the present state of mining throughout the world this book has a real value, and it supplies an actual want."—*Athenæum.*

Earthy Minerals and Mining.

A TREATISE ON EARTHY & OTHER MINERALS AND MINING. By D. C. DAVIES, F.G.S. Uniform with, and forming a Companion Volume to, the same Author's "Metalliferous Minerals and Mining." With 76 Wood Engravings. Second Edition. Crown 8vo, 12s. 6d. cloth.

"We do not remember to have met with any English work on mining matters that contains the same amount of information packed in equally convenient form."—*Academy.*

"We should be inclined to rank it as among the very best of the handy technical and trades manuals which have recently appeared."—*British Quarterly Review.*

Mineral Surveying and Valuing.

THE MINERAL SURVEYOR AND VALUER'S COMPLETE
GUIDE, *comprising a Treatise on Improved Mining Surveying and the Valua-
tion of Mining Properties, with New Traverse Tables.* By Wm. Lintern,
Mining and Civil Engineer. Third Edition, with an Appendix on "Magnetic
and Angular Surveying," with Records of the Peculiarities of Needle Dis-
turbances. With Four Plates of Diagrams. Plans, &c. 12mo, 4s. cloth.
" Mr. Lintern's book forms a valuable and thoroughly trustworthy guide."—*Iron and Coal
Trades Review.*
" This new edition must be of the highest value to colliery surveyors, proprietors and managers."—*Colliery Guardian.*

Asbestos and its Uses.

ASBESTOS : *Its Properties, Occurrence and Uses.* With some
Account of the Mines of Italy and Canada. By Robert H. Jones. With
Eight Collotype Plates and other Illustrations. Crown 8vo, 12s. 6d. cloth.
" An interesting and invaluable work."—*Colliery Guardian.*
" We counsel our readers to get this exceedingly interesting work for themselves ; they will
find in it much that is suggestive, and a great deal that is of immediate and practical usefulness."—
Builder.
" A valuable addition to the architect's and engineer's library."—*Building News.*

Underground Pumping Machinery.

MINE DRAINAGE. Being a Complete and Practical Treatise
on Direct-Acting Underground Steam Pumping Machinery, with a Description of a large number of the best known Engines, their General Utility and
the Special Sphere of their Action, the Mode of their Application, and
their merits compared with other forms of Pumping Machinery. By Stephen
Michell. 8vo, 15s. cloth.
" Will be highly esteemed by colliery owners and lessees, mining engineers, and students
generally who require to be acquainted with the best means of securing the drainage of mines. It
is a most valuable work, and stands almost alone in the literature of steam pumping machinery."—
Colliery Guardian.
" Much valuable information is given, so that the book is thoroughly worthy of an extensive
circulation amongst practical men and purchasers of machinery.' —*Mining Journal.*

Mining Tools.

A MANUAL OF MINING TOOLS. For the Use of Mine
Managers, Agents, Students, &c. By William Morgans, Lecturer on Prac-
tical Mining at the Bristol School of Mines. 12mo, 2s. 6d. cloth limp.
ATLAS OF ENGRAVINGS to Illustrate the above, contain-
ing 235 Illustrations of Mining Tools, drawn to scale. 4to, 4s. 6d. cloth.
" Students in the science of mining, and overmen, captains, managers, and viewers may gain
practical knowledge and useful hints by the study of Mr. Morgans' manual."—*Colliery Guardian.*
" A valuable work, which will tend materially to improve our mining literature."—*Mining
Journal.*

Coal Mining.

COAL AND COAL MINING : *A Rudimentary Treatise on.* By
the late Sir Warington W. Smyth, M.A., F.R.S., &c., Chief Inspector of the
Mines of the Crown. Seventh Edition, Revised and Enlarged. With
numerous Illustrations. 12mo, 4s. cloth boards.
" As an outline is given of every known coal-field in this and other countries, as well as of the
principal methods of working, the book will doubtless interest a very large number of readers."—
Mining Journal.

Subterraneous Surveying.

SUBTERRANEOUS SURVEYING, *Elementary and Practical
Treatise on,* with and without the Magnetic Needle. By Thomas Fenwick,
Surveyor of Mines, and Thomas Baker, C.E. Illust. 12mo, 3s. cloth boards.

Granite Quarrying.

GRANITES AND OUR GRANITE INDUSTRIES. By
George F. Harris, F.G.S., Membre de la Société Belge de Géologie, Lec-
turer on Economic Geology at the Birkbeck Institution, &c. With Illustra-
tions. Crown 8vo, 2s. 6d. cloth.
" A clearly and well-written manual for persons engaged or interested in the granite industry.'
—*Scotsman.*
" An interesting work, which will be deservedly esteemed."—*Colliery Guardian.*
" An exceedingly interesting and valuable monograph on a subject which has hitherto received
unaccountably little attention in the shape of systematic literary treatment."—*Scottish Leader.*

ELECTRICITY ELECTRICAL ENGINEERING, etc.

Electrical Engineering.

THE ELECTRICAL ENGINEER'S POCKET-BOOK OF MODERN RULES, FORMULÆ, TABLES AND DATA. By H. R. KEMPE, M.Inst.E.E., A.M.Inst.C.E., Technical Officer Postal Telegraphs, Author of "A Handbook of Electrical Testing," &c. With numerous Illustrations, royal 32mo, oblong, 5s. leather. [Just published.

"There is very little in the shape of formulæ or data which the electrician is likely to want in a hurry which cannot be found in its pages."—Practical Engineer.
"A very useful book of reference for daily use in practical electrical engineering and its various applications to the industries of the present day."—Iron.
"It is the best book of its kind."—Electrical Engineer.
"The Electrical Engineer's Pocket-Book is a good one."—Electrician.
"Strongly recommended to those engaged in the various electrical industries."—Electrical Review.

Electric Lighting.

ELECTRIC LIGHT FITTING: A Handbook for Working Electrical Engineers, embodying Practical Notes on Installation Management. By JOHN W. URQUHART, Electrician, Author of "Electric Light," &c. With numerous Illustrations, crown 8vo, 5s. cloth. [Just published.

"This volume deals with what may be termed the mechanics of electric lighting, and is addressed to men who are already engaged in the work or are training for it. The work traverses a great deal of ground, and may be read as a sequel to the same author's useful work on 'Electric Light.'"—Electrician.
"This is an attempt to state in the simplest language the precautions which should be adopted in installing the electric light, and to give information, for the guidance of those who have to run the plant when installed. The book is well worth the perusal of the workmen for whom it is written."—Electrical Review.
'Eminently practical and useful. . . . Ought to be in the hands of everyone in charge of an electric light plant."—Electrical Engineer.
"A really capital book, which we have no hesitation in recommending to the notice of working electricians and electrical engineers."—Mechanical World.

Electric Light.

ELECTRIC LIGHT : Its Production and Use. Embodying Plain Directions for the Treatment of Dynamo-Electric Machines, Batteries, Accumulators, and Electric Lamps. By J. W. URQUHART, C.E., Author of "Electric Light Fitting," &c. Fourth Edition, Revised, with Large Additions and 145 Illustrations. Crown 8vo, 7s. 6d. cloth. [Just published.

"The book is by far the best that we have yet met with on the subject."—Athenæum.
"It is the only work at present available which gives, in language intelligible for the most part to the ordinary reader, a general but concise history of the means which have been adopted up to the present time in producing the electric light."—Metropolitan.
"The book contains a general account of the means adopted in producing the electric light, not only as obtained from voltaic or galvanic batteries, but treats at length of the dynamo-electric machine in several of its forms."—Colliery Guardian.

Construction of Dynamos.

DYNAMO CONSTRUCTION : A Practical Handbook for the Use of Engineer Constructors and Electricians in Charge. With Examples of leading English, American and Continental Dynamos and Motors. By J. W. URQUHART, Author of "Electric Light," &c. Crown 8vo, 7s. 6d. cloth. [Just published.

"The author has produced a book for which a demand has long existed. The subject is treated in a thoroughly practical manner."—Mechanical World.

Dynamic Electricity and Magnetism.

THE ELEMENTS OF DYNAMIC ELECTRICITY AND MAGNETISM. By PHILIP ATKINSON, A.M., Ph.D. Crown 8vo. 400 pp. With 120 Illustrations. 10s. 6d. cloth. [Just published.

Text Book of Electricity.

THE STUDENT'S TEXT-BOOK OF ELECTRICITY. By HENRY M. NOAD, Ph.D., F.R.S., F.C.S. New Edition, carefully Revised. With an Introduction and Additional Chapters, by W. H. PREECE, M.I.C.E., Vice-President of the Society of Telegraph Engineers, &c. With 470 Illustrations. Crown 8vo, 12s. 6d. cloth.

"We can recommend Dr. Noad's book for clear style, great range of subject, a good index and a plethora of woodcuts. Such collections as the present are indispensable."—Athenæum.
"An admirable text book for every student — beginner or advanced — of electricity."—Engineering.

Electric Lighting.

THE ELEMENTARY PRINCIPLES OF ELECTRIC LIGHT-
ING. By ALAN A. CAMPBELL SWINTON, Associate I.E.E. Second Edition,
Enlarged and Revised. With 16 Illustrations. Crown 8vo, 1s. 6d. cloth.
"Anyone who desires a short and thoroughly clear exposition of the elementary principles of
electric-lighting cannot do better than read this little work."—*Bradford Observer.*

Electricity.

A MANUAL OF ELECTRICITY : Including Galvanism, Mag-
netism, Dia-Magnetism, Electro-Dynamics, Magno-Electricity, and the Electric
Telegraph. By HENRY M. NOAD, Ph.D., F.R.S., F.C.S. Fourth Edition.
With 500 Woodcuts. 8vo, £1 4s. cloth.
"It is worthy of a place in the library of every public institution."—*Mining Journal.*

Dynamo Construction.

HOW TO MAKE A DYNAMO : A Practical Treatise for Amateurs.
Containing numerous Illustrations and Detailed Instructions for Constructing a Small Dynamo, to Produce the Electric Light. By ALFRED CROFTS.
Third Edition, Revised and Enlarged. Crown 8vo, 2s. cloth.
"The instructions given in this unpretentious little book are sufficiently clear and explicit to
enable any amateur mechanic possessed of average skill and the usual tools to be found in an
amateur's workshop, to build a practical dynamo machine."—*Electrician.*

NATURAL SCIENCE, etc.

Pneumatics and Acoustics.

PNEUMATICS : including Acoustics and the Phenomena of Wind
Currents, for the Use of Beginners. By CHARLES TOMLINSON, F.R.S.
F.C.S., &c. Fourth Edition, Enlarged. 12mo, 1s. 6d. cloth.
" Beginners in the study of this important application of science could not have a better manual."
—*Scotsman.*   " A valuable and suitable text-book for students of Acoustics and the Pheno-
mena of Wind Currents."—*Schoolmaster.*

Conchology.

A MANUAL OF THE MOLLUSCA : Being a Treatise on Recent
and Fossil Shells. By S. P. WOODWARD, A.L.S., F.G.S., late Assistant
Palæontologist in the British Museum. With an Appendix on *Recent and*
Fossil Conchological Discoveries, by RALPH TATE, A.L.S., F.G.S. Illustrated
by A. N. WATERHOUSE and JOSEPH WILSON LOWRY. With 23 Plates and
upwards of 300 Woodcuts. Reprint of Fourth Ed., 1880. Cr. 8vo, 7s. 6d. cl.
" A most valuable storehouse of conchological and geological information."—*Science Gossip.*

Geology.

RUDIMENTARY TREATISE ON GEOLOGY, PHYSICAL
AND HISTORICAL. Consisting of "Physical Geology," which sets forth
the leading Principles of the Science; and "Historical Geology," which
treats of the Mineral and Organic Conditions of the Earth at each successive
epoch, especial reference being made to the British Series of Rocks. By
RALPH TATE, A.L.S., F.G.S., &c. With 250 Illustrations. 12mo, 5s. cloth.
" The fulness of the matter has elevated the book into a manual. Its information is exhaustive
and well arranged."—*School Board Chronicle.*

Geology and Genesis.

THE TWIN RECORDS OF CREATION ; or, Geology and
Genesis: their Perfect Harmony and Wonderful Concord. By GEORGE W.
VICTOR LE VAUX. Numerous Illustrations. Fcap. 8vo, 5s. cloth.
" A valuable contribution to the evidences of Revelation, and disposes very conclusively of the
arguments of those who would set God's Works against God's Word."—*The Rock.*

The Constellations.

STAR GROUPS : A Student's Guide to the Constellations. By
J. ELLARD GORE, F.R.A.S., M.R.I.A., &c., Author of " The Scenery of the
Heavens." With 30 Maps. Small 4to, 5s. cloth, silvered.   [*Just published.*

Astronomy.

ASTRONOMY. By the late Rev. ROBERT MAIN, M.A., F.R.S.,
formerly Radcliffe Observer at Oxford. Third Edition, Revised and Cor-
rected to the present time, by W. T. LYNN, B.A., F.R.A.S. 12mo, 2s. cloth.
" A sound and simple treatise, very carefully edited, and a capital book for beginners."—
Knowledge.   [*tional Times.*
" Accurately brought down to the requirements of the present time by Mr. Lynn."—*Educa-*

DR. LARDNER'S COURSE OF NATURAL PHILOSOPHY.

THE HANDBOOK OF MECHANICS. Enlarged and almost re-written by BENJAMIN LOEWY, F.R.A.S. With 378 Illustrations. Post 8vo, 6s. cloth.

"The perspicuity of the original has been retained, and chapters which had become obsolete have been replaced by others of more modern character. The explanations throughout are studiously popular, and care has been taken to show the application of the various branches of physics to the industrial arts, and to the practical business of life."—*Mining Journal.*

"Mr. Loewy has carefully revised the book, and brought it up to modern requirements."—*Nature.*

"Natural philosophy has had few exponents more able or better skilled in the art of popularising the subject than Dr. Lardner; and Mr. Loewy is doing good service in fitting this treatise, and the others of the series, for use at the present time."—*Scotsman.*

THE HANDBOOK OF HYDROSTATICS AND PNEUMATICS. New Edition, Revised and Enlarged, by BENJAMIN LOEWY, F.R.A.S. With 236 Illustrations. Post 8vo, 5s. cloth.

"For those 'who desire to attain an accurate knowledge of physical science without the profound methods of mathematical investigation,' this work is not merely intended, but well adapted."—*Chemical News.*

"The volume before us has been carefully edited, augmented to nearly twice the bulk of the former edition, and all the most recent matter has been added. . . . It is a valuable text-book."—*Nature.*

"Candidates for pass examinations will find it, we think, specially suited to their requirements." *English Mechanic.*

THE HANDBOOK OF HEAT. Edited and almost entirely re-written by BENJAMIN LOEWY, F.R.A.S., &c. 117 Illustrations. Post 8vo, 6s. cloth.

"The style is always clear and precise, and conveys instruction without leaving any cloudiness or lurking doubts behind."—*Engineering.*

"A most exhaustive book on the subject on which it treats, and is so arranged that it can be understood by all who desire to attain an accurate knowledge of physical science. . . . . Mr. Loewy has included all the latest discoveries in the varied laws and effects of heat."—*Standard.*

"A complete and handy text-book for the use of students and general readers."—*English Mechanic.*

THE HANDBOOK OF OPTICS. By DIONYSIUS LARDNER, D.C.L., formerly Professor of Natural Philosophy and Astronomy in University College, London. New Edition. Edited by T. OLVER HARDING, B.A. Lond., of University College, London. With 298 Illustrations. Small 8vo, 448 pages, 5s. cloth.

"Written by one of the ablest English scientific writers, beautifully and elaborately illustrated." *Mechanic's Magazine.*

THE HANDBOOK OF ELECTRICITY, MAGNETISM, AND ACOUSTICS. By Dr. LARDNER. Ninth Thousand. Edit. by GEORGE CAREY FOSTER, B.A., F.C.S. With 400 Illustrations. Small 8vo, 5s. cloth.

"The book could not have been entrusted to anyone better calculated to preserve the terse and lucid style of Lardner, while correcting his errors and bringing up his work to the present state of scientific knowledge."—*Popular Science Review.*

THE HANDBOOK OF ASTRONOMY. Forming a Companion to the "Handbook of Natural Philosophy." By DIONYSIUS LARDNER, D.C.L., formerly Professor of Natural Philosophy and Astronomy in University College, London. Fourth Edition. Revised and Edited by EDWIN DUNKIN, F.R.A.S., Royal Observatory, Greenwich. With 38 Plates and upwards of 100 Woodcuts. In One Vol., small 8vo, 550 pages, 9s. 6d. cloth.

"Probably no other book contains the same amount of information in so compendious and well-arranged a form—certainly none at the price at which this is offered to the public."—*Athenæum.*

"We can do no other than pronounce this work a most valuable manual of astronomy, and we strongly recommend it to all who wish to acquire a general—but at the same time correct—acquaintance with this sublime science."—*Quarterly Journal of Science.*

"One of the most deservedly popular books on the subject . . . We would recommend not only the student of the elementary principles of the science, but he who aims at mastering the higher and mathematical branches of astronomy, not to be without this work beside him."—*Practical Magazine.*

Dr. Lardner's Electric Telegraph.

THE ELECTRIC TELEGRAPH. By Dr. LARDNER. Re-vised and Re-written by E. B. BRIGHT, F.R.A.S. 140 Illustrations. Small 8vo, 2s. 6d. cloth.

"One of the most readable books extant on the Electric Telegraph."—*English Mechanic.*

DR. LARDNER'S MUSEUM OF SCIENCE AND ART.

THE MUSEUM OF SCIENCE AND ART. Edited by
Dionysius Lardner, D.C.L., formerly Professor of Natural Philosophy and
Astronomy in University College, London. With upwards of 1,200 Engravings on Wood. In 6 Double Volumes, £1 1s., in a new and elegant cloth binding; or handsomely bound in half-morocco, 31s. 6d.

*** Opinions of the Press.

"This series, besides affording popular but sound instruction on scientific subjects, with which
the humblest man in the country ought to be acquainted, also undertakes that teaching of 'Common Things' which every well-wisher of his kind is anxious to promote. Many thousand copies of
this serviceable publication have been printed, in the belief and hope that the desire for instruction
and improvement widely prevails; and we have no fear that such enlightened faith will meet with
disappointment."—*Times.*

"A cheap and interesting publication, alike informing and attractive. The papers combine
subjects of importance and great scientific knowledge, considerable inductive powers, and a
popular style of treatment."—*Spectator.*

"The 'Museum of Science and Art' is the most valuable contribution that has ever been
made to the Scientific Instruction of every class of society."—Sir David Brewster, in the
North British Review.

"Whether we consider the liberality and beauty of the illustrations, the charm of the writing,
or the durable interest of the matter, we must express our belief that there is hardly to be found
among the new books one that would be welcomed by people of so many ages and classes as a
valuable present."—*Examiner.*

*** *Separate books formed from the above, suitable for Workmen's Libraries,*
Science Classes, etc.

Common Things Explained. Containing Air, Earth, Fire, Water, Time,
Man, the Eye, Locomotion, Colour, Clocks and Watches, &c. 233 Illustrations, cloth gilt, 5s.

The Microscope. Containing Optical Images, Magnifying Glasses, Origin
and Description of the Microscope, Microscopic Objects, the Solar Microscope, Microscopic Drawing and Engraving, &c. 147 Illustrations, cloth
gilt, 2s.

Popular Geology. Containing Earthquakes and Volcanoes, the Crust of
the Earth, &c. 201 Illustrations, cloth gilt, 2s. 6d.

Popular Physics. Containing Magnitude and Minuteness, the Atmo-
sphere, Meteoric Stones, Popular Fallacies, Weather Prognostics, the
Thermometer, the Barometer, Sound, &c. 85 Illustrations, cloth gilt, 2s. 6d.

Steam and its Uses. Including the Steam Engine, the Locomotive, and
Steam Navigation. 89 Illustrations, cloth gilt, 2s.

Popular Astronomy. Containing How to observe the Heavens—The
Earth, Sun, Moon, Planets, Light, Comets, Eclipses, Astronomical Influ-
ences, &c. 182 Illustrations, 4s. 6d.

The Bee and White Ants: Their Manners and Habits. With Illustrations of Animal Instinct and Intelligence. 135 Illustrations, cloth gilt, 2s.

The Electric Telegraph Popularized. To render intelligible to all who
can Read, irrespective of any previous Scientific Acquirements, the various
forms of Telegraphy in Actual Operation. 100 Illustrations, cloth gilt,
1s. 6d.

Dr. Lardner's School Handbooks.

NATURAL PHILOSOPHY FOR SCHOOLS. By Dr. Lardner.
328 Illustrations. Sixth Edition. One Vol., 3s. 6d. cloth.

"A very convenient class-book for junior students in private schools. It is intended to convey,
in clear and precise terms, general notions of all the principal divisions of Physical Science."—
British Quarterly Review.

ANIMAL PHYSIOLOGY FOR SCHOOLS. By Dr. Lardner.
With 190 Illustrations. Second Edition. One Vol., 3s. 6d. cloth.

"Clearly written, well arranged, and ex'ently illustrated."—*Gardener's Chronicle.*

COUNTING-HOUSE WORK, TABLES, etc.

Introduction to Business.

LESSONS IN COMMERCE. By Professor R. GAMBARO, of the Royal High Commercial School at Genoa. Edited and Revised by JAMES GAULT, Professor of Commerce and Commercial Law in King's College, London. Crown 8vo, price about 3s. 6d. [In the press.

Accounts for Manufacturers.

FACTORY ACCOUNTS: Their Principles and Practice. A Handbook for Accountants and Manufacturers, with Appendices on the Nomenclature of Machine Details; the Income Tax Acts; the Rating of Factories; Fire and Boiler Insurance; the Factory and Workshop Acts, &c., including also a Glossary of Terms and a large number of Specimen Rulings. By EMILE GAROKE and J. M. FELLS. Third Edition. Demy 8vo, 250 pages, price 6s. strongly bound.

"A very interesting description of the requirements of Factory Accounts. . . . the principle of assimilating the Factory Accounts to the general commercial books is one which we thoroughly agree with."—Accountants' Journal.

"There are few owners of Factories who would not derive great benefit from the perusal of this most admirable work."—Local Government Chronicle.

Foreign Commercial Correspondence.

THE FOREIGN COMMERCIAL CORRESPONDENT: Being Aids to Commercial Correspondence in Five Languages—English, French, German, Italian and Spanish. By CONRAD E. BAKER. Second Edition, Revised. Crown 8vo, 3s. 6d. cloth.

"Whoever wishes to correspond in all the languages mentioned by Mr. Baker cannot do better than study this work, the materials of which are excellent and conveniently arranged."—Athenæum.

"A careful examination has convinced us that it is unusually complete, well arranged and reliable. The book is a thoroughly good one."—Schoolmaster.

Intuitive Calculations.

THE COMPENDIOUS CALCULATOR; or, Easy and Concise Methods of Performing the various Arithmetical Operations required in Commercial and Business Transactions, together with Useful Tables. By D. O'GORMAN. Corrected by Professor J. R. YOUNG. Twenty-seventh Ed., Revised by C. NORRIS. Fcap. 8vo, 2s. 6d. cloth; or, 3s. 6d. half-bound.

"It would be difficult to exaggerate the usefulness of a book like this to everyone engaged in commerce or manufacturing industry."—Knowledge.

"Supplies special and rapid methods for all kinds of calculations. Of great utility to persons engaged in any kind of commercial transactions."—Scotsman.

Modern Metrical Units and Systems.

MODERN METROLOGY: A Manual of the Metrical Units and Systems of the Present Century. With an Appendix containing a proposed English System. By LOWIS D'A. JACKSON, A.M.Inst.C.E., Author of "Aid to Survey Practice," &c. Large crown 8vo, 12s. 6d. cloth.

"The author has brought together much valuable and interesting information. . . . We cannot but recommend the work."—Nature.

"For exhaustive tables of equivalent weights and measures of all sorts, and for clear demonstrations of the effects of the various systems that have been proposed or adopted, Mr. Jackson's treatise is without a rival."—Academy.

The Metric System and the British Standards.

A SERIES OF METRIC TABLES, in which the British Standard Measures and Weights are compared with those of the Metric System at present in Use on the Continent. By C. H. DOWLING, C.E. 8vo, 10s. 6d. strongly bound.

"Their accuracy has been certified by Professor Airy, the Astronomer-Royal."—Builder.

"Mr. Dowling's Tables are well put together as a ready-reckoner for the conversion of one system into the other."—Athenæum.

Iron and Metal Trades' Calculator.

THE IRON AND METAL TRADES' COMPANION. For expeditiously ascertaining the Value of any Goods bought or sold by Weight, from 1s. per cwt. to 112s. per cwt., and from one farthing per pound to one shilling per pound. Each Table extends from one pound to 100 tons. To which are appended Rules on Decimals, Square and Cube Root, Mensuration of Superficies and Solids, &c.; also Tables of Weights of Materials, and other Useful Memoranda. By THOS. DOWNIE. Strongly bound in leather, 396 pp., 9s.

"A most useful set of tables. . . . Nothing like them before existed."—Building News.

"Although specially adapted to the iron and metal trades, the tables will be found useful in every other business in which merchandise is bought and sold by weight."—Railway News.

Calculator for Numbers and Weights Combined.

THE NUMBER, WEIGHT AND FRACTIONAL CALCU-LATOR. Containing upwards of 250,000 Separate Calculations, showing at a glance the value at 422 different rates, ranging from $\frac{1}{16}$th of a Penny to 20s. each, or per cwt., and £20 per ton, of any number of articles consecutively, from 1 to 470.—Any number of cwts., qrs., and lbs., from 1 cwt. to 470 cwts.—Any number of tons, cwts., qrs., and lbs., from 1 to 1,000 tons. By WILLIAM CHADWICK, Public Accountant. Third Edition, Revised and Improved. 8vo, price 18s., strongly bound for Office wear and tear.

  ** *This work is specially adapted for the Apportionment of Mileage Charges for Railway Traffic.*

  ☞ *This comprehensive and entirely unique and original Calculator is adapted for the use of Accountants and Auditors, Railway Companies, Canal Companies, Shippers, Shipping Agents, General Carriers, etc.*
  Ironfounders, Brassfounders, Metal Merchants, Iron Manufacturers, Ironmongers, Engineers, Machinists, Boiler Makers, Millwrights, Roofing, Bridge and Girder Makers, Colliery Proprietors, etc.
  Timber Merchants, Builders, Contractors, Architects, Surveyors, Auctioneers Valuers, Brokers, Mill Owners and Manufacturers, Mill Furnishers, Merchants and General Wholesale Tradesmen.

** OPINIONS OF THE PRESS.

  "The book contains the answers to questions, and not simply a set of ingenious puzzle methods of arriving at results. It is as easy of reference for any answer or any number of answers as a dictionary, and the references are even more quickly made. For making up accounts or estimates, the book must prove invaluable to all who have any considerable quantity of calculations involving price and measure in any combination to do."—*Engineer.*
  "The most perfect work of the kind yet prepared."—*Glasgow Herald.*

Comprehensive Weight Calculator.

THE WEIGHT CALCULATOR. Being a Series of Tables upon a New and Comprehensive Plan, exhibiting at One Reference the exact Value of any Weight from 1 lb. to 15 tons, at 300 Progressive Rates, from 1d. to 168s. per cwt., and containing 186,000 Direct Answers, which, with their Combinations, consisting of a single addition (mostly to be performed at sight), will afford an aggregate of 10,266,000 Answers; the whole being calculated and designed to ensure correctness and promote despatch. By HENRY HARBEN, Accountant. Fourth Edition, carefully Corrected. Royal 8vo, strongly half-bound, £1 5s.

  "A practical and useful work of reference for men of business generally; it is the best of the kind we have seen.' —*Ironmonger.*
  "Of priceless value to business men. It is a necessary book in all mercantile offices."—*Sheffield Independent.*

Comprehensive Discount Guide.

THE DISCOUNT GUIDE. Comprising several Series of Tables for the use of Merchants, Manufacturers, Ironmongers, and others, by which may be ascertained the exact Profit arising from any mode of using Discounts, either in the Purchase or Sale of Goods, and the method of either Altering a Rate of Discount or Advancing a Price, so as to produce, by one operation, a sum that will realise any required profit after allowing one or more Discounts: to which are added Tables of Profit or Advance from 1¼ to 90 per cent., Tables of Discount from 1¼ to 98¾ per cent., and Tables of Commission, &c., from ¼ to 10 per cent. By HENRY HARBEN, Accountant, Author of "The Weight Calculator." New Edition, carefully Revised and Corrected. Demy 8vo, 544 pp. half-bound, £1 5s.

  "A book such as this can only be appreciated by business men, to whom the saving of time means saving of money. We have the high authority of Professor J. R. Young that the tables throughout the work are constructed upon strictly accurate principles. The work is a mode of typographical clearness, and must prove of great value to merchants, manufacturers, and general traders."—*British Trade Journal.*

Iron Shipbuilders' and Merchants' Weight Tables.

IRON-PLATE WEIGHT TABLES: For Iron Shipbuilders, Engineers *and Iron Merchants.* Containing the Calculated Weights of upwards of 150,000 different sizes of Iron Plates, from 1 foot by 6 in. by ¼ in. to 10 feet by 5 feet by 1 in. Worked out on the basis of 40 lbs. to the square foot of Iron of 1 inch in thickness. Carefully compiled and thoroughly Revised by H. BURLINSON and W. H. SIMPSON. Oblong 4to, 25s. half-bound.

  "This work will be found of great utility. The authors have had much practical experience of what is wanting in making estimates; and the use of the book will save much time in making elaborate calculations."—*English Mechanic.*

INDUSTRIAL AND USEFUL ARTS.

Soap-making.

THE ART OF SOAP-MAKING : *A Practical Handbook of the Manufacture of Hard and Soft Soaps, Toilet Soaps, etc.* Including many New Processes, and a Chapter on the Recovery of Glycerine from Waste Leys. By ALEXANDER WATT, Author of " Electro-Metallurgy Practically Treated," &c. With numerous Illustrations. Fourth Edition, Revised and Enlarged. Crown 8vo, 7s. 6d. cloth.

"The work will prove very useful, not merely to the technological student, but o he practical soap-boiler who wishes to understand the theory of his art."—*Chemical News.*
"Mr. Watt's book is a thoroughly practical treatise on an art which has almost no literature in our language. We congratulate the author on the success of his endeavour to fill a void in English technical literature."—*Nature.*

Paper Making.

THE ART OF PAPER MAKING : *A Practical Handbook of the Manufacture of Paper from Rags, Esparto, Straw and other Fibrous Materials,* Including the Manufacture of Pulp from Wood Fibre, with a Description of the Machinery and Appliances used. To which are added Details of Processes for Recovering Soda from Waste Liquors. By ALEXANDER WATT. With Illustrations. Crown 8vo, 7s. 6d. cloth.

" This book is succinct, lucid, thoroughly practical, and includes everything of interest to the modern paper-maker. It is the latest, most practical and most complete work on the paper-making art before the British public."—*Paper Record.*
"It may be regarded as the standard work on the subject. The book is full of valuable information. The ' Art of Paper-making,' is in every respect a model of a text-book, either for a technical class or for the private student."—*Paper and Printing Trades Journal.*
" Admirably adapted for general as well as ordinary technical reference, and as a handbook for students in technical education may be warmly commended."—*The Paper Maker's Monthly Journal.*

Leather Manufacture.

THE ART OF LEATHER MANUFACTURE. Being a Practical Handbook, in which the Operations of Tanning, Currying, and Leather Dressing are fully Described, the Principles of Tanning Explained and many Recent Processes introduced. By ALEXANDER WATT, Author of " Soap-Making," &c. With numerous Illustrations. Second Edition. Crown 8vo, 9s. cloth.

"A sound, comprehensive treatise on tanning and its accessories. This book is an eminently valuable production, which redounds to the credit of both author and publishers."—*Chemical Review.*
" This volume is technical without being tedious, comprehensive and complete without being prosy, and it bears on every page the impress of a master hand. We have never come across a better trade treatise, nor one that so thoroughly supplied an absolute want."—*Shoe and Leather Trades' Chronicle.*

Boot and Shoe Making.

THE ART OF BOOT AND SHOE-MAKING. A Practical Handbook, including Measurement, Last-Fitting, Cutting-Out, Closing and Making, with a Description of the most approved Machinery employed. By JOHN B. LENO, late Editor of *St. Crispin,* and *The Boot and Shoe-Maker.* With numerous Illustrations. Third Edition. 12mo, 2s. cloth limp.

" This excellent treatise is by far the best work ever written on the subject. A new work, embracing all modern improvements, was much wanted. This want is now satisfied. The chapter on clicking, which shows how waste may be prevented, will save fifty times the price of the book." —*Scottish Leather Trader.*

Dentistry.

MECHANICAL DENTISTRY : *A Practical Treatise on the Construction of the various kinds of Artificial Dentures.* Comprising also Useful Formulæ, Tables and Receipts for Gold Plate, Clasps, Solders, &c. &c. By CHARLES HUNTER. Third Edition, Revised. With upwards of 100 Wood Engravings. Crown 8vo, 3s. 6d. cloth.

" The work is very practical."—*Monthly Review of Dental Surgery.*
" We can strongly recommend Mr. Hunter's treatise to all students preparing for the profession of dentistry, as well as to every mechanical dentist."—*Dublin Journal of Medical Science.*

Wood Engraving.

WOOD ENGRAVING: *A Practical and Easy Introduction to the Study of the Art.* By WILLIAM NORMAN BROWN. Second Edition. With numerous Illustrations. 12mo, 1s. 6d. cloth limp.

" The book is clear and complete, and will be useful to anyone wanting to understand the first elements of the beautiful art of wood engraving."—*Graphic.*

HANDYBOOKS FOR HANDICRAFTS. By PₙUL N. HASLUCK.

Metal Turning.

THE METAL TURNER'S HANDYBOOK. *A Practical Manual for Workers at the Foot-Lathe:* Embracing Information on the Tools, Appliances and Processes employed in Metal Turning. By PAUL N. HASLUCK, Author of " Lathe-Work." With upwards of One Hundred Illustrations. Second Edition, Revised. Crown 8vo, 2s. cloth.
" Clearly and concisely written, excellent in every way."—*Mechanical World.*

Wood Turning.

THE WOOD TURNER'S HANDYBOOK. *A Practical Manual for Workers at the Lathe:* Embracing Information on the Tools, Appliances and Processes Employed in Wood Turning. By PAUL N. HASLUCK. With upwards of One Hundred Illustrations. Crown 8vo, 2s. cloth.
" We recommend the book to young turners and amateurs. A multitude of workmen have hitherto sought in vain for a manual of this special industry."—*Mechanical World.*

WOOD AND METAL TURNING. By P. N. HASLUCK. (Being the Two preceding Vols. bound together.) 300 pp., with upwards of 200 Illustrations, crown 8vo, 3s. 6d. cloth.

Watch Repairing.

THE WATCH JOBBER'S HANDYBOOK. *A Practical Manual on Cleaning, Repairing and Adjusting.* Embracing Information on the Tools, Materials, Appliances and Processes Employed in Watchwork. By PAUL N. HASLUCK. With upwards of One Hundred Illustrations. Cr. 8vo, 2s. cloth.
" All young persons connected with the trade should acquire and study this excellent, and at the same time, inexpensive work."—*Clerkenwell Chronicle.*

Clock Repairing.

THE CLOCK JOBBER'S HANDYBOOK : *A Practical Manual on Cleaning, Repairing and Adjusting.* Embracing Information on the Tools, Materials, Appliances and Processes Employed in Clockwork. By PAUL N. HASLUCK. With upwards of 100 Illustrations. Cr. 8vo, 2s. cloth.
" Of inestimable service to those commencing the trade."—*Coventry Standard.*

WATCH AND CLOCK JOBBING. By P. N. HASLUCK. (Being the Two preceding Vols. bound together.) 320 pp., with upwards of 200 Illustrations, crown 8vo, 3s. 6d. cloth.

Pattern Making.

THE PATTERN MAKER'S HANDYBOOK. A Practical Manual, embracing Information on the Tools, Materials and Appliances employed in Constructing Patterns for Founders. By PAUL N. HASLUCK. With One Hundred Illustrations. Crown 8vo, 2s. cloth.
" This handy volume contains sound information of considerable value to students and artificers."—*Hardware Trades Journal.*

Mechanical Manipulation.

THE MECHANIC'S WORKSHOP HANDYBOOK. *A Practical Manual on Mechanical Manipulation.* Embracing Information on various Handicraft Processes, with Useful Notes and Miscellaneous Memoranda. By PAUL N. HASLUCK. Crown 8vo, 2s. cloth.
" It is a book which should be found in every workshop, as it is one which will be continually referred to for a very great amount of standard information."—*Saturday Review.*

Model Engineering.

THE MODEL ENGINEER'S HANDYBOOK : *A Practical Manual on Model Steam Engines.* Embracing Information on the Tools, Materials and Processes Employed in their Construction. By PAUL N. HASLUCK. With upwards of 100 Illustrations. Crown 8vo, 2s. cloth.
" By carefully going through the work, amateurs may pick up an excellent notion of the construction of full-sized steam engines."—*Telegraphic Journal.*

Cabinet Making.

THE CABINET WORKER'S HANDYBOOK : A Practical Manual, embracing Information on the Tools, Materials, Appliances and Processes employed in Cabinet Work. By PAUL N. HASLUCK, Author of " Lathe Work," &c. With upwards of 100 Illustrations. Crown 8vo, 2s. cloth.   [*Glasgow Herald.*
" Thoroughly practical throughout. The amateur worker in wood will find it most useful."—

Electrolysis of Gold, Silver, Copper, etc.

ELECTRO-DEPOSITION : A Practical Treatise on the Electrolysis of Gold, Silver, Copper, Nickel, and other Metals and Alloys. With descriptions of Voltaic Batteries, Magneto and Dynamo-Electric Machines, Thermopiles, and of the Materials and Processes used in every Department of the Art, and several Chapters on Electro-Metallurgy. By ALEXANDER WATT. Third Edition, Revised and Corrected. Crown 8vo, 9s. cloth.

"Eminently a book for the practical worker in electro-deposition. It contains practical descriptions of methods, processes and materials as actually pursued and used in the workshop."
—*Engineer.*

Electro-Metallurgy.

ELECTRO-METALLURGY; Practically Treated. By ALEXANDER WATT, Author of "Electro-Deposition," &c. Ninth Edition, Enlarged and Revised, with Additional Illustrations, and including the most recent Processes. 12mo, 4s. cloth boards.

"From this book both amateur and artisan may learn everything necessary for the successful prosecution of electroplating."—*Iron.*

Electroplating.

ELECTROPLATING : A Practical Handbook on the Deposition of Copper, Silver, Nickel, Gold, Aluminium, Brass, Platinum, &c. &c. With Descriptions of the Chemicals, Materials, Batteries and Dynamo Machines used in the Art. By J. W. URQUHART, C.E. Second Edition, with Additions. Numerous Illustrations. Crown 8vo, 5s. cloth.

"An excellent practical manual."—*Engineering.*
"An excellent work, giving the newest information."—*Horological Journal.*

Electrotyping.

ELECTROTYPING : The Reproduction and Multiplication of Printing Surfaces and Works of Art by the Electro-deposition of Metals. By J. W. URQUHART, C.E. Crown 8vo, 5s. cloth.

"The book is thoroughly practical. The reader is, therefore, conducted through the leading laws of electricity, then through the metals used by electrotypers, the apparatus, and the depositing processes, up to the final preparation of the work."—*Art Journal.*

Horology.

A TREATISE ON MODERN HOROLOGY, in Theory and Practice. Translated from the French of CLAUDIUS SAUNIER, by JULIEN TRIPFLIN, F.R.A.S., and EDWARD RIGG, M.A., Assayer in the Royal Mint. With 78 Woodcuts and 22 Coloured Plates. Second Edition. Royal 8vo, £2 2s. cloth ; £2 10s. half-calf.

"There is no horological work in the English language at all to be compared to this production of M. Saunier's for clearness and completeness. It is alike good as a guide for the student and as a reference for the experienced horologist and skilled workman."—*Horological Journal.*
"The latest, the most complete, and the most reliable of these literary productions to which continental watchmakers are indebted for the mechanical superiority over their English brethren —in fact, the Book of Books, is M. Saunier's 'Treatise.'"—*Watchmaker, Jeweller and Silversmith.*

Watchmaking.

THE WATCHMAKER'S HANDBOOK. A Workshop Companion for those engaged in Watchmaking and the Allied Mechanical Arts. From the French of CLAUDIUS SAUNIER. Enlarged by JULIEN TRIPPLIN, F.R.A.S., and EDWARD RIGG, M.A., Assayer in the Royal Mint. Woodcuts and Copper Plates. Third Edition, Revised. Crown 8vo, 9s. cloth.

"Each part is truly a treatise in itself. The arrangement is good and the language is clear and concise. It is an admirable guide for the young watchmaker."—*Engineering.*
"It is impossible to speak too highly of its excellence. It fulfils every requirement in a handbook intended for the use of a workman."—*Watch and Clockmaker.*
"This book contains an immense number of practical details bearing on the daily occupation of a watchmaker."—*Watchmaker and Metalworker* (Chicago).

Goldsmiths' Work.

THE GOLDSMITH'S HANDBOOK. By GEORGE E. GEE, Jeweller, &c. Third Edition, considerably Enlarged. 12mo, 3s. 6d. cl. bds.

"A good, sound educator, and will be accepted as an authority."—*Horological Journal.*

Silversmiths' Work.

THE SILVERSMITH'S HANDBOOK. By GEORGE E. GEE, Jeweller, &c. Second Edition, Revised, with numerous Illustrations. 12mo, 3s. 6d. cloth boards.

"Workers in the trade will speedily discover its merits when they sit down to study it."— *English Mechanic.*

*** *The above two works together, strongly half-bound, price 7s.*

Bread and Biscuit Baking.

THE BREAD AND BISCUIT BAKER'S AND SUGAR-BOILER'S ASSISTANT. Including a large variety of Modern Recipes. With Remarks on the Art of Bread-making. By ROBERT WELLS, Practical Baker. Second Edition, with Additional Recipes. Crown 8vo, 2s. cloth.
" A large number of wrinkles for the ordinary cook, as well as the baker."—*Saturday Review.*

Confectionery.

THE PASTRYCOOK AND CONFECTIONER'S GUIDE. For Hotels, Restaurants and the Trade in general, adapted also for Family Use. By ROBERT WELLS, Author of " The Bread and Biscuit Baker's and Sugar Boiler's Assistant." Crown 8vo, 2s. cloth.
" We cannot speak too highly of this really excellent work. In these days of keen competition our readers cannot do better than purchase this book."—*Bakers' Times.*

Ornamental Confectionery.

ORNAMENTAL CONFECTIONERY: A Guide for Bakers. Confectioners and Pastrycooks; including a variety of Modern Recipes, and Remarks on Decorative and Coloured Work. With 129 Original Designs. By ROBERT WELLS. Crown 8vo, 5s. cloth.
" A valuable work, and should be in the hands of every baker and confectioner. The illustrative designs are alone worth treble the amount charged for the whole work."—*Bakers' Times.*

Flour Confectionery.

THE MODERN FLOUR CONFECTIONER. Wholesale and Retail. Containing a large Collection of Recipes for Cheap Cakes, Biscuits, &c. With Remarks on the Ingredients used in their Manufacture, &c. By R. WELLS, Author of " Ornamental Confectionery," " The Bread and Biscuit Baker," " The Pastrycook's Guide," &c. Crown 8vo, 2s. cloth.

Laundry Work.

LAUNDRY MANAGEMENT. A Handbook for Use in Private and Public Laundries, Including Descriptive Accounts of Modern Machinery and Appliances for Laundry Work. By the EDITOR of " The Laundry Journal." With numerous Illustrations. Crown 8vo, 2s. 6d. cloth.

CHEMICAL MANUFACTURES & COMMERCE.

New Manual of Engineering Chemistry.

ENGINEERING CHEMISTRY: A Practical Treatise for the Use of Analytical Chemists, Engineers, Iron Masters, Iron Founders, Students, and others. Comprising Methods of Analysis and Valuation of the Principal Materials used in Engineering Work, with numerous Analyses, Examples, and Suggestions. By H. JOSHUA PHILLIPS, F.I.C., F.C.S. Analytical and Consulting Chemist to the Great Eastern Railway. Crown 8vo 320 pp., with Illustrations, 10s. 6d. cloth.   [*Just published*
" In this work the author has rendered no small service to a numerous body of practical men . . . The analytical methods may be pronounced most satisfactory, being as accurate as the despatch required of engineering chemists permits."—*Chemical News.*

Analysis and Valuation of Fuels.

FUELS: SOLID, LIQUID AND GASEOUS, Their Analysis and Valuation. For the Use of Chemists and Engineers. By H. J. PHILLIPS, F.C.S., Analytical and Consulting Chemist to the Great Eastern Railway. Crown 8vo, 3s. 6d. cloth.
" Ought to have its place in the laboratory of every metallurgical establishment, and wherever fuel is used on a large scale."—*Chemical News.*
" Cannot fail to be of wide interest, especially at the present time."—*Railway News.*

Alkali Trade, Manufacture of Sulphuric Acid, etc.

A MANUAL OF THE ALKALI TRADE, including the Manufacture of Sulphuric Acid, Sulphate of Soda, and Bleaching Powder. By JOHN LOMAS. 390 pages. With 232 Illustrations and Working Drawings. Second Edition. Royal 8vo, £1 10s. cloth.
" This book is written by a manufacturer for manufacturers. The working details of the most approved forms of apparatus are given, and these are accompanied by no less than 232 wood engravings, all of which may be used for the purposes of construction."—*Athenæum.*

The Blowpipe.
THE BLOWPIPE IN CHEMISTRY, MINERALOGY, AND
GEOLOGY. Containing all known Methods of Anhydrous Analysis, Work-
ing Examples, and Instructions for Making Apparatus. By Lieut.-Col. W. A
Ross, R.A. With 120 Illustrations. New Edition. Crown 8vo, 5s. cloth.
"The student who goes through the course of experimentation here laid down will gain a
better insight into inorganic chemistry and mineralogy than if he had 'got up' any of the best
text-books of the day, and passed any number of examinations in their contents."—*Chemical News.*

Commercial Chemical Analysis.
THE COMMERCIAL HANDBOOK OF CHEMICAL ANA-
LYSIS; or, Practical Instructions for the determination of the Intrinsic or
Commercial Value of Substances used in Manufactures,Trades, and the Arts.
By A. NORMANDY. New Edition by H. M. NOAO, F.R.S. Cr. 8vo, 12s. 6d. cl.
"Essential to the analysts appointed under the new Act. The most recent results are given,
and the work is well edited and carefully written."—*Nature.*

Brewing.
A HANDBOOK FOR YOUNG BREWERS. By HERBERT
EDWARDS WRIGHT, B.A. New Edition, much Enlarged. [*In the press.*

Dye-Wares and Colours.
THE MANUAL OF COLOURS AND DYE-WARES : Their
Properties, Applications, Valuation, Impurities, and Sophistications. For the
use of Dyers, Printers, Drysalters, Brokers, &c. By J. W. SLATER. Second
Edition, Revised and greatly Enlarged. Crown 8vo, 7s. 6d. cloth.
"A complete encyclopædia of the *materia tinctoria.* The information given respecting each
article is full and precise, and the methods of determining the value of articles such as these, so
liable to sophistication, are given with clearness, and are practical as well as valuable."—*Chemist
and Druggist.*
"There is no other work which covers precisely the same ground. To students preparing
for examinations in dyeing and printing it will prove exceedingly useful."—*Chemical News.*

Pigments.
THE ARTIST'S MANUAL OF PIGMENTS. Showing
their Composition, Conditions of Permanency, Non-Permanency, and Adul-
terations; Effects in Combination with Each Other and with Vehicles; and
the most Reliable Tests of Purity. By H. C. STANDAGE. Second Edition.
Crown 8vo, 2s. 6d. cloth.
"This work is indeed *multum-in-parvo,* and we can, with good conscience, recommend it to
all who come in contact with pigments, whether as makers, dealers or users."—*Chemical Review.*

Gauging. Tables and Rules for Revenue Officers, Brewers, etc.
A POCKET BOOK OF MENSURATION AND GAUGING :
Containing Tables, Rules and Memoranda for Revenue Officers, Brewers,
Spirit Merchants, &c. By J. B. MANT (Inland Revenue). Second Edition
Revised. Oblong 18mo, 4s. leather, with elastic band.
"This handy and useful book is adapted to the requirements of the Inland Revenue Depart
ment, and will be a favourite book of reference."—*Civilian.*
"Should be in the hands of every practical brewer."—*Brewers' Journal.*

AGRICULTURE, FARMING, GARDENING, etc.

Youatt and Burn's Complete Grazier.
THE COMPLETE GRAZIER, and FARMER'S and CATTLE-
BREEDER'S ASSISTANT. Including the Breeding, Rearing, and Feeding
of Stock; Management of the Dairy, Culture and Management of Grass
Land, and of Grain and Root Crops, &c. By W. YOUATT and R. SCOTT
BURN. An entirely New Edition, partly Re-written and greatly Enlarged, by
W. FREAM, B.Sc.Lond., LL.D. In medium 8vo, about 1,000 pp. [*In the press.*

Agricultural Facts and Figures.
NOTE-BOOK OF AGRICULTURAL FACTS AND FIGURES
FOR FARMERS AND FARM STUDENTS. By PRIMROSE MCCONNELL,
late Professor of Agriculture, Glasgow Veterinary College. Third Edition
Royal 32mo, 4s. leather.
"The most complete and comprehensive Note-book for Farmers and Farm Students that we
have seen. It literally teems with information, and we can cordially recommend it to all connected
with agriculture."—*North British Agriculturist.*

Flour Manufacture, Milling, etc.

FLOUR MANUFACTURE: A Treatise on Milling Science and Practice. By FRIEDRICH KICK, Imperial Regierungsrath, Professor of Mechanical Technology in the Imperial German Polytechnic Institute, Prague. Translated from the Second Enlarged and Revised Edition with Supplement. By H. H. P. POWLES, A.M.I.C.E. Nearly 400 pp. Illustrated with 28 Folding Plates, and 167 Woodcuts. Royal 8vo, 25s. cloth.

"This valuable work is, and will remain, the standard authority on the science of milling. . The miller who has read and digested this work will have laid the foundation, so to speak, of a successful career; he will have acquired a number of general principles which he can proceed to apply.   In this handsome volume we at last have the accepted text-book of modern milling in good, sound English, which has little, if any, trace of the German idiom."—*The Miller.*
"The appearance of this celebrated work in English is very opportune, and British millers will, we are sure, not be slow in availing themselves of its pages."—*Millers' Gazette.*

Small Farming.

SYSTEMATIC SMALL FARMING; or, The Lessons of my Farm. Being an Introduction to Modern Farm Practice for Small Farmers in the Culture of Crops; The Feeding of Cattle; The Management of the Dairy, Poultry and Pigs, &c. &c. By ROBERT SCOTT BURN, Author of "Outlines of Landed Estates' Management." Numerous Illusts., cr. 8vo, 6s. cloth.

"This is the completest book of its class we have seen, and one which every amateur farmer will read with pleasure and accept as a guide."—*Field.*
"The volume contains a vast amount of useful information.   No branch of farming is left untouched, from the labour to be done to the results achieved.   It may be safely recommended to all who think they will be in paradise when they buy or rent a three-acre farm."—*Glasgow Herald.*

Modern Farming.

OUTLINES OF MODERN FARMING. By R. SCOTT BURN. Soils, Manures, and Crops—Farming and Farming Economy—Cattle, Sheep, and Horses — Management of Dairy, Pigs and Poultry — Utilisation of Town-Sewage, Irrigation, &c. Sixth Edition. In One Vol., 1,250 pp., half-bound, profusely Illustrated, 12s.

"The aim of the author has been to make his work at once comprehensive and trustworthy, and in this aim he has succeeded to a degree which entitles him to much credit."—*Morning Advertiser.*   "No farmer should be without this book."—*Banbury Guardian.*

Agricultural Engineering.

FARM ENGINEERING, THE COMPLETE TEXT-BOOK OF. Comprising Draining and Embanking; Irrigation and Water Supply; Farm Roads, Fences, and Gates; Farm Buildings, their Arrangement and Construction, with Plans and Estimates; Barn Implements and Machines; Field Implements and Machines; Agricultural Surveying, Levelling, &c. By Prof. JOHN SCOTT, Editor of the "Farmers' Gazette," late Professor of Agriculture and Rural Economy at the Royal Agricultural College, Cirencester, &c. &c. In One Vol., 1,150 pages, half-bound, with over 600 Illustrations, 12s.

"Written with great care, as well as with knowledge and ability.   The author has done his work well; we have found him a very trustworthy guide wherever we have tested his statements. The volume will be of great value to agricultural students."—*Mark Lane Express.*
"For a young agriculturist we know of [no handy volume likely to be more usefully studied."
—*Bell's Weekly Messenger.*

English Agriculture.

THE FIELDS OF GREAT BRITAIN: A Text-Book of Agriculture, adapted to the Syllabus of the Science and Art Department. For Elementary and Advanced Students. By HUGH CLEMENTS (Board of Trade). Second Ed., Revised, with Additions. 18mo, 2s. 6d. cl.

"A most comprehensive volume, giving a mass of information."—*Agricultural Economist.*
"It is a long time since we have seen a book which has pleased us more, or which contains such a vast and useful fund of knowledge."—*Educational Times.*

Tables for Farmers, etc.

TABLES, MEMORANDA, AND CALCULATED RESULTS for Farmers, Graziers, Agricultural Students, Surveyors, Land Agents Auctioneers, etc.   With a New System of Farm Book-keeping.   Selected and Arranged by SIDNEY FRANCIS.   Second Edition, Revised.   272 pp., waistcoat-pocket size, 1s. 6d. limp leather.

"Weighing less than 1 oz, and occupying no more space than a match box, it contains a mass of facts and calculations which has never before, in such handy form, been obtainable. . Every operation on the farm is dealt with.   The work may be taken as thoroughly accurate, the whole of the tables having been revised by Dr. Fream.   We cordially recommend it."—*Bell's Weekly Messenger.*
"A marvellous little book. . . . The agriculturist who possesses himself of it will not be disappointed with his investment." —*The Farm.*

Farm and Estate Book-keeping.

BOOK-KEEPING FOR FARMERS & ESTATE OWNERS.
A Practical Treatise, presenting, in Three Plans, a System adapted for all Classes of Farms. By JOHNSON M. WOODMAN, Chartered Accountant. Second Edition, Revised. Cr. 8vo, 3s. 6d. cl. bds.; or 2s. 6d. cl. limp.
" The volume is a capital study of a most important subject."—*Agricultural Gazette.*
" Will be found of great assistance by those who intend to commence a system of book-keeping, the author's examples being clear and explicit, and his explanations, while full and accurate, being to a large extent free from technicalities."—*Live Stock Journal.*

Farm Account Book.

WOODMAN'S YEARLY FARM ACCOUNT BOOK. Giving a Weekly Labour Account and Diary, and showing the Income and Expenditure under each Department of Crops, Live Stock, Dairy, &c. &c. With Valuation, Profit and Loss Account, and Balance Sheet at the end of the Year, and an Appendix of Forms. Ruled and Headed for Entering a Complete Record of the Farming Operations. By JOHNSON M. WOODMAN, Chartered Accountant. Folio, 7s. 6d. half-bound. [*culture.*
"Contains every requisite form for keeping farm accounts readily and accurately."—*Agri-*

Early Fruits, Flowers and Vegetables.

THE FORCING GARDEN ; or, How to Grow Early Fruits, Flowers, and Vegetables. With Plans and Estimates for Building Glass-houses, Pits and Frames. By SAMUEL WOOD. Crown 8vo, 3s. 6d. cloth.
" A good book. and fairly fills a place that was in some degree vacant. The book is written with great care, and contains a great deal of valuable teaching."—*Gardeners' Magazine.*
" Mr. Wood's book is an original and exhaustive answer to the question 'How to Grow Early Fruits, Flowers and Vegetables ?'"—*Land and Water.*

Good Gardening.

A PLAIN GUIDE TO GOOD GARDENING ; or, How to Grow Vegetables, Fruits, and Flowers. With Practical Notes on Soils, Manures, Seeds, Planting, Laying-out of Gardens and Grounds, &c. By S. WOOD. Fourth Edition, with numerous Illustrations. Crown 8vo, 3s. 6d. cloth.
" A very good book, and one to be highly recommended as a practical guide. The practical directions are excellent."—*Athenæum.*
" May be recommended to young gardeners, cottagers, and specially to amateurs, for the plain, simple, and trustworthy information it gives on common matters too often neglected."—*Gardeners' Chronicle.*

Gainful Gardening.

MULTUM-IN-PARVO GARDENING ; or, How to make One Acre of Land produce £620 a-year by the Cultivation of Fruits and Vegetables ; also, How to Grow Flowers in Three Glass Houses, so as to realise £176 per annum clear Profit. By S. WOOD. Fifth Edition. Crown 8vo, 1s. sewed.
" We are bound to recommend it as not only suited to the case of the amateur and gentleman's gardener, but to the market grower."—*Gardeners' Magazine.*

Gardening for Ladies.

THE LADIES' MULTUM-IN-PARVO FLOWER GARDEN, and *Amateurs' Complete Guide.* By S. WOOD. With Illusts. Cr. 8vo, 3s. 6d. cl.
" This volume contains a good deal of sound, common sense instruction."—*Florist.*
" Full of shrewd hints and useful instructions, based on a lifetime of experience."—*Scotsman.*

Receipts for Gardeners.

GARDEN RECEIPTS. By C. W. QUIN. 12mo, 1s. 6d. cloth.
" A useful and handy book, containing a good deal of valuable information."—*Athenæum.*

Market Gardening.

MARKET AND KITCHEN GARDENING. By Contributors to "The Garden." Compiled by C. W. SHAW, late Editor of "Gardening Illustrated." 12mo, 3s. 6d. cloth boards.
" The most valuable compendium of kitchen and market-garden work published."—*Farmer.*

Cottage Gardening.

COTTAGE GARDENING ; or, *Flowers, Fruits, and Vegetables for Small Gardens.* By E. HOBDAY. 12mo, 1s. 6d. cloth limp.

Potato Culture.

POTATOES : How to Grow and Show Them. A Practical Guide to the Cultivation and General Treatment of the Potato. By JAMES PINK. Second Edition. Crown 8vo, 2s. cloth.

LAND AND ESTATE MANAGEMENT, LAW, etc.

Hudson's Land Valuer's Pocket-Book.

THE LAND VALUER'S BEST ASSISTANT: Being Tables on a very much Improved Plan, for Calculating the Value of Estates. With Tables for reducing Scotch, Irish, and Provincial Customary Acres to Statute Measure, &c. By R. HUDSON, C.E. New Edition. Royal 32mo, leather, elastic band, 4s.

"This new edition includes tables for ascertaining the value of leases for any term of years and for showing how to lay out plots of ground of certain acres in forms, square, round, &c., with valuable rules for ascertaining the probable worth of standing timber to any amount; and is of incalculable value to the country gentleman and professional man."—*Farmers' Journal.*

Ewart's Land Improver's Pocket-Book.

THE LAND IMPROVER'S POCKET-BOOK OF FORMULÆ, *TABLES* and *MEMORANDA required in any Computation relating to the Permanent Improvement of Landed Property.* By JOHN EWART, Land Surveyor and Agricultural Engineer. Second Edition, Revised. Royal 32mo, oblong, leather, gilt edges, with elastic band, 4s.

"A compendious and handy little volume."—*Spectator.*

Complete Agricultural Surveyor's Pocket-Book.

THE LAND VALUER'S AND LAND IMPROVER'S COM- *PLETE POCKET-BOOK.* Consisting of the above Two Works bound to-gether. Leather, gilt edges, with strap, 7s. 6d.

"Hudson's book is the best ready-reckoner on matters relating to the valuation of land and crops, and its combination with Mr. Ewart's work greatly enhances the value and usefulness of the latter-mentioned. . . . It is most useful as a manual for reference."—*North of England Farmer.*

Auctioneer's Assistant.

THE APPRAISER, AUCTIONEER, BROKER, HOUSE AND *ESTATE AGENT AND VALUER'S POCKET ASSISTANT,* for the Valua-tion for Purchase, Sale, or Renewal of Leases, Annuities and Reversions, and of property generally; with Prices for Inventories, &c. By JOHN WHEELER, Valuer, &c. Fifth Edition, re-written and greatly extended by C. NORRIS, Surveyor, Valuer, &c. Royal 32mo, 5s. cloth.

"A neat and concise book of reference, containing an admirable and clearly-arranged list of prices for Inventories, and a very practical guide to determine the value of furniture, &c."—*Standard.*

"Contains a large quantity of varied and useful information as to the valuation for purchase, sale, or renewal of leases, annuities and reversions, and of property generally, with prices for inventories, and a guide to determine the value of interior fittings and other effects."—*Builder.*

Auctioneering.

AUCTIONEERS: THEIR DUTIES AND LIABILITIES. A Manual of Instruction and Counsel for the Young Auctioneer. By ROBERT SQUIBBS, Auctioneer. Second Edition, Revised and partly Re-written. Demy 8vo, 12s. 6d. cloth.

"The position and duties of auctioneers treated compendiously and clearly."—*Builder.*

"Every auctioneer ought to possess a copy of this excellent work."—*Ironmonger.*

"Of great value to the profession. . . . We readily welcome this book from the fact that it treats the subject in a manner somewhat new to the profession."—*Estates Gazette.*

Legal Guide for Pawnbrokers.

THE PAWNBROKERS', FACTORS' AND MERCHANTS' *GUIDE TO THE LAW OF LOANS AND PLEDGES.* With the Statutes and a Digest of Cases on Rights and Liabilities, Civil and Criminal, as to Loans and Pledges of Goods, Debentures, Mercantile and other Se-curities. By H. C. FOLKARD, Esq., Barrister-at-Law, Author of "The Law of Slander and Libel," &c. With Additions and Corrections. Fcap. 8vo, 3s. 6d. cloth.

"This work contains simply everything that requires to be known concerning the department of the law of which it treats. We can safely commend the book as unique and very nearly perfect."—*Iron.*

"The task undertaken by Mr. Folkard has been very satisfactorily performed. . . Such ex-planations as are needful have been supplied with great clearness and with due regard to brevity." *City Press.*

Law of Patents.

PATENTS FOR INVENTIONS, AND HOW TO PROCURE THEM. Compiled for the Use of Inventors, Patentees and others. By G. G. M. HARDINGHAM, Assoc.Mem.Inst.C.E., &c. Demy 8vo, cloth, price 2s. 6d.

Metropolitan Rating Appeals.

REPORTS OF APPEALS HEARD BEFORE THE COURT OF GENERAL ASSESSMENT SESSIONS, from the Year 1871 to 1885. By EDWARD RYDE and ARTHUR LYON RYDE. Fourth Edition, brought down to the Present Date, with an Introduction to the Valuation (Metropolis) Act, 1869, and an Appendix by WALTER C. RYDE, of the Inner Temple, Barrister-at-Law. 8vo, 16s. cloth.

"A useful work, occupying a place mid-way between a handbook for a lawyer and a guide to the surveyor. It is compiled by a gentleman eminent in his profession as a land agent, whose specialty, it is acknowledged, lies i the direction of assessing property for rating purposes."—*Land Agents' Record.*

"It is an indispensable wo of reference for all engaged in assessment business."—*Journal of Gas Lighting.*

House Property.

HANDBOOK OF HOUSE PROPERTY. A Popular and Practical Guide to the Purchase, Mortgage, Tenancy, and Compulsory Sale of Houses and Land, including the Law of Dilapidations and Fixtures; with Examples of all kinds of Valuations, Useful Information on Building, and Suggestive Elucidations of Fine Art. By E. L. TARBUCK, Architect and Surveyor. Fourth Edition, Enlarged. 12mo, 5s. cloth.

"The advice is thoroughly practical."—*Law Journal.*
"For all who have dealings with house property, this is an indispensable guide."—*Decoration.*
"Carefully brought up to date, and much improved by the addition of a division on fine art."
"A well-written and thoughtful work."—*Land Agent's Record.*

Inwood's Estate Tables.

TABLES FOR THE PURCHASING OF ESTATES, Freehold, Copyhold, or Leasehold; Annuities, Advowsons, etc., and for the Renewing of Leases held under Cathedral Churches, Colleges, or other Corporate bodies, for Terms of Years certain, and for Lives; also for Valuing Reversionary Estates, Deferred Annuities, Next Presentations, &c.; together with SMART'S Five Tables of Compound Interest, and an Extension of the same to Lower and Intermediate Rates. By W. INWOOD. 23rd Edition, with considerable Additions, and new and valuable Tables of Logarithms for the more Difficult Computations of the Interest of Money, Discount, Annuities, &c., by M. FEDOR THOMAN, of the Société Crédit Mobilier of Paris. Crown 8vo, 8s. cloth.

"Those interested in the purchase and sale of estates, and in the adjustment of compensation cases, as well as in transactions in annuities, life insurances, &c., will find the present edition of eminent service."—*Engineering.*

"'Inwood's Tables' still maintain a most enviable reputation. The new issue has been enriched by large additional contributions by M. Fedor Thoman, whose carefully arranged Tables cannot fail to be of the utmost utility."—*Mining Journal.*

Agricultural and Tenant-Right Valuation.

THE AGRICULTURAL AND TENANT-RIGHT-VALUER'S ASSISTANT. A Practical Handbook on Measuring and Estimating the Contents, Weights and Values of Agricultural Produce and Timber, the Values of Estates and Agricultural Labour, Forms of Tenant-Right-Valuations, Scales of Compensation under the Agricultural Holdings Act, 1883, &c. &c. By TOM BRIGHT, Agricultural Surveyor. Crown 8vo, 3s. 6d. cloth.

"Full of tables and examples in connection with the valuation of tenant-right, estates, labour, contents, and weights of timber, and farm produce of all kinds."—*Agricultural Gazette.*
"An eminently practical handbook, full of practical tables and data of undoubted interest and value to surveyors and auctioneers in preparing valuations of all kinds."—*Farmer.*

Plantations and Underwoods.

POLE PLANTATIONS AND UNDERWOODS: A Practical Handbook on Estimating the Cost of Forming, Renovating, Improving and Grubbing Plantations and Underwoods, their Valuation for Purposes of Transfer, Rental, Sale or Assessment. By TOM BRIGHT, F.S.Sc., Author of "The Agricultural and Tenant-Right-Valuer's Assistant," &c. Crown 8vo, 3s. 6d. cloth. [Just published.

"Will be found very useful to those who are actually engaged in managing wood."—*Bell's Weekly Messenger.*
"To valuers, foresters and agents it will be a welcome aid."—*North British Agriculturist.*
"Well calculated to assist the valuer in the discharge of his duties, and of undoubted interest and use both to surveyors and auctioneers in preparing valuations of all kinds."—*Kent Herald.*

A Complete Epitome of the Laws of this Country.

EVERY. MAN'S OWN LAWYER: A Handy-Book of the *Principles of Law and Equity.* By A BARRISTER. Twenty-ninth Edition. Revised and Enlarged. Including the Legislation of 1891, and including careful digests of *The Tithe Act,* 1891; the *Mortmain and Charitable Uses Act,* 1891; the *Charitable Trusts (Recovery) Act,* 1891; the *Forged Transfers Act,* 1891; the *Custody of Children Act,* 1891; the *Slander of Women Act,* 1891; the *Public Health (London) Act,* 1891; the *Stamp Act,* 1891; the *Savings Bank Act,* 1891; the *Elementary Education ("Free Education") Act,* 1891; the *County Councils (Elections) Act,* 1891; and the *Land Registry (Middlesex Deeds) Act,* 1891; while other new Acts have been duly noted. ·Crown 8vo, 688 pp., price 6s. 8d. (saved at every consultation!), strongly bound in cloth.   [*Just published.*

*** THE BOOK WILL BE FOUND TO COMPRISE (AMONGST OTHER MATTER)—

THE RIGHTS AND WRONGS OF INDIVIDUALS—LANDLORD AND TENANT—VENDORS AND PURCHASERS—PARTNERS AND AGENTS—COMPANIES AND ASSOCIATIONS—MASTERS, SERVANTS AND WORKMEN—LEASES AND MORTGAGES—CHURCH AND CLERGY, RITUAL —LIBEL AND SLANDER—CONTRACTS AND AGREEMENTS—BONDS AND BILLS OF SALE— CHEQUES, BILLS AND NOTES—RAILWAY AND SHIPPING LAW—BANKRUPTCY AND IN-SURANCE—BORROWERS, LENDERS AND SURETIES—CRIMINAL LAW—PARLIAMENTARY ELECTIONS—COUNTY COUNCILS—MUNICIPAL CORPORATIONS—PARISH LAW, CHURCH-WARDENS, ETC.—PUBLIC HEALTH AND NUISANCES—FRIENDLY AND ¦BUILDING SOCIETIES—COPYRIGHT AND PATENTS—TRADE MARKS AND DESIGNS—HUSBAND AND WIFE, DIVORCE, ETC.—TRUSTEES AND EXECUTORS—INTESTACY, LAW OF—GUARDIAN AND WARD, INFANTS, ETC.—GAME LAWS AND SPORTING—HORSES, HORSE-DEALING AND DOGS—INNKEEPERS, LICENSING, ETC.—FORMS OF WILLS, AGREEMENTS, ETC. ETC.

NOTE.—*The object of this work is to enable those who consult it to help them-selves to the law; and thereby to dispense, as far as possible, with professional assistance and advice. There are many wrongs and grievances which persons sub-mit to from time to time through not knowing how or where to apply for redress; and many persons have as great a dread of a lawyer's office as of a lion's den. With this book at hand it is believed that many a* SIX-AND-EIGHTPENCE *may be saved; many a wrong redressed; many a right reclaimed; many a law suit avoided; and many an evil abated. The work has established itself as the standard legal adviser of all classes, and also made a reputation for itself as a useful book of reference for lawyers residing at a distance from law libraries, who are glad to have at hand a work em-bodying recent decisions and enactments.*

*** OPINIONS OF THE PRESS.

" It is a complete code of English Law, written in plain language, which all can understand. . . Should be in the hands of every business man, and all who wish to abolish lawyers' bills."— *Weekly Times.*

" A useful and concise epitome of the law, compiled with considerable care."—*Law Magazine.*

"A complete digest of the most useful facts which constitute English law."—*Globe.*

" Admirably done, admirably arranged, and admirably cheap."—*Leeds Mercury.*

" A concise, cheap and complete epitome of the English law   So plainly written that he who runs may read, and he who reads may understand."—*Figaro.*

" A dictionary of legal facts well put together.   The book is a very useful one."—*Spectator.*

"The latest edition of this popular book ought to be in every business establishment, and on every library table."—*Sheffield Post.*

Private Bill Legislation and Provisional Orders.

HANDBOOK FOR THE USE OF SOLICITORS AND EN-GINEERS Engaged in Promoting Private Acts of Parliament and Provi-sional Orders, for the Authorization of Railways, Tramways, Works for the Supply of Gas and Water, and other undertakings of a like character. By L. LIVINGSTON MACASSEY, of the Middle Temple, Barrister-at-Law, M.Inst.C.E.; Author of " Hints on Water Supply." 8vo, 950 pp., 25s. cloth.

" The volume is a desideratum on a subject which can be only acquired by practical experi-ence, and the order of procedure in Private Bill Legislation and Provisional Orders is followed. The author's suggestions and notes will be found of great value to engineers and others profession-ally engaged in this class of practice."—*Building News.*

" The author's double experience as an engineer and barrister has eminently qualified him for the task, and enabled him to approach the subject alike from an engineering and legal point of view.   The volume will be found a great help both to engineers and lawyers engaged in promoting Private Acts ot Parliament and Provisional Orders."—*Local Government Chronicle.*

𝔚eale's 𝔕udimentary 𝔖eries.

LONDON, 1862.
THE PRIZE MEDAL
Was awarded to the Publishers of
"WEALE'S SERIES."

A NEW LIST OF

WEALE'S SERIES
RUDIMENTARY SCIENTIFIC, EDUCATIONAL, AND CLASSICAL.

Comprising nearly Three Hundred and Fifty distinct works in almost every department of Science, Art, and Education, recommended to the notice of Engineers, Architects, Builders, Artisans, and Students generally, as well as to those interested in Workmen's Libraries, Literary and Scientific Institutions, Colleges, Schools, Science Classes, &c., &c.

☞ "WEALE'S SERIES includes Text-Books on almost every branch of Science and Industry, comprising such subjects as Agriculture, Architecture and Building, Civil Engineering, Fine Arts, Mechanics and Mechanical Engineering, Physical and Chemical Science, and many miscellaneous Treatises. The whole are constantly undergoing revision, and new editions, brought up to the latest discoveries in scientific research, are constantly issued. The prices at which they are sold are as low as their excellence is assured."—*American Literary Gazette.*

"Amongst the literature of technical education, WEALE'S SERIES has ever enjoyed a high reputation, and the additions being made by Messrs. CROSBY LOCKWOOD & SON render the series more complete, and bring the information upon the several subjects down to the present time."—*Mining Journal.*

"It is not too much to say that no books have ever proved more popular with, or more useful to, young engineers and others than the excellent treatises comprised in WEALE'S SERIES."—*Engineer.*

"The excellence of WEALE'S SERIES is now so well appreciated, that it would be wasting our space to enlarge upon their general usefulness and value."—*Builder.*

"The volumes of WEALE'S SERIES form one of the best collections of elementary technical books in any language."—*Architect.*

"WEALE'S SERIES has become a standard as well as an unrivalled collection of treatises in all branches of art and science."—*Public Opinion.*

PHILADELPHIA, 1876.
THE PRIZE MEDAL
Was awarded to the Publishers for
Books: Rudimentary, Scientific,
"WEALE'S SERIES," ETC.

CROSBY LOCKWOOD & SON,
7, STATIONERS' HALL COURT, LUDGATE HILL, LONDON, E.C.

WEALE'S RUDIMENTARY SCIENTIFIC SERIES.

*** The volumes of this Series are freely Illustrated with Woodcuts, or otherwise, where requisite. Throughout the following List it must be understood that the books are bound in limp cloth, unless otherwise stated; *but the volumes marked with a ‡ may also be had strongly bound in cloth boards for 6d. extra.*

N.B.—In ordering from this List it is recommended, as a means of facilitating business and obviating error, to quote the numbers affixed to the volumes, as well as the titles and prices.

CIVIL ENGINEERING, SURVEYING, ETC.

No.

31. *WELLS AND WELL-SINKING.* By JOHN GEO. SWINDELL, A.R.I.B.A., and G. R. BURNELL, C.E. Revised Edition. With a New Appendix on the Qualities of Water. Illustrated. 2s.

35. *THE BLASTING AND QUARRYING OF STONE,* for Building and other Purposes. B Gen. Sir J. BURGOYNE, Bart. 1s. 6d.

43. *TUBULAR, AND OTHER IRON GIRDER BRIDGES,* particularly describing the Britannia and Conway Tubular Bridges. By G. DRYSDALE DEMPSEY, C.E. Fourth Edition. 2s.

44. *FOUNDATIONS AND CONCRETE WORKS,* with Practical Remarks on Footings, Sand, Concrete, Béton, Pile-driving, Caissons, and Cofferdams, &c. By E. DOBSON. Seventh Edition. 1s. 6d.

60. *LAND AND ENGINEERING SURVEYING.* By T. BAKER, C.E. Fifteenth Edition, revised by Professor J. R. YOUNG. 2s.‡

80*. *EMBANKING LANDS FROM THE SEA.* With examples and Particulars of actual Embankments, &c. By J. WIGGINS, F.G.S. 2s.

81. *WATER WORKS,* for the Supply of Cities and Towns. With a Description of the Principal Geological Formations of England as influencing Supplies of Water, &c. By S. HUGHES, C.E. New Edition. 4s.‡

118. *CIVIL ENGINEERING IN NORTH AMERICA,* a Sketch of. By DAVID STEVENSON, F.R.S.E., &c. Plates and Diagrams. 3s.

167. *IRON BRIDGES, GIRDERS, ROOFS, AND OTHER WORKS.* By FRANCIS CAMPIN, C.E. 2s. 6d.‡

197. *ROADS AND STREETS.* By H. LAW, C.E., revised and enlarged by D. K. CLARK, C.E., including pavements of Stone, Wood, Asphalte, &c. 4s. 6d.‡

203. *SANITARY WORK IN THE SMALLER TOWNS AND IN VILLAGES.* By C. SLAGG, A.M.I.C.E. Revised Edition. 3s.‡

212. *GAS-WORKS, THEIR CONSTRUCTION AND ARRANGEMENT;* and the Manufacture and Distribution of Coal Gas. Originally written by SAMUEL HUGHES, C.E. Re-written and enlarged by WILLIAM RICHARDS, C.E. Eighth Edition, with important additions. 5s. 6d.‡

213. *PIONEER ENGINEERING.* A Treatise on the Engineering Operations connected with the Settlement of Waste Lands in New Countries. By EDWARD DOBSON, Assoc. Inst. C.E. 4s. 6d.‡

216. *MATERIALS AND CONSTRUCTION;* A Theoretical and Practical Treatise on the Strains, Designing, and Erection of Works of Construction. By FRANCIS CAMPIN, C.E. Second Edition, revised. 3s.‡

219. *CIVIL ENGINEERING.* By HENRY LAW, M.Inst. C.E. Including HYDRAULIC ENGINEERING by GEO. R. BURNELL, M.Inst. C.E. Seventh Edition, revised, with large additions by D. KINNEAR CLARK, M.Inst. C.E. 6s. 6d., Cloth boards, 7s. 6d.

268. *THE DRAINAGE OF LANDS, TOWNS, & BUILDINGS.* By G. D. DEMPSEY, C.E. Revised, with large Additions on Recent Practice in Drainage Engineering, by D. KINNEAR CLARK, M.I.C.E. Second Edition, Corrected. 4s. 6d.‡

☞ *The ‡ indicates that these vols. may be had strongly bound at 6d. extra.*

LONDON : CROSBY LOCKWOOD AND SON,

MECHANICAL ENGINEERING, ETC.

33. *CRANES*, the Construction of, and other Machinery for Raising Heavy Bodies. By JOSEPH GLYNN, F.R.S. Illustrated. 1s. 6d.
34. *THE STEAM ENGINE*. By Dr. LARDNER. Illustrated. 1s. 6d.
59. *STEAM BOILERS*: their Construction and Management. By R. ARMSTRONG, C.E. Illustrated. 1s. 6d.
82. *THE POWER OF WATER*, as applied to drive Flour Mills, and to give motion to Turbines, &c. By JOSEPH GLYNN, F.R.S. 2s.‡
98. *PRACTICAL MECHANISM*, the Elements of; and Machine Tools. By T. BAKER, C.E. With Additions by J. NASMYTH, C.E. 2s. 6d.‡
139. *THE STEAM ENGINE*, a Treatise on the Mathematical Theory of, with Rules and Examples for Practical Men. By T. BAKER, C.E. 1s. 6d.
164. *MODERN WORKSHOP PRACTICE*, as applied to Steam Engines, Bridges, Ship-building, &c. By J. G. WINTON. New Edition. 3s. 6d.‡
165. *IRON AND HEAT*, exhibiting the Principles concerned in the Construction of Iron Beams, Pillars, and Girders. By J. ARMOUR. 2s. 6d.‡
166. *POWER IN MOTION*: Horse-Power, Toothed-Wheel Gearing, Long and Short Driving Bands, and Angular Forces. By J. ARMOUR, 2s.‡
171. *THE WORKMAN'S MANUAL OF ENGINEERING DRAWING*. By J. MAXTON. 7th Edn. With 7 Plates and 350 Cuts. 3s. 6d.‡
190. *STEAM AND THE STEAM ENGINE*, Stationary and Portable. By J. SEWELL and D. K. CLARK, C.E. 3s. 6d.‡
200. *FUEL*, its Combustion and Economy. By C. W. WILLIAMS. With Recent Practice in the Combustion and Economy of Fuel—Coal, Coke, Wood, Peat, Petroleum, &c.—by D. K. CLARK, M.I.C.E. 3s. 6d.‡
202. *LOCOMOTIVE ENGINES*. By G. D. DEMPSEY, C.E.; with large additions by D. KINNEAR CLARK, M.I.C.E. 3s.‡
211. *THE BOILERMAKER'S ASSISTANT*. in Drawing, Templating, and Calculating Boiler and Tank Work. By JOHN COURTNEY, Practical Boiler Maker. Edited by D. K. CLARK, C.E. 100 Illustrations. 2s.
217. *SEWING MACHINERY*: Its Construction, History, &c., with full Technical Directions for Adjusting, &c. By J. W. URQUHART, C.E. 2s.‡
223. *MECHANICAL ENGINEERING*. Comprising Metallurgy, Moulding, Casting, Forging, Tools, Workshop Machinery, Manufacture of the Steam Engine, &c. By FRANCIS CAMPIN, C.E. Second Edition. 2s. 6d.‡
236. *DETAILS OF MACHINERY*. Comprising Instructions for the Execution of various Works in Iron. By FRANCIS CAMPIN, C.E. 3s.‡
237. *THE SMITHY AND FORGE*; including the Farrier's Art and Coach Smithing. By W. J. E. CRANE. Illustrated. 2s. 6d.‡
238. *THE SHEET-METAL WORKER'S GUIDE*; a Practical Handbook for Tinsmiths, Coppersmiths, Zincworkers, &c. With 94 Diagrams and Working Patterns. By W. J. E. CRANE. Second Edition, revised. 1s. 6d.
251. *STEAM AND MACHINERY MANAGEMENT*: with Hints on Construction and Selection. By M. POWIS BALE, M.I.M.E. 2s. 6d.‡
254. *THE BOILERMAKER'S READY-RECKONER*. By J. COURTNEY. Edited by D. K. CLARK, C.E. 4s.
⁎⁎⁎ *Nos.* 211 *and* 254 *in One Vol., half-bound, entitled* "THE BOILERMAKER'S READY-RECKONER AND ASSISTANT." By J. COURTNEY and D. K. CLARK. 7s.
255. *LOCOMOTIVE ENGINE-DRIVING*. A Practical Manual for Engineers in charge of Locomotive Engines. By MICHAEL REYNOLDS, M.S.E. Eighth Edition. 3s. 6d., limp; 4s. 6d. cloth boards.
256. *STATIONARY ENGINE-DRIVING*. A Practical Manual Engineers in charge of Stationary Engines. By MICHAEL REYNOLDS, M.S.E. Fourth Edition. 3s. 6d. limp; 4s. 6d. cloth boards.
260. *IRON BRIDGES OF MODERATE SPAN*: their Construction and Erection. By HAMILTON W. PENDRED, C.E. 2s.

☞ *The ‡ indicates that these vols. may be had strongly bound at 6d. extra.*

7, STATIONERS' HALL COURT, LUDGATE HILL, E.C.

MINING, METALLURGY, ETC.

4. *MINERALOGY,* Rudiments of; a concise View of the General
Properties of Minerals. By A. RAMSAY, F.G.S., F.R.G.S., &c. Third
Edition, revised and enlarged. Illustrated. 3s. 6d.‡

117. *SUBTERRANEOUS SURVEYING,* with and without the Magnetic Needle. By T. FENWICK and T. BAKER, C.E. Illustrated. 2s. 6d. ‡

135. *ELECTRO-METALLURGY;* Practically Treated. By ALEX-
ANDER WATT. Ninth Edition, enlarged and revised, with additional Illustrations, and including the most recent Processes. 3s. 6d.‡

172. *MINING TOOLS,* Manual of. For the Use of Mine Managers,
Agents, Students, &c. By WILLIAM MORGANS. 2s. 6d.

172*. *MINING TOOLS, ATLAS* of Engravings to Illustrate the above,
containing 235 Illustrations, drawn to Scale. 4to. 4s. 6d.

176. *METALLURGY OF IRON.* Containing History of Iron Manufacture, Methods of Assay, and Analyses of Iron Ores, Processes of Manufacture of Iron and Steel, &c. By H. BAUERMAN, F.G.S. Sixth Edition,
revised and enlarged. 5s.‡

180. *COAL AND COAL MINING.* By the late Sir WARINGTON W.
SMYTH, M.A., F.R.S. Seventh Edition, revised. 3s. 6d.‡ [*Just published.*

195. *THE MINERAL SURVEYOR AND VALUER'S COM-
PLETE GUIDE.* By W. LINTERN, M.E. Third Edition, including Magnetic and Angular Surveying. With Four Plates. 3s. 6d.‡

*14. *SLATE AND SLATE QUARRYING,* Scientific, Practical, and
Commercial. By D. C. DAVIES, F.G.S., Mining Engineer, &c. 3s.‡

264. *A FIRST BOOK OF MINING AND QUARRYING,* with the
Sciences connected therewith, for Primary Schools and Self-Instruction. By
J. H. COLLINS, F.G.S. Second Edition, with additions. 1s. 6d.

ARCHITECTURE, BUILDING, ETC.

16. *ARCHITECTURE—ORDERS*—The Orders and their Æsthetic
Principles. By W. H. LEEDS. Illustrated. 1s. 6d.

17. *ARCHITECTURE—STYLES*—The History and Description of
the Styles of Architecture of Various Countries, from the Earliest to the
Present Period. By T. TALBOT BURY, F.R.I.B.A., &c. Illustrated. 2s.
⁎ ORDERS AND STYLES OF ARCHITECTURE, *in One Vol.,* 3s. 6d.

18. *ARCHITECTURE—DESIGN*—The Principles of Design in
Architecture, as deducible from Nature and exemplified in the Works of the
Greek and Gothic Architects. By E. L. GARBETT, Architect. Illustrated. 2s.6d.
⁎ *The three preceding Works, in One handsome Vol., half bound, entitled*
" MODERN ARCHITECTURE," *price 6s.*

22. *THE ART OF BUILDING,* Rudiments of. General Principles
of Construction, Materials used in Building, Strength and Use of Materials,
Working Drawings, Specifications, and Estimates. By E. DOBSON, 2s.‡

25. *MASONRY AND STONECUTTING:* Rudimentary Treatise
on the Principles of Masonic Projection and their application to Construction. By EDWARD DOBSON, M.R.I.B.A., &c. 2s. 6d.‡

42. *COTTAGE BUILDING.* By C. BRUCE ALLEN, Architect.
Eleventh Edition, revised and enlarged. With a Chapter on Economic Cottages
for Allotments, by EDWARD E. ALLEN, C.E. 2s.

45. *LIMES, CEMENTS, MORTARS, CONCRETES, MASTICS,*
PLASTERING, &c. By G. R. BURNELL, C.E. Fourteenth Edition. 1s. 6d.

57. *WARMING AND VENTILATION.* An Exposition of the
General Principles as applied to Domestic and Public Buildings, Mines,
Lighthouses, Ships, &c. By C. TOMLINSON, F.R.S., &c. Illustrated. 3s.

111. *ARCHES, PIERS, BUTTRESSES, &c.:* Experimental Essays
on the Principles of Construction. By W. BLAND. Illustrated. 1s. 6d.

☞ *The ‡ indicates that these vols. may be had strongly bound at 6d. extra.*

LONDON : CROSBY LOCKWOOD AND SON,

Architecture, Building, etc., *continued.*

116. *THE ACOUSTICS OF PUBLIC BUILDINGS;* or, The Principles of the Science of Sound applied to the purposes of the Architect and Builder. By T. ROGER SMITH, M.R.I.B.A., Architect. Illustrated. 1s. 6d.

127. *ARCHITECTURAL MODELLING IN PAPER,* the Art of. By T. A. RICHARDSON, Architect. Illustrated. 1s. 6d.

128. *VITRUVIUS — THE ARCHITECTURE OF MARCUS VITRUVIUS POLLO.* In Ten Books. Translated from the Latin by JOSEPH GWILT, F.S.A., F.R.A.S. With 23 Plates. 5s.

130. *GRECIAN ARCHITECTURE,* An Inquiry into the Principles of Beauty in; with an Historical View of the Rise and Progress of the Art in Greece. By the EARL OF ABERDEEN. 1s.

⁎ *The two preceding Works in One handsome Vol., half bound, entitled* "ANCIENT ARCHITECTURE," *price 6s.*

132. *THE ERECTION OF DWELLING-HOUSES.* Illustrated by a Perspective View, Plans, Elevations, and Sections of a pair of Semi-detached Villas, with the Specification, Quantities, and Estimates, &c. By S. H. BROOKS. New Edition, with Plates. 2s. 6d.‡

156. *QUANTITIES & MEASUREMENTS* in Bricklayers', Masons', Plasterers', Plumbers', Painters', Paperhangers', Gilders', Smiths', Carpenters' and Joiners' Work. By A. C. BEATON, Surveyor. Ninth Edition. 1s. 6d.

175. *LOCKWOOD'S BUILDER'S PRICE BOOK FOR* 1892. A Comprehensive Handbook of the Latest Prices and Data for Builders, Architects, Engineers, and Contractors. Re-constructed, Re-written, and further Enlarged. By FRANCIS T. W. MILLER, A.R.I.B.A. 700 pages. 3s. 6d.; cloth boards, 4s. [*Just Published.*

182. *CARPENTRY AND JOINERY*—THE ELEMENTARY PRIN-CIPLES OF CARPENTRY. Chiefly composed from the Standard Work of THOMAS TREDGOLD, C.E. With a TREATISE ON JOINERY by E. WYNDHAM TARN, M.A. Fifth Edition, Revised. 3s. 6d.‡

182*. *CARPENTRY AND JOINERY.* ATLAS of 35 Plates to accompany the above. With Descriptive Letterpress. 4to. 6s.

185. *THE COMPLETE MEASURER;* the Measurement of Boards, Glass, &c.; Unequal-sided, Square-sided, Octagonal-sided, Round Timber and Stone, and Standing Timber, &c. By RICHARD HORTON. Fifth Edition. 4s.; strongly bound in leather, 5s.

187. *HINTS TO YOUNG ARCHITECTS.* By G. WIGHTWICK. New Edition. By G. H. GUILLAUME. Illustrated. 3s. 6d.‡

188. *HOUSE PAINTING, GRAINING, MARBLING, AND SIGN WRITING:* with a Course of Elementary Drawing for House-Painters, Sign-Writers, &c., and a Collection of Useful Receipts. By ELLIS A. DAVIDSON. Sixth Edition. With Coloured Plates. 5s. cloth limp; 6s. cloth boards.

189. *THE RUDIMENTS OF PRACTICAL BRICKLAYING.* In Six Sections: General Principles; Arch Drawing, Cutting, and Setting; Pointing; Paving, Tiling, Materials; Slating and Plastering; Practical Geometry, Mensuration, &c. By ADAM HAMMOND. Seventh Edition. 1s. 6d.

191. *PLUMBING.* A Text-Book to the Practice of the Art or Craft of the Plumber. With Chapters upon House Drainage and Ventilation. Sixth Edition. With 380 Illustrations. By W. P. BUCHAN. 3s. 6d.‡

192. *THE TIMBER IMPORTER'S, TIMBER MERCHANT'S,* and BUILDER'S STANDARD GUIDE. By R. E. GRANDY. 2s.

206. *A BOOK ON BUILDING,* Civil and Ecclesiastical, including CHURCH RESTORATION. With the Theory of Domes and the Great Pyramid, &c. By Sir EDMUND BECKETT, Bart., LL.D., Q.C., F.R.A.S. 4s. 6d.‡

226. *THE JOINTS MADE AND USED BY BUILDERS* in the Construction of various kinds of Engineering and Architectural Works. By WYVILL J. CHRISTY, Architect. With upwards of 160 Engravings on Wood. 3s.‡

228. *THE CONSTRUCTION OF ROOFS OF WOOD AND IRON.* By E. WYNDHAM TARN, M.A., Architect. Second Edition, revised. 1s. 6d.

☞ *The ‡ indicates that these vols. may be had strongly bound at 6d. extra.*

Architecture, Building, etc., *continued.*

229. *ELEMENTARY DECORATION:* as applied to the Interior and Exterior Decoration of Dwelling-Houses, &c. By J. W. FACEY. 2s.

257. *PRACTICAL HOUSE DECORATION.* A Guide to the Art of Ornamental Painting. By JAMES W. FACEY. 2s. 6d.

⁎ The two preceding Works, in One handsome Vol., half-bound, entitled "HOUSE DECORATION, ELEMENTARY AND PRACTICAL," price 5s.

230. *HANDRAILING.* Showing New and Simple Methods for finding the Pitch of the Plank, Drawing the Moulds, Bevelling, Jointing-up, and Squaring the Wreath. By GEORGE COLLINGS. Second Edition, Revised, including A TREATISE ON STAIRBUILDING. Plates and Diagrams. 2s. 6d.

247. *BUILDING ESTATES :* a Rudimentary Treatise on the Development, Sale, Purchase, and General Management of Building Land. By FOWLER MAITLAND, Surveyor. Second Edition, revised. 2s.

248. *PORTLAND CEMENT. FOR USERS.* By HENRY FAIJA, Assoc. M. Inst. C.E. Third Edition, corrected. Illustrated. 2s.

252. *BRICKWORK :* a Practical Treatise, embodying the General and Higher Principles of Bricklaying, Cutting and Setting, &c. By F. WALKER. Third Edition, Revised and Enlarged. 1s. 6d.

23. *THE PRACTICAL BRICK AND TILE BOOK.* Comprising :
189. BRICK AND TILE MAKING, by E. DOBSON, A.I.C.E.; PRACTICAL BRICKLAY-
265. ING, by A. HAMMOND; BRICKCUTTING AND SETTING, by A. HAMMOND. 534 pp. with 270 Illustrations. 6s. Strongly half-bound.

253. *THE TIMBER MERCHANT'S, SAW-MILLER'S, AND* IMPORTER'S FREIGHT-BOOK AND ASSISTANT. By WM. RICHARDSON. With a Chapter on Speeds of Saw-Mill Machinery, &c. By M. POWIS BALE, A.M.Inst.C.E. 3s.‡

258. *CIRCULAR WORK IN CARPENTRY AND JOINERY.* A Practical Treatise on Circular Work of Single and Double Curvature. By GEORGE COLLINGS. Second Edition, 2s. 6d.

259. *GAS FITTING :* A Practical Handbook treating of every Description of Gas Laying and Fitting. By JOHN BLACK. With 122 Illustrations. 2s. 6d.‡

261. *SHORING AND ITS APPLICATION :* A Handbook for the Use of Students. By GEORGE H. BLAGROVE. 1s. 6d.

265. *THE ART OF PRACTICAL BRICK CUTTING & SETTING.* By ADAM HAMMOND. With 90 Engravings. 1s. 6d. [*Just published.*

267. *THE SCIENCE OF BUILDING :* An Elementary Treatise on the Principles of Construction. Adapted to the Requirements of Architectural Students. By E. WYNDHAM TARN, M.A. Lond. Third Edition, Revised and Enlarged. With 59 Wood Engravings. 3s. 6d.‡

271. *VENTILATION :* a Text-book to the Practice of the Art of Ventilating Buildings, with a Supplementary Chapter upon Air Testing. By WILLIAM PATON BUCHAN, R.P., Sanitary and Ventilating Engineer, Author of "Plumbing," &c. 3s. 6d.‡ [*Just published.*

SHIPBUILDING, NAVIGATION, MARINE ENGINEERING, ETC.

51. *NAVAL ARCHITECTURE.* An Exposition of the Elementary Principles of the Science, and their Practical Application to Naval Constr. c-tion. By J. PEAKE. Fifth Edition, with Plates and Diagrams. 3s. 6d.‡

53*. *SHIPS FOR OCEAN & RIVER SERVICE*, Elementary a d Practical Principles of the Construction of. By H. A. SOMMERFELDT. 1s. d.

53**. *AN ATLAS OF ENGRAVINGS* to Illustrate the above. Twelve large folding plates. Royal 4to, cloth. 7s. 6d.

54. *MASTING, MAST-MAKING, AND RIGGING OF SHIPS,* Also Tables of Spars, Rigging, Blocks ; Chain, Wire, and Hemp Ropes, &c., relative to every class of vessels. By ROBERT KIPPING, N.A. 2s.

☞ *The ‡ indicates that these vols. may be had strongly bound at 6d. extra.*

Shipbuilding, Navigation, Marine Engineering, etc., *cont.*

54*. *IRON SHIP-BUILDING.* With Practical Examples and Details.
By JOHN GRANTHAM, C.E. Fifth Edition. 4s.

55. *THE SAILOR'S SEA BOOK:* a Rudimentary Treatise on Navigation. By JAMES GREENWOOD, B.A. With numerous Woodcuts and Coloured Plates. New and enlarged edition. By W. H. ROSSER. 2s. 6d.‡

80. *MARINE ENGINES AND STEAM VESSELS.* By ROBERT MURRAY, C.E. Eighth Edition, thoroughly Revised, with Additions by the Author and by GEORGE CARLISLE, C.E. 4s. 6d. limp; 5s. cloth boards.

83*bis.* *THE FORMS OF SHIPS AND BOATS.* By W. BLAND. Eighth Edition, Revised, with numerous Illustrations and Models. 1s. 6d.

99. *NAVIGATION AND NAUTICAL ASTRONOMY,* in Theory and Practice. By Prof. J. R. YOUNG. New Edition. 2s. 6d.

106. *SHIPS' ANCHORS,* a Treatise on. By G. COTSELL, N.A. 1s. 6d.

149. *SAILS AND SAIL-MAKING.* With Draughting, and the Centre of Effort of the Sails; Weights and Sizes of Ropes; Masting, Rigging, and Sails of Steam Vessels, &c. 12th Edition. By R. KIPPING, N.A., 2s. 6d.‡

155. *ENGINEER'S GUIDE TO THE ROYAL & MERCANTILE NAVIES.* By a PRACTICAL ENGINEER. Revised by D. F. M'CARTHY. 3s.

55 & 204. *PRACTICAL NAVIGATION.* Consisting of The Sailor's Sea-Book. By JAMES GREENWOOD and W. H. ROSSER. Together with the requisite Mathematical and Nautical Tables for the Working of the Problems. By H. LAW, C.E., and Prof. J. R. YOUNG. 7s. Half-bound.

AGRICULTURE, GARDENING, ETC.

61*. *A COMPLETE READY RECKONER FOR THE ADMEASUREMENT OF LAND,* &c. By A. ARMAN. Third Edition, revised and extended by C. NORRIS, Surveyor, Valuer, &c. 2s.

131. *MILLER'S, CORN MERCHANT'S, AND FARMER'S READY RECKONER.* Second Edition, with a Price List of Modern Flour-Mill Machinery, by W. S. HUTTON, C.E. 2s.

140. *SOILS, MANURES, AND CROPS.* (Vol. 1. OUTLINES OF MODERN FARMING.) By R. SCOTT BURN. Woodcuts. 2s.

141. *FARMING & FARMING ECONOMY,* Notes, Historical and Practical, on. (Vol. 2. OUTLINES OF MODERN FARMING.) By R. SCOTT BURN. 3s.

142. *STOCK; CATTLE, SHEEP, AND HORSES.* (Vol. 3. OUTLINES OF MODERN FARMING.) By R. SCOTT BURN. Woodcuts. 2s. 6d.

145. *DAIRY, PIGS, AND POULTRY,* Management of the. By R. SCOTT BURN. (Vol. 4. OUTLINES OF MODERN FARMING.) 2s.

146. *UTILIZATION OF SEWAGE, IRRIGATION, AND RECLAMATION OF WASTE LAND.* (Vol. 5. OUTLINES OF MODERN FARMING.) By R. SCOTT BURN. Woodcuts. 2s. 6d.

** *Nos.* 140-1-2-5-6, *in One Vol., handsomely half-bound, entitled* "OUTLINES OF MODERN FARMING." By ROBERT SCOTT BURN. *Price* 12s.

177. *FRUIT TREES,* The Scientific and Profitable Culture of. From the French of DU BREUIL. Revised by GEO. GLENNY. 187 Woodcuts. 3s. 6d.‡

198. *SHEEP; THE HISTORY, STRUCTURE, ECONOMY, AND DISEASES OF.* By W. C. SPOONER, M.R.V.C., &c. Fifth Edition, enlarged, including Specimens of New and Improved Breeds. 3s. 6d.‡

201. *KITCHEN GARDENING MADE EASY.* By GEORGE M. F. GLENNY. Illustrated. 1s. 6d.‡

207. *OUTLINES OF FARM MANAGEMENT,* and the Organization of Farm Labour. By R. SCOTT BURN. 2s. 6d.‡

208. *OUTLINES OF LANDED ESTATES MANAGEMENT.* By R. SCOTT BURN. 2s. 6d.

** *Nos.* 207 & 208 *in One Vol., handsomely half-bound, entitled* "OUTLINES OF LANDED ESTATES AND FARM MANAGEMENT." By R. SCOTT BURN. *Price* 6s.

☞ *The ‡ indicates that these vols. may be had strongly bound at 6d. extra.*

Agriculture, Gardening, etc., *continued.*

209. *THE TREE PLANTER AND PLANT PROPAGATOR.*
A Practical Manual on the Propagation of Forest Trees, Fruit Trees,
Flowering Shrubs, Flowering Plants, &c. By SAMUEL WOOD. 2s.

210. *THE TREE PRUNER.* A Practical Manual on the Pruning of
Fruit Trees, including also their Training and Renovation; also the Pruning
of Shrubs, Climbers, and Flowering Plants. By SAMUEL WOOD. 1s. 6d.

** Nos. 209 & 210 *in One Vol., handsomely half-bound, entitled* "THE TREE
PLANTER, PROPAGATOR, AND PRUNER." *By* SAMUEL WOOD. *Price* 3s. 6d.

218. *THE HAY AND STRAW MEASURER :* Being New Tables
for the Use of Auctioneers, Valuers, Farmers, Hay and Straw Dealers, &c.
By JOHN STEELE. Fifth Edition. 2s.

222. *SUBURBAN FARMING.* The Laying-out and Cultivation of
Farms, adapted to the Produce of Milk, Butter, and Cheese, Eggs, Poultry,
and Pigs. By Prof. JOHN DONALDSON and R. SCOTT BURN. 3s. 6d.‡

231. *THE ART OF GRAFTING AND BUDDING.* By CHARLES
BALTET. With Illustrations. 2s. 6d.‡

232. *COTTAGE GARDENING ;.* or, Flowers, Fruits, and Vegetables
for Small Gardens. By E. HOBDAY. 1s. 6d.

233. *GARDEN RECEIPTS.* Edited by CHARLES W. QUIN. 1s. 6d.

234. *MARKET AND KITCHEN.GARDENING.* By C. W. SHAW,
late Editor of "Gardening Illustrated." 3s.‡

239. *DRAINING AND EMBANKING.* A Practical Treatise, em-
bodying the most recent experience in the Application of Improved Methods.
By JOHN SCOTT, late Professor of Agriculture and Rural Economy at the
Royal Agricultural College, Cirencester. With 68 Illustrations. 1s. 6d.

240. *IRRIGATION AND WATER SUPPLY.* A Treatise on Water
Meadows, Sewage Irrigation, and Warping; the Construction of Wells,
Ponds, and Reservoirs, &c. By Prof. JOHN SCOTT. With 34 Illus. 1s. 6d.

241. *FARM ROADS, FENCES, AND GATES.* A Practical
Treatise on the Roads, Tramways, and Waterways of the Farm; the
Principles of Enclosures; and the different kinds of Fences, Gates, and
Stiles. By Professor JOHN SCOTT. With 75 Illustrations. 1s. 6d.

242. *FARM BUILDINGS.* A Practical Treatise on the Buildings
necessary for various kinds of Farms, their Arrangement and Construction,
with Plans and Estimates. By Prof. JOHN SCOTT. With 105 Illus. 2s.

243. *BARN IMPLEMENTS AND MACHINES.* A Practical
Treatise on the Application of Power to the Operations of Agriculture; and
on various Machines used in the Threshing-barn, in the Stock-yard, and in the
Dairy, &c. By Prof. J. SCOTT. With 123 Illustrations. 2s.

244. *FIELD IMPLEMENTS AND MACHINES.* A Practical
Treatise on the Varieties now in use, with Principles and Details of Con-
struction, their Points of Excellence, and Management. By Professor JOHN
SCOTT. With 138 Illustrations. 2s.

245. *AGRICULTURAL SURVEYING.* A Practical Treatise on
Land Surveying, Levelling, and Setting-out; and on Measuring and Esti-
mating Quantities, Weights, and Values of Materials, Produce, Stock, &c.
By Prof. JOHN SCOTT. With 62 Illustrations. 1s. 6d.

** Nos. 239 *to* 245 *in One Vol., handsomely half-bound, entitled* "THE COMPLETE
TEXT-BOOK OF FARM ENGINEERING." *By* Professor JOHN SCOTT. *Price* 12s.

250. *MEAT PRODUCTION.* A Manual for Producers, Distributors,
&c. By JOHN EWART. 2s. 6d.‡

266. *BOOK-KEEPING FOR FARMERS & ESTATE OWNERS.*
By J. M. WOODMAN, Chartered Accountant. 2s. 6d. cloth limp; 3s. 6d.
cloth boards.

☞ *The* ‡ *indicates that these vols. may be had strongly bound at* 6d. *extra.*

LONDON : CROSBY LOCKWOOD AND SON,

MATHEMATICS, ARITHMETIC, ETC.

32. *MATHEMATICAL INSTRUMENTS*, a Treatise on; Their Construction, Adjustment, Testing, and Use concisely Explained. By J. F. HEATHER, M.A. Fourteenth Edition, revised, with additions, by A. T. WALMISLEY, M.I.C.E., Fellow of the Surveyors' Institution. Original Edition, in 1 vol., Illustrated. 2s.‡

** *In ordering the above, be careful to say, " Original Edition " (No. 32), to distinguish it from the Enlarged Edition in 3 vols. (Nos. 168-9-70.)*

76. *DESCRIPTIVE GEOMETRY*, an Elementary Treatise on; with a Theory of Shadows and of Perspective, extracted from the French of G. MONGE. To which is added, a description of the Principles and Practice of Isometrical Projection. By J. F. HEATHER, M.A. With 14 Plates. 2s.

178. *PRACTICAL PLANE GEOMETRY:* giving the Simplest Modes of Constructing Figures contained in one Plane and Geometrical Construction of the Ground. By J. F. HEATHER, M.A. With 215 Woodcuts. 2s.

83. *COMMERCIAL BOOK-KEEPING.* With Commercial Phrases and Forms in English, French, Italian, and German. By JAMES HADDON, M.A., Arithmetical Master of King's College School, London. 1s. 6d.

84. *ARITHMETIC*, a Rudimentary Treatise on: with full Explanations of its Theoretical Principles, and numerous Examples for Practice. By Professor J. R. YOUNG. Eleventh Edition. 1s. 6d.

84*. A KEY to the above, containing Solutions in full to the Exercises, together with Comments, Explanations, and Improved Processes, for the Use of Teachers and Unassisted Learners. By J. R. YOUNG. 1s. 6d.

85. *EQUATIONAL ARITHMETIC*, applied to Questions of Interest, Annuities, Life Assurance, and General Commerce; with various Tables by which all Calculations may be greatly facilitated. By W. HIPSLEY. 2s.

86. *ALGEBRA*, the Elements of. By JAMES HADDON, M.A. With Appendix, containing miscellaneous Investigations, and a Collection of Problems in various parts of Algebra. 2s.

86*. A KEY AND COMPANION to the above Book, forming an extensive repository of Solved Examples and Problems in Illustration of the various Expedients necessary in Algebraical Operations. By J. R. YOUNG. 1s. 6d.

88. *EUCLID*, THE ELEMENTS OF: with many additional Propositions
89. and Explanatory Notes: to which is prefixed, an Introductory Essay on Logic. By HENRY LAW, C.E. 2s. 6d.‡

** *Sold also separately, viz. :—*

88. EUCLID, The First Three Books. By HENRY LAW, C.E. 1s. 6d.
89. EUCLID, Books 4, 5, 6, 11, 12. By HENRY LAW, C.E. 1s. 6d.

90. *ANALYTICAL GEOMETRY AND CONIC SECTIONS*, By JAMES HANN. A New Edition, by Professor J. R. YOUNG. 2s.‡

91. *PLANE TRIGONOMETRY*, the Elements of. By JAMES HANN, formerly Mathematical Master of King's College, London. 1s. 6d.

92. *SPHERICAL TRIGONOMETRY*, the Elements of. By JAMES HANN. Revised by CHARLES H. DOWLING, C.E. 1s.

** *Or with " The Elements of Plane Trigonometry," in One Volume, 2s. 6d.*

93. *MENSURATION AND MEASURING.* With the Mensuration and Levelling of Land for the Purposes of Modern Engineering. By T. BAKER, C.E. New Edition by E. NUGENT, C.E. Illustrated. 1s. 6d.

101. *DIFFERENTIAL CALCULUS*, Elements of the. By W. S. B. WOOLHOUSE, F.R.A.S., &c. 1s. 6d.

102. *INTEGRAL CALCULUS*, Rudimentary Treatise on the. By HOMERSHAM COX, B.A. Illustrated. 1s.

136. *ARITHMETIC*, Rudimentary, for the Use of Schools and Self-Instruction. By JAMES HADDON, M.A. Revised by A. ARMAN. 1s. 6d.
137. A KEY TO HADDON'S RUDIMENTARY ARITHMETIC. By A. ARMAN. 1s. 6d.

The ‡ indicates that these vols. may be had strongly bound at 6d. extra.

7, STATIONERS' HALL COURT, LUDGATE HILL, E.C.

Mathematics, Arithmetic, etc., *continued.*

168. *DRAWING AND MEASURING INSTRUMENTS.* Includ
ing—I. Instruments employed in Geometrical and Mechanical Drawing
and in the Construction, Copying, and Measurement of Maps and Plans
II. Instruments used for the purposes of Accurate Measurement, and fo
Arithmetical Computations. By J. F. HEATHER, M.A. Illustrated. 1s. 6c

169. *OPTICAL INSTRUMENTS.* Including (more especially) Tele
scopes, Microscopes, and Apparatus for producing copies of Maps and Plan
by Photography. By J. F. HEATHER, M.A. Illustrated. 1s. 6d.

170. *SURVEYING AND ASTRONOMICAL INSTRUMENTS*
Including—I. Instruments Used for Determining the Geometrical Feature
of a portion of Ground. II. Instruments Employed in Astronomical Observa
tions. By J. F. HEATHER, M.A. Illustrated. 1s. 6d.

* *The above three volumes form an enlargement of the Author's original worl
"Mathematical Instruments." (See No. 32 in the Series.)*

168.⎫ *MATHEMATICAL INSTRUMENTS.* By J. F. HEATHER
169.⎬ M.A. Enlarged Edition, for the most part entirely re-written. The 3 Parts a
170.⎭ above, in One thick Volume. With numerous Illustrations. 4s. 6d.‡

158. *THE SLIDE RULE, AND HOW TO USE IT;* containing
full, easy, and simple Instructions to perform all Business Calculations wit
unexampled rapidity and accuracy. By CHARLES HOARE, C.E. Sixt
Edition. With a Slide Rule in tuck of cover. 2s. 6d.‡

196. *THEORY OF COMPOUND INTEREST AND ANNUI*
TIES; with Tables of Logarithms for the more Difficult Computations c
Interest, Discount, Annuities, &c. By FÉDOR THOMAN. Fourth Edition. 4s.

199. *THE COMPENDIOUS CALCULATOR;* or, Easy and Concis
Methods of Performing the various Arithmetical Operations required i
Commercial and Business Transactions; together with Useful Tables. B
D. O'GORMAN. Twenty-seventh Edition, carefully revised by C. NORRIS
2s. 6d., cloth limp; 3s. 6d., strongly half-bound in leather.

204. *MATHEMATICAL TABLES,* for Trigonometrical, Astronomical
and Nautical Calculations; to which is prefixed a Treatise on Logarithms
By HENRY LAW, C.E. Together with a Series of Tables for Navigatioı
and Nautical Astronomy. By Prof. J. R. YOUNG. New Edition. 4s.

204*. *LOGARITHMS.* With Mathematical Tables for Trigonometrical
Astronomical, and Nautical Calculations. By HENRY LAW, M.Inst.C.E. Nev
and Revised Edition. (Forming part of the above Work). 3s.

221. *MEASURES, WEIGHTS, AND MONEYS OF ALL NA*
TIONS, and an Analysis of the Christian, Hebrew, and Mahometan Calen
dars. By W. S. B. WOOLHOUSE, F.R.A.S., F.S.S. Seventh Edition, 2s. 6d.

227. *MATHEMATICS AS APPLIED TO THE CONSTRUC*
TIVE ARTS. Illustrating the various processes of Mathematical Investi-
gation, by means of Arithmetical and Simple Algebraical Equations and
Practical Examples. By FRANCIS CAMPIN, C.E. Second Edition. 3s.‡

PHYSICAL SCIENCE, NATURAL PHILO-SOPHY, ETC.

1. *CHEMISTRY.* By Professor GEORGE FOWNES, F.R.S. With
an Appendix on the Application of Chemistry to Agriculture. 1s.

2. *NATURAL PHILOSOPHY,* Introduction to the Study of. By
C. TOMLINSON. Woodcuts. 1s. 6d.

6. *MECHANICS,* Rudimentary Treatise on. By CHARLES TOM-
LINSON. Illustrated. 1s. 6d.

7. *ELECTRICITY;* showing the General Principles of Electrical
Science, and the purposes to which it has been applied. By Sir W. SNOW
HARRIS, F.R.S., &c. With Additions by R. SABINE, C.E., F.S.A. 1s. 6d.

7*. *GALVANISM.* By Sir W. SNOW HARRIS. New Edition by
ROBERT SABINE, C.E., F.S.A. 1s. 6d.

8. *MAGNETISM;* being a concise Exposition of the General Principles of Magnetical Science. By Sir W. SNOW HARRIS. New Edition,
revised by H. M. NOAD, Ph.D. With 165 Woodcuts. 3s. 6d.‡

☞ *The ‡ indicates that these vols. may be had strongly bound at 6d. extra.*

LONDON: CROSBY LOCKWOOD AND SON,

Physical Science, Natural Philosophy, etc., *continued.*

11. *THE ELECTRIC TELEGRAPH;* its History and Progress; with Descriptions of some of the Apparatus. By R. SABINE, C.E., F.S.A. **3s.**

12. *PNEUMATICS,* including Acoustics and the Phenomena of Wind Currents, for the Use of Beginners. By CHARLES TOMLINSON, F.R.S. Fourth Edition, enlarged. Illustrated. **1s. 6d.**

72. *MANUAL OF THE MOLLUSCA;* a Treatise on Recent and Fossil Shells. By Dr. S. P. WOODWARD, A.L.S. Fourth Edition. With Plates and 300 Woodcuts. **7s. 6d.,** cloth.

96. *ASTRONOMY.* By the late Rev. ROBERT MAIN, M.A. Third Edition, by WILLIAM THYNNE LYNN, B.A., F.R.A.S. **2s.**

97. *STATICS AND DYNAMICS,* the Principles and Practice of; embracing also a clear development of Hydrostatics, Hydrodynamics, and Central Forces. By T. BAKER, C.E. Fourth Edition. **1s. 6d.**

173. *PHYSICAL GEOLOGY,* partly based on Major-General PORTLOCK's "Rudiments of Geology." By RALPH TATE, A.L.S., &c. Woodcuts. **2s.**

174. *HISTORICAL GEOLOGY,* partly based on Major-General PORTLOCK's "Rudiments." By RALPH TATE, A.L.S., &c. Woodcuts. **2s. 6d.**

173 & 174. *RUDIMENTARY TREATISE ON GEOLOGY,* Physical and Historical. Partly based on Major-General PORTLOCK's "Rudiments of Geology." By RALPH TATE, A.L.S., F.G.S., &c. In One Volume. **4s. 6d.‡**

183 & 184. *ANIMAL PHYSICS,* Handbook of. By Dr. LARDNER, D.C.L., formerly Professor of Natural Philosophy and Astronomy in University College, Lond. With 520 Illustrations. In One Vol. **7s. 6d.,** cloth boards.
*** *Sold also in Two Parts, as follows :—*

183. ANIMAL PHYSICS. By Dr. LARDNER. Part I., Chapters I.—VII. **4s.**

184. ANIMAL PHYSICS. By Dr. LARDNER. Part II., Chapters VIII.—XVIII. **3s.**

269. *LIGHT:* an Introduction to the Science of Optics, for the Use of Students of Architecture, Engineering, and other Applied Sciences. By E. WYNDHAM TARN, M.A. **1s. 6d.** *[Just published.*

FINE ARTS.

20. *PERSPECTIVE FOR BEGINNERS.* Adapted to Young Students and Amateurs in Architecture, Painting, &c. By GEORGE PYNE. **2s.**

40 *GLASS STAINING, AND THE ART OF PAINTING ON GLASS.* From the German of Dr. GESSERT and EMANUEL OTTO FROMBERG. With an Appendix on THE ART OF ENAMELLING. **2s. 6d.**

69. *MUSIC,* A Rudimentary and Practical Treatise on. With numerous Examples. By CHARLES CHILD SPENCER. **2s. 6d.**

71. *PIANOFORTE,* The Art of Playing the. With numerous Exercises & Lessons from the Best Masters. By CHARLES CHILD SPENCER. **1s. 6d.**

69-71. *MUSIC & THE PIANOFORTE.* In one vol. Half bound, **5s.**

181. *PAINTING POPULARLY EXPLAINED,* including Fresco, Oil, Mosaic, Water Colour, Water-Glass, Tempera, Encaustic, Miniature, Painting on Ivory, Vellum, Pottery, Enamel, Glass, &c. With Historical Sketches of the Progress of the Art by THOMAS JOHN GULLICK, assisted by JOHN TIMBS, F.S.A. Sixth Edition, revised and enlarged. **5s.‡**

186. *A GRAMMAR OF COLOURING,* applied to Decorative Painting and the Arts. By GEORGE FIELD. New Edition, enlarged and adapted to the Use of the Ornamental Painter and Designer. By ELLIS A. DAVIDSON. With two new Coloured Diagrams, &c. **3s.‡**

246. *A DICTIONARY OF PAINTERS, AND HANDBOOK FOR PICTURE AMATEURS;* including Methods of Painting, Cleaning, Relining and Restoring, Schools of Painting, &c. With Notes on the Copyists and Imitators of each Master. By PHILIPPE DARYL. **2s. 6d.‡**

☞ *The ‡ indicates that these vols. may be had strongly bound at 6d. extra.*

INDUSTRIAL AND USEFUL ARTS.

23. *BRICKS AND TILES*, Rudimentary Treatise on the Manufacture of. By E. DOBSON, M.R.I.B.A. Illustrated, 3s.‡

67. *CLOCKS, WATCHES, AND BELLS*, a Rudimentary Treatise on. By Sir EDMUND BECKETT, LL.D., Q.C. Seventh Edition, revised and enlarged. 4s. 6d. limp; 5s. 6d. cloth boards.

83**. *CONSTRUCTION OF DOOR LOCKS.* Compiled from the Papers of A. C. HOBBS, and Edited by CHARLES TOMLINSON. F.R.S. 2s. 6d.

162. *THE BRASS FOUNDER'S MANUAL;* Instructions for Modelling, Pattern-Making, Moulding, Turning, Filing, Burnishing, Bronzing, &c. With copious Receipts, &c. By WALTER GRAHAM. 2s.‡

205. *THE ART OF LETTER PAINTING MADE EASY.* By J. G. BADENOCH. Illustrated with 12 full-page Engravings of Examples. 1s. 6d.

215. *THE GOLDSMITH'S HANDBOOK,* containing full Instructions for the Alloying and Working of Gold. By GEORGE E. GEE, 3s.‡

225. *THE SILVERSMITH'S HANDBOOK,* containing full Instructions for the Alloying and Working of Silver. By GEORGE E. GEE. 3s.‡

* *The two preceding Works, in One handsome Vol., half-bound, entitled "*THE GOLDSMITH'S & SILVERSMITH'S COMPLETE HANDBOOK,*" 7s.*

249. *THE HALL-MARKING OF JEWELLERY PRACTICALLY CONSIDERED.* By GEORGE E. GEE. 3s.‡

224. *COACH BUILDING,* A Practical Treatise, Historical and Descriptive. By J. W. BURGESS. 2s. 6d.‡

235. *PRACTICAL ORGAN BUILDING.* By W. E. DICKSON, M.A., Precentor of Ely Cathedral. Illustrated. 2s. 6d.‡

262. *THE ART OF BOOT AND SHOEMAKING.* By JOHN BEDFORD LENO. Numerous Illustrations. Third Edition. 2s.

263. *MECHANICAL DENTISTRY:* A Practical Treatise on the Construction of the Various Kinds of Artificial Dentures, with Formulæ, Tables, Receipts, &c. By CHARLES HUNTER. Third Edition. 3s.‡

270. *WOOD ENGRAVING:* A Practical and Easy Introduction to the Study of the Art. By W. N. BROWN. 1s. 6d.

MISCELLANEOUS VOLUMES.

36. *A DICTIONARY OF TERMS used in ARCHITECTURE, BUILDING, ENGINEERING, MINING, METALLURGY, ARCHÆOLOGY, the FINE ARTS, &c.* By JOHN WEALE. Sixth Edition. Revised by ROBERT HUNT, F.R.S. Illustrated. 5s. limp; 6s. cloth boards.

50. *THE LAW OF CONTRACTS FOR WORKS AND SERVICES.* By DAVID GIBBONS. Third Edition, enlarged. 3s.‡

112. *MANUAL OF DOMESTIC MEDICINE.* By R. GOODING, B.A., M.D. A Family Guide in all Cases of Accident and Emergency. 2s.

112*. *MANAGEMENT OF HEALTH.* A Manual of Home and Personal Hygiene. By the Rev. JAMES BAIRD, B.A. 1s.

150. *LOGIC*, Pure and Applied. By S. H. EMMENS. 1s. 6d.

153. *SELECTIONS FROM LOCKE'S ESSAYS ON THE HUMAN UNDERSTANDING.* With Notes by S. H. EMMENS. 2s.

154. *GENERAL HINTS TO EMIGRANTS.* 2s.

157. *THE EMIGRANT'S GUIDE TO NATAL.* By ROBERT JAMES MANN, F.R.A.S., F.M.S. Second Edition. Map. 2s.

193. *HANDBOOK OF FIELD FORTIFICATION.* By Major W. W. KNOLLYS, F.R.G.S. With 163 Woodcuts. 3s.‡

194. *THE HOUSE MANAGER:* Being a Guide to Housekeeping. Practical Cookery, Pickling and Preserving, Household Work, Dairy Management, &c. By AN OLD HOUSEKEEPER. 3s. 6d.‡

194, *HOUSE BOOK (The).* Comprising :—I. THE HOUSE MANAGER.
112 & By an OLD HOUSEKEEPER. II. DOMESTIC MEDICINE. By R. GOODING, M.D.
112*. III. MANAGEMENT OF HEALTH. By J. BAIRD. In One Vol., half-bound, 6s.

☞ *The ‡ indicates that these vols. may be had strongly bound at 6d. extra.*

LONDON : CROSBY LOCKWOOD AND SON,

EDUCATIONAL AND CLASSICAL SERIES.

HISTORY.

1. **England, Outlines of the History of;** more especially with reference to the Origin and Progress of the English Constitution. By WILLIAM DOUGLAS HAMILTON, F.S.A., of Her Majesty's Public Record Office. 4th Edition, revised. 5s.; cloth boards, 6s.

5. **Greece, Outlines of the History of;** in connection with the Rise of the Arts and Civilization in Europe. By W. DOUGLAS HAMILTON, of University College, London, and EDWARD LEVIEN, M.A., of Balliol College, Oxford. 2s. 6d.; cloth boards, 3s. 6d.

7. **Rome, Outlines of the History of;** from the Earliest Period to the Christian Era and the Commencement of the Decline of the Empire. By EDWARD LEVIEN, of Balliol College, Oxford. Map, 2s. 6d.; cl. bds. 3s. 6d.

9. **Chronology of History, Art, Literature, and Progress,** from the Creation of the World to the Present Time. The Continuation by W. D. HAMILTON, F.S.A. 3s.; cloth boards, 3s. 6d.

50. **Dates and Events in English History,** for the use of Candidates in Public and Private Examinations. By the Rev. E. RAND. 1s.

NGLISH LANGUAGE AND MISCELLANEOUS.

11. **Grammar of the English Tongue,** Spoken and Written. With an Introduction to the Study of Comparative Philology. By HYDE CLARKE, D.C.L. Fifth Edition. 1s. 6d.

12. **Dictionary of the English Language,** as Spoken and Written. Containing above 100,000 Words. By HYDE CLARKE, D.C.L. 3s. 6d.; cloth boards, 4s. 6d.; complete with the GRAMMAR, cloth bds., 5s. 6d.

48. **Composition and Punctuation,** familiarly Explained for those who have neglected the Study of Grammar. By JUSTIN BRENAN. 18th Edition. 1s. 6d.

49. **Derivative Spelling-Book:** Giving the Origin of Every Word from the Greek, Latin, Saxon, German, Teutonic, Dutch, French, Spanish, and other Languages; with their present Acceptation and Pronunciation. By J. ROWBOTHAM, F.R.A.S. Improved Edition. 1s. 6d.

51. **The Art of Extempore Speaking:** Hints for the Pulpit, the Senate, and the Bar. By M. BAUTAIN, Vicar-General and Professor at the Sorbonne. Translated from the French. 8th Edition, carefully corrected. 2s. 6d.

54. **Analytical Chemistry,** Qualitative and Quantitative, a Course of. To which is prefixed, a Brief Treatise upon Modern Chemical Nomenclature and Notation. By WM. W. PINK and GEORGE E. WEBSTER. 2s.

THE SCHOOL MANAGERS' SERIES OF READING BOOKS,

Edited by the Rev. A. R. GRANT, Rector of Hitcham, and Honorary Canon of Ely; formerly H.M. Inspector of Schools.

INTRODUCTORY PRIMER, 3d.

	s. d.					s. d.
FIRST STANDARD	0 6	FOURTH STANDARD	.	.	.	1 2
SECOND „	0 10	FIFTH „	.	.	.	1 6
THIRD „	1 0	SIXTH „	.	.	.	1 6

LESSONS FROM THE BIBLE. Part I. Old Testament. 1s.

LESSONS FROM THE BIBLE. Part II. New Testament, to which is added THE GEOGRAPHY OF THE BIBLE, for very young Children. By Rev. C. THORNTON FORSTER. 1s. 2d. *₄* Or the Two Parts in One Volume. 2s.

FRENCH.

24. **French Grammar.** With Complete and Concise Rules on the Genders of French Nouns. By G. L. STRAUSS, Ph.D. 1s. 6d.
25. **French-English Dictionary.** Comprising a large number of New Terms used in Engineering, Mining, &c. By ALFRED ELWES. 1s. 6d.
26. **English-French Dictionary.** By ALFRED ELWES. 2s.
25,26. **French Dictionary** (as above). Complete, in One Vol., 3s.; cloth boards, 3s. 6d. *** Or with the GRAMMAR, cloth boards, 4s. 6d.
47. **French and English Phrase Book :** containing Introductory Lessons, with Translations, several Vocabularies of Words, a Collection of suitable Phrases, and Easy Familiar Dialogues. 1s. 6d.

GERMAN.

39. **German Grammar.** Adapted for English Students, from Heyse's Theoretical and Practical Grammar, by Dr. G. L. STRAUSS. 1s. 6d.
40. **German Reader :** A Series of Extracts, carefully culled from the most approved Authors of Germany; with Notes, Philological and Explanatory. By G. L. STRAUSS, Ph.D. 1s.
41-43. **German Triglot Dictionary.** By N. E. S. A. HAMILTON. In Three Parts. Part I. German-French-English. Part II. English-German-French. Part III. French-German-English. 3s., or cloth boards, 4s.
41-43 **German Triglot Dictionary** (as above), together with German
& 39. Grammar (No. 39), in One Volume, cloth boards, 5s.

ITALIAN.

27. **Italian Grammar,** arranged in Twenty Lessons, with a Course of Exercises. By ALFRED ELWES. 1s. 6d.
28. **Italian Triglot Dictionary,** wherein the Genders of all the Italian and French Nouns are carefully noted down. By ALFRED ELWES. Vol. 1. Italian-English-French. 2s. 6d.
30. **Italian Triglot Dictionary.** By A. ELWES. Vol. 2. English-French-Italian. 2s. 6d.
32. **Italian Triglot Dictionary.** By ALFRED ELWES. Vol. 3. French-Italian-English. 2s. 6d.
28,30, **Italian Triglot Dictionary** (as above). In One Vol., 7s. 6d.
32. Cloth boards.

SPANISH AND PORTUGUESE.

34. **Spanish Grammar,** in a Simple and Practical Form. With a Course of Exercises. By ALFRED ELWES. 1s. 6d.
35. **Spanish-English and English-Spanish Dictionary.** Including a large number of Technical Terms used in Mining, Engineering, &c. with the proper Accents and the Gender of every Noun. By ALFRED ELWES 4s.; cloth boards, 5s. *** Or with the GRAMMAR, cloth boards, 6s.
55. **Portuguese Grammar,** in a Simple and Practical Form. With a Course of Exercises. By ALFRED ELWES. 1s. 6d.
56. **Portuguese-English and English-Portuguese Dic-**tionary. Including a large number of Technical Terms used in Mining, Engineering, &c., with the proper Accents and the Gender of every Noun. By ALFRED ELWES. Second Edition, Revised, 5s.; cloth boards, 6s. *** Or with the GRAMMAR, cloth boards, 7s.

HEBREW.

46*. **Hebrew Grammar.** By Dr. BRESSLAU. 1s. 6d.
44. **Hebrew and English Dictionary,** Biblical and Rabbinical; containing the Hebrew and Chaldee Roots of the Old Testament Post-Rabbinical Writings. By Dr. BRESSLAU. 6s.
46. **English and Hebrew Dictionary.** By Dr. BRESSLAU. 3s.
44,46. **Hebrew Dictionary** (as above), in Two Vols., complete, with
46*. the GRAMMAR, cloth boards, 12s.

LATIN.

19. **Latin Grammar.** Containing the Inflections and Elementary Principles of Translation and Construction. By the Rev. THOMAS GOODWIN, M.A., Head Master of the Greenwich Proprietary School. 1s. 6d.

20. **Latin-English Dictionary.** By the Rev. THOMAS GOODWIN, M.A. 2s.

22. **English-Latin Dictionary;** together with an Appendix of French and Italian Words which have their origin from the Latin. By the Rev. THOMAS GOODWIN, M.A. 1s. 6d.

20,22. **Latin Dictionary** (as above). Complete in One Vol., 3s. 6d. cloth boards, 4s. 6d. ** Or with the GRAMMAR, cloth boards, 5s. 6d.

LATIN CLASSICS. With Explanatory Notes in English.

1. **Latin Delectus.** Containing Extracts from Classical Authors, with Genealogical Vocabularies and Explanatory Notes, by H. YOUNG. 1s. 6d.

2. **Cæsaris** Commentarii de Bello Gallico. Notes, and a Geographical Register for the Use of Schools, by H. YOUNG. 2s.

3. **Cornelius Nepos.** With Notes. By H. YOUNG. 1s.

4. **Virgilii** Maronis Bucolica et Georgica. With Notes on the Bucolics by W. RUSHTON, M.A., and on the Georgics by H. YOUNG. 1s. 6d.

5. **Virgilii** Maronis Æneis. With Notes, Critical and Explanatory, by H. YOUNG. New Edition, revised and improved With copious Additional Notes by Rev. T. H. L. LEARY, D.C.L., formerly Scholar of Brasenose College, Oxford. 3s.

5* —— Part 1. Books i.—vi., 1s. 6d.
5** —— Part 2. Books vii.—xii., 2s.

6. **Horace;** Odes, Epode, and Carmen Sæculare. Notes by H. YOUNG. 1s. 6d.

7. **Horace;** Satires, Epistles, and Ars Poetica. Notes by W. BROWNRIGG SMITH, M.A., F.R.G.S. 1s. 6d.

8. **Sallustii** Crispi Catalina et Bellum Jugurthinum. Notes, Critical and Explanatory, by W. M. DONNE, B.A., Trin. Coll., Cam. 1s. 6d.

9. **Terentii** Andria et Heautontimorumenos. With Notes, Critical and Explanatory, by the Rev. JAMES DAVIES, M.A. 1s. 6d.

10. **Terentii** Adelphi, Hecyra, Phormio. Edited, with Notes, Critical and Explanatory, by the Rev. JAMES DAVIES, M.A. 2s.

11. **Terentii** Eunuchus, Comœdia. Notes, by Rev. J. DAVIES, M.A. 1s. 6d.

12. **Ciceronis** Oratio pro Sexto Roscio Amerino. Edited, with an Introduction, Analysis, and Notes, Explanatory and Critical, by the Rev. JAMES DAVIES, M.A. 1s. 6d.

13. **Ciceronis** Orationes in Catilinam, Verrem, et pro Archia. With Introduction, Analysis, and Notes, Explanatory and Critical, by Rev. T. H. L. LEARY, D.C.L. formerly Scholar of Brasenose College, Oxford. 1s. 6d.

14. **Ciceronis** Cato Major, Lælius, Brutus, sive de Senectute, de Amicitia, de Claris Oratoribus Dialogi. With Notes by W. BROWNRIGG SMITH, M.A., F.R.G.S. 2s.

16. **Livy:** History of Rome. Notes by H. YOUNG and W. B. SMITH, M.A. Part 1. Books i., ii., 1s. 6d.

16*. —— Part 2. Books iii., iv., v., 1s. 6d.
17. —— Part 3. Books xxi., xxii., 1s. 6d.

19. **Latin Verse Selections,** from Catullus, Tibullus, Propertius, and Ovid. Notes by W. B. DONNE, M.A., Trinity College, Cambridge. 2s.

20. **Latin Prose Selections,** from Varro, Columella, Vitruvius, Seneca, Quintilian, Florus, Velleius Paterculus, Valerius Maximus Suetonius, Apuleius, &c. Notes by W. B. DONNE, M.A. 2s.

21. **Juvenalis** Satiræ. With Prolegomena and Notes by T. H. S. ESCOTT, B.A., Lecturer on Logic at King's College, London. 2s.

GREEK.

14. Greek Grammar, in accordance with the Principles and Philo-logical Researches of the most eminent Scholars of our own day. By HANS CLAUDE HAMILTON. 1s. 6d.

15,17. Greek Lexicon. Containing all the Words in General Use, with their Significations, Inflections, and Doubtful Quantities. By HENRY R. HAMILTON. Vol. 1. Greek-English, 2s. 6d.; Vol. 2. English-Greek, 2s. Or the Two Vols. in One, 4s. 6d.: cloth boards, 5s.

14,15. Greek Lexicon (as above). Complete, with the GRAMMAR, in **17.** One Vol., cloth boards, 6s.

GREEK CLASSICS. With Explanatory Notes in English.

1. Greek Delectus. Containing Extracts from Classical Authors, with Genealogical Vocabularies and Explanatory Notes, by H. YOUNG. New Edition, with an improved and enlarged Supplementary Vocabulary, by JOHN HUTCHISON, M.A., of the High School, Glasgow. 1s. 6d.

2, 3. Xenophon's Anabasis; or, The Retreat of the Ten Thousand. Notes and a Geographical Register, by H. YOUNG. Part 1. Books i. to iii., 1s. Part 2. Books iv. to vii., 1s.

4. Lucian's Select Dialogues. The Text carefully revised, with Grammatical and Explanatory Notes, by H. YOUNG. 1s. 6d.

5-12. Homer, The Works of. According to the Text of BAEUMLEIN. With Notes, Critical and Explanatory, drawn from the best and latest Authorities, with Preliminary Observations and Appendices, by T. H. L. LEARY, M.A., D.C.L.

THE ILIAD:	Part 1. Books i. to vi., 1s.6d.	Part 3. Books xiii. to xviii., 1s. 6d.
	Part 2. Books vii. to xii., 1s.6d.	Part 4. Books xix. to xxiv., 1s. 6d.
THE ODYSSEY:	Part 1. Books i. to vi., 1s.6d	Part 3. Books xiii. to xviii., 1s. 6d.
	Part 2. Books vii. to xii., 1s. 6d.	Part 4. Books xix. to xxiv., and Hymns, 2s.

13. Plato's Dialogues: The Apology of Socrates, the Crito, and the Phædo. From the Text of C. F. HERMANN. Edited with Notes, Critical and Explanatory, by the Rev. JAMES DAVIES, M.A. 2s.

14-17. Herodotus, The History of, chiefly after the Text of GAISFORD. With Preliminary Observations and Appendices, and Notes, Critical and Explanatory, by T. H. L. LEARY, M.A., D.C.L.
Part 1. Books i., ii. (The Clio and Euterpe), 2s.
Part 2. Books iii., iv. (The Thalia and Melpomene), 2s.
Part 3. Books v.-vii. (The Terpsichore, Erato, and Polymnia), 2s.
Part 4. Books viii., ix. (The Urania and Calliope) and Index, 1s. 6d.

18. Sophocles: Œdipus Tyrannus. Notes by H. YOUNG. 1s.

20. Sophocles: Antigone. From the Text of DINDORF. Notes, Critical and Explanatory, by the Rev. JOHN MILNER, B.A. 2s.

23. Euripides: Hecuba and Medea. Chiefly from the Text of DIN-DORF. With Notes, Critical and Explanatory, by W. BROWNRIGG SMITH, M.A., F.R.G.S. 1s. 6d.

26. Euripides: Alcestis. Chiefly from the Text of DINDORF. With Notes, Critical and Explanatory, by JOHN MILNER, B.A. 1s. 6d.

30. Æschylus: Prometheus Vinctus: The Prometheus Bound. From the Text of DINDORF. Edited, with English Notes, Critical and Explanatory, by the Rev. JAMES DAVIES, M.A. 1s.

32. Æschylus: Septem Contra Thebes: The Seven against Thebes. From the Text of DINDORF. Edited, with English Notes, Critical and Explanatory, by the Rev. JAMES DAVIES, M.A. 1s.

40. Aristophanes: Acharnians. Chiefly from the Text of C. H. WEISE. With Notes, by C. S. T. TOWNSHEND, M.A. 1s. 6d.

41. Thucydides: History of the Peloponnesian War. Notes by H. YOUNG. Book 1. 1s. 6d.

42. Xenophon's Panegyric on Agesilaus. Notes and Intro-duction by LL. F. W. JEWITT. 1s. 6d.

43. Demosthenes. The Oration on the Crown and the Philippics. With English Notes. By Rev. T. H. L. LEARY, D.C.L., formerly Scholar of Brasenose College, Oxford. 1s. 6d.

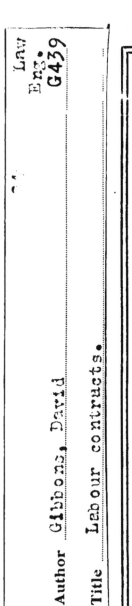

Lightning Source UK Ltd.
Milton Keynes UK
UKHW051105271218
334505UK00017B/766/P

9 781330 837917